Public Voices

American Catholic Identities
A Documentary History

Christopher J. Kauffman, General Editor

American Catholic Identities is a nine-volume series that makes available to the general reader, the student, and the scholar seminal documents in the history of American Catholicism. Subjects are wide-ranging and topically ordered within periods to encounter the richly textured experiences of American Catholics from the earliest years to the present day. The twenty-six editors of these volumes reveal a command of trends in historiography since the publication of John Tracy Ellis's three-volume work, *Documents of American Catholic History*. Hence the American Catholic Identities series shows developments in our understanding of social history — the significance of gender, race, regionalism, ethnicity, and spirituality, as well as Catholic thought and practice before and since the Second Vatican Council.

The series elucidates myriad meanings of the American Catholic experience by working with the marker of religious identity. It brings into relief the historical formations of religious self-understandings of a wide variety of Catholics in a society characterized by the principles of religious liberty, separation of church and state, religious pluralism, and voluntarism.

American Catholic Identities is united by such dominant factors in American history as waves of immigration, nativism, anti-Catholicism, racism, sexism, and several other social and ideological trends. Other aspects of unity are derived from American Catholic history: styles of episcopal leadership, multiple and various types of Catholic institutions, and the dynamic intellectual interaction between the United States and various national centers of Catholic thought. Woven into the themes of this documentary history are the protean meanings of what constitutes being American and Catholic in relation to the formations of religious identities.

Titles of books in the series are:

Public Voices: Catholics in the American Context, Steven M. Avella and Elizabeth McKeown

The Frontiers and Catholic Identities, Anne M. Butler, Michael E. Engh, S.J., and Thomas W. Spalding, C.F.X.

Creative Fidelity: U.S. Catholic Intellectual Identities, Scott Appleby, Patricia Byrne, C.S.J., and William Portier

Keeping Faith: European and Asian Immigrants, Jeffrey Burns, Ellen Skerrett, and Joseph White

Prayer and Practice in the American Catholic Community, Joseph P. Chinnici, O.F.M., and Angelyn Dries, O.S.F.

Gender Identities in American Catholicism, Paula Kane, James Kenneally, and Karen Kennelly, C.S.J.

"Stamped with the Image of God": African-Americans as God's Image in Black, Cyprian Davis, O.S.B., and Jamie Phelps, O.P.

¡Presente! Latino Catholics from Colonial Origins to the Present, Timothy Matovina and Gerald E. Poyo, in collaboration with Jaime Vidal, Cecilia González, and Steven Rodríguez

The Crossing of Two Roads: Being Catholic and Native in the United States, Marie Therese Archambault, O.S.F., Mark Thiel, and Christopher Vecsey

A workshop for the editors of these books was entirely funded by a generous grant from the Louisville Institute.

American Catholic Identities
A Documentary History
Christopher J. Kauffman, General Editor

Public Voices

Catholics in the
American Context

Steven M. Avella
Elizabeth McKeown
Editors

ORBIS BOOKS
Maryknoll, New York 10545

Copyright © 1999 by Steven M. Avella and Elizabeth McKeown

Published by Orbis Books, Maryknoll, New York, U.S.A.

Documents 92, 93, and 94 are reprinted with the permission of America Press, Inc., 106 West 56th Street, New York, NY 10019. Copyright © 1955, 1958, 1964, all rights reserved. For subscription information call (800) 627-9533 or (212) 581-4640.

Manufactured in the United States of America

Library of Congress Cataloging-in-Publication Data

Public voices : Catholics in the American context / Steven M. Avella, Elizabeth McKeown, editors.
    p. cm.
    Includes bibliographical references.
    ISBN 1-57075-266-4 (pbk.) – ISBN 1-57075-267-2 (cloth)
    1. Catholic Church – United States – History – Sources. 2. Catholics – United States – History – Sources. I. Avella, Steven M. II. McKeown, Elizabeth.
BX1405 .P83 1999
282′.73 – dc21

99-048732

To

David O'Brien

For God, who said, "Let light shine out of darkness,"
has shone in our hearts, that we in turn might make known
the glory of God shining on the face of Christ. (2 Cor. 4:6)

CONTENTS

Part 1
1776–1865

Part 2
1865–1920

Part 3
1920–45

Part 4
1945 TO THE PRESENT

Race 251

War and Peace 261

Education 278

FOREWORD

Christopher J. Kauffman

To orchestrate the public voices heard in these pages — voices that come in several movements over the span of more than two centuries — is an achievement of almost symphonic proportions. Drawing upon their experiences as scholars of American religious history and their expertise at organizing an abundance of material, Steven M. Avella and Elizabeth McKeown treat their readers to a wide range of fascinating materials organized topically within well-defined periods. Dedicated to David O'Brien, a seasoned composer of several rhapsodies on the theme of public Catholicism, this volume of documents is indeed a fitting testimony to the historian who has analyzed the significance of the protean terms "Catholic" and "American," particularly as they help to break open meanings of religious identities in a pluralist society.

David O'Brien's notion of republican Catholicism is clearly evident in the public voice of John Carroll, the first bishop of the United States. Based upon a positive anthropology that was in accord with the principles of self-government, the ecclesiology of John Carroll was congenial with the republican ethos. For example, he adapted to the drive among the laity to take an active role in parish government as lay trustees but demanded his right as bishop to name their pastors. Also in accord with O'Brien's republican Catholicism is the diocesan constitution composed by Bishop John England of Charleston, South Carolina. It was a model of Catholic adaptation to the contemporary principles of federalism and separation of powers. Indeed, England's preface explicitly draws parallels between president and governor, on the one hand, and pope and bishop, on the other; it also proposes a two-house legislature, a house of priest delegates and one of lay delegates. The editors balance England's engagement with the progressive elements of American society with a document on the bishop's defensive posture toward Pope Gregory XVI's condemnation of the slave trade; the document explains to a Southerner that the pope did not actually condemn slavery.

O'Brien's notion of immigrant Catholicism is represented by Bishop John Hughes of New York, particularly his struggle with the Protestant guardians of the public schools, a struggle which led to widespread support for the Catholic parochial schools. In response to nativism and anti-Catholicism, Bishop Hughes articulated a hostile, defensive voice of Catholic identity in counterpoint to the regnant religious discrimination of the era. Besides documents illustrative of O'Brien's concept of immigrant Catholicism, several selections deal with what O'Brien referred to as reform Catholicism. These include the selections from the writings of Father John A. Ryan on the "living wage," "social reconstruction," and other social issues; a large section on organized labor is also clearly illustrative of O'Brien's model of reform Catholicism as well as his notion of social Catholicism. The editors also feature several little-known women of the 1920s and 1930s — Helen P. McCormick, Rose J. McHugh, Sister Mary Martina — and others associated with child care; together they resound as a polyphonic response to the social problems of the era.

David O'Brien was the first historian to identify evangelical Catholicism, which, in contrast to the liberal reform perspective of John A. Ryan, placed an emphasis upon a radical critique of capitalism blended with a gospel call to respond to the poor and the marginalized in light of the Sermon on the Mount. Dorothy Day's Houses of Hospitality and the Catholic Worker movement — with its emphasis upon personal conversion and a commitment to a life of poverty and pacifism — also entailed a critique of capitalism and its individualistic ethos, a critique grounded in scripture. The editors chose one of Day's foundational writings to capture her unique public voice.

Martin E. Marty's five continuities in American religious history work as complements to O'Brien's models. Pluralism, the wide array of religious beliefs in the United States, is Marty's first continuity, one that is of course based upon religious liberty and the separation of church and state. This is analogous to O'Brien's concept of republican Catholicism, which was articulated by several bishops and priests committed to mediating Catholicity in the American republican language. Until the election of John Kennedy in 1960 and the passage of the Declaration on Religious Freedom in 1965 at the last session of Vatican II, the church was in principle opposed to pluralism and the separation of church and state, but tolerated them as practical necessities. This volume includes a selection from a book by John A. Ryan that endorses the traditional opposition to the principle of religious liberty. In contrast, John Courtney Murray, S.J., represents progressive views on the issue, views most bishops implicitly endorsed by affirming that the church thrived within American society because of its religious freedom. The opposite of a respect for pluralism is tribalism, a trend represented by the Ku Klux Klan attempt in the 1920s to promote an extremist "Christian" society with the public school as its icon and the antirepublican and pro-Vatican parochial school as the enemy that should be made illegal. The document on the Oregon school case illustrates the development of tribalism in the 1920s.

Voluntarism, Marty's second continuity, flows from the separation of church and state. The term simply indicates that churches run on the voluntary contributions from the people. This condition has allowed the Catholic laity in the United States to assume a sense of ownership of their parishes, schools, and hospitals, a condition that does not have an analogue in traditional European countries. Federal aid to higher education and to hospitals are consensus countertrends to a rigid voluntarism.

Experimentalism, the third of Marty's continuities, underscores the penchant for pragmatism and the provisional dimensions of religion in the United States. The Catholic adjustment to coeducation, the church's relation to the rise of organized labor, and its many social-welfare projects are developments that were perceived as a blend of principle and pragmatism; Avella and McKeown have selected several documents revealing these trends.

The fourth continuity, the role of the Enlightenment in the foundation story of the nation, emphasizes the rational natural-rights basis of the nation's seminal documents, a theme trumpeted in the Fourth of July oratory accompanied by our national "hymns." Referred to as civil religion by several scholars, this Enlightenment influence has been contradicted by slavery and other exclusive boundaries to full citizenship, tendencies well documented in this book.

The final continuity, scripturalism, emphasizes the finger of divine providence in the design of the new nation, "the new Jerusalem." Catholic scripturalism is evident in several documents in this volume, including the justice and peace documents, particularly those against racism and poverty (an example is the text by Dorothy Day). Further, the strident voices against communism were often expressed in the apocalyptic language of scripture.

Several documents in this work are unrelated to O'Brien's styles and Marty's continuities; such is the originality of this book. Elizabeth McKeown's publications on Catholic social provision, on the intellectual life, on the national organizations of Catholic bishops, and on other areas of public Catholicism have sharpened her wide-angled vision, a vision that assisted her in selecting stimulating and wide-ranging documents. Steven Avella's research in publications on diocesan histories of Chicago, Milwaukee, and Sacramento has enriched his perspective for selecting documents in several spheres of public life. Because so much of American Catholic life and thought has a public dimension, the editors' principal challenge was to discern those documents among an abundant supply that would illustrate the myriad topics and themes of their book and simultaneously respect the boundaries of the other eight volumes. They have achieved these goals with a sensitivity to the needs of students and a concern for the scholarship of their colleagues in history and theology.

ACKNOWLEDGMENTS

Several institutions and colleagues have sustained us in the present effort. We would like to thank our respective universities (Marquette and Georgetown) for supporting this project and to acknowledge the contributions of our hard-working and conscientious research assistants (Stephanie Bauer Ferguson, Kate Fuller, Paula Dicks, Agnes King, and Deborah Koller) in gathering, reproducing, and editing these texts. We are deeply grateful to them. We would also like to acknowledge the support of Christopher Kauffman, who has conceptualized and guided this entire nine-volume collection and who hosted a very productive session for all volume editors at the Catholic University of America in the summer of 1997. And finally, special thanks go to the people at Orbis Books who helped make this series a reality and who have given generous assistance in bringing it to fruition.

We have dedicated this volume to David O'Brien, Loyola Professor of History at the College of the Holy Cross in Worcester, Massachusetts. It was David who coined the term "public Catholicism" years ago. He is a model scholar and a good friend. To him we pay the highest tribute, "Blessed are they who hear the word of God and live it."

GENERAL INTRODUCTION

Steven M. Avella and Elizabeth McKeown

The following collection of documents is intended to introduce readers to the historical development of a Catholic presence in the political and social life of the United States. It is divided into four periods: 1776 to 1865, 1865 to 1920, 1920 to 1945, and 1945 to the present. Three rules have guided our selection process: we have chosen authors who made a deliberate effort to relate the church to issues of importance in the wider culture; we have chosen documents that provide evidence of the impact of the wider culture on the church; and we have chosen documents that suggest a range of Catholic views and practices on public questions.

On the one hand, there are persistent concerns recorded here that provide strong threads of continuity in this development. Chief among these are the issues of church-state relations, education, and social welfare. On the other hand, there are debates — over slavery, industrialization, abortion, and nuclear war, for instance — which have been signature issues during particular periods of American history. Documents in this collection mark the range of Catholic voices on these issues, and they also suggest the shape of the influence exercised by the larger culture on Catholic thinking and practice. There is indeed no singular Catholic identity on most of these public issues. There are instead multiple "public identities" among American Catholics, and those identities are related in complex ways to an evolving tradition of Catholic teaching and practice.

Given the criteria that guided our selection, there is a certain inevitability about the social characteristics of the "voices" in the collection. The majority of these documents have been written by educated and self-conscious men who held positions of privilege and power in American Catholic life. Many of them were priests and bishops. But there are exceptions to this pattern. There are documents in this collection that suggest the exceptional contribution of women religious who sustained American Catholic social and educational efforts, and other documents bear witness to the growing public influence of Catholic laity in twentieth-century American life.

The magnitude of material pertinent to our subject at this point in time leads us to think ahead to those who may attempt the task of documenting the history of "public Catholicism" in the United States in the future. We extend our sympathies and wish them well. Perhaps they, too, will be comforted by the careful scholarship of Msgr. John Tracy Ellis, whose three-volume *Documents of American Catholic History* (1987) reached far beyond the rubric of "public Catholicism" and marked the American Catholic documentary trail for all of us.

Part 1

1776–1865

Introduction

A new nation emerged from the transitional period of the confederation. The new Constitution created a central government which would demonstrate itself to be fully capable of seizing the direction of national affairs and propelling the infant republic into its future.

Simultaneously, the fledgling American Catholic community, under the leadership of former-Jesuit John Carroll, was also erecting its necessary institutional infrastructure. Carroll's new diocese, headquartered at Baltimore, provided the visible base of leadership Catholics needed to have a public voice in the "new order of the ages." Politically astute and well connected with the leaders of the Revolution, Carroll reassured American society about the loyalty of his co-religionists to the new republic. At the same time he kept wary Roman officials secure in the knowledge that American Catholics were holding fast to the tradition they had received. Subsequent bishops would follow this lead and be the primary spokesmen on the public issues which impinged on and demanded a response from the church.

Of special interest to Catholic leaders was the federal government's policies governing the relations between church and state. The new government enshrined in the First Amendment to the Constitution its decision to remove itself as much as possible from the sphere of religious life and practice. This principled withdrawal of the federal government from religious affairs provided an opening for the Catholic minority (and others) to develop a distinctive presence in American public life even as it acted as a guard against the dominance of any denomination which might seek to use its political and persuasive skills to secure an advantage over others.

One of the most important social and political trends of the early nineteenth century was the impulse characterized by historian Gordon Wood as the "democratization of the mind." Embedded in an extension of suffrage and in a greater respect for the common citizen, this new mind-set reshaped American self-consciousness and framed the political discourse of the early nineteenth century. New political leadership succeeded the founding generation of Washington and Adams and even Jefferson. This era brought forth Clay, Calhoun, Jackson, Webster, and Lincoln as well as a host of other lumi-

1

naries who dominated the political landscape. America moved dynamically in the first half of the nineteenth century as its natural resources, its geographical isolation from Europe, its energetic population, and its embrace of liberal capitalism all combined to transform the infant republic into a mature nation. This was most visibly exemplified by the great move westward. Whatever arguments later historians would have about the significance of the frontier, clearly many Americans saw it as a place of opportunity and an arena to work out their own personal destiny and that of the nation. Americans spilled into the Ohio Valley and claimed new lands in the South and Middle West. The Oregon country's lush valleys lured settlers to the shores of the Pacific while the lure of gold in 1849 sent them scurrying to California. Brand new urban communities such as Chicago, Salt Lake City, and San Francisco popped up virtually overnight. American life was never static or stable, but growing, expanding, and demanding more and more.

Expansion brought new population as immigration from northern and western Europe accelerated after the War of 1812. Immigrant strangeness provoked xenophobic fears that demanded response and defense. Expansion also brought conflict with powers such as Britain and Mexico. A wave of high-powered Protestant revivalism generated an interest in personal and cultural reform in the first decades of the nineteenth century. The imperatives of expansion and reform coalesced into a massive national debate over the institution of slavery — a national discussion which could not of its very nature maintain the boundaries of civility. Ultimately, it tested every preconception about the nation's unity in diversity. And in April 1861, the tensions inherent in a public culture that claimed both republican ideals of civic virtue and a philosophy of individual rights anchored in a commitment to economic growth finally erupted into civil war.

Church and Society

The creation of the American republic shaped the backdrop for the first elements of a public identity for the Catholic Church of the United States. The existence of universal religious toleration and the establishment of a new government officially indifferent to the internal workings of the church created the context for the emergence of a distinctly American Catholic public identity. In a certain sense, the issues that are surfaced in this set of documents form the infrastructure of Catholic public identity in America.

The letters of John Carroll, the first leader of the American Catholic community and later its first bishop, suggest the nature of these circumstances and articulate a modus vivendi for Catholics in America.

As the address of William Gaston to the constitutional convention of North Carolina and the observations of Alexis de Tocqueville suggest, Catholics in America came to feel comfortable with the juxtaposition of their faith and citizenship. Indeed, the emphasis on religious freedom came to be viewed in a wholly positive light. If imitation is the highest form of flattery, Catholics in America emulated the lesson of constitutionalism that had reshaped American civic life after the Revolution. John England's "Constitution of the Roman Catholic Churches" is the clearest evidence that the impulses of the world around them shaped the reaction and public stance of at least some American Catholics.

But other questions shaped this stance as well. Some came from the hostility of American society, which raised doubts as to the loyalty of American Catholics to the republic. Others came from church officials in Rome who needed regular reassurance that American Catholics were not slipping into a fuzzy indifference through their support for religious toleration and pluralism. The letter of Archbishop John Hughes to *New York Tribune* editor Horace Greeley emphasizes the continuing sense of distance between Catholics and the larger society.

The emergence of a theology of lay governance in church affairs and the rise of a strong lay trustee movement demonstrated an important adaptation of American Catholics to the realities of public life in the early national period. At a time when the rising tide of democratization was reshaping public institutions everywhere, Catholics repaired to the traditional division of spiritual and temporal powers to justify the role and influence of lay trustees. As the people of the United States were the sovereigns in their civic life, so also would that sovereignty be expressed within the proper theological boundaries in their ecclesial life.

Although lay trustee controversies flared in different locations, one document here relates to the controversy that raged in Norfolk, Virginia, early in the nineteenth century. The level and quality of arguments and especially their dependence on certain principles of American law and practice as their justification provide a clear expression on one facet of the church's public identity.

Education became a central point of the encounter between American Catholics and the wider society. John Carroll insisted on Catholic schools as the "main sheet anchor of religion." Requiring major financial and personnel resources, Catholic schools grew steadily, aided by the introduction of religious orders of women and men to the country. Meanwhile, public schools became one of the flash points between American Catholics and American society. Because the earliest public schools in America were heavily influenced and dominated by evangelical Protestants, Catholics retreated from them to found their own institutions. The onset of heavy European immigration in the nineteenth century accentuated this trend toward institutional separatism as schools became the locus for the preservation of immigrant culture. The uncertain standards for the provision of public funding for schools led Catholics to demand a share of the commonly collected tax moneys for their own schools. Vocal opposition to these Catholic demands once again called into question the loyalty of Catholics to the American republic and fueled the rise of a virulent anti-Catholicism in the nineteenth century. The letter of John Hughes and the response of Catholic citizens to the so-called Bible Riots in Philadelphia in 1844 offer a view on the public response to these issues.

1. Rev. John Carroll to Cardinal Vitaliano Borromeo, 10 November 1783

Dr. Sir...

You are not ignorant, that in these United States our Religious system has undergone a revolution, if possible, more extraordinary, than our political one. In all of them, free toleration is allowed to Christians of every denomination; and particularly in the States of Pennsylvania, Delaware, Maryland, and Virginia, a communication of all Civil rights, without distinction or diminution, is extended to those of our Religion. This is a blessing and advantage, which is our duty to preserve & improve with the utmost prudence, by demeaning ourselves on all occasions as subjects zealously attached to our government & avoiding to give any jealousies on account of any dependence on foreign jurisdictions, more than that, which is essential to our Religion an[d] acknowledgement of the Pope's spiritual Supremacy over the whole Christian world. You know that we of the Clergy have heretofore resorted to the Vicar Apostolick of the London district for the exercise of spiritual powers, but being well acquainted with the temper of Congress, of our assemblies and the people at large, we are firmly of opinion, that we shall not be suffered to continue under such a jurisdiction, whenever it becomes known to the publick. You may be assured of this from the following fact. The Clergy of the church of England were heretofore subject to the Bishop of London: but the umbrage taken at this dependence was so great, that notwithstanding the power & prevalence of that sect, they could find no other method to allay jealousies, than by withdrawing themselves, as they have lately done, from all obedience to him.

Being therefore thus circumstanced, we think it not only advisable in us, but, in a manner obligatory to solicit the Holy See to place the Episcopal powers at least such as recommended are most essential, in the hands of one amongst us, whose recognized virtue, knowledge, and integrity of faith, shall be certified by ourselves. We shall annex to this letter such powers, as we judge it absolutely necessary he should be invested with. We might add many very cogent reasons for having amongst us a person thus empowered, and for want of whom it is impossible to conceive the inconveniences happening every day. If it be possible to obtain a grant from Rome for vesting these powers in our Superior *pro tempore,* it would be most desirable. We shall endeavor to have you aided in this application by a recommendation if possible from our own country and the Minister of France. You will know how to avail yourself of the residence of so favourable a Russian minister at Rome; and if Mr. Thorpe will be pleased to undertake the management of the business there we will with cheerfulness and gratitude answer all expenses which he may incur in the prosecution of it. He will be the judge, how and whether the annexed petition ought in prudence to be presented to His Holiness, but at all events the powers therein contained, are those which we wish our Superior to be invested with.

Thomas O'Brien Hanley, S.J., ed., *The John Carroll Papers* (Notre Dame, Ind.: University of Notre Dame Press, 1976), 1:80–81.

2. Rev. John Carroll to John Thorpe, 17 February 1785

Dear Sir

The official information of the advices sent by you June 9th 1784, was only received Novr. 26th. I did myself the honour of writing to you on the subject, immediately after receiving your letter, which was about the 20th of August, and of thanking you most cordially for your active & successful endeavours to render service to this country. I say successful, not because of your partiality, as I presume, joined to that of my old cheerful friend Dr. Franklin suggested me to the consideration of his holiness; but because you have obtained some form of spiritual government to be adopted for us. It is not indeed quite such, as we wish; and it cannot continue long in its present form. You well know, that in our free and jealous government, where Catholics are admitted into all public councils equally with the professors of any other Religion, it will never be suffered, that their Ecclesiastical Superior (be he a Bishop, or Prefect Apostolic) receive his appointment form a foreign state, and only hold it at the discretion of a foreign tribunal or congregation. If even the present temper, or inattention of our Executive, and legislative bodies were to overlook it for this & perhaps a few more instances, still ought we not to acquiesce & rest quiet in actual enjoyment: for the consequence, sooner or later, would certainly be that some malicious or jealous-minded person would raise a spirit against us, & under pretence of rescuing the state from foreign influence, & dependance, strip us perhaps of our common civil rights. For these reasons, every thinking man amongst us is convinced, that we neither must request or admit any other foreign interference than such, as being essential to our religion, is implied in the acknowledgement of the Bishop of Rome being, by divine appointment, head of the universal Church; and the See of S. Peter being the center of ecclesiastical unity.

I am well aware, that these suggestions will sound ungrateful at Rome; and that the mention of them from us will be perhaps imputed by some of the officers of the propaganda to a remaining spirit of Jesuitism: but I own to you, that tho' I wish to treat them upon terms of sincere unanimity & cordial concurrence in all matters tending to the service of God; yet I do not feel myself disposed to sacrifice, to the fear of giving offence, the permanent interests of Religion. I mean candidly and respectfully to state our present situation; the spirit of our people; & the sentiments of the R. Catholics, the principal of whom are ready & desirous to transmit to Rome their opinion under their own signature, I am yet uncertain [*sic*]; I would wish to avoid giving the Congregation, or any other person the smallest reason to suspect a cabal to defeat their measures; and if plain and honest representation will not succeed with them, I shall fear the effects of intemperate obstinacy....

Our objections...are — 1st We conceive our situation no longer as that of missioners; and the Ecclesiastical constitution here no longer a mission. By acquiring civil and religious rights in common with other Christians, we are become a national catholic clergy; Colleges are now erecting [*sic*] for giving general & liberal education; these colleges are open, both to Masters and Scholars, of every religious denomination and as we have every reason to believe, that amongst the youth trained in these different colleges, there will be frequently some inclined to the Ecclesiastical state, we Catholics propose instituting a seminary to form them to the virtues of their future state, & to instruct them in Divinity. Thus we shall, in a few years, with the blessing of providence be able to supply this country with labourers in the Lord's vineyard, & keep up a succession if we are indulged in a Bishop. We are not in immediate want of one, and it will be more agreeable to many of my Brethren not to have any yet appointed; but whenever the time for it comes, we conceive that it will be more advantageous to Religion, & less [*indecipherable*] that he be an ordinary Bishop; and not a Vicar-Apostolic & be chosen and presented to his holiness by the American Cat. Clergy. 2ly For two reasons we think it improper to be subject in our Ecclesiastical government to the Propaganda: the first is, that not being missioners, we conceive ourselves not a proper object of their institution: and the second is, that tho' our free and tolerant forms of Government (in Virg[ini]a, Maryl[an]d & Pennsylva.) admit us to equal civil rights with other Christians, yet the leading men in our respective states often express a jealousy of any foreign jurisdiction; and surely will be more offended with our submitting to it in matters not essential to our faith. I hope they will never object to our depending on the pope in things purely spiritual; but I am sure there are men, at least in this state, who would blow up a flame of animosity against us, if they suspected that we were to be so much under the government of any Cong[regatio]n at Rome, as to receive our Superior from it, commissioned only during their good will; and that this Superior was restricted from employing any Clergyman here, but such as that Congregation should direct. I dread so much the consequences of it being known; that this last direction was even given that I have not thought proper to mention it to several of my Brethren....

Thomas O'Brien Hanley, S.J., ed., *The John Carroll Papers* (Notre Dame, Ind.: University of Notre Dame Press, 1976), 1:162–64.

3. Rev. John Carroll, "Proposals to Establish an Academy at George Town, Patowmack River, Maryland," 1788[1]

The object of the proposed Institution is to unite the means of communicating Science with an effectual provision for guarding and preserving the Morals of Youth. With this View, the Seminary will be superintended by those who,

---

1. By reason of the penal legislation against Catholics in colonial America it had never been possible to have a Catholic school. The brief existence of the furtive little academy at Bohemia

having had Experience in similar Institutions, know that an undivided Attention may be given to the Cultivation of Virtue and literary Improvement, and that a System of Discipline may be introduced and preserved incompatible with Indolence and Inattention in the Professor, or with incorrigible habits of Immorality in the Student.

The Benefit of this Establishment should be as general as the Attainment of its Object is desirable. It will therefore receive Pupils as soon as they have learned the first Elements of Letters, and will conduct them through the several Branches of Classical Learning to that Stage of Education from which they may proceed with Advantage to the Study of higher Sciences in the University of this or those of the neighboring States. Thus it will be calculated for every Class of Citizens; — as Reading, Writing, Arithmetic, the earlier Branches of the Mathematics, and the Grammar of our native Tongue, will be attended to no less than the learned Languages.

Agreeably to the liberal Principal [*sic*] of our Constitution, the Seminary will be open to Students of every religious profession. They, who, in this Respect differ from the Superintendent of the Academy, will be at Liberty to frequent the places of Worship and Instruction appointed by their Parents; but with Respect to their moral Conduct, all must be subject to general and uniform Discipline.

In the choice of Situation, Salubrity of Air, Convenience of Communication and Cheapness of Living have been principally consulted, and George Town offers these united Advantages.

The Price of Tuition will be moderate; in the Course of a few Years it will be reduced still lower, if the System formed for this Seminary be effectually carried into execution.

Such a plan of Education solicits, and, it is not presumption to add, deserves public Encouragement. The following gentlemen, and others that may be named hereafter will receive subscriptions and inform the subscribers to whom and in what proportion payments are to be made. In Maryland, the Hon. Charles Carroll of Carrollton; Henry Rozer, Notley Young, Robert Darnall, George Digges, Edmond Plowden, Esq'rs, Mr. Joseph Millard, Captain John Lancaster, Mr. Baker Brooke, Chandler Brent, Esq., Mr. Bernard O'Neill and Mr. Marsham Waring, merchants; John Darnall and Ignatius Wheeler, Esq., on the western shore; and on the eastern, Rev. Mr. Joseph Mosley, John

---

Manor was but the exception that proved the rule. But with the coming of religious liberty the Catholics were free to have a school of their own, and John Carroll took the lead among the clergy in urging its establishment. At a meeting of priests on May 15, 1789, it was agreed to issue a prospectus which would explain the nature of the school they had in mind and to solicit subscriptions. This document was printed later that year, and the work got under way. After some delays caused by lack of funds, Georgetown Academy opened in November 1791 with William Gaston of North Carolina, future associate justice of the state's supreme court, as the first student. As will be noted, the academy welcomed students of all religious faiths. Thus was begun the institution from which developed the first Catholic college in the United States. See John Gilmary Shea, *Memorial of the First Centenary of Georgetown College, D.C., Comprising a History of Georgetown University* (New York: P. F. Collier, 1891), 12–13.

Blake, Francis Hall, Charles Blake, William Matthews and John Tuitte, Esq'rs. In Pennsylvania, George Mead and Thomas Fitzsimmons, Esq'rs, Mr. Joseph Cauffman, Mr. Mark Wilcox and Mr. Thomas Lilly. In Virginia, Colonel Fitzgerald and George Brent, Esq'rs, and at New York, Dominick Lynch, Esq.

Subscriptions will also be received and every necessary Information given by the following Gentlemen, Directors of the Undertaking: The Rev. Messrs. John Carroll, James Pellentz, Robert Molyneux, John Ashton and Leonard Neale.

John Tracy Ellis, ed., *Documents of American Catholic History* (Wilmington, Del.: Michael Glazier, 1987), 1:168–69. (Footnotes in Ellis.) Printed with permission of the estate of John Tracy Ellis.

4. Rev. John Carroll et al. to George Washington [undated, late in 1789], and Reply, 12 March 1790

To George Washington, President of the United States of America.

Sir,

We have been long impatient to testify our joy and unbounded confidence in your being called, by an unanimous vote, to the first station of a country, in which that unanimity could not have been obtained without the previous merit of unexampled services, of eminent wisdom, and unblemished virtue. Our congratulations have not reached you sooner, because our scattered situation prevented the communication, and the collection of those sentiments, which warmed every breast. But the delay has furnished us with the opportunity, not merely of presaging the happiness to be expected under your administration, but of bearing testimony to that which we experience already. It is your peculiar talent, in war and in peace, to afford security to those, who commit their protection into your hands. In war, you shield them from the ravages of armed hostility: in peace you establish public tranquillity by the justice and moderation, not less than by the vigour, of your government. By example as well as by vigilance, you extend the influence of laws on the manners of our fellow-citizens. You encourage respect for religion, and inculcate, by words and actions, that principle, on which the welfare of nations so much depends, that a superintending providence governs the events of the world, and watches over the conduct of men. Your exalted maxims and unwearied attention to the moral and physical improvement of our country have produced already the happiest effects. Under your administration, America is animated with zeal for the attainment and encouragement of useful literature. She improves her agriculture, extends her commerce, and acquires with foreign nations a dignity, unknown to her before. From these happy events, in which none can feel a warmer interest than ourselves, we derive additional pleasure by recollection, that you, Sir, have been the principal instrument to effect so rapid a change in our political situation. This prospect of national prosperity is peculiarly pleasing to us on another account; because whilst our country preserves her freedom and independence, we shall have a well founded title to claim from her justice [and] equal rights of citizenship, as the price of our blood spilt under your eyes, and of our common exertions for her defence, under your auspicious conduct, rights rendered more dear to us by the remembrance of former hardships. When we pray for the preservation of them, where they have been granted; and expect the full extension of them from the justice of those States, which still restrict them; when we solicit the protection of Heaven over our common country: we neither omit nor can omit recommending your preservation to the singular care of divine providence; because we conceive that no human means are so available to promote the welfare of the United States, as the prolongation of your health and life, in which are included the energy of your example, the wisdom of your counsels, and the persuasive eloquence of your virtues.

J. Carroll, in behalf of the Roman Catholic Clergy

Charles Carroll of Carrollton, Daniel Carroll, Thos. FitzSimons, Domk. Lynch. — in behalf of the Roman Catholic Laity.

•

To the Roman Catholics in the United States of America.

Gentlemen, — While I now receive with much satisfaction your congratulations on my being called, by an unanimous vote, to the first station in my country; I cannot but duly notice your politeness in offering an apology for the unavoidable delay. As that delay has given you an opportunity of realizing, instead of anticipating, the benefits of the general government; you will do me the justice to believe that your testimony of the increase of public prosperity enhances the pleasure which I should otherwise have experienced from your affectionate Address.

I feel that my conduct in war and in peace has met with more general approbation than could reasonably have been expected: and I find myself disposed to consider that fortunate circumstance, in a great degree, resulting from the able support and extraordinary candor of my fellow-citizens of all denominations.

The prospect of national prosperity now before us is truly animating, and ought to excite the exertions of all good men to establish and secure the happiness of their Country, in the permanent duration of its freedom and independence. America, under the smiles of a Divine Providence — the protection of a good government — the cultivation of manners, morals and piety, can hardly fail of attaining an uncommon degree of eminence in literature, commerce, agriculture, improvements at home, and respectability abroad.

As mankind become more liberal, they will be more apt to allow, that all those who conduct themselves as worthy members of the community are equally entitled to the protection of civil government. I hope ever to see America among the foremost nations in examples of justice and liberality. And I presume that your fellow-citizens will not forget the patriotic part which you took in the accomplishment of their Revolution, and the establishment of their government; or the important assistance which they received from a nation in which the Roman Catholic religion is professed.

I thank you, Gentlemen, for your kind concern for me. While my life and my health shall continue, in whatever situation I may be, it shall be my constant endeavor to justify the favorable sentiments you are pleased to express of my conduct. And may the members of your Society in America, animated alone by the pure spirit of christianity, and still conducting themselves as faithful subjects of our free government, enjoy every temporal and spiritual felicity.

G. Washington.

John Tracy Ellis, ed., *Documents of American Catholic History* (Wilmington, Del.: Michael Glazier, 1987), 1:170–72. Printed with permission of the estate of John Tracy Ellis.

5. Bishop John Carroll, Prayer for Civil Authorities, 10 November 1791

We pray Thee, O almighty and eternal God! Who through Jesus Christ hast revealed Thy glory to all nations, to preserve the works of Thy Mercy, that Thy Church, being spread through the whole world may continue with unchanging faith in the confession of Thy name.

We pray Thee, Who alone art good and holy, to endow with heavenly knowledge, sincere zeal, and sanctity of life, our chief bishop, N.N., the vicar of Our Lord Jesus Christ, in the government of His Church; our own bishop, N.N. (or archbishop); all other bishops, prelates, and pastors of the Church; and especially those who are appointed to exercise amongst us the functions of the holy ministry, and conduct Thy people into the ways of salvation.

We pray Thee, O God of might, wisdom, and justice! through Whom authority is rightly administered, laws are enacted, and judgment decreed, assist with Thy holy spirit of counsel and fortitude the President of the United States, that his administration may be conducted in righteousness, and be eminently useful to Thy people over whom he presides; by encouraging due respect for virtue and religion; by a faithful execution of the laws in justice and mercy; and by restraining vice and immorality. Let the light of Thy divine wisdom direct the deliberations of Congress, and shine forth in all the proceedings and laws framed for our rule and government, so that they may tend to the preservation of peace, the promotion of national happiness, the increase of industry, sobriety, and useful knowledge; and may perpetuate to us the blessing of equal liberty.

We pray for his excellency, the Governor of this State, for the members of the Assembly, for all judges, magistrates, and other officers who are appointed to guard our political welfare, that they may be enabled, by Thy powerful protection, to discharge the duties of their respective stations with honesty and ability.

We recommend likewise, to Thy unbounded mercy, all our brethren and fellow citizens throughout the United States, that they may be blessed in the knowledge and sanctified in the observance of Thy most holy law; that they may be preserved in union, and in that peace which the world cannot give; and after enjoying the blessings of this life, be admitted to those which are eternal.

Finally, we pray to Thee, O Lord of mercy, to remember the souls of Thy servants departed who are gone before us with the sign of faith, and repose in the sleep of peace; the souls of our parents, relatives, and friends; of those who, when living, were members of this congregation, and particularly of such as are lately deceased; of all benefactors who, by their donations or legacies to this church, witnessed to their zeal for the decency of divine worship and proved their claim to our grateful and charitable remembrance. To these, O Lord, and to all that rest in Christ, grant, we beseech Thee, a place of refreshment, light, and everlasting peace, through the same Jesus Christ, our Lord and Saviour. Amen.

John Tracy Ellis, ed., *Documents of American Catholic History* (Wilmington, Del.: Michael Glazier, 1987), 1:174–75. Printed with permission of the estate of John Tracy Ellis.

6. A Norfolk Trustee to President Thomas Jefferson and Members of Congress, December 1818[1]

Sir:

Although a stranger, the patriotic exertions, which distinguished your conduct in vindicating the rights of your country have made your name familiar to me. But your wisdom in fixing those rights upon principles, which will shed unceasing blessings upon millions yet unborn, shall forever endear your character to every benevolent heart. Under this conviction I feel encouraged to submit with all deference and respect to the consideration of so luminous a mind, a subject, which at some future day must be deserving the attention of those whom Providence may call to the general government of the States. Religion has been always deemed a necessary auxiliary to the sound and enlightened policy of every State. To derive from it those salutary benefits, it is calculated to bestow, and to obviate those evils that might arise from a collision of those religious and civil institutions, which are alike the work of man, the various governments that have prevailed in the world have endeavoured to assimilate the outward character of those institutions....

The different religionists of these countries, if I am well informed, already elect the ministers of their faith of whatever grade or dignity. Besides this system having a merit of being perfectly conformable to the fundamental and vital principles of the American constitution, it is in itself most just and

1. Peter Guilday notes that this broadside was also distributed to state governors and members of state legislatures, to judges, "and to all who held any position of prominence in the United States" (*The Catholic Church in Virginia, 1815–1922* [New York: United States Catholic Historical Society, 1924], 93).

reasonable, that those who are most interested in the good conduct of their Pastors, and remunerate them for their labours, should have a right of selecting those whom they deem most suitable to their wishes and in their judgment most deserving of their confidence. This was also the discipline and practice of the Catholic Church for near a thousand years, nor was it tamely resigned by the people without many a violent struggle, and until an unnatural connection between the church and the state, overwhelmed and extinguished their civil and religious rights. This right is recognized even now by the Court of Rome in conceding to the King of England the title of interfering in the appointment of Catholic Bishops in Ireland. The Pope affects to establish, that this right, which originally belonged to the people, may be now transferred to their governors. Upon the accuracy of this reasoning it is needless to remark any further, than that he lays down a fundamental principle of this government in Europe, upon which he is unwilling to act in America, because so advised by the emmissaries [sic] of the Sulpicians at Paris and at Rome, or because his Ministers tell him, if such a concession should be required by the government of the United States, he might be allowed some equivalent in return, which only betrays an ignorance of the principles which guide the policy of those countries. But whatever the views of the court of Rome may be, in its conduct towards the Catholics of North America, who now insist upon this right, as originally belonging to them; as conformable to the fundamental principles of the constitution; and as acted upon by other religionists in this country...it is evident, that nothing but intrigue can induce the court of Rome not to accede to the just demands of the Catholics in North America.

It only now remains to examine the objections to the enactment of a Law excluding all those from being Pastors or Ministers of congregations, or Bishops in any State of the Union, unless elected by the people of their persuasion. It cannot create any jealousy, or give any umbrage to the other religionists, as they all act as if such a law existed, and most of them have established it by their bye laws in almost the whole Union. The Catholics alone, I believe, are the only religionists, whose clergy are differently appointed, of whom 19/20ths. are Irish and who are extremely anxious for such a law. Their complaints are loud and universal, that French, Dutch and German Clergymen are imposed upon them without their knowledge or consent, whose language they do not understand, and whose jargon in preaching they consider a burlesque upon their religion. Such a law cannot then meet the disapprobation of any religionist except of those, who are desirous to keep up a foreign influence, which may prove injurious to the State at some future period. This is already apprehended by the sensible Catholics, especially the Irish, who have been already the victims of French and Italian influence in the land of their birth. They have remarked with regret in Maryland and Pennsylvania where the Catholics are most numerous, that the eternal subject of the harangues of the foreign influenced Clergy in those States, is obedience to the Church, that is to themselves. They dread the influence of such doctrine upon ignorant and weak minds, and suspect that is so incessantly inculcated for some sinister purpose. They remember to hear it constantly vociferated in Europe, that the French revolution, so odious to the legitimates has sprung from that of America, and that a durable peace could not be established on earth, while such a hotbed of democracy exists, and that this is the language of the Royalist Priests even in America.

I have heard it remarked that such a law would be regarded as interfering with the liberty of Conscience, so sacred in this country. But I am satisfied that this is viewing the question in a very wrong light. It does not relate to any doctrine of religion, but merely to a municipal regulation, to which it is the duty of every Government to attend. It simply comes to this, whether a foreign power shall exercise a right over the Citizens, which only belongs to themselves, and impose persons upon them without their knowledge, and contrary to their wishes; or whether the State will pass a law to protect them in those rights, which are exercised by those, who have rejected the authority of that foreign power: or whether they will allow that foreign power to exercise an authority in this country, which it would not be allowed in any other, and enjoy an influence here which no foreign power ought to have within the State. No letter rescript or bull, issuing from the court of Rome, is allowed to be published in any Catholic State in the world, without the expressed consent and approbation of the Government, while in countries not Catholic, the most arbitrary and despotic laws are clandestinely enforced by the Clergy appointed by the Pope, without the knowledge of the governments in such States, and have been generally submitted to by the people for nearly two centuries, on account of the acrimonious spirit of religious intolerance, which generally prevailed, but since a more bland and benevolent temper has gradually arisen among Christians, the unlimited power of the court of Rome has been proportionably contracting. Such a law regards not what doctrine is taught, but whether the teachers be imposed upon the citizens contrary to their will, which is against true liberty, and whether those teachers hold political principles dangerous to the State, and which they may spread under the mask of religion.

The other religionists have no connection with those of Europe, except in the identity of faith, but the Catholics have a common church polity with those of their communion all over the world, although under Catholic governments, that polity is regulated and governed by the municipal laws of the States, (and this is what they warmly desire to be similarly established by law in America) to prevent the evils, that may possibly arise from an abuse of foreign influence. Such cannot happen among other religionists, because in their church governments, they have nothing to do with those of other States, and it is conducted by free citizens born in those States, who have common principles and common interests with the people. In short viewing it on all sides, it is as in Catholic countries, more a question of policy than of religion. But it may be asked why they do not exclude those teachers of their own accord. This would be most assuredly the shortest way, if all men could view every object in the same light: if all were alike capable of forming a correct judgment upon all subjects: if all were equally prepared to divest themselves of prejudices, especially when these are of a long standing; cherished from habit, diversified by education, and by different manners of strangers to each other, by birth, by language and by country. You will see at a glance the difficulty, not to say impossibility of bringing order, unity and harmony out of such heterogeneous materials, and that nothing but the sanction of law can make them subside in concord and peace, by closing every avenue against the influence of prejudices of passion and of foreign intrigue.

It is also said, and what may not be said by envy, or by ambition to blame men in power, that the discussion of such a law would occasion unpopularity. This might be possible among the ignorant or interested, but it certainly never could influence the thinking and wise nor should this weigh for a moment with any man, who sincerely wishes the tranquillity and safety of the Nation to rest for ever upon a firm and solid foundation. I cannot conceive how an able and honest statesman, can with consistency, with honour to himself, and justice to this country sit down cooly to calculate the quantum of obliquy he may possibly bring upon himself, in promoting a measure, which may avert not only a possible but also a probably and positive evil from this country.

France is now not only the Ally, but also the dependant of England as far as relates to the government and must continue so for half a century, and if we be allowed to assume that a war might break out between this country and Britain, the former will probably be compelled to become a party. Perhaps were she in condition to enter upon a war even her inclination, or at least that of her government would urge her to that evil, thus to rid herself of the friends of Napoleon and of his family. But allowing her to be indisposed to embark in a war with this country, Britain unless she joined with her cordially, might place the late Emperor in her embraces. His return from Elba tells the present Dynasty, how great its peril would be, and must in spite even of inclination, or interest become your enemy. She lacks not in soldiers, and England has ships. Would it then be wise to cherish in the heart of the country, or to dispose in the ranks of your army, a large body of men, who might be so far seduced by an hired, or mistaken Priesthood to countenance the enemies of your government in the interior, or to desert to the standard of the enemy on the frontiers[?] You have seen in the late war, the Clergy of those States in which your revolution began, seduced, as is supposed, by promises of ascendency, become the allies of that nation, which they once so enthusiastically opposed; and can it be supposed, that men of monarchical principles, and national attachments and prejudices could not be more easily arrayed against you, seduced by promises, and allured by privileges[,] dignity and honours, whenever personal safety shall permit[?] But by placing the appointment in the hands of citizens by law, and citizens too to whom the recollection of past injuries has rendered the British name odious, you check the influence of foreign powers within your State, you will have a clergy among those religionists of their own choice who will command their confidence, and whose political principles will be in unison with their own, and with those of the country they have adopted.

The right of the people to choose their civil governors is the fundamental principle of your constitution, and the unbounded liberty of conscience is also another fundamental principle, and as the law guarantees and secures the right of election in the former case, so the latter is nugatory without it, and tends to excite a spirit of discord among the citizens, fomented and fanned by the policy, intrigue, and craft of foreign governments. How readily foreign politicians can avail themselves of such an order of things, we are instructed by the history of nations, and that some underplot of that nature is now acting in the world, we have some ground to suspect, when we reflect on the extraordinary phenomenon in the politics of Europe, of the Pope being restored to his temporal rank among the legitimates, and the order of the Jesuits being re-established through the influence of the English Cabinet, and that, notwithstanding the noise made about it in the House of Commons by Cox Hippesly, it has received the most marked attention in Washington from the English Ambassador, promising that it would be indemnified by his Government for the losses it sustained from the British troops in their incursion to the capital.

Whatever the views of the British Government may be, in affording such countenance to the Pope and the Jesuits, while it is promoting a propaganda of Methodism as well in America as in the most distant regions (Catholic countries excepted) time will develop, but it must be evident to common sense, that some object is in contemplation, and that consequently it behoves the Pilots of every State to be vigilant, lest any power claiming unlimited authority over the minds and opinions of men, may not feel an interest, or be influenced by other power, to favour such religious teachers and guides, who are likely to prove fit instruments in misleading the people upon points, where it may not be easy for the multitude to discriminate between religious and civil duties. The clearsighted and penetrating may discover the imposition, and resist, but the many are not so easily enlightened, and feuds, contention and discord may arise to the prejudice of good order and Christian charity, and religion in the hands of an ignorant[,] misguided and corrupted Priesthood, will whenever it suits the views of politicians, become a bane and a scourge instead of a blessing bearing comfort and consolation to its votaries.

It is clear, that at all times, but more especially in those in which we live, and considered as the United States are, with an evil eye by the Kings, Nobility, and Clergy of Europe, that her own safety, her interest and sound policy should urge America to limit the power of every foreign government within her territory, even in matters of religion, so far as regards the teachers to be employed for the instruction of the people; and that none should be suffered to officiate in that capacity unless by the suffrages of such American citizens as profess the same religion, worship in the same congregation, and are united in the same faith, whatever that may be.

I am with respect, your Most H'mble and Obt. Servt.

Peter Guilday, *The Catholic Church in Virginia, 1815–1922* (New York: United States Catholic Historical Society, 1924), 93–101.

7. Alexis de Tocqueville, *Democracy in America,* 1835

About fifty years ago Ireland began to pour a Catholic population into the United States; and on their part, the Catholics of America made proselytes, so that, at the present moment more than a million Christians professing the truths of the Church of Rome are to be found in the Union.[1] These Catholics are faithful to the observances of their religion; they are fervent and zealous in the belief of their doctrines. Yet they constitute the most republican and the most democratic class in the United States. This fact may surprise the observer at first, but the cause of it may easily be discovered upon reflection.

I think the Catholic religion has erroneously been regarded as the natural enemy of democracy. Among the various sects of Christians, Catholicism seems to me, on the contrary, to be one of the most favorable to equality of condition among men. In the Catholic Church the religious community is composed of only two elements: the priest and the people. The priest alone rises above the rank of his flock, and all below him are equal.

On doctrinal points the Catholic faith places all human capacities upon the same level; it subjects the wise and ignorant, the man of genius and the vulgar crowd, to the details of the same creed; it imposes the same observances upon the rich and the needy, it inflicts the same austerities upon the strong and the weak; it listens to no compromise with mortal man, but, reducing all the human race to the same standard, it confounds all the distinctions of society at the foot of the same altar, even as they are confounded in the sight of God. If Catholicism predisposes the faithful to obedience, it certainly does not prepare them for inequality; but the contrary may be said of Protestantism, which generally tends to make men independent more than to render them equal. Catholicism is like an absolute monarchy; if the sovereign be removed, all the other classes of society are more equal than in republics.

It has not infrequently occurred that the Catholic priest has left the service of the altar to mix with the governing powers of society and to take his place among the civil ranks of men. This religious influence has sometimes been used to secure the duration of that political state of things to which he belonged. Thus we have seen Catholics taking the side of aristocracy from a religious motive. But no sooner is the priesthood entirely separated from the government, as is the case in the United States, than it is found that no class of men is more naturally disposed than the Catholics to transfer the doctrine of the equality of condition into the political world.

If, then, the Catholic citizens of the United States are not forcibly led by the nature of their tenets to adopt democratic and republican principles, at least they are not necessarily opposed to them; and their social position, as well as their limited number, obliges them to adopt these opinions. Most of the Catholics are poor, and they have no chance of taking a part in the government unless it is open to all the citizens. They constitute a minority, and

---

1. Tocqueville was in error on the number of Catholics in the United States in 1831; the best estimate for the year 1830 was 318,000.

all rights must be respected in order to ensure to them the free exercise of their own privileges. These two causes induce them, even unconsciously, to adopt political doctrines which they would perhaps support with less zeal if they were rich and preponderant.

The Catholic clergy of the United States have never attempted to oppose this political tendency; but they seek rather to justify it. The Catholic priests in America have divided the intellectual world into two parts: in the one they place the doctrines of revealed religion, which they assent to without discussion; in the other they leave those political truths which they believe the Deity has left open to free inquiry. Thus the Catholics of the United States are at the same time the most submissive believers and the most independent citizens. . . .

I showed in the first Part of this work how the American clergy stand aloof from secular affairs. This is the most obvious but not the only example of their self-restraint. In America religion is a distinct sphere, in which the priest is sovereign, but out of which he takes care never to go. Within its limits he is master of the mind; beyond them he leaves men to themselves and surrenders them to the independence and instability that belong to their nature and their age. I have seen no country in which Christianity is clothed with fewer forms, figures, and observances than in the United States, or where it presents more distinct, simple, and general notions to the mind. Although the Christians of America are divided into a multitude of sects, they all look upon their religion in the same light. This applies to Roman Catholicism as well as to other forms of belief. There are no Roman Catholic priests who show less taste for the minute individual observances, for extraordinary or peculiar means of salvation, or who cling more to the spirit and less to the letter of the law than the Roman Catholic priests of the United States. Nowhere is that doctrine of the church which prohibits the worship reserved to God alone from being offered to the saints more clearly inculcated or more generally followed. Yet the Roman Catholics of America are very submissive and very sincere. . . .

America is the most democratic country in the world, and it is at the same time (according to reports worthy of belief) the country in which the Roman Catholic religion makes most progress. At first sight this is surprising.

Two things must here be accurately distinguished: equality makes men want to form their own opinions; but, on the other hand, it imbues them with the taste and the idea of unity, simplicity, and impartiality in the power that governs society. Men living in democratic times are therefore very prone to shake off all religious authority; but if they consent to subject themselves to any authority of this kind, they choose at least that it should be single and uniform. Religious powers not radiating from a common center are naturally repugnant to their minds; and they almost as readily conceive that there should be no religion as that there should be several.

At the present time, more than in any preceding age, Roman Catholics are seen to lapse into infidelity, and Protestants to be converted to Roman Catholicism. If you consider Catholicism within its own organization, it seems to be losing; if you consider it from outside, it seems to be gaining. Nor is this difficult to explain. The men of our days are naturally little disposed to believe; but as soon as they have any religion, they immediately find in themselves a latent instinct that urges them unconsciously towards Catholicism. Many of the doctrines and practices of the Roman Catholic Church astonish them, but they feel a secret admiration for its discipline, and its great unity attracts them. If Catholicism could at length withdraw itself from the political animosities to which it has given rise, I have hardly any doubt but that the same spirit of the age which appears to be so opposed to it would become so favorable as to admit of its great and sudden advancement.

One of the most ordinary weaknesses of the human intellect is to seek to reconcile contrary principles and to purchase peace at the expense of logic. Thus there have ever been and will ever be men who, after having submitted some portion of their religious belief to the principle of authority, will seek to exempt several other parts of their faith from it and to keep their minds floating at random between liberty and obedience. But I am inclined to believe that the number of these thinkers will be less in democratic than in other ages, and that our posterity will tend more and more to a division into only two parts, some relinquishing Christianity entirely and others returning to the Church of Rome.

Alexis de Tocqueville, *Democracy in America,* ed. Phillips Bradley (New York: Alfred A. Knopf, 1945), 1:300–302, 2:26–30; also in John Tracy Ellis, ed., *Documents of American Catholic History* (Wilmington, Del.: Michael Glazier, 1987), 1:233–36. Printed with permission of the estate of John Tracy Ellis.

8. William Gaston, Address to the Constitutional Convention of North Carolina, 1835

Mr. Chairman—The peculiar situation in which I am known to stand with respect to the question now under consideration, and the character of the debate which has already taken place upon it, may be thought to render it indelicate in me to interfere at all in the discussion. But no considerations of delicacy ought to deter me from the full and faithful performance of my duties as a Delegate of the People of this Convention. Besides, silence is likely to subject me to much greater misconstruction than the most frank and fearless exposition of my opinions. At all events, the latter is the course to which I am prompted by inclination as well as by a sense of propriety, and therefore is it, that I must ask the patient and kind attention of this Committee.... I am not, indeed, aware that any one decent citizen of this State has called in question the purity of my motives or questioned the propriety of my conduct, or has expressed dissatisfaction at my course. But this is an age of detraction. Calumnies are the ordinary weapons of warfare with religious as well as political factions; and if I have not yet been assailed by slander on this subject, it is not unlikely that I soon shall be. This explanation is therefore due, not only to my character, but to the character of the State, whose honor is always involved in the fair fame of her sons. [Gaston then entered upon a detailed explanation of how he came to accept appointment to the Supreme Court of North Carolina in 1833 in view of the controverted article thirty-two of the state constitution barring those who denied the truth of the Protestant religion.]

Prejudice and cupidity are formidable foes, and will no doubt oppose an obstinate resistance to every effort which may be made to dislodge them from their hold. But we should be false to this people, if we distrusted their ability to decide correctly on this question. Lay it *fairly* before them, and no man need doubt the issue. The question is, ought there to be any Religious test in the Constitution? Shall any man be debarred from office, merely because of his *opinions* on matters of Religion? To me it seems, if there can be any certainty in moral or political science, the answer must be in the negative. It is an invasion of the right of the people to select those whom they deem worthy of confidence, and a violation of the right of the citizen to acquire the confidence of his fellow men, and to enjoy the rewards which they wish to bestow on his intelligence, industry, patriotism and virtue. In those governments which undertake to prescribe a religious faith to their subjects, and command its profession as a part of civil duty, there is at least a congruity in visiting disobedience by appropriate penalties. Incapacitation for office is *there* a punishment for disloyalty — and if it be supposed not adequate to its end, it is followed up by imprisonment, fine, confiscation, exile, torture and death. The *principle* is the same in all these grades of punishment. It is a visitation of the vengeance of the State upon those who offend against its institutions. But where a State is avowedly based on Religious Freedom, where it proclaims that every man has from nature a right, which he cannot surrender, and which none may take away — a "natural and unalienable right" to worship Almighty God according to the dictates of *his own conscience* — a right, of the correct exercise of which, his conscience is the sole judge — how can that State, without a violation of first principles, punish him by degradation because of the exercise of that very right? To this question, an answer is attempted to be given; and if the indefensible character of the cause did not forbid all wonder at any sophism that might be pressed into its defence, I should find it difficult either to restrain, or fitly to express my surprise at the nature of the pretended answer. It is very gravely said, that no man has any natural right to office, and therefore, the refusal of an office to him cannot be a punishment....

Sir, I am opposed, out and out, to any interference of the State with the *opinions* of its citizens, and more especially with their opinion on Religious subjects. The good order of society requires that *actions* and *practices* injurious to the public peace and public morality, should be restrained, and but a moderate portion of practical good sense is required to enable the proper authorities to decide what conduct is really thus injurious. But to decide on truth or error, on the salutary or pernicious consequences of *opinions,* requires a skill in dialectics, a keenness of discernment, a forecast and comprehension of mind, and above all, an exemption from bias, which do not ordinarily belong to human tribunals. The preconceived opinions of him, who is appointed to try, become the standard by which the opinions of others are measured, and as these correspond with, or differ from his own, they are pronounced true or false, salutary or pernicious.... Law is the proper judge of *action*, and reward or punishment its proper sanction. Reason is the proper umpire of *opinion*, and argument and discussion its only fit advocates. To denounce opinions by law is as silly, and unfortunately much more tyrannical, as it would be, to punish crime by logic. Laws [*sic*] calls out the force of the community to compel obedience to its mandates. To operate an opinion by law, is to enslave the intellect and oppress the soul — to reverse the order of nature, and make reason subservient to force. But of all the attempts to arrogate unjust dominion, none is so pernicious as the efforts of tyrannical men to rule over human conscience. Religion is exclusively an affair between man and his God. If there be any subject upon which the interference of human power is more forbidden, than on all others, it is on Religion. Born of Faith — nurtured by Hope — invigorated by Charity — looking for its rewards in a world beyond the grave — it is of Heaven, heavenly. The evidence upon which it is founded, and the sanctions by which it is upheld, are addressed solely to the understanding and the purified affections. Even He, from whom cometh every pure and perfect gift, and to whom Religion is directed as its author, its end, and its exceedingly great reward, imposes no coercion on his children. They believe, or doubt, or reject, according to the impression which the testimony of revealed truth makes upon their minds. He causes His Sun to shine, alike on the believer and the unbeliever, and His dews to fertilize equally the soil of the orthodox and the heretic.... [Gaston here described the services of George Calvert, Roger Williams, and William Penn to religious freedom in colonial America, and how that principle had won out in most of the United States.] But finally, in every other of the twenty-four States of this Union, *perfect Religious Freedom*, perfect equality of sects, an entire exemption from religious tests, are now solemnly declared to be the basis on which rest all their Institutions. This salutary principle has spread across the Atlantic, and triumphed over the misrule and inveterate usages of the ancient Governments there. With scarcely an exception, it now prevails throughout *all* Europe, and Religious opinions are no longer there a qualification for, or an incapacity for Civil employment. And can it be, that *we* shall prove recreant in this noble strife for securing the sanctity of conscience and purity of religion? Shall we afford to the bigots, the fanatics, and the friends of arbitrary power abroad, an apology for claiming this State as an ally in the cause of Intolerance? — I hope not. I trust that we shall act *up* to the axiom proclaimed in our Bill of Rights, and permit no man to suffer inconvenience or to incur incapacity, because of religion, whether he be Jew or Gentile, Christian or Infidel, Heretic or Orthodox. Pollute not the ark of God with unholy touch. Divine Truth *needs* not the support of human power, either to convince the understanding or to regulate the heart. Dare not to define divine truth, for it belongs not to your functions, and you may set up falsehood and error in its stead. Prohibit, restrain and punish, as offences against human society, all practices insulting to the faith, the institutions, and the worship of your people, but offer no bribes to lure men to profess a faith which they do not believe, inflict no penalties to deter them from embracing what their understandings approve, and make no distinction of ranks and orders in the community because of religious opinions....

Proceeding and Debates of the Convention of North Carolina, Called to Amend the Constitution of the State, Which Assembled at Raleigh, June 4, 1835 (Raleigh, N.C.: Joseph Gales and Son, 1836), 264–65, 283–85, 292; also in John Tracy Ellis, ed., *Documents of American Catholic History* (Wilmington, Del.: Michael Glazier, 1987), 1:243–46. (Bracketed summaries in Ellis.)

9. The Constitution of the Roman Catholic Churches of North Carolina, South Carolina, and Georgia: Which are Comprised in the Dioceses of Charleston, and Province of Baltimore, U.S.A., As Fully Agreed To, and Accepted, After Repeated Discussion, By the Clergy and the Several Congregations, and Regularly Confirmed by the Bishop, and Subsequently Amended According to the Form Prescribed, 1839

Preface

The system of government which exists in the Roman Catholic Church is divided into two parts; the one of divine institution; the other, the result of human regulation; this second part must, necessarily, be so far dependent upon the first as that no one of its provisions shall in any way counteract any principle or provision of the former. Hence it has always, in the Roman Catholic Church, been an invariable and essential rule, that in making those secondary regulations, the principal, if not the exclusive power of legislation should be vested in those persons who were, by the ordinance of our Saviour, made the judges and witnesses and preservers of his institutions. A distinction of parts was again made in that portion of the system which was to be the result of human regulation; it comprises ecclesiastical discipline, and the regulation of those temporalities, or that property, which is necessary for the support of religion; the first portion, that is, ecclesiastical discipline, was necessarily to be under the exclusive regulation of those whom the Holy Ghost had placed as bishops to govern the Church of God; it was never known in the Catholic Church that any other body or individual was admitted to have any power therein. Respecting the second part of this head, three questions presented themselves, viz.: How are those means to be procured? In whom are they to be vested? In what manner are they to be expended? A few principles are clear, viz.: That the Church had no divine power of taxation. That there was a general obligation on those who partook of the benefit of religion to contribute to its support, and that they who served the altar had a right to live by the altar. Therefore it was plain, that this general right and general obligation should be made operative by some special regulations. These regulations should necessarily be found at different times: hence they could never be permanent, invariable, or uniform throughout the world; but it was plain that unless there existed a power of restraint as to the mode of regulation, they might in some instances be made in direct opposition to, or incompatible with the divine institution itself. Thus the readiest and most effectual mode of raising money might be direct simony, or some other mode equally criminal. Church property might be vested in persons who, though professing a regard for religion, were its worst enemies. In its expenditure, it might be applied to ends subversive of religion; and in actual contradiction to that object for which it was contributed. The spiritual governors of the church might on one side feel it their conscientious duty to prescribe to a clergyman a special line of conduct commanded by the divine law; and the person who controlled the expenditure of the fund, including the means for the support of the priest, might withhold from him those means because of his obedience to the lawful command of his proper superior; and give them to create opposition to the laws of the Church.

We need not have resource to ancient history, or to foreign nations, to show that those evils have frequently occurred. The scandalous accounts of several churches of the United States, too flagrantly exhibit the exemplification. The experience of the early ages also proved it. We find that originally all this power was vested in the apostles; they distributed portions of it amongst others, deputing deacons principally to the charge and management of the property. When the churches became more numerous, the bishop constituted an arch-deacon to receive the reports and accounts of the deacons of the several churches; from him the bishop received the general report, and through him he gave the general directions; and thus the management of the temporalities of the church was under his control, for the reasons above specified.

In process of time, in some places, the most prudent and zealous of the laity were either appointed by the people or by the bishop *to aid* the priests and deacons in the management of the property. In the confusion of feudal times, powerful barons and others took the property into their care as patrons, and several new abuses were the consequence. But those abuses were frequently withstood, and in other instances a portion of the right of the Church was yielded to preserve the rest. One great principle, however, was kept sacred and inviolable throughout, viz.: That the management of ecclesiastical affairs was solely in the prelates, and that they had *at least a negative* [veto] upon the management of church property.

It is useless to inquire minutely, how attempts to establish a different principle have originated in some of our congregations. A general remark will suffice; they have as their guide, not a knowledge of the laws of their own church, but the example of churches which protested against its doctrines, and its discipline too frequently served as their model: and a bad custom originating in accident, was soon quoted as an established usage. The constitution of this diocese was formed, for the purpose of preventing in future the recurrence of evils of this description within its limits.

The portions of our church government are very like to those of the government of this Union. The entire consists of dioceses [*sic*], the bishop of each of which holds his place, not as the deputy of the Pope, but as a successor to the Apostles; as the governor of each state holds his place not as the deputy of the President, but as vested therewith by the same power which vests the President with his own authority. And as all the states are bound together in one federation, of which the President is the head, so are the dioceses collected into one church, of which the Pope is the head. Each state has power to make its own laws, provided they do not contravene the general Constitution of the United States; so in each diocess there exists the power of legislation, provided the statutes made therein be not incompatible with the faith or general discipline of the Catholic Church. The legislature of the Union is collected from all the states, and the decisions of the majority bind the individuals and the states which they represent; the general legislative body of the church is a council composed of the representatives of each diocess, and the decision of the majority binds the members and their dioceses. It is the duty of the President to have the laws of the Union executed in every state, as it is the duty of the Pope to have the general laws of the church executed in every diocess. The bishop is also bound to have them carried into execution within his own diocess, and he has power, and it is his duty to make such special regulations and laws as circumstances may render necessary for their more effectual observance, and for the spiritual benefit of his own district. As our states are subdivided, so are our dioceses: and as the laws of Congress and those of the state are binding in each subdivision, so are the general laws of the church and the laws of the diocess in each parish or district the same; but in each subdivision, special regulations are made, each corporate city, town, or district, has its own by-laws which would be invalid if incompatible with the general laws of Congress or those of the states, otherwise they are of force; so in each parish or district by-laws which are incompatible with the general law of the church or the law of the diocess, are invalid.

With this general view, the frame of the following Constitution will be the more easily understood. The object of its formation was to lay down those general principles of law, and to show their special bearing in the most usual cases; and then upon the mode of raising, vesting, and managing church property, to fix the special manner in which the great principles that are recognised by the church should be carried into practice. This was done by consultation, discussion, and arrangement between the bishop, the clergy, and the laity, in several meetings in the several districts; and the outline of the entire, together with some of the most important of its special provisions, was laid before the Holy See, after it had been adopted, on the 25th of September, 1822. No objection having been received from that quarter, and its provisions having been more maturely examined and tested by some experience, it is now published for the use of the members...Charleston, Dec. 31, 1839.

General appendix to Sebastian G. Messmer, ed., *The Works of the Rt. Rev. Dr. John England* (Cleveland: Arthur H. Clarke, 1908).

10. John Hughes, Bishop of New York, "Address of the Catholics to Their Fellow Citizens of the City and State of New York," 10 August 1840

Fellow Citizens:

We, the Roman Catholics of the City of New York, feeling that both our civil and religious rights are abridged and injuriously affected by the operation of the Common School System,[1] and by the construction which the Common Council have lately put on the laws authorizing that system, beg leave to state our grievances, with the deepest confidence in the justice of the American character; that if our complaints are well founded, you will assist us in obtaining the redress to which we are entitled — if they are not well founded, we are ready to abandon them.

We are Americans and American citizens. If some of us are foreigners, it is only by the accident of birth. As citizens, our ambition is to be Americans — and if we cannot be so by birth, we are so by choice and preference, which we deem an equal evidence of our affection and attachment to the Laws and Constitution of the country. But our children, for whose rights as well as our own we contend in this matter, are Americans by nativity. So that we are either, like yourselves, natives of the soil, or, like your fathers from the Eastern world, have become Americans under the sanction of the Constitution, by the birthright of selection and preference.

We hold, therefore, the same idea of our rights that you hold of yours. We wish not to diminish yours, but only to secure and enjoy our own. Neither have we the slightest suspicion that you would wish us to be deprived of any privilege, which you claim for yourselves. If then we have suffered by the operation of the Common School System in the City of New York, it is to be imputed rather to our own supineness, than to any wish on your part that we should be aggrieved.

The intention of the Legislature of this State in appropriating public funds for the purposes of popular schools, *must have been* (whatever construction the lawyers of the Common Council put upon it) to diffuse the blessings

---

1. "After reading the address, the Right Rev. Prelate said ... it might be proper that he should mention some of the circumstances authorizing the language adopted in it.... For what purpose does the first charter of this incorporated Public School Society purport to have been given? They had read the language of the report drawn up by the Common Council, in which it was stated that anything sectarian or religious in the instruction given in a school was a disqualification, and cut off that school from all participation in the Common School Fund; but this was not the language of the charter by which the Public School Society was incorporated; for in that it was recited that it was given for the education of children belonging to no known denomination, and for implanting in their minds the principles of *religion* and morality.... From that time this Public School Society, thus incorporated, passed on, step by step, enlarging their powers, and becoming favorites with the State and City authorities, until this private incorporation took charge of the children — not of no known denomination, that they might be taught religion and morality, but of all classes, and upon a principle that operated to exclude religion altogether" (secretary's notes from the meeting in which Hughes delivered his address and accompanying remarks, in Lawrence Kehoe, ed., *Complete Works of the Most Rev. John Hughes, D.D., Archbishop of New York* [New York: Lawrence Kehoe, 1865], 1:65).

of education among the people, without encroachment on the civil and religious rights of the citizens. It was, *it must have been,* to have implanted in the minds of youth, principles of knowledge and virtue, which would secure to the State a future population of enlightened and virtuous, instead of ignorant and vicious members.

This was certainly their general intention, and no other would have justified their bountiful appropriation of the public funds. But in carrying out the measure, this patriotic and wise intention has been lost sight of; and in the City of New York, at least, under the late arbitrary determination of the present Common Council, such intention of the legislature is not only disregarded, but the high public ends to which it was directed, are manifestly being defeated. Here knowledge, according to the late decision, mere secular knowledge, is what we are to understand by education, in the sense of the legislature of New York. And if you should allow the smallest ray of religion to enter the school-room; if you should teach the children that there is an eye that sees every wicked thought, there is a God, a state of rewards and punishment beyond this life; then, according to the decision of the Common Council, you forfeit all claim to the bounty of the State, although your scholars should have become as learned as Newton, or wise as Socrates. Is then, we would ask you, fellow citizens, a practical rejection of the Christian religion in all its forms, and without the substitution of any other, the basis on which you would form the principles and character of the future citizens of this great Commonwealth? Are the meek lessons of religion and virtue, which pass from the mother's lips into the heart of her child, to be chilled and frozen by icy contact with a system of education thus interpreted?

Is enlightened villainy so precious in the public eye, that science is to be cultivated whilst virtue is neglected, and religion, its only adequate groundwork, is formally and authoritatively proscribed? Is it your wish that vice should thus be elevated from its low and natural companionship with ignorance, and be married to knowledge imparted at the public expense?

We do not say that even the Common Council profess to require that the Christian religion should be excluded from the Common Schools. They only contend that the inculcation of each or any of its doctrines would be sectarianism, and thus lest sectarianism should be admitted Christianity is substantially excluded. Christianity in this country is made up of the different creeds of the various denominations, and since all these creeds are proscribed, the Christian religion necessarily is banished from the hall of public education.

The objections which we have thus far stated, fellow citizens, ought to appear to you, in our opinion, as strong to you as they do to us. For though we may differ in our definition of the religion of Christ, still we all generally profess to believe, to revere it, as the foundation of moral virtue and social happiness. Now we know of no fixed principle of infidelity, except in the *negation* of the Christian religion. The adherents of this principle may differ in other points of skepticism, but in rejecting Christianity they are united. Their confession of faith is a belief in the *negative* of Christianity — but they reject it *in toto* — whilst the Common School rejects it only in all its several parts, under the name of Sectarianism.

It is manifest, therefore, that the Public School System of the City of New York, is entirely favorable to the sectarianism of infidelity, and opposed only to that of positive Christianity. And is it your wish, fellow citizens, is it your wish more than ours, that infidelity should have a predominancy and advantages, in the public schools, which are denied to Christianity? Is it your wish that your children should be brought up under a system of education so called, which shall detach them from the Christian belief which you profess, whatever it may be — and prepare them for initiation into the mysteries of Fanny Wrightism, or any other scheme of infidelity which may come in their way? Are you willing that your children, educated at your expense, shall be educated on a principle *antagonist* [sic] to the Christian religion? that you shall have the toil and labor of cultivating the ground, and sowing the seed, in order that infidelity may reap the harvest?

With us it is a matter of surprise that conscientious persons of all Christian denominations have not been struck with this bad feature of the system as understood by the Common Council. A new sectarianism antagonist to all *Christian* sects has been generated in, not the common schools, as the State originally understood the term, but in the *public* schools of the Public School Society; this new sectarianism is adopted by the Common Council of the City, and is supported, *to the exclusion of all others,* at the public expense. Have the conscientious Methodists, Episcopalians, Baptists, Lutherans, and others, no scruples of conscience at seeing their children, and the children of their poor brought up under this new sectarianism? It is not for us to say, but for ourselves we can speak. And we cannot be parties to such a system, except by legal compulsion against conscience.

Let us not be mistaken. We do not deny to infidels for unbelief any rights to which any other citizen is entitled.

But we hold that the Common School System as it has been lately interpreted by the Common Council of the City, necessarily transfers to the interest of infidel sectarianism, the advantages which are denied to Christian sectarianism of every kind. Again, let us not be misunderstood. We are opposed to the admission of sectarianism of any and of every kind, whether Christian or anti-Christian in the schools that are supported by the State.

But we hold also that, as far as the Commonwealth is concerned in the character of her future citizens, even the least perfect religion of Christian sectarianism would be better than no religion at all. And we hold that of all bad uses to which the public money can be perverted, among the worst would be the expending of it, in the shape of a bounty to education, for the spread and propagation of sectarian infidelity. Far be it from us to suppose that either the Legislature, Common Council or School Commissioners, ever intended such perversion. We hold, nevertheless, that the consequence which we have pointed out and the apprehension of which is one of the reasons why the

Roman Catholics cannot conscientiously participate in the benefits of these schools, is necessary and inevitable.

The education which each denomination might under proper restraints and vigilance give to its *own poor*, has passed and become a monopoly in the hands of "The Public School Society of New York." That corporation is in high and almost exclusive standing with the Common Council.

Now, the education which is imparted on the principles of the schools of that society, is, in our decided opinion, calculated from its defectiveness to disappoint the benevolent hope of legislative bounty, and to make bad and dangerous citizens. We all know that the belief of another world is ultimately at the base of all that is just and sacred in this. The love of God — the hope of future rewards — the dread of future punishment — one or all of these constitute and must be the foundation of conscience in the breast of every man.

When neither of them exists, conscience is but an idle word. Religion is but the development of these important truths, governing man by their internal influence on his passions and affections, regulating the order of his duties, to God, to his country, to his neighbor and himself. If they have their full force he will be a man of justice, probity and truth. And in proportion as such men are numerous in the Commonwealth, in the same proportion will the State enjoy security and happiness from within — honor and high estimation from without....

Thus far, fellow-citizens, we have stated our objections to the present system of common school education, not as they affect us more than any other denomination of Christians. We have stated them in view of the bearing which that system is likely to have on interests in which you are concerned as much as, or more, than ourselves, viz.: religion, morals, individual and social happiness, and the welfare of the State....

We now come to the statement of grievances which affect us in our civil and religious rights, as Roman Catholics. Under the guarantee of liberty of conscience, we profess the religion which we believe to be true and pleasing to God. We inherit it, many of us, from our persecuted fathers, for we are the sons of martyrs in the cause of religious freedom. Our conscience obliges us to transmit it to our children.

A brief experience of the Public School System in the city of New York convinced us that we could not discharge our conscientious duty to our offspring, if we allowed them to be brought up under the influence of the irreligious principles on which those schools are conducted, and to some of which we have already alluded. But besides these, there were other grounds of distrust and danger which forced on us the conclusion that the benefits of public education were not for *us*. Besides the introduction of the Holy Scriptures without note or comment, with the prevailing theory that from these even children are to get their notions of religion, contrary to our principles, there were in the class books of those schools false (as we believe) historical statements respecting the men and things of past times calculated to fill the minds of our children with errors of fact, and at the same time to excite in them prejudice against the religion of their parents and guardians. These passages were not considered as sectarian, inasmuch as they had been selected as mere reading lessons, and were not in *favor* of any particular sect, but merely *against* the Catholics. We feel it is unjust that such passages should be taught at all in schools, to the support of which we are contributors as well as others. But that such books should be put into the hands of *our own* children, and that in part at our own expense, was in our opinion unjust, unnatural, and at all events to us intolerable. Accordingly, through very great additional sacrifices, we have been obliged to provide schools, under our churches and elsewhere, in which to educate our children as our conscientious duty required. This we have done to the number of some thousands for several years past, during all of which time we have been obliged to pay taxes; and we feel it unjust and oppressive that whilst we educate our children, as well we contend as they would be at the public schools, we are denied our portion of the school fund, simply because we at the same time endeavor to train them up in principles of virtue and religion. This we feel to be unjust and unequal. For we pay taxes in proportion to our numbers, as other citizens. We are supposed to be from one hundred and fifty to two hundred thousand in the State.

And although most of us are poor, still the poorest man amongst us is obliged to pay taxes, from the sweat of his brow, in the rent of his room or little tenement. Is it not then hard and unjust that such a man cannot have the benefit of education for his child without sacrificing the rights of his religion and conscience? He sends his child to a school under the protection of his Church, in which these rights will be secure. But he has to support this school also. In Ireland he was compelled to support a church hostile to his religion, and here he is compelled to support schools in which his religion fares but little better, and to support his own schools besides....

Nothing can be more false than some statements of our motives, which have been put forth against us. It has been asserted that we seek our share of the school funds for the support and advance of our religion. We beg to assure you with respect that we would scorn to support or advance our religion at any other than our own expense. But we are unwilling to pay taxes for the purpose of destroying our religion in the minds of our children. This points out the sole difference between what we seek and what some narrow-minded or misinformed journals have accused us of seeking.

If the public schools could have been constituted on a principle which would have secured a perfect NEUTRALITY of influence on the subject of religion, then we should have no reason to complain. But this has not been done, and we respectfully submit that it is impossible. The cold indifference with which it is required that all religion shall be treated in those schools — the Scriptures without note or comment — the selection of passages, as reading lessons, from Protestants and prejudiced authors, on points in which our creed is supposed to be involved — the comments of the teacher, of which the Commissioners cannot be cognizant — the school libraries, stuffed with sectarian works against us — form against our religion a combination of influences prejudicial to our religion, and to whose action it would be criminal in us to expose our children at such an age.

Such, fellow-citizens, is a statement of the reasons of our opposition to the public schools, and the unjust and unequal grievances of which we complain....

> Lawrence Kehoe, ed., *Complete Works of the Most Rev. John Hughes, D.D., Archbishop of New York* (New York: Lawrence Kehoe, 1865), 1:56–63.

11. *Address to the Catholic Lay Citizens, of the City and County of Philadelphia, to Their Fellow-Citizens, in Reply to the Presentment of the Grand Jury of the Court of Quarter Sessions of May Term 1844, in Regard to the Causes of the Late Riots in Philadelphia*[1]

Fellow-Citizens: — The calamities which have recently befallen us, are already known to you all, through the public papers, which have also made you somewhat acquainted with their immediate occasion. It was thought proper by the Honorable Court of Quarter Sessions, to direct the attention of the Grand Jury of May Term, to these events; and to request of them a full and accurate investigation of their causes; in consequence of which, they examined a number of witnesses, and at length, on the 15th inst., made a presentment, signed by seventeen of their number.

We must confess our surprise at the avowal of the Grand Jury, in the presentment, that they necessarily depended on *"Ex parte evidence"* in the investigation of *public facts regarding the community at large*, into which it was plainly their duty to inquire most fully, as they were instructed by the Court, and encouraged to do, with assurances of protection to all witnesses whose attendance might be sought or offered.

We conceive that it was their duty to hear the evidence on both sides, in regard to all facts connected with the late riots, and we regret that *"ex parte evidence"* should have been received in a matter of public interest, where *no bill of indictment nor any particular charge* had been laid before them.

They seem to have assumed that one party were rioters and the others the assailed, and to have consequently, taken the evidence of the latter, without summoning the others before them to hear their accounts of the transaction, and thus, we are not surprised, at the result of their investigations. Speaking of the causes which led to the riots, the Grand Jury ascribe them —

> "To the efforts of a portion of the community to exclude the Bible from our Public Schools. The Jury are of the opinion that these efforts in some measure gave rise to the formation of a new party, which called

---

1. This...pamphlet was published by a group of Catholics for the purpose of stating obliquely their opinion regarding the alleged causes of the first stage of the riots. The activity of the Catholic laymen contrasts with the silence of [Philadelphia's] Bishop [Francis] Kenrick, who later expressed his unreserved approbation of the actions of the laity.

and held public meetings in the District of Kensington, in the peaceful exercise of the sacred rights and privileges guaranteed to every citizen by the Constitution and laws of our State and Country. These meetings were rudely disturbed and fired upon by a band of lawless irresponsible men, some of whom had resided in our country only for a short period. This outrage, causing the death of a number of our unoffending citizens, led to immediate retaliation, and was followed up by subsequent acts of aggression in violation and open defiance of all law."

We regret that the Grand Jury had not the moral courage to utter, in distinct terms, what they are now avowed and admitted to have meant. They have, in the paragraph just quoted, without using the name Catholic, wantonly charged that denomination with "an attempt to exclude the Bible from the Public Schools," and they have also, though more guardedly, insinuated, that they "have attempted to interfere with the sacred rights, and privileges guaranteed to every citizen, by the Constitution and Laws of our State." THESE CHARGES ARE UNFOUNDED. If the Grand Jury, on what is avowed to have been *"ex parte testimony,"* came to these conclusions, it was their duty to have presented the names of those who constitute "the portion of the community" with specific charges against them, to the end that they might be tried and punished. If they did not come to these conclusions, they have stated what they know to be untrue. So that, in either aspect, the Grand Jury, both in the manner of its investigations and conclusions, has given great reason for complaint, not only to the 60,000 citizens whom they have condemned without a hearing, but to every man in the community who respects the laws and desires that its administrators be *both wise and pure.*

In the name and in behalf of the Catholic community, we explicitly deny that they have at any time, or in any manner made any effort "to exclude the Bible from the Public Schools." In the most solemn manner we declare that they have never designed, desired, or attempted to exclude the Bible from the Schools. We have uniformly contended, not only for ourselves, but on behalf of our Protestant and Jewish brethren, for the fullest freedom of conscience both for children and adults in Schools or elsewhere.

We confidently refer to the letter of the Right Rev. the Bishop of Philadelphia, to the Controllers of the Public Schools, dated 14th November, 1842, as evidence that the Catholic body, in whose name he spoke, only asked the liberty of using the version of the Bible, approved of and authorised in their own communion. Speaking of the School regulations he says —

"Among them (the regulations) I am informed one is, that the teacher shall read, and cause to be read, the Bible; by which is understood the version published by command of King James. To this regulation we are forced to object, inasmuch as Catholic children are thus led to view as authoritative, a version which is rejected by the Church. It is not expected that I should state in detail the reason of this rejection. I shall only say, that we are persuaded that several books of Divine Scripture are wanting in that version, and that the meaning of the original text is not faithfully expressed. It is not incumbent on us to prove either position, since we do not ask you to adopt the Catholic version for general use; but we feel warranted in claiming that our conscientious scruples to recognize or use the other, be respected. In Baltimore, the Directors of the Public Schools have thought it their duty to provide Catholic children with the Catholic version. Is it too much for us to expect the same measure of justice?"

From this it is clear that no attempt was made by the Catholic body, or their official and authorised representative, "to exclude the Bible from the Schools." The use, by themselves, of their own version was asked. In a neighboring city, where the Catholic faith prevails, and where peace and harmony on this subject have always existed, Catholics use their own Bible, and Protestants theirs. In the capital of the ancient Catholic province of Maryland — the city of Baltimore, both sides are protected, and neither side is oppressed....

We have heard it affirmed that because Catholics are a minority, they must submit to the regulations which the majority may please to adopt. We are willing that the principle should be applied to all things wherein public interest and order are concerned, saving always those principles and rights which the Constitution holds to be inviolable. We are the minority; and for us, therefore, does the Constitution exist. The majority need not its protection, for they have the power to take care of their own interests. Unless for the shield which the Constitution gives to those who are the smaller, and therefore, the weaker party, this government would be a despotism, for the governing power would be uncontrolled. To-day one class may be lashed by the tyrant of numbers, and to-morrow another class may feel the scourge. No man, no sect, no party, would ever be safe. Peace and order would be destroyed, and soon the wreck of the Republic would add another to the many melancholy instances of the danger which always attends the conferring of unbounded power.

UNDER NO CIRCUMSTANCES IS CONSCIENCE AT THE DISPOSAL OF A MAJORITY. It is the feeling of a duty which springs from the law of nature engraved on the heart, or from the revealed law of God, and cannot be subject to the control of any authority not immediately derived from Him. We plead then on our natural and indefeasible right recognized by the Constitution and laws....

We yield to none of our fellow-citizens in attachment to republican institutions, we own no allegiance whatever to foreign prince or potentate; the obedience which as children of the church, we render to the chief Bishop, regards not the things that appertain to this world.

As Catholics, we are free in our political sentiments, uninfluenced by our religious tenets or by our spiritual guides. We belong to different political parties, according to our judgment and choice, and we have political opinions and predilections over which we acknowledge no control, other than the constitutional and legal restrictions. We do not object to the formation of any new party, which respects the Constitution and laws, and pursues its objects without infringing on rights already guaranteed and public faith and the dictates of natural justice and humanity. But if any party takes its rise in opposition to the peaceable efforts of citizens to protect and preserve the rights of conscience to the growing youth of our country, it is of ill omen to our peace and prosperity. We trust that the Grand Jury has been mistaken in tracing its origin; but we pretend not to decide the question, for our desire is, not to attack others, but to defend ourselves....

In the meantime we would observe that we are credibly informed, and firmly believe, that Irish Catholics did not go to the meeting of the 6th of May, which unfortunately adjourned to the market-house, where the first collision took place, and that the first death occurred at the time when the houses were being sacked, the second when the school-house was being put on fire. The conflict of the following day was not sought for. The Catholics remained at their homes, until the arrival of the immense crowd which had illegally met at the State House Square, "armed for defence," and had adjourned to the scene of the preceding conflict. We however disclaim all sympathy for the men, whoever they may have been, who rudely disturbed any public meeting; we detest, with all our hearts, the crime of murder by whomsoever perpetrated; we deeply regret the loss of human life, in whatever way it occurred; and we leave to the public law, all who have been guilty of shedding human blood wantonly and maliciously. We care not to dispute the allegations at the present time, but await the calm action of public justice....

For ourselves, and the Catholic community at large, we deprecate all violence, intimidation, and other illegal means of checking the expression of public sentiment, and the exercise of political privileges. We wish the right of assembling peaceably to be guarded with jealousy, but we confess our alarm for the safety of our civil institutions, when public meetings are called, and invited to come "armed for defence."

We forbear, fellow-citizens, entering into further details. We complain not of the soft tones and delicate phrases in which the Grand Jury has hinted at the burning of two churches, one of them within the city, and far removed from the scene of riot; the residence of the clergy, and a house of education; a Presbytery, that, when pestilence overspread the land, received within its walls the afflicted, without regard to their creed; of a library of great value; of ancient paintings, which had existed through ages in the old world, to become models of art in the new world; of the threats uttered and the attempts made to burn all our churches; we will even repress our indignation of the conduct of those who burned the letters and papers, and picture of George Washington, preserved with religious care in the Church of St. Augustine, of which he was one of the earliest benefactors. — The Grand Jury complaisantly alludes to all these as "acts of retaliation." Retaliation against whom? Is any reckless enough to deny that the Bishop, the Clergy, and the immense majority of the Catholics of the city and county were no parties to the disturbance of any meeting, or any acts of lawless violence? And yet acts of unprovoked and unprecedented outrage inflicted on them are called — RETALIATION!

We are Philadelphians, and we love our city. Many of us can say it is the home of our childhood, the habitation of our wives and children — it contains the ashes of our fathers. Willingly would we bury in oblivion those awful scenes, which (though painful and injurious to us) we deeply deplore on higher grounds than any selfish personal feelings.

It had been our pride and our glory that religious freedom was here enjoyed in its plenitude, and that any attempt to diminish it would meet with the reprobation and successful opposition of all classes of citizens.

Here we fondly hoped the shrines of religion were safe; here the seminaries of learning were fostered; here the ministers of religion were respected. Alas! after the scenes through which we have passed, when even the resting place of the dead was invaded, can we speak the same language of exultation? We trust still in the good sense and feeling of our fellow-citizens, that they will unite with us in maintaining that liberty of conscience, for which our fathers and theirs bled, and the supremacy of the law, and that the sympathies of life will be renewed and increased among us; so that united by the bonds of our social harmony, we shall continue to enjoy the blessings of which we have hitherto been proud; and in the day of danger we shall *all* remember, that life is well sacrificed, if sacrificed for our country.

We desire not to proscribe any one; we ask for no peculiar privileges; we make no merit of the purity of our Pennsylvania descent, but WE DEMAND that the exclamation, "I AM AN AMERICAN CITIZEN," shall continue to be the protection of our rights, and the guarantee of our freedom.

ARCH. RANDALL, Chairman
William A. Stokes, Secretary

First published in Philadelphia by M. Fithian, 1844; reprinted from *Records of the American Catholic Historical Society of Philadelphia* 80 (June–September 1969): 135–44. (Footnote from *Records.*) Reprinted with permission of *Records* of the Catholic Historical Society of America.

12. John Hughes, Archbishop of New York, to Horace Greeley, Editor, *New York Tribune,* 21 November 1851

Sir — You have continued to manifest, for some time past, a great desire to know my opinion on certain questions of which I have said nothing, whilst you manifest great dissatisfaction with certain other opinions which I have expressed, or which have been imputed to me. Hence, I have but little hope that your opinions and mine are likely to be found coincident. I do not take you to task for the opinions which you publish, nor am I prepared to admit your right to abridge the liberty or interfere with the expression of mine. And yet, if I understand you, you have made the attempt to do so in the concluding sentence of your article of Thursday morning, in which you proclaim that "it is a sad day for our country, when a prelate so able and powerful as Archbishop Hughes is heard instilling into the minds of his flock distrust of, and aversion to, secular Common Schools." In other words, it is a sad day for our country when Archbishop Hughes does not agree in opinion with Hon. Horace Greeley.

Permit me, sir, to indicate the extent to which I respect opinion, whether public or private. If it is composed of conclusions legitimately deduced from facts which are certain, I bow with reverence to its authority. If it be deductions from facts which are assumed on grounds of probability, and which cannot be disproved, I take it for what it is worth; but it is no authority for me. If I know it to be founded, not on facts, but on fallacies and falsehoods, then I do not honor it with the name of public or private opinion, but I rank it under the head of ignorance, prejudice, and presumption. All the votes of mankind, all the newspapers on earth, cannot change false into true, nor true into false. Hence, therefore, neither your opinions nor mine can have any worth, except in so far as they are deduced from facts.

Now the basis of opinion is not the same in your mind as it is in mine. I am a Catholic, and the truths of my religion are to me facts from which I draw my deductions. You, on the other hand, have the disbelief of the Catholic religion as one great element in the groundwork of your opinions. There is no great probability, therefore, that our opinions, respectively, will be found to harmonize with each other. And yet, I trust no great evil will befall the country, even if I should have the misfortune to differ with you in opinion.

Still, you have exhibited great curiosity to know what I think on certain questions, touching civil and religious liberty, and, especially, in Rome. Have patience with me, then, while I lay them before you, as briefly as possible.

I. As regards myself, I claim to be a friend of civil and religious liberty, in a sense more just and true — that is, my opinion, of course — than any which you are in the habit of attaching to those words. God is the author of truth. The Devil is the father of lies. I am not sure that you believe in the existence of a devil, but certainly you cannot deny the existence of falsehood. Now, in my opinion, your system of religious liberty goes to put God and the Devil, truth and falsehood, on the same level. You hold it as a religious right no less sacred to deny God, if a man thinks proper, than to worship Him; and hence, you implicitly deny to God Himself the right to impose on man the obligation of worship, for that would take away the freedom of his right to be an Atheist.

II. I deny, with the Catholic Church, any right of one man, by physical coercion, to compel the conscience of another man. Hence, therefore, I am opposed to all penal laws having the coercion of conscience for their object. In countries which are already divided and broken up into religious sects, mutual toleration, kindness, and good-will, in all the civil and social relations of life, constitute at once, in my opinion, the duties and the rights of all. But, I am not aware that a Protestant State, such as Sweden, is bound, by way of granting religion liberty to place Atheism on the same footing as Lutheranism. Neither am I of opinion that the Sovereign Pontiff, whose subjects are entirely Catholic and united in belief, is bound to throw his States open for the preaching of every form of Protestantism and infidelity. As spiritual head of the Catholic Church on earth, he is bound to preserve the revelation which has Christ for its author. To encourage opposition to that religion would be to take sides with the father of lies, and I am sure, sir, that you would hardly expect the Pope to go so far. Besides, as a temporal prince, he knows the horrors of civil war which have desolated other countries, springing out of the ambitions of religious sects, each struggling for political ascendency in the State. But, besides all this, he knows that it is a fundamental article of the Protestant religion to believe that he is Antichrist. Liberty of conscience, therefore, in your sense, would require that the Pope should become directly a party to the introduction of every species of error and impiety, and the overthrow of his own authority both as temporal prince and sovereign pontiff....

V. You have taken what I consider the unwarrantable liberty of throwing personal suspicion on my sincerity and loyalty as a Republican, and a citizen of these United States. I will not stoop to argue that question with you. It is a question not to be settled. A voluntary exile in early life from the land of my nativity, the first honor that was conferred upon me was the right of freedom and citizenship in the United States. No word or action of my life has ever dimmed, or shall ever tarnish that honor. No dignity in the Church has ever diminished value in my estimation; and no further honor, even if offered, could be accepted by me on conditions that would vitiate my obligations to my country, or diminish my right as one of her citizens. It is true I have not preached Red Republicanism in Europe, for, so far is it has hitherto made itself known, I despise it everywhere.

But in circles in which Americans have rarely an opportunity of making their sentiments known, I have uniformly vindicated the Government and institutions of the United States; and I will say, briefly, that of the twenty-four millions which compose their population, there is not a more sincere or more loyal citizen than the humble individual whose integrity you have seen fit to call in question. It does not follow, however, that I hold our Government and institutions to be the best for all nations at all times; and if on this subject I hold a different opinion from you, I hope you will tolerate my weakness, and not proclaim the event as marking a sad day for our country....

VIII. It is again my misfortune to differ with you in opinion regarding common-school education. It is not necessary for me, I hope, to say that I am an advocate for general, nay, universal education. My efforts to establish colleges, seats of learning, and even day-schools, for the education of youth in this diocese, will be a sufficient proof that I am no advocate of ignorance. Our disagreement, therefore, is not in regard to education itself, but in regard to the circumstances under which it is imparted. The divided condition of the community on the subject of religion has led to a system which affects to divorce the religious doctrine of each denomination from the rudiments of primary science in schools. If we were a people of unbelievers in Christianity, this system would be in perfect harmony with our condition. And yet, happily, it is understood that the welfare of society and the State must rest, ultimately, on a religious basis of some kind. We are still a Christian country, composed, indeed, of many sects in religion, and if you exclude from education the peculiar doctrines of each sect, one after another, you necessarily exclude Christianity itself; for all the Christianity of the land is made up of the several "sectarian" doctrines which are severally excluded. Hence if we had one other sect among us, having for its peculiar doctrine a belief in the expediency of excluding from the minds of youth all knowledge of and faith in Christianity, our present common schools might be denominated "a legal establishment for the purpose of causing Christianity to die out, and of promoting the interests and purposes of one anti-Christian sect." Now, sir, your opinion may be that such a result is desirable. Mine is directly the reverse. I believe it would be more beneficial to the country and to society that the religious influences of the least desirable sect of professing Christians in the land should be felt in the common school, than that all Christianity, under the pretence of excluding all *sectarianism*, should be eliminated. Whether any other system could be adopted in the actual state of the case, it is not for me to decide; but I am very strong in the opinion that the present system is not calculated to meet the requirements which Catholic parents, at least, are bound to fulfil towards their Catholic offspring. It may suit other denominations to have their children brought up without any admixture of religious teaching in their education, but it does not suit us. I was not ignorant that common schools existed in New England before they did in Prussia; but you will remember that the people of New England contended strenuously for the unity and exclusiveness of religion, whereas the Prussian system was framed, in contempt of distinctive dogmas, for the purpose of amalgamating, in the new generation, religions hitherto separate.

IX. I have thus, sir, given you my opinions on nearly all the topics in regard to which you have called for them. I fear they will be as little agreeable to you as the silence of which you seem to complain. I can only say of them, however, that they are entirely sincere, and I am sure if they were not you would not think them worth having. But my position will be rather singular, if, after having called them forth, you should be among the first to censure me for their utterance. In conclusion, whatever may be our differences of opinion on these or other topics, I trust that we are both actuated by a desire of promoting the good of our country, the interests of society, and the happiness of mankind.

Lawrence Kehoe, ed., *Complete Works of the Most Rev. John Hughes, D.D., Archbishop of New York* (New York: Lawrence Kehoe, 1865), 2:464–70.

Slavery

Virtually every aspect of American life and culture was polarized over the issue of slavery. While the issue soon situated itself at the heart of a great moral debate, the arguments also reflected regional realities. Like other Americans, Catholics in the United States tended to sort out their feelings on slavery according to their region. On the one hand, Catholics below the

Mason-Dixon Line, such as the Jesuits of Maryland, owned slaves. Southern lay Catholics, like Chief Justice Roger Brooke Taney, and southern bishops, like John England, looked kindly on "the peculiar institution" and, in the case of England, deployed carefully reasoned interpretations of papal documents which seemed to cast doubt on the perpetuation of involuntary human servitude. On the other hand, many northern Catholics deplored African American slavery. Since relatively few Catholics lived in the American South, the Catholic Church in the United States did not break apart over the issue of slavery. Indeed, few Catholic voices could be found who asserted the equality of African Americans.

13. Peter Kenny, S.J., Provincial Visitor, " 'Temporalities': Report Submitted to Corporation Leadership re: Conditions on Plantations owned and operated by the Society of Jesus," 1820

The [province] Consultors are requested to make an arrangement on the treatment, which the slaves are to receive on all our farms, from which the local procurator cannot depart. Almost every where there is a sort of arbitrary regulation, which is different from that of other farms, & which is frequently changed by the new manager. This gives these querulous creatures cause to complain, even when they are not ill used — They are in general disaffected towards their immediate manager — At St. Inigoes they are furious against B[rother] Mobberly, nor can it be hoped that he can do good by remaining with them — Indeed there have been instances of undue treatment, even allowing for exaggerations: all this should be prevented: it can only be done effectively by the Corporation — Let then

1. their Rations be fixed — in some places they have only had one pound & a quarter of meat: often this has not been sound —

2. Whether they are to be allowed to rear poultry or not? — & hogs —

3. Whether they are to have half of Saturday to themselves?

4. That pregnant women should not be whipped —

5. That this chastise[ment] should not be inflicted on any female in the house, where the priest lives — sometimes they have been tied up in the priest's own parlour, which is very indecorous —

6. that they should all be sent to Church on Ash-Wednesday & Good Friday, & on the patron Saint of the Churchs [*sic*] or place, *if kept with solemnity*, tho of course, they be made to work the rest of the day —

7. To devise more effectual means to promote morality & the frequentation of the sacram[ents] — The crimes, that are reported of our slaves & their neglect of duties the most sacred to a Christian, are a reproach to a Society, that taught sanctity to Savages; but when these Crimes are committed in the very threshold of the Sanctuary, the scandal is enormous —

Great zeal, piety, prudence & charity with a regular system are requisite to check the evils attendant on the possession of slaves — as long as our farms are cultivated by them, such constant exertions alone can keep them from becoming scenes of iniquity & disorder. Should the day ever come that the Corporation will esteem it feasible to get rid of the Slaves, either by employing whites, or letting out their lands to *reputable* tenants or any other way, in which it can be effected without injury to the property, it is unnecessary to say, that such an event will relieve this mission of an immense burthen, & a painful responsibility & the whole society of the odium, which is thrown on it, by people, who speak without consideration or the knowledge of the actual state of things in this country.

Maryland Province Archives, Georgetown University Special Collections, Washington, D.C. Printed with permission.

14. Bill of Sale for Negroes of the Maryland Mission, 1835

I. That they have the free exercise of the Catholic religion and the opportunity of practicing it. Therefore,

a) They are not to be sold except to proprietors of plantations so that the purchasers may not separate them indiscriminately and sell them;

b) it must be stipulated in the sale, that the negroes have the advantage of practicing their religion, and the assistance of a priest;

c) that husbands and wives be not at all separated, and children not from their parents, quantum fieri potest;

d) if a servant, male or female, have wife and husband on another plantation they are to be brought together, otherwise, they are no means to be sold to a distant place;

e) that those who cannot be sold or transported on account of old age or incurable diseases be provided for as justice and charity demands.

II. That the money received from the sale be in no way spent in making purchases, nor in paying of debts, but it must be invested as Capital which fructifies. The best way would perhaps be *ground rents* in the cities especially of Pennsylvania and New York — but in this you shall have to ask counsel both from Ours and externs.

Of everything that is done in this matter your Rev. will inform me as on it depends the subsistence of the Province, namely for the Novitiate and scholasticate. Therefore act with consideration and consultation and prayer, in order that the business may proceed for the good of the Province and the Glory of God.

Maryland Province Archives, Georgetown University Special Collections, Washington, D.C. Printed with permission.

15. Unsigned Editorial, "The Catholic Church, Domestic Slavery, and the Slave Trade," *United States Catholic Miscellany,* 9 December 1843

We understand that considerable attention has been excited by a document going the rounds of the papers under the title of a "Bull of Pope Gregory XVI against slavery," and several inquiries are made as to the meaning of the document and the truth of the charge that the Catholics have concealed or suppressed it in the United States for the last four years.

On recurring to our own files we find that the document itself, not a *Bull,* but an Apostolic Letter, was published in the *Miscellany* of March 14th 1840, and that our late lamented Bishop [John England], in his two first letters to the Hon. John Forsyth, then secretary of State, published likewise in the *Miscellany,* Oct. 3d and Oct. 10th 1840, fully explained its true meaning. We cannot now say whether it was published in the other Catholic papers of the day, as we have not regular files; but we are under the impression that such was the case. In the Acts of the councils of Baltimore, there is a record of its having been formally read and accepted by the Prelates in the Council of 1840. So much for catholics [*sic*] concealing or suppressing it. It was likewise given to the public through other channels. It is found, for example, in the Appendix to Mr. Forsyth's address to the people of Georgia on the nomination of General Harrison for the Presidency. And yet in just three years it is again trumpeted through the land as something new and hitherto unknown! Truly, we can sometimes be hoaxed.

As to the meaning of the Apostolic Letter, we can see no room for doubt. His Holiness speaks of reducing Indians, Negroes, and such others, into slavery; of assisting those who engage in that inhuman traffic, and through desire of gain and to foster their trade, go so far as to excite quarrels and wars among them in their native country. He opposes the continuance of the evil which several of his predecessors, whom he names, endeavoured with imperfect success to repress. They speak explicitly of reducing freemen, Indians in South America, and Negroes in Guinea, to slavery. In one word he condemns what our own laws condemn as felony, — the slave trade. Domestic Slavery as it exists in the Southern States, and in other parts of the Christian world, he does not condemn. This is evident from the tenor of the Apostolic Letter itself, from the declarations made concerning it in Rome, and from the fact that at the fourth provincial Council of Baltimore, in which the majority of Bishops were from the Slaveholding States, it was accepted, without any one's thinking it interfered at all with our domestic polity. We apprehend there is a vast difference between the Slave-Trade and Domestic slavery. At least our own laws make the distinction — punishing the one and sanctioning the other. It is absurd then to conclude, that because the Apostolical Letter condemns the piratical Slave-Trade, it is also aimed against Domestic Servitude.

There is no danger, no possibility on our principles, that Catholic theology should ever be tinctured with the fanaticism of abolition. Catholics may and do differ in regard to slavery, and other points of human policy, when considered as ethical or political questions. But our Theology is fixed, and it must be the same now as it was for the first eight or nine centuries of Christianity. During that period, as Bishop England has ably shown in his series of *Letters to the Hon. John Forsyth,* the Church ... by the admonitions of her earliest and holiest pastors; by the decrees of her councils made on a variety of occasions; by her synodical condemnation of those who under pretext of religion, would teach the slave to despise his master; by her sanction and support of those laws by which the civil power sought to preserve the rights of the owner; by her own acquiring such property, by deeds of gift or of sale, for the cultivation of her lands, the maintenance of her clergy, the benefit of her monasteries, of her hospitals, of her orphans, and of her other works of Charity, repeatedly and evidently testified that she regarded the possession of slave property as fully compatible with the doctrines of the Gospel: and this whilst she denounced the pirate who made incursions to reduce into bondage those who were free and unoffending, and regarded with just execration the men who fitted out ships and hired others to engage in the inhuman traffic. In Catholic Theology the question is a settled one and no one would be recognised as a Catholic who would utter the expressions we have heard from the lips of American Abolitionists, who call themselves protestants: "If the Bible allows slavery, it should be amended." "The Christianity of the nineteenth century should as far excel the Christianity of the Early Church, as that did the old Jewish law" &c. The line of conduct prescribed especially to the Catholic clergy is laid down by the venerable and learned Bishop of Philadelphia, in his standard work, *Theologia Moralis.* ... From the first ... chapter we translate the following paragraph:

37. But what is to be thought of the domestic servitude which exists in most of the southern and western states, where the posterity of those who were brought from Africa, still remains in slavery? It is indeed to be regretted that in the present fulness of liberty in which all glory, there should be so many slaves, and that to guard against their movements, it has been necessary to pass laws prohibiting their education, and in some places greatly restricting their exercise of religion. Nevertheless since such is the state of things, nothing should be attempted against the laws, nor anything be done or said that would make them bear their yoke unwillingly. But the prudence and the charity of the sacred Ministers should appear in their effecting that the slaves, imbued with christian morals, render service to their masters, venerating God, the supreme master of all; and that the masters be just and kind, and by their humanity and care for their salvation, endeavour to mitigate the condition of their slaves. The Apostles have left us these rules; which if any one should neglect and through a feeling of humanity endeavour to overturn the entire established order, he would in most cases but aggravate the condition of the slaves. The Pope, in the before-mentioned constitution, omitted not to lay this before us. "For the Apostles, in-

spired by the Holy Ghost, taught slaves to obey their temporal masters, as they would Christ himself and to do the will of God cheerfully: and they also gave a precept to the masters to act kindly towards their slaves, to give them what is just and reasonable, and to refrain from threatening them, knowing that the Lord of both is in heaven, and that with Him there is no acceptation of persons."

How strictly this instruction is complied with, and how beneficial are its effects, is known to every one who has any knowledge of the character of Catholic slaves. They are every where distinguished as a body for orderly habits and fidelity to their masters; so much so that in Maryland, where they are numerous, their value is 20 or 25 per cent above that of others.

We have said this much, not to vindicate the Southern Clergy of our church from the charge of Abolitionism, for we believe it has never been preferred against them, but simply to satisfy the inquiries of some of our fellow citizens, whose attention has been drawn by recent events to this subject.

United States Catholic Miscellany, 9 December 1843, 182.

16. Roger Brooke Taney, Chief Justice, U.S. Supreme Court, to Rev. Samuel Nott of Wareham, Massachusetts, 19 August 1857

Sir, — I received some time ago your letter, and pamphlet on "Slavery, and the Remedy," which you have been kind enough to send me. They were received when I was much out of health, and about to leave home for the summer. And it was not in my power to give the pamphlet an attentive perusal until within a few days past. I have read it with great pleasure. The just, impartial, and fraternal spirit in which it is written entitles it to a respectful consideration, in the South as well as the North. And if any thing can allay the unhappy excitement which is daily producing so much evil to the African as well as the white race, it is the discussion of the subject in the temper in which you have treated it. For you have looked into it and considered it in all its bearings, in the spirit of a statesman as well as a philanthropist. I am glad to find that it has been so well received as to reach the fifth edition.

Every intelligent person whose life has been passed in a slave holding State, and who has carefully observed the character and capacity of the African race, will see that a general and sudden emancipation would be absolute ruin to the negroes, as well as to the white population. In Maryland and Virginia every facility has been given to emancipation where the freed person was of an age and condition of health that would enable him to provide for himself by his own labor. And before the present excitement was gotten up, the freed negro was permitted to remain in the State, and to follow any occupation of honest labor and industry that he might himself prefer. And in this state of the law manumissions were frequent and numerous. They sprang from the kindness and sympathy of the master for the negro, or from scruples of conscience; and were often made without sufficiently considering his capacity and fitness for

freedom. And in the greater number of cases that have come under my observation, freedom has been a serious misfortune to the manumitted slave; and
he has most commonly brought upon himself privations and sufferings which
he would not have been called on to endure in a state of slavery. In many
cases, however, it has undoubtedly promoted his happiness. But all experience
proves that the relative position of the two races, when placed in contact with
each other, must necessarily become such as you describe. Nor is it felt as a
painful degradation by the black race. On the contrary, upon referring to the
last census, you will find that more free negroes remain in Maryland than in
any one of the Northern States, notwithstanding the disabilities and stricter
police to which they are subjected. And there is a still greater number in Virginia. I speak from memory, without having the census before me. But I think
I am not mistaken in the fact.

It is difficult for any one who has not lived in a slaveholding State to
comprehend the relation which practically exist between the slaves and their
masters. They are in general kind on both sides, unless the slave is tampered
with by ill-disposed persons; and his life is usually cheerful and contented,
and free from any distressing wants or anxieties. He is well taken care of in
infancy, in sickness, and in old age. There are indeed exceptions, — painful
exceptions. But this will always be the case, where power combined with bad
passions or a mercenary spirit is on one side, and weakness on the other. It frequently happens when both parties are of the same race, although the weaker
and dependent one may not be legally a slave.

Unquestionably it is the duty of every master to watch over the religious
and moral culture of his slaves, and to give them every comfort and privilege
that is not incompatible with the continued existence of the relations between
them. And so far as my knowledge extends, this duty is faithfully performed
by the great body of hereditary slaveholders in Maryland and Virginia. I speak
of these States only, because with respect to them I have personal knowledge
of the subject. But I have no reason to suppose it is otherwise in States farther
south. And I know it has been the desire of the statesmen of Maryland to
secure to the slave by law every protection from maltreatment by the master
that can with safety be given, and without impairing that degree of authority
which is essential to the interest and well-being of both. But this question is
a very delicate one, and must at all times be approached with the utmost caution. The safe and true line must always depend upon existing circumstances,
and they must be thoroughly inquired into and understood before there can
be any safe or useful legislation in a State.

The pains which have unhappily been taken for some years past to produce discontent and ill-feeling in the subject race, has rendered any movement
in that direction still more difficult. For it has naturally made the master more
sensitive and jealous of any new restriction upon the power he has heretofore
exercised, and which he has been accustomed to think essential to the maintenance of his authority as master. And he also feels that any step in that
direction at the present time might injuriously affect the minds of the slaves.

They are for the most part weak, credulous, and easily misled by stronger minds. And if in the present state of things additional restrictions were placed on the authority of the master, or new privileges were granted to them, they would probably be told that they were wrung from the master by their Northern friends; and be taught to regard them as the first step to a speedy and universal emancipation, placing them on a perfect equality with the white race. It is easy to foresee what would be the sad result of such an impression upon the minds of this weak and credulous race.

Your review of the decision in the case of Dred Scott is a fair one, and states truly the opinion of the Court.[1] It will, I hope, correct some of the misrepresentations which have so industriously been made; and made too, I fear, by many who must have known better. But I do not mean to publish any vindication of the opinion; or of my own consistency, or the consistency of the Court. For it would not become the Supreme Court, or any member of it, to go outside of the appropriate sphere of judicial proceedings; and engage in a controversy with any one who may choose from any motive to misrepresent its opinion. The opinion must be left to speak for itself. And it is for that reason that I hope you will pardon me for requesting that you will not permit this letter to be published in the newspapers or otherwise. Not that I am not perfectly ready on all proper occasions to say publicly every thing I have said in this letter. But in the judicial position I have the honor to occupy, I ought not to appear as a volunteer in any political discussion; and still less would it become me out of Court and off the bench to discuss a question that has been there determined. And I have written to you (although a stranger) thus freely from the personal respect with which the perusal of your pamphlet has inspired me. I am not a slaveholder. More than thirty years ago I manumitted every slave I ever owned, except two, who were too old, when they became my property, to provide for themselves. These two I supported in comfort as long as they lived. And I am glad to say that none of those whom I manumitted disappointed my expectations, but have shown by their conduct that they were worthy of freedom; and know how to use it.

Proceedings of the Massachusetts Historical Society, 1871–1873 (Boston: Massachusetts Historical Society, 1873), 445–47; also in John Tracy Ellis, ed., *Documents of American Catholic History* (Wilmington, Del.: Michael Glazier, 1987), 1:322–25. Printed with permission of the estate of John Tracy Ellis.

17. Rev. Edward Purcell, "The Church and Slavery," 8 April 1863

In some remarks lately made on the emancipation of the serfs in Russia, we observed that the Church and slavery could never get along well together. The New York *Freeman's Journal* condemns our remarks, quotes St. Paul and Church Councils, and says that we are ignorant of ecclesiastical history. The writer in the *Freeman* also observes that he does not wish for a controversy

---

1. Taney wrote the opinion, which was handed down 6 March 1857.

with us. As the *Freeman,* on this occasion, is mild and uses no very offensive language, we reply to his comments at some length.

We assure our contemporary that we, too, have no desire to enter into a controversy. It would be useless now, because the subject of slavery is dead. The first canon fired at Sumter, sounded its knell. It would be much easier to take Richmond or open the Mississippi, than restore slavery in the United States. The thing is gone forever.

But our contemporary suggests that we are not acquainted with ecclesiastical history and that slavery and the Church have got along well together, and quotes St. Paul and certain Councils. Our cotemporary [*sic*] has a right to entertain any opinion he pleases about our ignorance. His opinion is his own. But without acrimony we can write on this subject of slavery. It must be discussed; there is no help for it — and whilst we accord to those who are its advocates all liberty of speech, we hope that some license will be extended to us when we give our reasons on the other side. It is not in a factious spirit or a fanatical spirit that we write, but under the strong conviction that a great change is at hand in the political welfare of the country, and that it is of some consequence to Catholics to decide wisely what part to take. This cannot be done by crying out "ignorance," "abolition," but by friendly discussion. Whether we like it or not, slavery is extinguished in the United States, and all that we have to do is to decide how we shall accommodate ourselves "to coming events."

We have said and we now repeat it, that slavery and the Catholic Church could never get along well together. The Church never tries to correct evils by revolutionary means. When she has not the legislative power in her hands she is patient, long-suffering, gentle. What she could not suppress she tolerated. But she found slavery little disposed to imitate her meekness. When the slave power predominates, religion is nominal. There is no life in it. It is the hard-working laboring man who builds the church, the schoolhouse and the orphan asylum, not the slaveholder, as a general rule. Religion flourishes in a slave State only in proportion to its intimacy with a free State, or as it is adjacent to it. There are more Catholics in the Cathedral congregation of this city than in North and South Carolina and Georgia! There are more Catholics in one of our second-rate congregations than in the whole State of Alabama! Louisiana ought to be a Catholic State, but it has never sent a Senator or Representative to Congress who identified himself with the Catholic cause, so far as we know. The slave-owners are not the zealous men of the Church in that State.

What help is Cuba, with all its riches, to the Catholic cause? The poorest Irish or German congregation in the free States does more for religion than Havana, if we can rely on the representations of those who ought to know and whose character forbids deception. It appears to us, therefore, that slavery is not friendly to the propagation of the Catholic Faith — or to its charity and fervor when it happens to be professed. If for telling these plain truths any subscriber wishes to withdraw his patronage, we hope he will do so at once.

And if for telling these truths the ladies of a community in a slave State choose to burn our Paper again, they have our liberty, if that be of any consequence, to prove their amiability and piety by doing so. The time is near at hand when they will wish that they had been more tolerant to the expression of an opinion.

But to our knowledge of ecclesiastical history: "No one now ventures to doubt," says Balmes, "that the Church exercised a powerful influence on the abolition of slavery: this is a truth too clear and evident to be questioned.... It did all that was possible in favor of human liberty; if it did not advance more rapidly in the work, it was because it could not do so without compromising the undertaking — without creating serious obstacles to the desired emancipation. Such is the result at which we arrive when we have thoroughly examined the charges made against some proceedings of the Church.... That slavery endured for a long time in the presence of the Church is true; but it was always declining, and only lasted as long as was necessary to realize the benefit without violence — without a shock — without compromitting [sic] its universality and its continuation."[1] These few words from the fifteenth chapter of Balmes' incomparable work, show the exact position occupied by the Church in reference to slavery. To say that she ever favored the system is a calumny. She proclaimed men's fraternity with each other, and their equality before God, and therefore could not be the advocate of slavery.

With respect to the words of St. Paul, so often quoted, we find a full justification of our position. He writes to Philemon, commending his faith and charity, and he says — "wherefore, though I might have much confidence in Christ Jesus *to command thee that which is to the purpose,* for charity's sake I rather beseech, *thou being such a one,* as Paul the aged and now also a prisoner of Jesus Christ, I beseech thee for my son Onesimus, whom I have begotten in my chains — whom I have sent back to thee. And do thou receive him as my own bowels.... Not now as a servant, but instead of a servant a most dear brother, especially to me; but how much more to thee, both in the flesh and in the good?"[2]

Any one who can find anything in this in favor of slavery, must have piercing optics. Would St. Paul have sent him back to a Heathen master — or one who would have the power and the will to despise him — to sell his wife and children into slavery? The thought is not to be entertained of the blessed apostle.

If a fugitive slave in this country was to be sent back to some master in Mississippi or Texas by a Catholic Bishop of our days, bearing such an epistle as the above, how would the master mock and the world laugh at the Bishop? What a joke it would be considered in the South!

But what did the Popes think of slavery? This will probably throw some

---

1. James Balmes, *Protestantism and Catholicity Compared in Their Effects on the Civilization of Europe* (Baltimore: n.p., 1851), 91–94.
2. Philemon 1:8–16.

light on ecclesiastical history. Paul III. in 1537, and Urban VIII. in 1639, condemned in the strongest terms the crime of reducing men to slavery, separating them from their wives and children, or in any manner depriving them of their liberty, or upon any pretext to preach or teach that it is lawful. Pius II. in 1462, also denounces the system in the strongest terms. Gregory XVI., who, in his Apostolic Letter of the 3d of December, 1839, refers to the foregoing, uses this vehement language on the same subject — "Wherefore, we, desiring to turn away so great a reproach as this from all the boundaries of Christians, and the whole matter being maturely weighed, certain Cardinals of the Holy Roman Church, our venerable brethren being also called into Council, treading in the footsteps of our predecessors with Apostolic authority, do vehemently admonish and adjure in the Lord, all believers in Christ, that no one hereafter may dare unjustly to molest Indians, negroes or other men of this sort, or to spoil them of their goods or reduce them to slavery. We, therefore, with Apostolic authority do reprobate all the aforesaid actions as utterly unworthy of the Christian name; and by the same Apostolic authority do strictly prohibit and interdict that any ecclesiastic or lay person shall presume to defend that very trade in negroes *as lawful under any pretext or studied excuse,* or otherwise to preach, or in any manner, publicly or privately, to teach contrary to those things which we have charged in this, our Apostolic Letter."[3]

This is tolerably showy language. Its import, we think, is clear enough to any one who has a human mind. There can be "no pretext or studied excuse," says the good and great Pontiff. Are Catholics afraid or unwilling to read the admonition of the Vicar of Jesus Christ?

But it will be said that Gregory XVI. alluded to the foreign slave trade! This, however, is a pretext, and has not even the dignity of a "studied excuse." We have a word to say on the point.

Shortly before the appearance of this Apostolic letter, a religious order in the United States, by their close communication with Rome, received information of its existence and approaching publication. With more wit than piety the Superiors of that order collected together a large number of their slaves and sold them all to a Southern *gentleman,* we will call him so, who hurried them into Louisiana, and they were scattered over the South without reference to their relationship one to another. The whole Catholic community was shocked at the occurrence. Pope Gregory's letter appeared soon after, and it did not moderate the feeling of indignation. When the fact was known in Rome, such was the emotion felt by His Holiness, that the Superiors, on whom the responsibility rested, were ordered forthwith to proceed to the Eternal City and they did not return for years. Why they were detained it is unnecessary to discuss.

This shows that slavery in every shape, is condemned and reprobated by the Church. In the meantime she did nothing violently. She only spoke the

---

3. For the text of Gregory XVI's apostolic letter, *In supremo apostolatus,* cf. Antonius Maria Bernasconi, ed., *Acta Gregorii papae XVI* (Rome, 1901), 2:387–88.

solemn words of admonition. Events have hurried on — what the Church would not or could not do the politicians have done. The door is now made open without any agency of Catholics, and those who wish to despise the venerable Pontiffs and be the jailors of their fellowmen, may endeavor to close and lock and bolt it. We take no part in any such proceeding.

Catholic Telegraph (Cincinnati), 8 April 1863; also in John Tracy Ellis, ed., *Documents of American Catholic History* (Wilmington, Del.: Michael Glazier, 1987), 1:378–83. (Footnotes in Ellis.) Printed with permission of the estate of John Tracy Ellis.

War

American expansionism was reignited in the 1840s, and tensions with Mexico over its former colony of Texas erupted in war in 1846. Since certain elements of American society made the Catholic identity of Mexico an issue in the decision to go to war, American Catholics were compelled to reply to the religious issues raised by the conflict. The war with Mexico resulted in the cession of vast lands to the United States, and it also provoked a major confrontation among the sections over the question of slavery in the newly acquired territories. Because their religious allegiances were tempered by their regional loyalties, American Catholics fought on both sides of the Civil War. Catholics' political allegiances in the North were tenuous. Many did not support Lincoln or the Republicans because of the party's nativist and Know-Nothing taint. Because many of the same elements were pressing hard for abolitionism, Catholics did not find much common ground with the Lincoln administration. Vocal critics of the sixteenth president included James A. McMaster, editor of the New York *Freeman's Journal*. Yet northern and southern bishops did differ on the causes and solution of the war. The telling exchange of correspondence between Archbishop John Hughes of New York and Bishop Patrick N. Lynch of Charleston accentuates the public feature of this debate.

Northern leaders took advantage of this cleavage in Catholic opinion to neutralize the prosouthern sympathies of Pope Pius IX, as evidenced in the letter of Archbishop John Hughes to Secretary of State William H. Seward, a former governor of New York.

18. "The Washington Union and the Sequestration of Church Property in Mexico during the War," 22 May 1847

The *Washington Union*, of the 11th inst., has broached a project unworthy of our age, and still more unworthy of our government, of which it is sometimes called the *official organ* — it is nothing more nor less than a proposal to turn

the war against Mexico into a war against the priests and the religion of that
unfortunate country.

Having had no reason hitherto to suppose that our government was actuated by other motives than those of a real or imaginary necessity to undertake
and prosecute the war in which we are now engaged, and that too, in a high-
minded, honorable, and humane manner, as becomes the greatness of *our*
country and the weakness of our enemy, we must say that we have read the article in the *Union* with pain and regret, and if we could believe for a moment,
that its spirit or purpose could have had the sanction of our government, we
would add with disgust and horror. In the earlier stages of this unhappy contest we were exceedingly anxious to convince the Mexican people that on the
score of religion they should have nothing to apprehend from the triumph of
our arms. Every means were taken to disabuse them of the prejudices which
their military demagogues infused and fomented among the people of Mexico, as if, to use the language of the papers of the time, we were a nation of
church-burners.

The question will arise, whether or not we were sincere at that period.
Whether or not we do not now leave ourselves open to the charge of duplic-
ity, when something as bad as church-burning is advocated by a newspaper
supposed to be in the confidence of the public authorities — whether or not
our first disclaimer was not intended to inspire a confidence in the Mexican
people for the purpose of betraying it only the more readily when the time
should arrive. We think that the article in the *Washington Union* of the 11th
inst. will do more to inflame the Mexican people and to confirm in their
obstinacy of resistance even to desperation, than anything which has been
published in the American papers since the commencement of the war. Nay
we fear that it will destroy the hope of gaining a powerful influence to the
side of peace from the only stable and permanent element of nationality that
survives in Mexico, and that at last there will be no power left in the country competent even to make a peace or to sustain it if made. As long as there
was nothing on the part of our government to warrant the suspicion of hostility to the religion and church of Mexico, there was every reason to hope
that, at least the clergy of that country, seeing the ruin that must result from
so unequal a contest, would at the earliest opportunity use their influence to
bring around a peaceful adjustment of the unhappy difficulties, but the spirit
and language and purpose of the article we have just alluded to, and which
in Mexico will be regarded as semi-official, at least, will go far to throw the
weight of clerical influence into the opposite scale; for if the church property
must be sacrificed they will judge it more in accordance with their duty, to see
it sacrificed in support of their own country than to see it sequestered as an
additional means to enable the invaders to extinguish the last hopes of their
religion, their nation and their race.

But in truth, we will not allow ourselves to believe for an instant, that
the cabinet at Washington, exercising the powers of the freest, and one of the
mightiest nations of the earth, could ever have stooped to sanction a project so

contrary to dignity, to justice, to sound policy, as that which is recommended by the *Washington Union,* which would place this mighty Republic in the attitude of making war on the priests of a hostile nation.

The crime of the Church in Mexico, would be a virtue, if the similar case had occurred in our own country, if during the Revolutionary war the clergy of the country had furnished from their own resources means to clothe the naked troops of Gen. Washington; the fact would be recorded as one of the noblest instances of patriotism. And if for this the British government were to have singled out the clerical body as special victims of military or civil vengeance, the whole world would have cried out shame!

It is known that but a little while ago one of the factions in Mexico had proposed a general confiscation of church property by the state, for the purpose of carrying on the war. Against this it does not appear that the *Washington Union* had any objection. But that party being overthrown on this very ground, the *Union* proposes that we shall accomplish, under the name of sequestration during the war, a sacrilege which the Mexicans themselves, even to preserve their nation, have hesitated to accomplish. The *Union* very gratuitously assumes a distinction between the Catholics of Mexico and the rest of the community. This is hardly fair, for whatever religion there is in Mexico, is professed by all its population.

But there is another view under which we regret still more the appearance of this article. It is the indirect encouragement which it holds out to the possible excesses from which it is difficult to restrain troops, such as ours are, in the enemy's country. Already we hear of their deliberate irreverence in the temples of religion — of their wearing their hats in the churches, of smoking cigars around the sanctuary, and other trifling insults that inflict deeper wounds on the feelings of the Mexicans than the loss of a battle. We are aware that every precaution is taken to prevent any excess of this kind among the troops, but if they should find countenance in a higher, though more remote, quarter than the authority of the camp, it is to be feared that they may go still farther.

It appears to us clear, that unless it be our intention to extinguish the independence of Mexico — to break it utterly down and reconstruct its government according to our own will, without considering either the cost or the consequences, we should, as well from policy as from justice, be on our guard against the dangerous advice which the *Union* suggests. No civilized nation, having regard for its own honor, or its own interest, makes war on the religion of its enemy. No great statesman has ever recommended, no great general has ever practiced, a policy so well calculated to make resistance desperate and interminable.

If, on the other hand, we shall desire Mexico to continue as a distinct nation, after we shall have compelled her to discharge the duties and responsibilities of independent sovereignty by doing justice to *our* claims, let us be careful not to destroy all the elements of national existence, before the period of negotiation arrives. Otherwise a treaty of peace will have to be made between Gen. Scott and Gen. Taylor, the one signing for Mexico, and the other for the United States.

19. James A. McMaster, "The Ship on the Breakers," 8 June 1861

Abraham Lincoln, county court lawyer of the village of Springfield, Illinois, elected President according to the letter of the Constitution — and whom we are ready to sustain in the place he so unworthily fills, *according to the Constitution* — has been playing some infamous tricks, of late. He has been creating new regular armies, and establishing an additional navy, without any act of Congress. By a certain stretch of executive authority he has the *right*, in the present exigency, under the act of 1795, to call out the *militia of such States as may be necessary*, but the legal limit of that authority expires *"thirty days after the next assembling of Congress."* Abraham Lincoln made demure protestations, in his inaugural, that it was his devotion to the Constitution of the United States, and the laws made in pursuance thereof, that would *compel* him to act in a manner disagreeable to millions of his "dissatisfied countrymen." Why, then, in view of the crisis, did he not call Congress together at an *earlier* day? Why did he not limit his proclamation, calling for seventy-five thousand militia men, to the term for which *alone* he had Constitutional power to call them — the expiration of thirty days after the next meeting of Congress? Why, in his subsequent proclamation, calling for a much larger force, did he not, in the same way, confine himself to his legal and Constitutional power, of calling on *the militia of States,* for the term for which alone he had power to call them — ending *thirty days after the meeting of Congress?* Why has he undertaken, without act of Congress, to increase the regular army and the navy of the United States? Why has he assumed the peculiar and restrictive prerogative of Congress — the *law-making* power — in *creating* military offices and commissions, in order that he may fill those assumed offices with officers selected by him? Congress, which *alone* has the power, has recognized but *one* Major-General of the United States regular army — Gen. Winfield Scott.[1] Mr. Abe Lincoln, who has no more authority to do so than Mr. Dogberry Kennedy of the New York Police, has *named* Major George B. McClellan,[2] a very meritorious Captain of the United States Cavalry; Benjamin F. Butler,[3] an unusually clever Brigadier of the Massachusetts State Militia; and some others, to be Major-Generals of the United States Army — that is, to fill offices that *do*

---

1. Winfield Scott (1786–1866), although Virginia-born, remained loyal to the Union and as commander of the United States Army made the preparations for defending Washington.

2. George B. McClellan (1826–85), an officer of the Ohio Volunteers, was appointed a major general of the regular army on May 13, 1861, and placed in command of the Department of the Ohio.

3. Benjamin F. Butler (1818–93) was nominated a major general on 16 May 1861, after having been chosen to occupy Baltimore, which he had done peacefully with 900 troops three days before.

not exist by the law-making power — Congress — which can *alone* create them, according to the Constitution of the United States.

The Constitution of the United States confers no such power on Mr. President Lincoln. And the contemporaneous writings of the framers of that constitution say *why* they did not. They say that they withheld such powers, because history showed them that a people "*in proportion as they are free,* will disarm the executive of the influence to exercise a war-making propensity."

In light of the Constitution of the United States, and of the authoritative expositors and commentators of that instrument, there can be but one judgment — that Lincoln has sought to absorb and confound in his own action the legislative and the executive functions, which the Constitution of the United States, with such pre-eminent care, has distinguished and placed in separate hands.

It appears, also, that Mr. Abe Lincoln, as chief Executive of the United States, has directed various military Commandants, at their discretion, or in case of certain emergencies, to suspend the Writ of *Habeas Corpus.*[4] It is difficult, in a country so blessed as ours has been for three quarters of a century, to attract popular attention to the fundamental guarantee of public security. Perhaps *Habeas Corpus* seems like an abstraction, or a pettifogger's trick. But it is the symbol of our rights as freemen. It is not simply a guarantee for personal liberty, demanded and gained from Charles II., but, in essence and in virtue, it is the characteristic of our free and superior civilization. In substance it was recognized in the *Magna Charta,* and had its origin far back of that, in the old *Frank law.* We call attention to the documents we furnish in another column on this subject. From them it will appear, so far as has been ascertained, that Lincoln — having been *constitutionally* elected by a minority vote to the executive office of President — has at one and the same time thought he could absorb the law-making power, and set at defiance — as he did even in his inaugural — the judicial branch of the Government. The *Constitution* divides our Government into three distinct and co-ordinate branches — the Legislative, the Judicial, and the Executive. The latter assumes to *dispense* with the other two, and to exert autocratic power, as completely as any Asiatic or Turkish despot could do, over a nation of slaves.

We have no *party* quarrel to wage against any one. Alas, we have, now, no *party* to sustain. Our wish, above all things, is that Lincoln's Administration *could,* and then *would,* adopt a course which, as loyal American freemen, we can sustain. The present course of the Executive is unconstitutional, outrageous, and *an open rebellion* against the United States Government as established and recognised. We cannot sustain it in this course, and we will not. We declare and protest, on the contrary, with the Chief Justice of the United States,[5] that it subverts all law as recognized by freemen, and attempts

---

4. On 2 July 1861, Lincoln empowered General Scott to suspend the privilege of habeas corpus.

5. Roger Brooke Taney (1777–1864) was Chief Justice of the United States Supreme Court from March 1836 to his death.

to place our persons, our property, liberty, and life, at the will of one or another army office.

We have often adverted to the fact that, under anti-slavery as a cry, the anti-Democratic coalition known as "Republicans," have been seeking the substitution of a *centralized despotism* in place of the Constitutional Government of the United States. The very ridiculousness of the controlling elements of this coalition is an occasion of danger. If we cite the Red-Republican ravings of the *Tribune*[6] and *Post*,[7] it is replied: "Who regards such bran-bread socialists and poetasters!" If we cite the *Daily Times*,[8] we are told that the writers are "ninnies — nobody heeds them." If we hunt up a copy of the *Courier and Enquirer*, it raises a laugh. But, be it remembered, it was the influence of these papers, and others no whit more respectable, that brought into executive office Abraham Lincoln and his coterie of incapables. The mistake is made of supposing that the dangers of the country come from *able* or from *great* men. Its dangers and its ruin are to be found in *weak* and *little* men — where great men ought to be. Despotism is a *petty* thing, and petty fellows are they who exercise it.

The *Daily Times*, one day last week, elaborates an article to show that we must, hereafter, keep up a large standing army — even when peace is restored. A large standing army, in time of peace — that is, a hundred thousand men or so, standing idle, with muskets in their hands, at the beck of the Government that pays them — would be the death-knell of political liberty. This is too plain — has been too often insisted on by our greatest statesmen — to render it necessary to argue it. It seems that the *minority*, who have climbed to power, through licentious presses and desecrated pulpits, playing on the ignorance and fanaticism of the country — recognizes that the American people, if left free, will take good care that they never attain a second, nor another, term of administration. It seems that the deliberate purpose has been formed of *subverting, from top to bottom,* the American system of government, and of trying to rule this people by an armed despotism. We do not say that the accursed project may not be accomplished, but we do say that the cowardly and incapable clique who inaugurate the system, will inevitably pay the forfeit of their crime, like Robespierre and Danton, in their own blood.

We have said that our chief danger is from the incapacity, the mental and moral weakness, of the faction now attempting to rule us — not from their strength. This will be our apology for quoting the following from a bombastic article of Webb,[9] in his *Courier and Enquirer*, published a few days before he was appointed Minister to Brazil. It is *his* offering of incense to the attempted

---

6. Horace Greeley (1811–72) was editor of the *New York Tribune* at the time.

7. William Cullen Bryant (1794–1878) was editor of the New York *Evening Post*.

8. Henry J. Raymond (1820–69), editor of the New York *Times*, was the most steadfast of all the New York editors in their support of Lincoln.

9. James W. Webb (1802–84) was editor of the New York *Courier and Enquirer* from the time he merged the two papers in 1829 to his retirement in 1861. He was named minister to Brazil on 31 May 1861.

military despotism, which he will help by keeping his Brigadier Generalship out of harm's way, while playing courtier at a South American court. He says:

> The war may soon pass away — we may have a quick and vital battlefield, and the North prove its prowess, as certainly it will; but the truth of *national unity* and *power* that these events have given, endures–combined–condensed–*concentrated in army and navy.*
>
> ... We shall ask the question — *Why all these State lines? Why all this needless, cumbersome, intricate entanglement of different powers to make law and to decree judgment? We can afford now to efface the old Colonial Geography. It is the admitted powers of States within the nation that has been the source of all our trouble. Nor will the removal of State power, and the creation of a nationality, be a task so formidable.*

"Nonsense!" Certainly it is; but we beg thoughtful and intelligent men who turn from it contemptuously, to remember that the miseries the country is now enduring have been brought on it by nonsense as palpable. Webb, who put this in his *Courier,* was, a few days after, named Minister to Brazil, by Lincoln's Administration. It is fair to conclude that he uttered the sentiments that are governing Lincoln's Administration. He says that the *national unity* is to *endure "concentrated in army and navy."*

He says that "State forms," recognized in the Constitution of the country as fundamental and essential, are to be blotted out. Nay, he asks, "why all this *needless, cumbersome, intricate* entanglement of *different* powers to *make law* and to *decree judgment."* It is true, it seems out of place for us to occupy our columns with language worthy only of a negro, or a John Chinaman; but consider the relations of the *Courier* and its editor to Lincoln's Administration, and a reason appears.

Nay, what is Lincoln doing, but *simplifying* the "cumbersome intricate entanglement of *different* powers," as prescribed in the Constitution of the United States, which three months ago, at the hands of Chief Justice Taney, he swore to observe inviolate?

The county court lawyer may not understand what he is doing. His Cabinet may not understand what they are doing. But ideas will rule. Causes will produce results. Men must reap the same that they sow.

Let those heed it who, one year ago, scoffed when we said that the election of Lincoln would cause civil war! We say, now, that if there be not conservatism enough in the country to stop and to rebuke the course of Lincoln and his Cabinet, we will have a bloody revolution and anarchy, resulting in a military despotism, with a different man from Lincoln at its head. We speak what we see and know. Our conscience forces us to speak, whether it please or offend.

New York *Freeman's Journal,* 8 June 1861; also in John Tracy Ellis, ed., *Documents of American Catholic History* (Wilmington, Del.: Michael Glazier, 1987), 1:342–47. (Footnotes in Ellis.) Printed with permission of the estate of John Tracy Ellis.

20. Patrick N. Lynch,[1] Bishop of Charleston, to John Hughes, Archbishop of New York, 4 August 1861

Most Reverend Dear Sir: — The mails are so completely paralyzed that it is hard to get a letter from outside the Confederacy. Papers are scarcely ever seen. That, however, Jefferson would think a blessing, on the ground that "he who is simply ignorant is wiser than the one that believes error." A paragraph which has gone the rounds of the Southern papers, states that your Grace has spoken strongly against the war policy of the Government of the United States, fraught with much present suffering, and not calculated to attain any real advantage. What a change has come over these States since I wrote you a long letter last November, and even since I have had the pleasure of seeing you last March. All that I anticipated in that letter has come to pass, and more than I looked for. All the hopes cherished last spring of a peaceful solution have vanished before the dreadful realities of war. What is before us, who can say? Missouri, Maryland and Kentucky are nearer secession now than Virginia, North Carolina and Tennessee were four months ago. Missouri is a battlefield. I think that President Davis, after the victory of Stone Bridge, will probably throw a column into Maryland. Kentucky will, ere long, be drawn into the struggle, and the United States will, in less than ten months, be divided in two now unequal parts, marshalling hundreds of thousands of men against each other.

This war is generally dated from the bombardment of Fort Sumter. There we fired the first gun, and the responsibility is charged on us. But, in reality that responsibility falls on those who rendered the conflict unavoidable — The South, years ago, and a hundred times, declared that the triumph of the abolition or anti-slavery policy, would break up the Union. They were in earnest. When that party, appealing to the people on the Chicago platform, elected their candidate by every free State vote (excepting New Jersey, which was divided) South Carolina seceded, and other States were preparing to do so. They were in earnest. Yet, as the people disbelieved it, or heeded it not at the ballot, so Congress heeded it not at Washington, and stood doggedly on the Chicago platform endorsed by the people. — This consummated success. The Confederate Government was formed. The dogged obstinacy of the Black Republicans at Washington last winter made all the South secessionists. Still there was peace. The new Administration professed an intention to preserve it. Peace gave time, and time can work wonders. The Confederate Government did not put much faith in those professions. The same hallucination as to their power, which rendered the Black Republicans arrogant and impracticable in Congress, would, it was apprehended, lead them to attempt to

---

1. Patrick N. Lynch was consecrated as third bishop of Charleston on 15 March 1858. In the spring of 1864 he received an official commission from President Jefferson Davis to go to Rome with the hope that he could win recognition for the Confederacy from Pope Pius IX. The mission ended in failure, however, and it was not until late in 1865 that Lynch was able to return to his diocese after a presidential pardon had been won for him through the efforts of Archbishop Martin J. Spalding of Baltimore. He liberated over two hundred slaves just before the Civil War.

crush out secession by force. — And nothing was left undone to be prepared for this event should it occur.

Meanwhile Commissioners were at Washington to arrange a peaceful separation. Favorable intimations were privately given them, and they had hopes of success.

Nine Governors, however, it is said, put the screws on the Cabinet, which resolved on a war policy, and, as silently as they could, made warlike naval preparations. Then, after a month, the Commissioners were refused admission or dismissed, and it was plainly announced that there would be no negotiation. At this time other facts were coming to light here, in Charleston, where our batteries had, for a month or more silently looked on Fort Sumter. During the time of peaceful professions two special messengers (Fox[2] and Lamon[3]) from President Lincoln visited Fort Sumter. Before being allowed to go thither they gave their word of honor to our Governor that their object was really peaceful. The hotel conversation of the latter was very frank, it is said. Gentlemen here supposed that President Lincoln before ordering the evacuation wished, by these personal friends, to see, as it were, personally, and not simply to learn through official channels, how matters stood at Fort Sumter. When time rolled by without such an order, and it was rumored that the Cabinet had succumbed to the pressure of the Governors, the mails were stopped to and from Fort Sumter. Among the letters seized was one from Major Anderson[4] to President Lincoln, discussing the details of the plan of reinforcement, forwarded to him from Washington by these messengers. Our authorities were thus made aware of the breach of faith towards them, and of the details of the plan itself.

Then came the special messenger of the President, announcing that he intended revictualing the fort, quietly, if permitted, forcibly, if resisted; then the account of the sailing of the fleet from New York. The fort was at once attacked and taken without waiting their arrival. The attack was not made until the offer of negotiation and peaceful arrangement had been rejected, and until the United States Government was in the act of sending an armed force. But it is of little use now to inquire on whom the responsibility rests; we have the war on us, with all its loss of life and long train of evils of every kind. It is the latest, perhaps the strangest instance history gives us, *quam parva sapientia regitur mundus.* Here was a country, vast, populous, prosperous and blessed in all material interest, if any country was. The South producing Cotton, tobacco, sugar, rice and naval stores for the supply, as far as needed, of the North and Northwest, to the value of perhaps, $50,000,000 a year, and exporting to foreign countries over $220,000,000; the Northwest producing chiefly grain, and supplying the North and the South, and when the European crops failed, having, as last winter, a large European market; the North manufacturing and

---

2. Gustavus V. Fox (1821–83) was named assistant secretary of the navy by Lincoln's government in August 1861.

3. Ward H. Lamon (1828–93), a former law partner of Lincoln in Illinois, had been sent to Charleston as the president's personal agent in March 1861.

4. Robert Anderson (1805–71) was the Union commander at Fort Sumter.

supplying the South and the Northwest, and struggling to compete with foreign goods abroad, and doing the trading and commerce of the South and the Northwest.

Could the material interests of all the sections be more harmoniously and advantageously combined than in this Union, where each was free to develop to the fullest extent those branches of industry in which it could excel, and could draw from the others those products which it needed, but could not produce as well or as cheaply as they could? Even a child could see the vast benefits to all from this mutual co-operation. No wonder that in all material interests the country was prospering to an extent that intoxicated us and astonished the world. We claimed to be pre-eminently sagacious in money matters. The Yankees, I believe, ranked next after the Chinese, in their keenness in business; yet they especially, with an inconceivable blindness, have originated, fostered and propagated a fanatical party spirit which has brought about a result foretold from the beginning, both North and South, as the inevitable consequence of its success.

Taking up anti-slavery, making it a religious dogma, and carrying it into politics, they have broken up the Union. While it was merely an intellectual opinion they might discuss it as they pleased; they might embrace it as they did any other ism. Even their virulent use and misrepresentation we scarcely heeded, provided they did not obtrude them upon us at home. We, as Catholics, might everywhere smile at this additional attempt to "reform" the teachings of our Savior. And the Protestants, South, could have churches and associations of their own. But when they carried it into politics, gaining one State Government after another, and defining their especial policy by unconstitutional laws and every mode of annoying and hostile action, and finally, with increased enthusiasm and increased bitterness, carrying the Presidential election in triumph, and grasping the power of the Federal Government, what could the South do but consult its own safety by withdrawing from the Union? What other protection had they? The Senate, which had still a Democratic majority? They had seen the House of Representatives pass into the hands of their enemies, and each session saw an increasing majority there. The Executive had gone for four years. Their own majority in the Senate was dwindling fast, while on the Territorial question not a few of the Northern Democrats were unsound. To the Supreme Court? That had spoken in the Dred Scott decision. The North would not sustain it, and the Black Republicans scouted it; and moreover, in a few years President Lincoln would have the privilege of placing on the bench new judges from the ranks of his party. To the sober second thought of the people? But this was no new issue on which they were taken by surprise. For years and years it had been discussed; North and South it had been denounced as fraught with disunion and ruin; and yet the Northern people had gradually come to accept it. But the South had spoken so often and so strongly of disunion, without doing anything, that the Northern people had no real belief that any evil consequences would ensue; they did not understand the full bearing of their action. At least, let them understand something of this before all hope of appeal to them is abandoned. Well, South Carolina seceded — other States were preparing to follow her. The matter was taken up in Congress. Many Southerners hoped that then, when the seriousness of the questions could no longer be doubted, something might be done. How vainly they hoped, the Committees of Congress showed. The alternative was thus forced on the South either of tame submission or of resistance. They did not hesitate. They desired to withdraw in peace. This war has been forced upon them.

It was necessary in the beginning. It brings ruin to thousands in its prosecution. It will be fruitless of any good. At its conclusion the parties will stand apart exhausted and embittered by it; for every battle, however, won or lost, will have served but to widen the chasm between the North and South, and to render more difficult, if not impossible, any future reconstruction. Will it be a long war, or a short and mighty one? The Cabinet and the Northern press has pronounced for the last. Yet this is little more than an idle dream. What could 400,000 men do?

I do not think there is a General on either side able to fight 50,000 men. And the North would need eight or ten such Generals. Certainly the 40,000 under McDowell,[5] after five hours' fighting, fought on mechanically without any generalship. The higher officers had completely lost the guiding reins. On our side the Southern troops ought to have been in Washington within forty-eight hours. But the 40,000 on the Confederate side was, I apprehend, too unwieldy a body for our Generals. Did not Bonaparte say that not one of his Marshals could general fifty thousand men?

Soult[6] could bring them to the field, and place them properly, but could go no further.

But without Generals, what could 400,000 men do against the South? By force of numbers, and a great loss, they might take city after city. But unless they left large permanent garrisons, their authority would die out with the sound of their drums. Such an army marching through a country covered with forests and thickets and occupied by a population hostile to a man, and where even school-boys can "bark a squirrel," would be decimated every hundred miles of its progress by a guerrilla warfare, against which it could find no protection. This mode of attacking the South can effect nothing beyond the loss of life it will entail, and the temporary devastation that will mark the track of the armies. But it is probable that circumstances would again, as they have done, overrule the designs of the Washington Cabinet, and make the war slow, long and expensive — one to be decided, less by battles than by the resources and endurance of the combatants.

That portion of the former United States will suffer most in such a contest and must finally succumb, which is least able to dispense with the support

5. General Irwin McDowell (1818–85) and his Union army were routed by the Confederate forces at Manassas Junction, Virginia, on 21 July 1861.

6. Marshal Nicolas-Jean-de-Dieu Soult (1769–1851) was one of the most prominent of Napoleon's generals.

it received from the other two sections. How the North can do without our Southern trade, I presume it can judge after three or four months' trial. But it would seem that the failure to sell to the South one hundred and twenty millions of their shipping interest as was engaged in the two hundred and twenty millions of our foreign exports and the return importations, and in our internal costing trade, together with the loss of the profits and commissions on so vast a business, must have a very serious effect, too, that I see no way of escaping. Truly the North has to pay dearly for its whistle of Black Republicanism. The Northwest depended partially on the South for a market for its productions, and so far will suffer from the loss of it. It must also be incidentally affected by commercial embarrassments at the North. They will assuredly have enough to eat and to wear, but the "fancy" prices of real estate and stocks, by which they computed their rapidly increasing wealth, must fall in a way to astonish Wall-street. Should their own crops fail, as they sometimes do, or should the European crops be abundant, their commerce will fall. Yet, as the mass of the poor will have all that they ever get anywhere — food and raiment, and that without stint — the Northwest will suffer comparatively little.

How long will it fare with the South should the war be long and so powerfully waged as to require the Southern Confederation to keep say 100,000 men-in-arms, and if the ports are strictly blockaded? This is an important question, and one that can be answered only from a practical knowledge of the habits, resources and disposition of the Southern people. Our needs will be provisions, clothing, money for the government and war expenses, and for the purchase from abroad of what we absolutely require, and are not already supplied with.

As for provisions, I am satisfied that this season we are gathering enough for two years' abundant supply. Every one is raising corn, wheat and stock. On this point the South need not envy the Northwest. Again, manufactures are springing up on all sides. In this State we are providing for our wants — from lucifer matches and steam engines to powder and rifled cannon. Clothing, too, though of a ruder texture and sometimes inferior quality, is abundantly made and easily procured. The supply of tea and coffee will, I presume, in time run out. This will put us to some trouble, but otherwise, neither for provisions nor for clothes, will the South be seriously inconvenienced.

The blacks (by-the-bye more quiet and orderly now, if possible, than before) will remain devoted to agriculture, while the rapidly increasing demand for home productions of every kind gives ready employment to the poorer classes of the whites.

What amount of gold and silver there is within the Confederate States I can only guess at — I suppose about $25,000,000. But as the greater part of our expenses are at home, any currency we are satisfied to use will do, whether Bank bills, Confederate bonds or Treasury notes. When we go abroad, it must be with gold or with Cotton. This last is the spinal column of our financial system. The following is the proposed mode of operating with it: Two millions, or two and a half of bales will be conveyed to the Confederate Government, to be paid for in bonds or Treasury notes. This Cotton will be worth, at ordinary prices, one hundred millions of dollars. If it can be exported at once, it is so much gold. If it is retained, it will form the security for any loan that may be required abroad. The other third of the Cotton will be sold by the planters as best they can on their own account.

The chief difficulty is the blockade, which may prevent the export and sale abroad of the Cotton. A loan on it as security, while it is still unshipped, and scattered in numberless small warehouses, could not easily be affected.

Up to the present time, and for six months more, the blockade, so far from doing any serious injury, has, on the contrary, benefitted, and will continue to benefit the South, forcing us to be active, and to do for ourselves much that we preferred formerly to pay others to do for us. I presume that next January, with a crop of three and a half or four millions of bales on hand, the South would become very restive under a strict blockade. *Should it continue twelve months longer property at the South would go down as they say it has in New York.*

But, before that time comes, another very serious complication arises — how England and France will stand the cutting off their supply of an article on which depend two-thirds of the manufacturing interests of the one and one-third of those of the other? They cannot, try they ever so much, supply the deficiency. As far as the feelings of England are concerned, and, I presume, those of France, too, both nations are decidedly and bitterly anti-slavery; but neither will be guilty of the mistake of the North, and utterly sacrifice vast interests for the sake of a speculative idea. If they find that they cannot do without Southern Cotton, they will interfere, first probably to make peace, and if that effort fails, then in such other manner as will secure for them what will be a necessity. Mr. Seward's[7] letter to Dayton,[8] and its reception in Europe, the transportation of troops to Canada, and Admiral Milne's declaration as to the inefficiency of the blockade, are straws already showing the possible course of future events. Is the Federal Government strong enough for a war with England and France in addition to that with the South?

One other warlike course remains — to capture and hold all the Southern ports, and thus seek to control commerce, independent of secession, leaving the interior of the South to fret and fume as it pleases. This is the problem of belling the cat. The Northern forces would have to capture Norfolk, Charleston, Savannah, Wilmington, N.C., Pensacola, Mobile, New Orleans and Galveston, besides some fifteen other smaller points. At each of them they would find a Stone Bridge; and even if they succeeded, they could only hold military possession and be forever in arms against the attacks of the State authorities. Peace would never be established by any such course. It would not

---

7. William H. Seward (1801–72) was Lincoln's secretary of state.
8. William L. Dayton (1807–64) had been appointed American minister to France in 1861.

be successful, and even if successful, it would only hamper the South, it would never subjugate it.

The separation of the Southern States is *un fait accompli.* The Federal Government has no power to reverse it. Sooner or later it must be recognized. Why preface the recognition by a war equally needless and bloody? Men at the North may regret the rupture; as men at the South may do. The Black Republicans overcame the first at the polls, and would not listen to the second in Congress, when the evil might have been repaired. They are responsible. If there is to be fighting, let those who voted the Black Republican ticket shoulder their musket and bear the responsibility. Let them not send Irishmen to fight in their stead, and then stand looking on at the conflict, when, in their heart of hearts, they care little which of the combatants destroy the other.

Most Reverend dear Sir, I am surprised and somewhat ashamed of the length to which my pen has run. But the night is hot — too hot for sleep. I arose from my couch, and have spent a couple of hours speaking to you as frankly and unreservedly as you have ever kindly allowed me to do. A trip to New York would be agreeable for more reasons than one. But that is impossible. Next to that I would like to see a file of the Record.[9] That, too, is impossible. Nothing seems now to span the chasm but that bridge of Catholic union and charity, of which your grace spoke so eloquently last St. Patrick's Day....

Commending myself to your holy sacrifices, I have the honor to remain, most Reverend dear Sir, your Grace's sincere and respectful son in Christ.

Catholic Miscellany (Charleston), 14 September 1861; also in John Tracy Ellis, ed., Documents of American Catholic History (Wilmington, Del.: Michael Glazier, 1987), 1:347–56. (Footnotes in Ellis.) Printed with permission of the estate of John Tracy Ellis.

21. John Hughes, Archbishop of New York, to Patrick N. Lynch, Bishop of Charleston, 23 August 1861

Right Rev. Dear Sir — I have received your letter of the 4th instant. How it reached me I can hardly conjecture. But it came to hand within about the usual period required for the transmission of mail matter between Charleston and New York during happier years, when all the States, North and South, found their meaning in the words *"E pluribus Unum."*

It must have run the blockade, or dodged the pickets on hostile borders. I have read it with very deep interest, increased, if anything, by the perils of *flood and field* through which it must have passed.

If even the innocent lightning of the North were permitted to carry a message into Southern latitudes, I would telegraph you for permission to publish your calm and judicious communication. As it is, however, my only chance of acknowledging it is through the *Metropolitan Record,* and without special

---

9. Hughes had started the *Metropolitan Record* in July 1859, after falling out with McMaster of the *Freeman's Journal.*

permission publish your letter at the same time. In this way it may happen that during the war, or afterwards, my answer will come under your inspection. Yours is, in my judgment, one of the most temperate views of the present unhappy contest that has ever come under my notice from any son of South Carolina. It is not to be inferred, however, that because I admire so much the calmness of its tone and temper I therefore agree with all its arguments and speculations.

You say I am "reported to have spoken strongly against the war policy of the Government of the United States, as fraught with much present suffering, and not calculated to obtain any real advantage." Be assured that previous to the outbreak of military violence, I was most ardently desirous of preserving peace and union; but, since violence, battle, and bloodshed have occurred, I dare not hope for peace unless you can show me a foundation of rock or solid ground (but no quicksand basis) on which peace can be re-established. The nature of your ministry and mine necessarily implies that we should be the friends of peace. It was the special legacy of our Divine Master to His flock. And it would be strange if we, His appointed ministers, should be found in the ranks of its enemies. His words were, as we find in St. John, "Peace I leave to you, my peace I give you; not as the world giveth do I give to you." And yet St. Paul, in writing to the Christian converts of Rome, says: "If it be possible, as much as it is in you, have peace with all men." I think this latter inspired quotation has at least a remote bearing on our present sad difficulties.

Your explanations of the causes which have led to this war are entirely Southern in their premises and conclusions. But they are so mildly, and even plausibly stated, that I leave them uncontroverted. Your description of the evils resulting from the war is too correct to be gainsayed by me. Still, here we are in the midst of a sanguinary context, which, so far as I can see, like a hurricane on the ocean, must exhaust its violence before we can expect the return of national calm. There is no one who desires more ardently than I do the advent of that bright day on which we shall all be re-united in one great prosperous and happy country.

Instead of controverting the correctness of your views in regard to the causes of our actual troubles, or determining where or on whom the responsibility of their existence rests, I shall beg leave to make my own statement from a point of view which is found in the general sentiment of the people north of Mason and Dixon's line.

They say that whatever may have been the anterior origin of this war, its immediate cause was the overt act of turning guns, put in place by the State of South Carolina, against a public military defence of the country at large, which of right belonged to all the States in common. Then it is thought, or at least stated, in these quarters that the South, for many years past, would not be satisfied with less than a paramount control of the Federal Government. The South, it is well known, has been in a fretful mood for many years under Northern assaults, made upon her civil and domestic institutions. It would be, on my part, very uncandid to disguise the conviction that in this respect the South has had much reason to complain. Leaving, however, opinions to fluctuate as they may, I will simply give you my own as to the primary causes of our present strife.

You know that free speech and a free press are essential constituents of the first notions of Anglo-Saxon liberty. These were the shibboleth of its existence, prosperity, and prospects. In this exercise of these peculiar privileges, the North of this country has used its type and its tongue offensively against the South. Neither was the South backward in the work of retaliation on the same principle. But the Anglo-Saxon, whether of the South or of the North, would see the whole world set in a blaze rather than put limits to the freedom of the press or the unbridled license of the tongue, except when the laws interpose for the protection of public authority or individual rights of character and property.

At the commencement of our national institution as an independent State, slavery for instance, was found to exist, almost universally, in the North as well as in the South. The word itself was not used in any of the paragraphs found in the Magna Charta of our Government. The slave-trade from the western coast of Africa had been encouraged by the subjects and the Government of Great Britain. The Government of England did not hesitate to affix its veto on some of the enactments made by the recognized local authorities of the Colonies for the diminution of the slave-trade. It would appear that from this trade, so abominable in its primary origin, there were certain emoluments accruing to the treasury of the mother country. And these emoluments were looked to as a source of revenue, just as some countries in Europe, in their sovereign capacity, monopolize the largest portion of profits resulting from commerce in salt and tobacco.

After the Revolution slavery was gradually dispensed with in all the Northern States. Whether this was done from what would appear a sense of humanity, or from motives of domestic or political lucre, it will be for you, as for me, a private right to determine, each according to his own opinion. But slavery was a social element recognized in all the States at the period of the Revolution. So far the changes that have supervened in reference to slavery have been all in the North, and the South is to-day as to this matter in *statu quo* just as she was at the period of the Declaration of Independence. The Northern States, in the exercise of their acknowledged right, repudiated slavery within their own borders. The Southern States, in the equal exercise of theirs, have done just the reverse. The North, unrepenting of many sins of its own, has exhibited great remorse for the sins of its neighbors. A portion of its inhabitants talk in a certain style, not only of this subject, but of a great many others, about national sins which, according to its solution of Pagan ethics or of Christian duty, every human being is bound to correct. Yet, the biggest sin in our day known to the North is not what occurs in its own immediate neighborhood or State, but the monster iniquity of the South, which, between you and me, and as the world goes, might have been permitted to manage its own affairs in its own way, so that its acts should be found either in harmony with, or not in violation of, the Constitution of the United States.

I am an advocate for the sovereignty of every State in the Union within the limits recognized and approved of by its own representative authority, when the Constitution was agreed upon. As a consequence, I hold that South Carolina has no State right to interfere with the internal affairs of Massachusetts. And, as a further consequence, that Massachusetts has no right to interfere with South Carolina, or its domestic and civil affairs, as one of the sovereign States of this now threatened Union. But the Constitution having been formed by common consent of all the sovereign parties engaged in the framework and approval thereof, I maintain that no State has a right to secede, except in the manner provided for in the document itself.

The revolt of the Colonies against the authority of Great Britain is quite another thing. If England had extended to these Colonies the common rights and privileges nominally secured by the British Constitution, we have high authority for believing that the Colonies would not have gone, at least when they did, into rebellion. Indeed, it might be asserted and maintained that it was not the Americans, but the British Ministry and Government, that supplied legitimate reasons for the American Revolution.

In the present case it would be difficult, by parity of reasoning, to justify the grounds on which the South have acted.

I think a few remarks will satisfy you of the correctness of this statement. You say that for many years the South has proclaimed its dissatisfaction, and announced its determined purpose of secession, if certain complaints should not be attended to, and their causes redressed; that the South was all the time in earnest, and the North would never believe in their sincerity or their predictions. This may be so; but it gives me an occasion to remark that the Federal Government as such had given no special reason for the secession of the South at this time more than there was ten, or even fifteen years ago. The Personal Liberty Bill was unconstitutional in the few States that adopted it. New York was too wise and too patriotic to be caught in that trap. The so-called Personal Liberty Bill was never adopted, so far as documents are evidence, either directly or indirectly, by the Government at Washington. Indeed I am not aware of any statute passed by the Federal authority which could give the South additional reasons for discontent or complaint within the last ten or fifteen years.

I have thus alluded to the unofficial causes for Southern resentment. Even in your own letter the cause alleged is the election of the present Chief Magistrate. This does not seem at all sufficient to warrant the course which the South has adopted.

The Government originally agreed upon by all the States has lasted during a period of between seventy and eighty years. During this time its executive administration was enjoyed by the South for fifty-two years. No Northern President has ever been re-elected. Washington, Jefferson, Madison, Monroe, and Jackson, have each discharged that office for a term of eight years. The conclusion is, then, that out of seventy or eighty years of the administration of our Government, fifty-two years have enured to our patriotic men of the South. This fact involves the potentialities and powers of the Government as having been exercised by supremacy on the part of the South. The navy, the army, the incumbents of the Supreme Court were not ignorant of or insensible to this fact. Now, I put it to your candor to say whether, after such a history of the administration of our country, the South might not have tolerated the occupancy of the presidential chair by the present incumbent, who, with his Northern predecessors in that office, could hardly expect to survive officially the ordinary four years of a Northern Supreme Magistrate?

You say that President Lincoln was elected by Black Republicans in the North. I am inclined to think that he was indirectly or negatively elected by Democrats, North and South. The Black Republicans presented one candidate; and, in order to defeat his election, the Democrats, North and South, presented *three*. If the latter had only selected one candidate, it is probable that the Black Republicans, as you call them, would have been found as *minus habentes*. But when the Democrats distributed their votes, apparently with a view of rendering them inefficient, then, of course, the one man of choice was elected over the three candidates and competitors that had been placed in rivalship with each other, and, in the aggregate, all against him alone. That he was constitutionally elected under these circumstances is not denied either in the South or in the North. Then, if so elected, he is the Chief Magistrate of all the United States of America, and by his very oath of office is bound by their own common consent so see that neither Maine, on the northeast, nor Texas, on the southwest, be permitted to overthrow the original Federal compact agreed upon in the Constitution of this Government. If States shall be allowed, in the face of that Federal Constitution, to kick over the traces of a common Union, as agreed upon in the primitive days of our Government, then it is difficult to see why counties, and townships, and villages may not be at liberty to do the same thing just as often as a freak or fancy to do so may or shall come upon them.

There appears to be an idea in the South that the Federal Government and the people of the North are determined to conquer and subjugate them. This, I think, is a great mistake. First, in the sterner sense of the word "conquer," it seems to me utterly impossible; and, if possible, I think it would be undesirable and injurious both to the North and to the South. Unless I have been deceived by statements considered reliable, I would say that the mind of the North looks only to the purpose of bringing back the seceded States to their organic condition — *ante bellum.*

There remains now scarcely a hope of peace, and the issue is apparently that the North must triumph on the field of Mars, or that the South shall prove itself victorious on the same bloody arena. But, after all, we must not despair in reference to a coming peace. The idea of an armistice, even for six months, is now utterly hopeless; but I think that the North, if the chance were presented, would be as willing to enter on terms of peace as the South itself.

Still, I am bound to say, under deep conviction of the truth, that, of both sections unhappily launched on the swelling current of our domestic troubles, the North will be the latter to sink or swim in the sanguinary tide on which both are now afloat.

You make mention of the Commissioners sent to Washington at an early period of the struggle with kind, fair, and liberal propositions, as you consider them, for the arrangement of the whole difficulty. Before reaching the point of settlement there would be found a vast amount of principle involved. Commissioners should have some recognized authority to warrant them in attempting to discharge the duties of their official office. Those of the South, in the circumstances, so far as I can see, had no authority whatever.

The people of your region (when I say people, of course, I mean the voters, as commonly understood in this country) had scarcely been consulted on this vital question. Their Government, so-called, was unrecognized by any civil principality on the face of the earth. Commissioners presented themselves before the public servants of a Government universally recognized by all nations. The terms of these Southern Commissioners were more of dictation than of petition. The Government at Washington had to choose one or another of two alternatives. The President and his Cabinet might have chosen the alternative of perjury, and acceded to the demands of those Commissioners; or they might, as they surely did, decline every official intercourse with them.

They chose the latter course. And now it only remains to see whether the Government is what it calls itself — the Government of the United States, or merely the Government of a fraction thereof, and that fraction measured out to them by the Southern Commissioners, who could not show a legitimate title for the commission which they professed to execute.

You think it hard that foreigners and Catholics should be deluded into the service of the recognized Federal Government, in order to be immolated in the front of battles, and made food for Southern powder. If this end were a deliberate policy in the North, I should scout and despise it. I admit and maintain, that foreigners now naturalized, whether Catholics or not, ought to bear their relative burden in defence of the only country on these shores which they have recognized, and which has recognized them as citizens of the United States.

Mr. Russell, the correspondent of the London *Times*, reports a conversation which he had with "a very intelligent Southern gentleman, formerly editor of a newspaper," who stated, on behalf of the Confederacy — "Well, sir, when things are settled we'll just take the law into our own hands. Not a man shall have a vote unless he's American born, and by degrees we'll get rid of these men who disgrace us." Mr. Russell inquired: "Are not many of your regiments composed of Germans and Irish — of foreigners, in fact?" "Yes sir."

This very "intelligent Southern gentleman, formerly editor of a newspaper," is certainly no true representative of the gentlemen whom it was my good fortune and pleasure to meet whenever I travelled in the South. But no matter. If the statement be true, it only shows that for Irish and foreigners in general the South is nearly as unfriendly as the North can be. It proves, further, that, so far as the Irish are concerned, the hereditary calamities of their native land follow them up wherever they go, in one form or another. Here, and now, they are called upon by both sides to fight in the battles of the country; and no matter who triumphs, they need not look for large expressions of thanks or gratitude from either side. Still, whether in peace or war, take them for all in all, they are as true to the country as if they had been born on its once free and happy soil.

Pardon me this digression, and let me return to the other sentiment touching the hope of a prospective peace.

That word "peace" is becoming more or less familiar here in the North. In a crisis like this it is not, in my opinion, expressive of a sound principle or a safe policy. Its meaning changes the basis and issue of this melancholy war. If changed, it will be a war, not between the South and the North, geographically considered, but a war between two great political parties that divide the country. Instead of this partisan hostility, wise patriots should rival each other in restoring or preserving the Union as one nation, its prosperity, and the protection and happiness of its entire people in all their legitimate rights. But all this is to be judged of by others, and the opinion of any individual is of the smallest account. If a word of mine could have the slightest influence, I would suggest that, even whilst the war is going on, there might be a convention of the seceded States held within their own borders. There might be one representative appointed from each of those States by the governor, to meet and examine the whole case as it now stands; arrange and draw up a report of their grievances, or what they consider such; and report to their respective governors the result of their deliberations, and the conclusions at which they shall have arrived.

The same process might be adopted in the States that have not seceded, and similar reports be made to their respective governors. This would be only a preparatory measure for something more important. If a better feeling or understanding could be even partially arrived at, a future convention of all the States by their representatives would have something to act upon. The difficulties might be investigated and provided for; the Constitution might be revised by general consent, and if the platform — sufficiently ample for 3,000,000 at the period when the Constitution was formed — is found to be neither of breadth nor strength to support a population of 33,000,000, wise and patriotic men might suggest, according to the rules prescribed in the original document, the improvements which the actual condition of the country would seem to require. The Constitution itself, in its letter and spirit, is no doubt the same as it was when first framed; but every thing around has been undergoing a change for nearly eighty years. For a peace of that kind I would be a very sincere, if not an influential, advocate. But to expect that a peace will spring up by the advocacy of individuals, in the midst of the din and clash of arms, amidst the mutually alienated feelings of the people, and the widening of the breach which has now separated them, would be, in my opinion, hoping against hope. Still, we must trust that the Almighty will overrule and direct the final issues of this lamentable contest.

I had no intention to write so long a response to your kind letter. Enough, and perhaps more than enough, has been said; and it only remains for me to add, that the Catholic faith and Catholic charity which unites us in the spiritual order, shall remain unbroken by the booming of cannon along the lines that unfortunately separate a great and once prosperous community into two hostile portions, each arrayed in military strife against the other.

Lawrence Kehoe, ed., *Complete Works of the Most Rev. John Hughes, D.D., Archbishop of New* York (New York: Lawrence Kehoe, 1865), 2:515–21.

22. John Hughes, Archbishop of New York, to William H. Seward, Secretary of State of the United States, 1 November 1862

My Dear Governor — It is now more than twenty-three years since I had the pleasure of being introduced to you on the railroad train between Albany and Utica. Opportunities for cultivating more intimately that first acquaintance have been few and far between. Still, as a personal friend, apart from what they commonly call politics, I have always recognized you, in my own mind, as a true, unflinching man of upright principle.

As for myself, I cannot say that I ever belonged to any political party, and yet, since my return from Europe, certain nominally Catholic papers have written me down as a politician. Much allowance must be made for such writers. They assume that my going to Europe was for a political, not a national purpose; in fact, they seem, or choose to appear, as incompetent to distinguish between what is vulgarly called a politician and a patriot. Of the two, I would prefer to be considered a patriot rather than a politician. Before the outbreak of this melancholy civil war, it is known to you, my dear Governor,[1] that I foresaw the coming calamity. I wrote to distinguished persons in the South, praying and beseeching that they should exercise their influence for the perpetuation of peace, or rather against the disruption of the Union. In my own sphere, in New York, I left nothing undone to soothe bitter prejudices, especially on the part of abolitionists, with a view, and even in hope, that the domestic strife which has since overtaken us might be arrested and turned aside.

It is just one year and eight days since it was desired, by a telegraphic communication, that I should visit the city of Washington on public business. I obeyed the summons. I spoke my mind freely. It was thought that, in the perils of the nation, at that time, I could be useful in promoting the interests of the commonwealth and of humanity if I would go to Europe and exercise whatever little influence I might possess in preventing France and England from intermeddling in our sad quarrel.

---

1. Seward was formerly governor of New York.

It has, no doubt, escaped your memory that, during the fourteen or fifteen hours which I spent in Washington, *I declined the acceptance of what would be to persons, not of my rank, a great honor.* I did not absolutely refuse before deciding, but I wished to consult one or two persons very near and dear to me in New York. Finally, and at the very last hour, there was a word uttered to me, not by any special member of the Cabinet to which you belong, but by the authority which it possesses, to the effect that my acting as had been suggested was a personal request, and would be considered as a personal favor. In three minutes I decided that, without consulting any body, I should embark as a volunteer to accomplish what might be possible on the other side of the Atlantic in favor of the country to which I belong.

What occurred on the other side, I think it would be, at present, improper for me to make public. I am not certain that any word, or act, or influence of mine has had the slightest effect in preventing either England or France from plunging into the unhappy divisions that have threatened the Union of these once prosperous States. On the other hand, I may say that no day — no hour even — was spent in Europe in which I did not, according to opportunity, labor for peace between Europe and America. So far that peace has not been disturbed. *But let America be prepared. There is no love for the United States on the other side of the water.* Generally speaking, *on the other side of the Atlantic, the United States are ignored, if not despised;* treated in conversation in the same contemptuous language as we might employ towards the inhabitants of the Sandwich Islands, or Washington Territory, or Vancouver's Island, or the settlement of the Red River, or of the Hudson's Bay Territory.

This may be considered very unpolished, almost unchristian language proceeding from the pen of a Catholic Archbishop. But, my dear governor, it is unquestionably true, and I am sorry that it is so. If you, in Washington, are not able to defend yourselves in case of need, I do not see where, or from what source, you can expect friendship or protection. Since my return I made a kind of familiar address to my people, but not for them exclusively, in St. Patrick's Cathedral. Some have called it not a sermon, but a discourse, and even a war blast, in favor of blood spilling. Nothing of that kind could be warranted by a knowledge of my natural temperament or of my ecclesiastical training. From the slight correspondence between us, you can bear me witness that I pleaded in every direction for the preservation of peace, so long as the slightest hope of its preservation remained. When all hope of this kind had passed away *I was for a vigorous prosecution of our melancholy war, so that one side or the other should find itself in the ascendency.*

On my return from Europe, I knew it was expected that I should make, in writing or otherwise, some observations of my experience abroad that would reach the public generally. These observations were made in the Cathedral of St. Patrick, on the 18th of August. They consisted of a very simple narrative of my experience in different countries of Europe during my absence from New York. Towards the close of my remarks, two ideas I ventured to express with perhaps more energy than had been employed in the simple narrative.

One was the advocacy of conscription, in preference to the dragging business of enlistment and volunteering. Perhaps some may have thought that it was unbecoming for me in a Catholic pulpit to have expressed my opinion on this topic. But I know that the country, which I had no reason not to love, was being agonized by civil war. And besides, on reflection, I consider that conscription, sometimes called drafting, is the only fair, open, honest mode by which a nation can support its rights, and, in case of danger, its own independence.

Many of my hearers on that occasion confounded the principle of conscription with the abominable practice of the "press gang," during the war between England and France. This, of course, was their mistake, not mine. France is a military nation, and a great nation; and its system of conscription, although at periods of great national necessity, verging in its operation to almost cruelty, in taking from the family one after another of the sons who might be otherwise the hope, and the stay, and consolation of their aged parents, is, notwithstanding, still the impartial mode of providing for national defence and honor. Yet, on the whole, there is no system in civilized countries so just, so equitable, and so efficient in raising an army of defence, as the system of conscription rightly administered. If it can be dispensed with by the multitude of volunteers, of course there would be no objection to that result. But a government must execute the office for which it was appointed, and for the execution of the functions of which it is supposed to have ample means, or else it should abdicate.

Lawrence Kehoe, ed., *The Complete Works of the Most Rev. John Hughes, D.D., Archbishop of New York* (New York: Lawrence Kehoe, 1865), 2:539–42.

Part 2

1865–1920

Introduction

Industrialization and urbanization were the major motifs of post–Civil War America. The United States was remade in this period, evolving from a rural, decentralized, and technologically underdeveloped nation to an urban, rationalized, and progress-oriented society.

America's rise to industrial power was first fueled by the railroads. Not only did they create tremendous demands for raw materials and human labor; they also revolutionized business practices and opened up vast new markets for American manufactured goods. Expanding on the base of textile manufacturing, the new heavy industries of steel and oil led the way in creating a new industrial order in America. Upstart cities like Cleveland, Detroit, Chicago, and Milwaukee spouted smokestacks and developed an insatiable demand for unskilled laborers, who helped generate the fantastic wealth created by these industries. Managing wealth itself became a full-time enterprise for some, and the management of major industries came to be determined not by the practitioners of the skills themselves but by new capitalist barons who cut deals in oak-paneled boardrooms and over cigars and brandy in men's clubs.

Urban life was the nexus of much that happened in this period — the city was the concentrated image of the excesses and blessings of the new socioeconomic order. Cities evolved from small walking communities, where commercial buildings bumped up against the houses of the wealthy, to spatially differentiated metropolises linked together by urban transit systems. The human geography and culture of American cities changed dramatically as scores of immigrants poured into them. The immigrant presence was perceived by many as both a blessing and a curse. Immigrant labor provided the needed workers to build industrial might and necessary services to rapidly expanding cities. But it also raised important questions of national identity and evoked nativist reaction. In the West, Chinese and later Japanese immigrants were the first to feel the sting of a suspicious and aroused population. Their restriction led to a debate that ultimately imposed additional restrictions on immigrants who did not share Anglo-American physical or cultural traits.

71

Political institutions on every level found themselves befuddled by the new realities and for a time coped as best they could with measures and movements intended to alleviate the worst problems. Farm distress had its panacea in monetary inflation, the problems of monopoly in some limited toleration of skilled-worker unionism, governmental corruption in efforts to reform the standards of government service. However, full-scale efforts to address serious dislocations created by the new circumstances came when government overcame the ideological barriers of laissez-faire and social Darwinian ideologies — both of which had come to be enshrined as national dogma. Once convinced that government could make a difference, any number of independent reformers on city, state, and federal levels swung into action to deal with various issues. The progressive movement, as historians package this concatenation of reforms, attempted to help Americans cope with the massive changes that had reconfigured their social and economic life since the middle of the nineteenth century. Using the government as an effective partner in equalizing some of the imbalances created by large-scale industrialization, progressive reform left an important imprint not only on the American Constitution but even more importantly on the average American's expectation of the role of government. It also enshrined as indispensable the techniques and principles of the managerial revolution, a revolution that affected virtually every facet of American life.

The American metamorphosis of the late nineteenth and early twentieth century brought with it wealth, prestige, and international stature. If the vast American continent seemed to shrink due to the transportation and communication revolutions of the era, so also did the world community. American commercial and ideological interests propelled the shaping of a coherent foreign policy. American intervention in external affairs grew steadily throughout the nineteenth century as the nation discerned its role in the rekindled expansionism that affected all parts of the globe. Military preparedness and a heightened awareness of hemispheric order led to a "splendid little war" with Spain in 1898 and a major role in the shaping of the destiny of the Americas because of the construction of a long-planned canal in Panama. Indifference to European imperialism or Asian events was no longer a luxury as the Spanish-American War created a niche for the stars and stripes in the far-off Philippines and in China. Caught up in the whirlwind of all the intersecting events of global trade, politics, and ideology, the United States eventually found itself enmeshed in a major world conflict that erupted with fury in August 1914. Ideologically and strategically driven to support Great Britain, the United States made war on resurgent Germany and its allies. Emerging a virtually unscathed victor, the American president, Woodrow Wilson, attempted to impose his vision of a new world order on the victorious Allies — and failed the test of domestic politics. The election of an affable and comfortable Republican by the name of Warren Harding created a watershed for the epoch that had begun when Lee's sword was gallantly refused by General Grant at Appomattox.

Education

The spectacular growth of parochial schools after the Civil War reignited earlier discussions of the use of public funds for these enterprises. Deliberate efforts of President Ulysses S. Grant to actively prohibit the use of these funds for parochial schools fell short of approval. Faced with a growing secularization of the schools, Catholics became even more intent on forming their own distinct institutions.

23. Ulysses S. Grant's Proposal and James G. Blaine's Amendment, 29 September–14 December 1875

Grant's Message to Congress, December 7, 1875

As we are now about to enter upon our second centennial — commencing our manhood as a nation — it is well to look back upon the past and study what will be best to preserve and advance our future greatness. From the fall of Adam for his transgression to the present day, no nation has ever been free from threatened danger to its prosperity and happiness. We should look to the dangers threatening us, and remedy them so far as lies in our power. We are a republic whereof one man is as good as another before the law. Under such a form of government it is of the greatest importance that all should be possessed of education and intelligence enough to cast a vote with the right understanding of its meaning. A large association of ignorant men cannot, for any considerable period, oppose a successful resistance to tyranny and oppression from the educated few, but will inevitably sink into acquiescence to the will of intelligence, whether directed by the demagogue or by priestcraft. Hence the education of the masses becomes of the first necessity for the preservation of our institutions. They are worth preserving, because they have secured the greatest good to the greatest proportion of the population of any form of government yet devised. All other forms of government approach it just in proportion to the general diffusion of education and independence of thought and action. As the primary step, therefore, to our advancement in all that has marked our progress in the past century, I suggest for your earnest consideration — and most earnestly recommend it — that a constitutional amendment be submitted to the Legislatures of the several States for ratification making it the duty of the several States to establish and forever maintain free public schools adequate to the education of all the children in the rudimentary branches within their respective limits, irrespective of sex, color, birthplace, or religions; forbidding the teaching in said schools of religious, atheistic, or pagan tenets; and prohibiting the granting of any school funds, or school taxes, or any part thereof, either by the legislative, municipal, or other authority, for the benefit or in aid, directly or indirectly, of any religious sect or denomination, or in aid for the benefit of any other object of any nature or kind whatever.[1]

Blaine's Proposed Amendment, December 14, 1875

Resolved by the Senate and House of Representatives, That the following be proposed to the several States of the Union as an amendment to the Constitution:

Article XVI: No State shall make any law respecting an establishment of religion or prohibiting the free exercise thereof; and no money raised by taxation in any State for the support of public schools, or derived from any public fund therefor, nor any public lands devoted thereto, shall ever be under the control of any religious sect, nor shall any money so raised or lands so devoted be divided between religious sects or denominations.

> Frank A. Burr, *A New, Original, and Authentic Record of the Life and Deeds of General U. S. Grant* (St. Paul: Empyreal Publishing House, 1885), 871–72; *Congressional Record*, 44th Cong., 1st Sess. (1876), 4, pts. 175, 205; also in John Tracy Ellis, ed., *Documents of American Catholic History* (Wilmington, Del.: Michael Glazier, 1987), 2:395–97. (Footnote in Ellis.) Printed with permission of the estate of John Tracy Ellis.

24. Instruction of the Congregation de Propaganda Fide concerning Catholic Children Attending American Public Schools, 24 November 1875

The Sacred Congregation of Propaganda has been many times assured that for the Catholic children of the United States of America evils of the gravest kind are likely to result from the so-called public schools.

The sad intelligence moved the Propaganda to propose to the illustrious prelates of that country a series of questions, with the object of ascertaining, first, why the faithful permit their children to attend non-catholic schools, and secondly, what may be the best means of keeping the young away from schools of this description. The answers, as drawn up by the several prelates, were submitted, owing to the nature of the subject, to the Supreme Congregation of the Holy Office. The decision reached by their Eminences, Wednesday, June 30, 1875, they saw fit to embody in the following *Instruction*, which the Holy Father graciously confirmed on Wednesday, November 24, of the same year.

1. The first point to come under consideration was the system of education itself, quite peculiar to those schools. Now, that system seemed to the S. Congregation most dangerous and very much opposed to Catholicity. For

---

1. Grant's message to Congress also contained the following proposal: "I would suggest the taxation of all property equally, whether church or corporation, exempting only the last resting-place of the dead, and possibly, with proper restrictions, church edifices." The New York League for the Separation of Church and State, founded in 1938, carried on its letterhead a picture of Grant and a phrase from his Des Moines speech as its slogan.

the children in those schools, the very principles of which exclude all religious instruction, can neither learn the rudiments of the faith nor be taught the precepts of the Church; hence, they will lack that knowledge, of all else, necessary to man without which there is no leading a Christian life. For children are sent to these schools from their earliest years, almost from their cradle; at which age, it is admitted, the seeds sown of virtue or of vice take fast root. To allow this tender age to pass without religion is surely a great evil.

2. Again, these schools being under no control of the Church, the teachers are selected from every sect indiscriminately; and this, while no proper precaution is taken to prevent them injuring the children, so that there is nothing to stop them from infusing into the young minds the seeds of error and vice. Then evil results are certainly to be dreaded from the fact that in these schools, or at least in very many of them, children of both sexes must be in the same class and class-room and must sit side by side at the same desk. Every circumstance mentioned goes to show that the children are fearfully exposed to the danger of losing their faith and that their morals are not properly safeguarded.

3. Unless this danger of perversion can be rendered remote, instead of proximate, such schools cannot in conscience be used. This is the dictate of natural as well as of divine law. It was enunciated in unmistakable terms by the Sovereign Pontiff, in a letter addressed to a former Archbishop of Freiburg, July 14, 1864. He thus writes: "There can be no hesitation; wherever the purpose is afoot or carried out of shutting out the Church from all authority over the schools, there the children will be sadly exposed to loss of their faith. Consequently the Church should, in such circumstances, not only put forth every effort and spare no pains to get for the children the necessary Christian training and education, but would be further compelled to remind the faithful and publicly declare that schools hostile to Catholicity cannot in conscience be attended." These words only express a general principle of natural and divine law and are consequently of universal application wherever that most dangerous system of training youth has been unhappily introduced.

4. It only remains, then, for the prelates to use every means in their power to keep the flocks committed to their care from all contact with the public schools. All are agreed that there is nothing so needful to this end as the establishment of Catholic schools in every place, — and schools no whit inferior to the public ones. Every effort then, must be directed towards starting Catholic schools where they are not, and, where they are, towards enlarging them and providing them with better accommodations and equipment until they have nothing to suffer, as regards teachers or equipment, by comparison with the public schools. And to carry out so holy and necessary a work, the aid of religious brotherhoods and of sisterhoods will be found advantageous where the bishop sees fit to introduce them. In order that the faithful may the more freely contribute the necessary expenses, the bishops themselves should not fail to impress on them, at every suitable occasion, whether by pastoral letter, sermon or private conversation, that as bishops they would be recreant to

their duty if they failed to do their very utmost to provide Catholic schools.[1] This point should be especially brought to the attention of the more wealthy and influential Catholics and members of the legislature.

5. In that country there is no law to prevent Catholics having their own schools and instructing and educating their youth in every branch of knowledge. It is therefore in the power of Catholics themselves to avert, with God's help, the dangers with which Catholicity is threatened from the public school system. Not to have religion and piety banished from the school-room is a matter of the very highest interest, not only to certain individuals and families, but to the entire country, — a country now so prosperous and of which the Church has had reason to conceive such high hopes.

6. However, the S. Congregation is not unaware that circumstances may be sometimes such as to permit parents conscientiously to send their children to the public schools. Of course they cannot do so without having sufficient cause. Whether there be sufficient cause in any particular case is to be left to the conscience and judgment of the bishop. Generally speaking, such cause will exist when there is no Catholic school in the place, or the one that is there cannot be considered suitable to the condition and circumstances in life of the pupils. But even in these cases, before the children can conscientiously attend the public school, the danger, greater or less, of perversion, which is inseparable from the system, must be rendered remote by proper precaution and safeguards. The first thing to see to, then, is whether the danger of perversion, as regards the school in question, is such as cannot possibly be rendered remote; as, for instance, whether the teaching there is such, or the doings of a nature so repugnant to Catholic belief and morals, that ear cannot be given to the one, nor part taken in the other without grievous sin. It is self-evident that danger of this character must be shunned at whatever cost, even life itself.

7. Further, before a child can be conscientiously placed at a public school, provision must be made for giving it the necessary Christian training and instruction, at least out of school hours. Hence parish priests and missionaries in the United States should take seriously to heart the earnest admonitions of the Council of Baltimore,[2] and spare no labor to give children thorough catechetical instructions, dwelling particularly on those truths of faith and morals which are called most in question by Protestants and unbelievers: children beset with so many dangers they should guard with tireless vigilance, induce them to frequent the sacraments, excite in them devotion to the Blessed Virgin and on all occasions animate them to hold firmly by their religion. The par-

---

1. That the American bishops had not been unmindful of their duty in this regard was evident from the decree passed in their First Plenary Council of Baltimore in May 1852, which read: "We exhort the bishops, and in view of the very grave evils which usually result from the defective education of youth, we beseech them through the bowels of the mercy of God, to see that schools be established in connection with all the churches of their dioceses" (*Concilium plenarium totius Americae septentrionalis foederatae Baltimori habitum anno 1852* [Baltimore, 1853], 47).

2. The Second Plenary Council of Baltimore, in October 1866, went beyond the legislation of 1852 and devoted an entire chapter to the subject "De scholis parochialibus ubique fundandis" (*Concilii plenarii Baltimorensis II... Acta et decreta* [Baltimore, 1868], 218–25).

ents or guardians must look carefully after those children. They must examine them in their lessons, or if not able themselves, get others to do it. They must see what books they use and, if the books contain passages likely to injure the child's mind, explain the matter. They must keep them from freedom and familiarity with those of the other school children whose company might be dangerous to their faith or morals, and absolutely away from the corrupt.

8. Parents who neglect to give this necessary Christian training and instruction to their children, or who permit them to go to schools in which the ruin of their souls is inevitable, or finally, who send them to the public school without sufficient cause and without taking the necessary precautions to render the danger of perversion remote, and do so while there is a good and well-equipped Catholic school in the place, or the parents have the means to send them elsewhere to be educated, — that such parents, if obstinate, cannot be absolved, is evident from the moral teaching of the Church.

> Latin text in *Acta et decreta concilii plenarii Baltimorensis tertii* (Baltimore, 1886), 279–82; English translation in *The Pastor* 4 (June 1886): 232–37; also in John Tracy Ellis, ed., *Documents of American Catholic History* (Wilmington, Del.: Michael Glazier, 1987), 2:405–8. (Footnotes in Ellis.) Printed with permission.

Church and Economic Order

Industrialization and urbanization reconfigured the social, economic, and political realities of life in the United States in the latter part of the nineteenth century. The massive imbalance in the distribution of wealth and challenging conditions of urban life presented a special challenge to American Catholics, many of whom were in the swelling labor force and the burgeoning cities. Catholic leaders were fearful of the in-roads of European-style radicalism, which carried with it some serious criticism of the church. European fears of proletarian organizations were equally strong. These concerns are manifested in the reaction to the ideas of Henry George, the rise of socialism, and the proliferation of secret societies.

25. The Pastoral Letter of the Third Plenary Council of Baltimore on Forbidden Societies, 7 December 1884

One of the most striking characteristics of our times is the universal tendency to band together in societies for the promotion of all sorts of purposes.[1] This

---

1. That the bishops were not exaggerating the phenomenon may be seen from the fact that between 1880 and 1900 at least 490 new societies were organized in the United States, and by 1900 there were over six million names on the rolls of these societies. Arthur M. Schlesinger has stated, "So thoroughly did the 'habit of forming associations' — James Bryce's phrase — interpenetrate American life that it becomes possible to understand practically all the important economic and social developments merely by examining the activities of voluntary organizations" ("Biography of a Nation of Joiners," *American Historical Review* 50 [October 1944]: 16).

tendency is the natural outgrowth of an age of popular rights and representative institutions. It is also in accordance with the spirit of the Church, whose aim, as indicated by her name Catholic, is to unite all mankind in brotherhood. It is consonant also with the spirit of Christ, who came to break down all walls of division, and to gather all in the one family of the one heavenly Father.

But there are few good things which have not their counterfeits, and few tendencies which have not their dangers. It is obvious to any reflecting mind that men form bad and rash as well as good and wise designs; and that they may band together for carrying out evil or dangerous as well as laudable and useful purposes. And this does not necessarily imply deliberate malice, because, while it is unquestionably true that there are powers at work in the world which deliberately antagonize the cause of Christian truth and virtue, still the evil or the danger of purposes and associations need not always spring from so bad a root. Honest but weak and erring human nature is apt to be so taken up with one side of a question as to do injustice to the other; to be so enamored of favorite principles as to carry them to unjustifiable extremes; to be so intent upon securing some laudable end as to ignore the rules of prudence, and bring about ruin instead of restoration. But no intention, no matter how honest, can make lawful what is unlawful. For it is a fundamental rule of Christian morals that "evil must not be done that good may come of it," and "the end can never justify the means," if the means are evil. Hence it is the evident duty of every reasonable man, before allowing himself to be drawn into any society, to make sure that both its ends and its means are consistent with truth, justice, and conscience.

In making such a decision, every Catholic ought to be convinced that his surest guide is the Church of Christ. She has in her custody the sacred deposit of Christian truth and morals; she has the experience of all ages and all nations; she has at heart the true welfare of mankind; she has the perpetual guidance of the Holy Ghost in her authoritative decisions. In her teaching and her warnings therefore, we are sure to hear the voice of wisdom, prudence, justice and charity. From the hill-top of her Divine mission and her worldwide experience, she sees events and their consequences far more clearly than they who are down in the tangled plain of daily life. She has seen associations that were once praiseworthy, become pernicious by change of circumstances. She has seen others, which won the admiration of the world by their early achievements, corrupted by power or passion or evil guidance, and she has been forced to condemn them. She has beheld associations which had their origin in the spirit of the Ages of Faith, transformed by lapse of time, and loss of faith, and the manipulation of designing leaders, into the open or hidden enemies of religion and human weal. Thus our Holy Father Leo XIII has lately shown that the Masonic and kindred societies, — although the offspring of the ancient Guilds, which aimed at sanctifying trades and tradesmen with the blessings of religion; and although retaining, perhaps, in their "ritual," much that tells of the religiousness of their origin; and although in some countries still professing entire friendliness toward the Christian religion, — have nevertheless already gone so far, in many countries, as to array themselves in avowed hostility against Christianity, and against the Catholic Church as its embodiment; that they virtually aim at substituting a world-wide fraternity of their own, for the universal brotherhood of Jesus Christ, and at disseminating mere Naturalism for the supernatural revealed religion bestowed upon mankind by the Saviour of the world. He has shown, too, that, even in countries where they are as yet far from acknowledging such purposes, they nevertheless have in them the germs, which under favorable circumstances, would inevitably blossom forth in similar results.[2] The Church, consequently, forbids her children to have any connection with such societies, because they are either an open evil to be shunned or a hidden danger to be avoided. She would fail in her duty if she did not speak the word of warning, and her children would equally fail in theirs, if they did not heed it.

Whenever, therefore, the Church has spoken authoritatively with regard to any society, her decision ought to be final for every Catholic. He ought to know that the Church has not acted hastily or unwisely, or mistakenly; he should be convinced that any worldly advantages which he might derive from his membership of such society, would be a poor substitute for the membership, the sacraments, and the blessings of the Church of Christ; he should have the courage of his religious convictions, and stand firm to faith and conscience. But if he be inclined or asked to join a society on which the Church has passed no sentence, then let him, as a reasonable and Christian man, examine into it carefully, and not join the society until he is satisfied as to its lawful character.

There is one characteristic which is always a strong presumption against a society, and that is secrecy. Our Divine Lord Himself has laid down the rule: "Every one that doth evil, hateth the light and cometh not to the light, that his works may not be reproved. But he that doth truth cometh to the light that his works may be made manifest, because they are done in God."[3] When, therefore, associations veil themselves in secrecy and darkness, the presumption is against them, and it rests with them to prove that there is nothing evil in them.

But if any society's obligation be such as to bind its members to secrecy, even when rightly questioned by competent authority, then such a society puts itself outside the limits of approval, and no one can be a member of it and at the same time be admitted to the sacraments of the Catholic Church. The same is true of any organization that binds its members to a promise of blind obedience — to accept in advance and to obey whatsoever orders, lawful or unlawful, that may emanate from its chief authorities; because such a promise is contrary both to reason and conscience. And if a society works or plots, either openly or in secret, against the Church, or against lawful authorities,

---

2. See Leo XIII's encyclical *Humanum genus*, 20 April 1884, in John J. Wynne, S.J., ed., *The Great Encyclical Letters of Pope Leo XIII* (New York, 1903), 83–106.

3. John 3:20–21.

then to be a member of it is to be excluded from the membership of the Catholic Church.

These authoritative rules, therefore, ought to be the guide of all Catholics in their relations with societies. No Catholic can conscientiously join, or continue in, a body in which he knows that any of these condemned features exist. If he has joined it in good faith and the objectionable features become known to him afterwards, or if any of these evil elements creep into a society which was originally good, it becomes his duty to leave it at once. And even if he were to suffer loss or run the risk by leaving such a society or refusing to join it, he should do his duty and brave the consequences regardless of human consideration.

To these laws of the Church, the justice of which must be manifest to all impartial minds, we deem it necessary to add the following admonition of the Second Plenary Council: "Care must be taken lest workingman's societies, under the pretext of mutual assistance and protection, should commit any of the evils of condemned societies; and lest the members should be induced by the artifices of designing men to break the laws of justice, by withholding labor to which they are rightfully bound, or by otherwise unlawfully violating the rights of their employers."[4]

But while the Church is thus careful to guard her children against whatever is contrary to Christian duty, she is no less careful that no injustice should be done to any association, however unintentionally. While therefore the Church, before prohibiting any society, will take every precaution to ascertain its true nature, we positively forbid any pastor, or other ecclesiastic, to pass sentence on any association or to impose ecclesiastical penalties or disabilities on its members without the previous explicit authorization of the rightful authorities....[5]

> Peter Guilday, ed., *The National Pastorals of the American Hierarchy, 1792–1919* (Washington: National Catholic Welfare Conference, 1923), 256–60; also in John Tracy Ellis, ed., *Documents of American Catholic History* (Wilmington, Del.: Michael Glazier, 1987), 2:418–21. (Footnotes in Ellis.)

26. Cardinal James Gibbons to Cardinal Simeoni, 25 February 1887

Your Eminence:

I have already had the honor of presenting to your Eminence my views on the social questions which agitate America, especially with regard to their bearing on the association of the Knights of Labor. But recently another form of social debate has developed relating to the doctrines of Mr. Henry George,

---

4. *Concilii plenarii Baltimorensis II...Acta et decreta* (Baltimore, 1868), 263.

5. The plenary council of 1884 constituted the archbishops of the United States as a commission to investigate and pass judgment on all suspect societies. For a treatment of how the commission operated, the condemnation of three American societies by the Holy Office in August 1894, and the final solution given to the problem, see Fergus Macdonald, *The Catholic Church and the Secret Societies in the United States* (New York, 1946), 100ff.

an American author identified with the working classes. And since my arrival in Rome I have heard the idea discussed that the writings of Henry George should be put on the Index.[1] After having fully thought over the subject I believe it my duty to submit to your Eminence the reasons which seem to me to demonstrate that a formal condemnation of the works of Henry George would be neither opportune nor useful.

1. Henry George is in no way the originator of the theory which he advocates concerning the right of ownership in land. In his principal book, "Progress and Poverty," he cites precisely the teachings of Herbert Spencer and John Stuart Mill, two of England's chief authors. And in the English periodical work, the "Contemporary Review," of November 1886, a distinguished Professor quotes them more fully to prove, as he says, that Mr. George is only a plagiarist of these celebrated authors.[2] Now it seems to me that the world will judge it a bit singular if the Holy See attacks the work of a humble American artisan instead of attacking his great masters. And if there are some who, therefore, think that it is the duty of the Holy See to pronounce judgment on Spencer and Mill, perhaps it would be prudent first to take counsel with their Eminences Cardinals Manning and Newman on the opportuneness of such action.[3]

2. It is well to remark that the theory of Henry George differs from that which is ordinarily called Communism and Socialism. Because as Father Valentine Steccanella shows very well in his work on Communism, published by the Propaganda Press in 1882,[4] this implies "the abolition of private property and the collectivization of all goods in the hands of the State." Now anyone who has read the books of Henry George ought to recognize that he neither teaches this nor does he at all wish it. On the contrary, he maintains the absolute ownership of all the fruits of human energy and industry, even when they amount to great riches acquired either by labor or heredity. It is only with regard to land itself that he would wish to limit the ownership of individuals by an extension of the *supremum dominum* of the state; and on this point he has expressly stated that he would in no way dispossess the actual owners; but he would desire simply that our system of taxation be changed in such a way that only the land would provide taxes and not the fruits of human industry. One can see, therefore, that in the practical form in which the controversy presents itself to the American public it is simply a question of the government's power over individual ownership of land. And on that there is this to be noted:

---

1. Up to 1887 George's principal works were *Progress and Poverty* (1879), *Social Problems* (1883), and *Protection or Free Trade* (1886).

2. Henry Sidgwick, "Economic Socialism," *Contemporary Review* 50 (November 1886): 629.

3. Perhaps the only ecclesiast who knew George personally was Cardinal Manning, who, in the previous year (1885), had discussed with him his proposals to alleviate the world as written in his book *Progress and Poverty*. (Shane Leslie, *Henry Edward Manning: His Life and Labours* [London, 1921], 353.)

4. Valentino Steccanella, S.J., *Del communismo esame critico filosofico e politico* (Rome, 1882).

a) Anyone who studies properly the question of the relations of the State to the right of ownership of land, as it is treated by Father Steccanella and by other Catholic writers, or as it is regulated by the laws of taxation and the care of the poor in some countries, and especially in England, cannot help but understand that it is a very complex question, very much subject to the diverse circumstances of time and place, and not yet ready to be resolved by a decisive judgment.

b) The question is already before the American public as a political issue, and in so practical an arena it will soon find its end;[5]

c) As Mr. George himself realizes, it is only the legislative power of the country which could bring about such a disposition of affairs; and it is quite certain that neither a Congress nor a legislature ever be found that would vote for such a profound change in social relations, nor a President who would approve it,

d) In a country such as ours, which is by no means a country of doctrinaires and visionaries, speculative theory will not be dangerous, nor will it live long after its practical application will have been rejected; one may, therefore, in all certainty, let it die by itself.

3. Certain recent events in our country have occasioned a profound and widespread popular excitement having an intimate relation to this question.[6] Therefore, your Eminence understands better than I how necessary it is for us to have care not only to speak the truth, but also to choose well the time and the circumstances to say it, so that our action may produce salutary and not fatal results. It seems evident, therefore, that even if there is certainly a need for condemnation, now is not the time to speak out.

4. Finally, it would be prudent to apply here the principle of morality which counsels one not to pronounce a sentence the consequences of which will probably be adverse rather than favorable to the good end proposed. Now I am sure that such would result of a condemnation of the works of Mr. George. It would give them a popular importance that they would not ever otherwise have, and would excite an appetite of curiosity that would make them sell by the thousands of copies, and would thus extend immensely the influences that the condemnation sought to restrain and prevent.

Once again, in dealing with so practicable a people as the Americans, in whose genius bizarre and impractical ideas quickly find their grave, it seems to me that prudence suggests that absurdities and fallacies be allowed to perish

---

5. Gibbons was referring to George's unsuccessful effort to be elected mayor of New York City in the fall elections of 1886, when he was defeated by Abram S. Hewitt.

6. Here the cardinal was alluding to the removal of Father Edward McGlynn from the pastorate of St. Stephen's Church, New York, by Archbishop Corrigan on January 14, 1887, and the storm that this action stirred up among McGlynn's many followers. For the role of McGlynn in the single tax movement of Henry George, see John Tracy Ellis, *The Life of James Cardinal Gibbons, Archbishop of Baltimore, 1834–1921* (Milwaukee, 1952), 1:547–94.

by themselves, and not run the risk of giving them an importance, a life and an artificial force by the intervention of the tribunals of the Church.

Archives of the Archdiocese of Baltimore, unclassified; printed copy in French entitled "La question des ecrits de Henri George"; English text also in John Tracy Ellis, ed., *Documents of American Catholic History* (Wilmington, Del.: Michael Glazier, 1987), 2:458–60. (Footnotes in Ellis.) Printed with permission of the estate of John Tracy Ellis.

27. "Mgr. Ireland's Social Views: He Pleads for Material Welfare as a Means, Not an End," 14 October 1894

The interviewer laureate of the Paris press, Jules Huret[1] reports in *Le Figaro*[2] the following conversation with Archbishop Ireland:

Q. — What do you think of the Socialist predictions? Do you believe that transformations in social organizations are imminent?

A. — The transformations predicted by the Socialists seem to me to be neither imminent nor probable. What is probable, what I desire to realize as soon as possible is improvement in the condition of the mass of working men, their elevation from an intellectual and moral point of view, as much as from a material point of view. This improvement and this elevation shall have as consequences the advent of democracy and the disappearance of what is called, in Europe, the reign of the bourgeoisie. This will be accomplished without much resistance. As was said to me by a Belgian statesman, Minister Northamb:[3] "In our days, more than ever, nobody remains immovable. Some turn to reaction, others to democracy."

Observe that true democracy does not exclude, but, on the contrary, presupposes social influences. There shall always be in society men of genius, men of talent, and men of elevated character, and these men will always exert influence. A society where social influences are weak, where natural legitimate influences are replaced by others, is a society in an abnormal state. It was a great mistake of writers in France to write of directing classes. The expression is unfortunate; there are no directing classes, but there are, and there always will be, directing men.

I do not believe that there will be an extreme condensation of capital in the future. I think, on the contrary, that money shall be more generally distributed, that the workingmen shall be better paid, and, consequently, shall have more instruction. Notice what Leo XIII[4] says of diffusion of property, while talking of capital. Doubtless there shall always be great fortunes, but

---

1. Jules Huret (1864–1915) was a famous French journalist who won early notice by his series of articles on controverted questions for *l'Echo de Paris*, and later for a series on European social questions for *Le Figaro*.

2. *Le Figaro* began in 1825 and went through a number of changes, becoming in 1866 a daily paper which was monarchical in sympathies after the Franco-Prussian War and which continued to be an organ of conservative opinion.

3. An effort to identify Northamb was not successful.

4. Leo XIII's encyclical *Rerum novarum* on the condition of the working classes had been issued on 15 May 1891.

great fortunes are an evil only when they have been acquired by fraud and injustice, and, moreover, they are not incompatible with small fortunes; on the contrary, often small fortunes are formed in the shadow of great ones. No other country possesses as many millionaires as the United States, and no other country possesses as small a number of poor people, whereas, no country possesses a smaller number of millionaires than Russia, and no other country contains more poor people. There shall always be great capitalists, great capitalists shall always have influence, and this influence will be increased naturally by association, but association in its turn will protect small capitalists and workingmen. Between the interests of the two classes, independently of moral and religious influences, there is and will remain the civil power, the mission of which is to enact wise laws which insure liberty, rights, the activity of all, especially of the weakest. In transitory times these laws are not easily made. But this is a fault inherent in human nature.

Q. — You are called here "the Socialist Bishop." Do you accept the adjective? Would your ideas be accepted by the Scholastic schools?

A. — The word "Socialist" has an evil ring, and before applying it to my ideas it should be defined. If by Socialists you understand those who are preoccupied by social necessities and miseries, who desire to improve the state of society, and who ask, in view of this improvement, not only action of individuals and influence of voluntary associations, but also a reasonable intervention of the civil power, yes, I am a Socialist. But if by "Socialist" you understand those who share the theories of Marx, of Benoit Malon,[5] of Greef, and others — theories which consist in denying the rightfulness of private property in land and in instruments of labor — no, I am not a Socialist.

I do not doubt that my ideas would be rejected by the Socialistic sects. Everywhere the Socialist sects are opposed to the Christian social movement. In laboring for the disappearance of the just grievances of the working class, the Christian movement takes from sectarian socialism the reason for its existence.

This is not because the promoters of the Christian social movement preach only charity and resignation. Far from this, they preach, above all, right and justice; natural right of the workingman; complete justice, social as well as individual. It is said that justice is a foundation of societies; it is also the foundation of economic order. Therefore, in the first place, justice; after justice, charity; charity may not be substituted for justice; one completes the other; in places where justice has ceased to command, charity intervenes.

Doubtless our conception of life differs essentially from that of the materialists; our reason and our faith teach us that present life is a preparation for a better life. But we are not led by this to neglect material welfare. Material welfare is not our end; it is our means. Its profession to a reasonable degree is of the highest importance for the moral and religious life of men.

---

5. Benoit Malon (1841–93) was a French socialist who participated in the Paris Commune of 1870–71 and later fled to Geneva where he founded *La Revanche;* Guillaume-Joseph de Greef (1842–1924) was a professor of sociology in the University of Brussels.

Q. — Do you admit as legitimate the actual aspirations of the masses toward absolute social equality? Do you think that the natural inequalities might be reconciled with social equality?

A. — Aspirations of the masses toward social equality — I mean reasonable equality — are perfectly legitimate. Social equality is, after all, only the expression of equality from the point of view of human dignity and of Christian dignity. We must take care, however, that social equality should not be opposed to social hierarchy; parentage, service, and authority engender rights and social duties which are not the same for all; genius, talent, virtue, and riches entail consideration and give a certain moral pre-eminence which shall always be admitted. This observation is sufficient to show that social equality may be reconciled with natural inequality. Natural inequality is that of intelligence, of strength, and of health. This inequality is more or less corrected by society, which protects the weak. Social hierarchy is natural; and indestructible. Something not as natural, and which may be abolished, is the great distance between the two ends of this hierarchy. It is not necessary that some should be so elevated and that others should be so degraded.

Q. — Since you admit that societies may pass through transformations, think you that the trilogy — family, religion, and property — should necessarily escape these transformations?

A. — The action of Providence, which brings everything to its end, does not prevent the natural course of things and does not suppress the liberty of man. Modifications in the form of societies are therefore possible, but family, religion, and property are essential elements of all human society. Family is the principle of human society; religion is its crown; property — considered in itself, independently of variable forms — is a condition of life, of liberty, and of progress.

The form of the family is determined by the nature of man, his physical forces, his intellectual faculties, his sentiments, and his instincts, and this form was sanctioned by Christ. It will not change, but what may be desired, what may be hoped, is more perfect realization of this form, and this realization may not be obtained except by progress in manners, customs, and laws.

The form of religion is also determined in a general manner by nature as regards its object and its principal acts. It was also determined in a special and positive manner by Christ. There shall not therefore be a new form of religion, but one may hope for a more complete intelligence and a more general and more perfect realization of the Christian idea, and consequently a more powerful influence of the Gospel on the life of individuals and of nations. Outside of Christianity there may be new religious forms, as was Mohammedanism, but these forms shall not be progressive. As for Neo-Christianity,[6] it will never be anything but amateurish religion.

Property is essential, but there is nothing absolute in its forms. These de-

---

6. Ireland may have been referring here to the followers of Claude-Henri de Rouvroy, Comte de Saint-Simon (1760–1825), who fostered in his last years a sort of mystical fraternalism.

pend on the social, industrial, political, and moral situation of peoples. The history of property has occupied in France and elsewhere many learned men. Their studies cannot but throw light on questions of social philosophy.

Q. — Among the possible modifications of property, which ones would you regard favorably? What do you think of the Communist theory?

A. — The form of property was not always the same at all epochs, and even to-day it is not absolutely the same in all countries. What modifications are possible, useful, and necessary depends on the conditions under which each people finds itself. Modifications may not be made by legislation. This can only give sanction. They are accomplished slowly, by progress in manners and under the sway of circumstances. An example of such modifications is the introduction and disappearance of feudal property.

The system of property which appears to me to be the most desirable should reunite the following qualities: Stimulate human activity and individual labor by assurance of just retribution; maintain the stability of the family, and favor an equitable distribution of the good things of this world.

The Communist theory takes no account of the nature of things or of the nature of man. It does not seem possible to me that it may be realized, and if it were realized the result would be fatal to civilization. Herbert Spencer[7] recently demonstrated this in the introduction which he wrote for "The Man Versus the State." Community of goods may exist among a certain number of men devoted to celibacy and to the cult of God. It might have existed in the age of gold and in a state of innocence; but it does not answer to the real state of present humanity.

Yet the present movement contains very complex elements, which may not be judged in their entirety from the point of view of morality and of civilization. There are few theories, however false they may be in their entirety, which do not contain elements of truth and of justice. The errors which they contain are often an occasion determining a more complete intelligence of the truth. Thus, it may not be denied that the Communist agitation has provoked a more adequate understanding of certain social principles and a more profound sentiment of social justice.

Q. — What is the state of the social question in America? Where, think you, do the Socialist theories have a better chance to succeed, in Europe or in the United States?

A. — The social question exists in America. Read on this subject Prof. Ely's[8] book, "The Labor Movement in America." In my opinion, the difference between our situation and that of Europe is as follows:

The social movement is expressed in the United States by numerous and powerful workingmen's associations. These associations have for their princi-

---

7. *Man versus the State,* to which Herbert Spencer (1820–1903) wrote an introduction, was first published in 1884 and was reprinted in 1940 by the Caxton Printers, Caldwell, Idaho.

8. Richard T. Ely (1854–1943), at this time professor of political economy at the University of Wisconsin, was a prolific writer on social and economic questions. The latest edition of his volume *The Labor Movement in America* appeared in 1905.

pal object to maintain good wages; they are preoccupied by the morality of their members and by professional education. You know that there are some associations which labor to maintain harmony between bosses and workmen, and to prevent strikes. I think that among the American people there are few Anarchists, few Communists, and that the number of collectivists cannot be large. They come from other countries. European immigration supplies their principal contingent. The details which Mr. Ely gives on these subjects are very interesting. As for Henry George's[9] agrarian movement, it is far from powerful.

Socialist theories have far less chance in America than in Europe. In the first place, the sentiment of personal dignity and responsibility and the spirit of enterprise are much developed in the American people. It likes and appreciates individual liberty and respects the law. These dispositions do not lead to social revolution. Furthermore, there is room in the United States for all kinds of energy. Labor there insures honorable life; then, the greater number of Americans have conquered their situation by personal valor, at the price of efforts, perils, and heroic sacrifices. They are not disposed to share with others what they have gained by so much work. Then there are philosophical, moral, and political causes which elsewhere favor the development of Socialism, and have no force in the United States. I allude to administrative centralization, intervention of the Government in the affairs of citizens, to the military regime, and to authoritative traditions.

New York Times, 14 October 1894; also in John Tracy Ellis, ed., *Documents of American Catholic History* (Wilmington, Del.: Michael Glazier, 1987), 2:489–94. (Footnotes in Ellis.) Printed with permission of the estate of John Tracy Ellis.

Coping with Modernity

Although the rise of large-scale business brought about serious dislocations among many sectors of American society, the implementation of principles of the "organizational revolution" had a pervasive influence on every facet of American life. Rational structures of organization, specialization, and the rise of bureaucracies made it possible for large-scale organizations to function effectively in modern times, and Catholic University's William Kerby assessed the challenge to Catholic life posed by these new forms of association. For Catholics these consolidationist impulses dovetailed to a certain degree with the ever-increasing centralization of the Roman Catholic Church in the early years of the twentieth century. The formation of the National Catholic Welfare Conference was one of the watershed moments of the impulse to organize among Catholics. Ironically, in one of the earliest statements issued

---

9. Henry George (1839–97) was chiefly notable for his theory of the single tax on land.

by the conference, its leadership cautioned Catholics to beware of the rise of bureaucracy.

Another form of caution about the dislocations of modernity came from moral theologian John A. Ryan, whose analysis of the threat of "race suicide" contained arguments and themes that would become prominent in Catholic responses to the birth control movement of the early decades of the century.

28. John A. Ryan, Professor of Moral Theology, St. Paul Seminary, St. Paul, Minnesota, "The Small Family and National Decadence," 1904

The controversy occasioned by President Roosevelt's letter some time ago on "race suicide" has included three distinct questions: Is the decline in the American birth-rate abnormal? If it is, are the causes physical or moral? Is there anything, either in the phenomenon or its causes, to fill us with alarm?

The first of these questions has been pretty generally answered in the affirmative. The diminishing fecundity of our people is not in accordance with what have always been regarded as the normal and healthy conditions of human reproduction. The decline in our birth-rate has, indeed, been partially obscured by our comparatively rapid increase in population — from five and one-half millions in 1800 to seventy-six millions a century later. While these figures seem impressive, the increase is far less than might reasonably have been expected....

Two of the causes to which the diminished size of the American family have frequently been attributed may be disposed of very briefly. The first is the alleged physical deterioration of the parents, due, we are told, to the artificial and nerve-destroying life of our cities. This explanation is not without some foundation, but it is far from being adequate to account for the facts. Certainly the average American is not yet the physical weakling that this theory assumes. The second cause alleged is late marriages, and consequently the shortened period of child-bearing. As a matter of fact, the average American marriage takes place early enough to allow of the birth of seven or eight children. Each of these factors will account for a slight decrease in the number of children born to our native parents, but neither deserves serious consideration in the face of the decrease that has actually taken place. The simple truth — which sometimes is concealed from motives of shame or hypocrisy — is that the American family is small because the parents wish it to be so, and, to quote Dr. John Billings, "know how to obtain their wish." The cause is not physical but moral. As President Roosevelt has well said, "the difficulty is one of character; it lies in the will."

The number of children brought into the world is, then, abnormally small, and the causes thereof are within the control of the parents. The most important and most disputed question remains: Is this so-called race suicide to be deplored? The answer depends entirely on the point of view from which the phenomenon is regarded. An anonymous writer in the *North American*

Review for June, 1903, asserts that the primary purpose of marriage is the happiness of the parents, and that the rearing of children is desirable only in so far as it contributes to this result. This is what he calls a "common-sense" view, and it is really the best that could be expected from one handicapped by his very palpable moral and intellectual limitations. His view has, at any rate, the merit of simplicity. . . .

Judged by the standard of the moralist, the small family is, of course, condemned as an immoral institution. It is immoral because the positive means by which it is effected (and in the overwhelming majority of instances the means are positive) are often criminal — the murder of the unborn offspring — and always perverse, unnatural, and degrading. They are perverse, inasmuch as they defeat the primary end of marriage; unnatural, inasmuch as they are in direct conflict with the definite standard set up by nature; and degrading, inasmuch as they brutalize the most sacred of marital relations. The small family is likewise immoral because it tends inevitably to the degeneracy and extinction of the human race, implying therefore the refusal of the individual to discharge one of his primary duties toward society.

The viewpoint that I wish to consider more fully is neither that of the groveling egoist nor that of the scientific moralist. I desire to examine the question through the eyes of the patriot. Under this aspect it has been discussed by the majority of those who have taken sides with the President. Generally speaking, they have failed to make out a strong case, for the reason that they have confined their attention to a minor phase of the problem. They have insisted too much on the danger of national extinction through a sheer decline in numbers. Of course, it is inevitable that the number of immigrants will some day become so small as to exert but a very slight influence in neutralizing the low birth-rate among native-born parents; but when that day finally comes, the total population of the country will be so large as to render the disappearance of the nation, either through depopulation or foreign aggressions, quite remote. This statement assumes, of course, that the birth-rate will not become lower than it is at present among native Americans, and secondly, that the *quality* of the population will not degenerate. If these assumptions will be granted, it is evident that even after all increase of population has ceased, the country will still have sufficient numbers to secure her a considerably longer term of life.

The fundamental reason of the alarm felt by the intelligent lover of America on account of the small family, is that it spells *enervating self-indulgence.* It means a decline not merely in the number, but in the quality of our people. The small family is the most striking symptom and result of the craving for material happiness, for the goods that minister to the senses. As an institution, it has arisen out of the desire to have more time and money for indulging the emotional and animal appetites. It means that the married regard material enjoyments as the chief end of life, and subordinate thereto such ideals as duty and self-sacrifice. The persistence of the small family serves to diffuse these views among all classes of the population; thus it becomes in turn a cause —

the most powerful cause — contributing to the increase and continuance of the deplorable tendencies to which it owes its origin. The small family is another mighty force, in addition to those already existing, which makes for the spread of groveling views of life and low standards of morality. It will inevitably bring about the progressive, mental, moral and physical deterioration of the individuals who make up the American nation, and consequently prove destructive of the welfare and progress of the nation itself....

Consider, in the first place, the direct influence of the small family and its attendant phenomena upon the parents themselves. The question of health may be passed over with the observation that, according to the unanimous testimony of the most competent physicians, the means by which the limitations of offspring generally is secured, are all physically injurious to those who make use of them. What we are most concerned with is the moral injury. The primary moral effects of the practices in question are a decline in the self-respect of husband and wife, and in their respect for each other. The sacred instincts of parenthood are shocked and outraged by conduct which perverts that portion of the marital relation which was destined to cooperate with the Creator in giving life to human beings, into a mere means of sensual gratification. From being co-workers with God in His highest creative act, they degenerate into mutual instruments of pleasure. This loss of reverence for the most sacred and most intimate relation of the conjugal union, this decline in self-respect and mutual respect, are followed sooner or later by the disappearance of *true* conjugal love, and a decline in the sense of conjugal obligation. Hence a pronounced weakening of the motives for resisting temptations to conjugal infidelity. For if husband and wife deliberately cease to look upon each other as parents of the children with which God may possibly bless them, they deprive themselves of the highest and strongest incentives for refusing to gratify their passions elsewhere. Hand in hand with this result go a lessening respect for the marriage bond itself and an increased impetus to divorce. A perusal of the records of the divorce courts for any considerable period will show that a significantly large proportion of those applying for a dissolution of marriage have either small families or no children at all. The desire for divorce is strengthened both by the decline of respect for the marriage bond, just mentioned, and by the absence of the deterrent influence exercised by children, or small children, or a normal number of children.

The phenomena that we are discussing produce, furthermore, a damaging effect on the entire moral life. For it is a law of nature that faculties and instincts exerting a profound and far-reaching influence on the life of the individual can be perverted and violated only at the cost of a general deterioration of the moral and emotional nature. The moral sense becomes blunted, and the belief in the essential superiority of moral actions and purposes becomes weak and uncertain. Men and women who can accustom themselves to disregard and stifle their most elementary instincts of what is decent, and pure, and becoming, cannot retain in full vigor their conviction of the sacredness of other moral instincts. Under the stress of temptation these, too, will more easily give way to considerations of utility or pleasure. In one word, there is brought about a weakening of the moral fibre, with a lowering of the moral tone. In this connection it is worth while to take particular note of the moral injury done to the wife. "The mother," says Henry Drummond, "represents the last and most elaborately wrought pinnacle in the temple of nature." Some idea of this commanding position, this almost sacred dignity, dawns upon the mind of every normal woman. This idea it was which found such frequent expression in the longing of the Hebrew women of old for offspring, for numerous offspring. When this longing was not realized, they felt incomplete and disgraced. Something of the same feeling still lives in the normal woman. She realizes in some way her dignity and importance as the mother of the race, the being who is most intimately identified with the development, physical and moral, of the newly created life. When, therefore, she deliberately deprives herself of this privilege, or deliberately curtails its exercise, she does a violence to her ideals of worth and sacredness which cannot but have a most baneful effect on her belief in lofty ideals of every kind. She makes herself less than a woman, and deliberately brutalizes all her views of life and conduct. With the woman who foregoes the privilege of motherhood from motives of religion or charity, the case is different. She chooses to exercise a still higher function, and ennobles the choice by an act of self-sacrifice. But the woman who restricts her possibilities of motherhood from motives of self-indulgence, declines to a lower level of moral and emotional life, and renders herself incapable of that large self-sacrifice and inspiring example that society needs and expects from its women....

The direct effect of the small family on parents is, therefore, physical and moral deterioration; and the indirect effect is the increasing pursuit of and belief in low ideals of life and conduct. The effect on children is not less baneful, though possibly not so apparent. Of late we have heard much concerning the desirability of "quality rather than quantity" in the matter of children, and of the superiority of the small family as a means to this end. We might with some show of reason raise the question whether we are justified in instituting a comparison between quality and quantity in respect of beings endowed with human souls, each of which has consequently an intrinsic and, in a sense, an infinite value. We might ask whether a method of evaluation that is sufficiently legitimate in the case of hogs or machinery, may without modification reasonably be applied to human persons. Waiving this consideration, and keeping to the viewpoint of social welfare, we deny that a "better quality" of citizens will emerge from the small family than from a large one. Other things being equal, the children in a small family will, of course, enjoy superior ability, advantages in the matter of food, clothing, housing, amusements, and education. In the majority of instances, however, they will have fewer opportunities of experiencing the conditions that are essential to the formation of character. They will stand in grave danger of being over-indulged and under-disciplined. Parents who have deliberately sacrificed one class of unpleasant duties — the rearing of *many* children — to the desire of self-indulgence, will not infrequently adopt such methods of dealing with their children as will give to themselves a minimum of present inconvenience and present mental distress. Devotees of a life of ease are prone to shrink from inflicting pain *of which they are obliged to be witnesses.* The result of this selfish leniency is that the children are deprived of the salutary correction which is an essential element in character-building. Again, the parental affections that normally and in the designs of nature should be distributed among a large number of children, are concentrated upon two or three. This means an immoderate tenderness, an excess of attentions which enervate the children and convert them into pets. The ideals of life which are apparent in the lives and conversation of the parents — the whole atmosphere of the home, in fact — is detrimental to the formation of habits of self-denial. Because of the small number of brothers and sisters, the children have no sufficient opportunity of cultivating habits of unselfishness, of caring for others, of taking into account the claims of others. They grow up, therefore, self-centered, and with an exaggerated sense of their own importance. We are all sufficiently familiar with the type as it is found in so many small families. The child is nicely dressed, and exhibits certain superficial indications of budding refinement, but is nervous, disobedient, ignorant of the meaning of self-repression, and devoid of that naturalness and artlessness that are proper to childhood. We are satisfied that this is not the child that will possess the patience or the self-denial required for the hard work of intellectual formation, or who will grow into the strong character that is essential to good citizenship. We feel that if this is the best "quality" that the small family can produce, we shall continue to wish that the interests of the society be committed to those of "inferior" quality who have had fewer opportunities of development in externals, but who have stronger, nobler, more altruistic characters.

I have sketched, then, in imperfect outline, the manner in which the small family promotes enervating self-indulgence. As there is undoubtedly a large number of families of one, and two, and three children that exhibit no indications of these baneful tendencies, the picture may seem to be overdrawn. These, however, are of the nature of exceptions to the general rule, or are explained by the fact that the theory of life and conduct fostered by the small family has not yet had time to work out its full results. Large families are still numerous in every section of the country, and many of the parents of small families can recall the saner and loftier views of life and duty that prevailed in the families of which they were children. Both of these facts exert some influence in the small family. As the small-family idea becomes more prevalent these correctives will become less and less effective; hence the full realization of the evil tendencies that we are discussing is merely a question of time.

The effects of this enervating self-indulgence upon the nation is obvious. It means physical and mental deterioration, growing disregard for property rights and the sanctity of human life, and a decline in efficient patriotism. Over-indulgence of the animal appetites and an unwillingness to endure hardship produce weak bodies. The desire to follow the line of least resistance leads men to select that kind of education which will soonest and most effectively transform them into money-getters. The culture of the mind that costs long and arduous toil is waved contemptuously aside by the overwhelming majority. Hence the growing tendency to shorten the college term, in order that college graduates may not be outstripped in the race for money by those who have had an earlier start. The excessive estimate put upon material goods tends to blur the distinction between "mine" and "thine," and to introduce gradually the principle underlying

> "The simple rule, the good old plan,
> That he shall take who has the might,
> And he shall keep who can."

And evil is none the less grave because "might" no longer means physical prowess, but represents contempt for law, double-dealing, extortion, and the exercise of superior cunning. The widespread practice of abortion tends to weaken very materially the belief in the sacredness of human life. If it be lawful to kill the child unborn for no other reason than that its birth would involve a certain amount of inconvenience to the parents, why may not the fully developed human being be likewise eliminated, if his presence interferes with the plans of his fellows for "wider and fuller life"? Finally, the cult of selfishness fostered by the small family will result in a decline of effective patriotism. For if individuals are to become less and less capable of self-sacrifice, and less responsive to ideals that do not appeal to the senses, how can they reasonably be expected to subordinate the pursuit of happiness to the interests of the commonweal? They will find it easier to hand over the task of withstanding foreign foes to those who can be got for hire, and to leave the management of internal affairs to those who look upon public office as an opportunity for gain....

A recent defender of the small family maintains that, although the Anglo-Saxon must ultimately cease to be the dominating political factor in America, he can continue to hold his intellectual preeminence. The hope is vain. The small family has made the Anglo-Saxon too small a proportion of the population to retain first place in any sphere of effort. Everywhere in the struggle for existence and supremacy numbers seem to be necessary in order that the field for selection may be sufficiently large, and the resulting survivors sufficiently numerous. In this connection it is of interest to note that Bishop Potter [of the Episcopal Church] recently refused to say whether their large families would give Catholics an advantage over Protestants. His hesitancy is quite natural; for all the signs point to a time not remotely distant when — if Catholics remain true to their consciences and their traditions — mere preponderating numbers will enable them to dominate American life. Moreover, it must be kept in mind that, as Huxley pointed out in the "Romanes lecture," in the *human* struggle it is the *morally* fittest that survive finally. Those foreigners who are gradually supplanting the native stock in so many fields of activity, will continue the process as long as they continue to be the fittest in the moral sense of fitness. Those sections of the population that place self-indulgence before duty will grow more and more insignificant, and finally disappear. The only disquieting question is: will they disappear before their pestilent example shall have corrupted the whole population, and made it physically, mentally and morally decadent?

Ecclesiastical Review 30 (February 1904): 140–55. Printed with permission.

29. Rev. William Kerby, "Reinforcement of the Bonds of Faith," January 1907

A recent issue of a Catholic magazine contains a reference to "the undeniable leakage among educated Catholics."... A late Catholic paper complains that "the touchstone of Catholicity is applied, and they (Catholics) are found wanting." A prominent priest, in a sermon a short time ago, complained that men, in very large numbers, systematically neglect Sunday Mass. One hears frequently the statement that many Catholics seem not to have a Catholic point of view.

Are these conditions symptoms of a process of disintegration from which Catholicity may be suffering? Do Catholics find themselves in the midst of a conflict between necessary and unavoidable facts of life and actual demands of Church loyalty? If they do, there is some danger of attempt on their part to frame a practice of religion which will enable them to meet social conditions without seeming to surrender conscience. The spiritual vigor and loyalty of the individual Catholic must be protected....

One can scarcely doubt that a problem exists. It may be timely to discuss the natural social reinforcements of the bond of faith, as in them is to be found protection against some of the conditions which we face.

Social groups represent particular interests and sympathies in life. Individuals are always unequal to their own wants and possibilities. Hence, they are continually forming associations or entering them to seek what nature or interests or sympathy craves, but cannot unaided give. Groups thus become larger selves; group consciousness fills the members' minds, group point of view controls their sympathies, and feelings of loyalty, devotion, and enthusiasm are developed. Social groups which represent vital human interests gradually gain an ascendency in the individual's life, until principles, character, and ambitions are largely under their control....

The laboring class without unions, symbols, conventions, leaders, opposition, could never hope to express or defend its philosophy. Socialism depends more on propaganda literature, catch phrases, and symbols than on argument. Federal and State elections, with all of their delirium, waste, confusion, and debate, are worth many times what they cost, because they make real, concrete, personal, the fact of government and the citizens' share in it. The cult of the flag is shrewd, for that symbol touches deep national feeling and fosters the sense of group unity, power, and interest....

State, Church, Labor Union, Party represent but partial views of human interests, fragmentary efforts to care for man. Each in its own sphere aims to form, direct, and win its members. If men belonged exclusively to one or another of these groups, the process of upbuilding group supremacy and point of view would be simple. If the groups, to which men in the course of life belong, were in harmony with one another, co-ordinated and subordinated in perfect form, the process would be simple. But, in fact, these great vital groups are now indifferent, again antagonistic to one another; sometime in principle, again in emphasis, or administration, or method. As a result, men find many claims on mind, on sympathy, on loyalty which are mutually exclusive, with the result that every kind of compromise is attempted. The Catholic lives, we will say, in a business atmosphere in which the soul cannot thrive; on Sunday he hears teaching from the pulpit in which his quest of wealth is condemned; he spends his evenings reading literature which represents every point of view or none at all. He belongs to clubs which have still other atmospheres. The result is seen in a general endeavor to mark off sections of interest and attention, leaving each group supreme on its day or in its field, and charged not to interfere beyond. Thus a Catholic is supposed to be not a Catholic, but a citizen, when he votes; a labor unionist is not a Catholic, he is merely a unionist when he strikes....

Although in this country the several groups that represent our chief interests profess to let one another alone, in the nature of the case they cannot succeed. Business is tolerant of only such form of religion as allows its own point of view to remain supreme; the labor union would antagonize any form of religion which denied one of its fundamental principles; the State constitutes itself sole judge of the limits of its own jurisdiction, and while tolerant of religions and willing to protect them, imposes its views in some matters, regardless of what a given church would say. Individuals who share intensely the spirit of any of these groups, tend necessarily to modify allegiance to the others whenever conflict arises among them....

In view, then, of the need of loyalty to the spirit and point of view of a social group; in view of the complex social relations that affect the growth of a group and the conflict in points of view to which we are every day subjected, it is of interest to look into the situation by which the Catholic group as a group is confronted.

Usually a group spirit is greatly fostered by mass meetings of great numbers who reinforce one another. Gatherings impress individuals deeply with a sense of the reality, vitality, and power of the group, and instill the group consciousness into individual minds: extended social contact among members; active participation in group government; knowledge of group history and pride in it; a distinctive group literature actively read, are powerful factors in sustaining a social group, yet, on the whole, they play a lesser *role* in the development of the Catholic group spirit in the United States than one would suppose.

The individual Catholic has few opportunities to come into direct contact with great numbers of his fellow-believers, brought together under some common inspiration. Occasions are rare when one may stand in the presence of thousands, or among them, all feeling, thinking, acting under one great conviction or purpose. The presence and influence of leaders, the fusing of wills and awakening of enthusiasm, the strengthening of the sense of the group's reality, the contagion of loyalty, even when questions of policy or view may on the surface divide the group, all of these reach deeply into imagination and feeling, strengthen conviction, renew spirit, and clarify point of view to a marked degree. The local parish or diocese is, of course, actual, but these themselves do not have many occasions for energetic mass action. When they do, the result is seen. There is symbolism of power in numbers brought together for action, but the routine of parish life, the rare occasions when the Catholics of a city or a diocese come together, permit us to lose this important inspiration in our efforts to upbuild a group point of view. The regular meeting of Catholics for Sunday worship has, of course, its social value, but reference is now made to meetings where the numbers are active, aggressive, and at work on an interest felt as a social reality.

This loss is sometimes overcome by antagonism from without. Attack on the Church, misunderstanding which provokes explanation, self-assertion, and advertence to group interests, have very great value in developing group spirit and loyalty. Every social process, positive or negative, which provokes the assertion of the group point of view, and calls for defence of its interest, contributes to its vigor and establishes its spirit among members.

The social value of anniversaries, jubilees, commemorations; the importance of striking events in the group's life and growth become at once apparent. Many were heard to remark on the occasion of the centenary of the Baltimore Cathedral that never before had they so felt the grandeur, power, and reality of the Church. Our occasional Congresses, such as those of Baltimore and Chicago, have value in the same way, but the rarity of such events reminds us of what we lose in group inspiration by not having them more frequently. The meaning of these features of Catholic activity in Europe can scarcely be overestimated.

Association with fellow-members is another important factor in fostering group spirit and protecting the integrity of its point of view. Americans very generally associate independently of religious views. Business, locality, like taste or culture, similar pursuits or ambitions, are usually final in fixing our associations. Conditions in America make this largely a practical necessity. There is consequently a tendency to indifference concerning a man's religion. Men may do business with one another for years, and never know one another's religion. The interests and sympathies which men have in common monopolize conversation, attention, while religion and its particular interests silently recede from our social intercourse. Hence our own religion tends to become a matter of more personal concern; it fails to be in any particular way a social concern, and we are thus deprived of another aid usually of avail in building up a group spirit. Much in the way of understanding, increase in knowledge, strengthening of attachment to group institutions results when our religion becomes a real human interest to us, when it forms the basis of discussion, of reading, and is intermingled with the real concerns of daily life....

Active share in the government of a group is another powerful stimulant of group consciousness and spirit. In the Church, however, the great mass of members have no voice in government, no intervention in Church policy, and no control of her authoritative institutions. As the constitution of Church authority has developed, this is, of course, to be expected, nor is there any specific reason why it should be otherwise. However, among social groups, this share in government by members is of great importance. It is a right jealously guarded, if not always nobly or zealously exercised. Democracy consists largely in this; the vigor of a nation's spirit depends on it. Campaign, election, discussion, party, vote, convention, meeting, all such activities which result from the individual's share in government, foster, in a marked way, political consciousness. It is no shortsighted policy in a great school like Harvard that it permits its graduates to vote for overseers. This share by former students in government plays its part in fostering the spirit of loyalty among them when a hundred other actual interests claim their attention.

Of course the Church is unlike any other group, since the teaching, governing, and sanctifying powers derive from a divine source and are independent of members. However, lay participation in Church affairs, though at present uncalled-for in this country except in a minor degree, was not unknown in the past. Attention is directed to the point merely because the age is democratic and practically all great social groups depend on this share in government to foster interest and loyalty among their members....

We find, too, as a last social factor to be referred to, that in the Catholic family, very often, insufficient attention is paid to the home as the most important channel for the awakening of Catholic inspiration and transmitting of Catholic ideals and traditions. On the whole, it appears that the integrity of the family spirit is suffering. Industrial, social forces are reducing its power. Strong bonds that should hold family consciousness intact are relaxing, and the home is too often merely a place where blood relations stay when not at business or in society or visiting. The family spirit, sacred, powerful, chastening, with every dearest memory of home united with manifestations of faith and love of Church, should be a powerful factor in awakening attachment to faith and fostering its spirit. Everything seems to indicate, however, that the spiritual, religious, and moral power of homes is decreasing; that outside social influences, business, worldliness, companions, social pursuits and tastes other than domestic are disintegrating them. Catholicity loses one of its mainstays, in as far as this is true of Catholic homes.

Turning from these social facts, which bear directly on the development of the group spirit among Catholics, we find that in the social atmosphere in which we live there are elements which may affect our point of view and lead us to misunderstand the essential truths for which the Church stands. The lack of social confirmation of our group existence, lack of occasions when the vitality and power of the Church are impressed on us socially, poor development of our sense of solidarity as Catholics, leave us exposed to such elements in the social atmosphere about us, as tend to harm our belief in the doctrine of the Church as a divinely constituted social body.

We are surrounded by the belief and assertion that religion is a private matter between individual and Creator. The Church, or any church, as a divinely constituted society is not recognized. Insistence on the political dignity and self-assertion of the individual is close akin to similar insistence on religious independence. We see and know and speak daily with hundreds who, believing in some way in Christ, believe in no divinely organized Church. Lacking frequent large social expressions of our own group consciousness, tending under pressure of all manner of worldly interests to confine our own religious sympathy, interest, and practice to the details of personal, individual sanctification, we miss the thousand beautiful expressions of the communion of saints in worship, liturgy, and devotion; we live without much contact with whole group consciousness, and we are thus prepared to hear without much protest and meet without recoil, the general sentiment that religion is individual, that there is no organic Church, no corporate teaching agency instituted by Christ. As a doctrinal proposition, the Catholic will not accept such a view, but in the loss of sympathy with the works of the Church; in indifference to her policies, and an apathy toward many of her appeals, we show at times that some influence has reduced the zeal and dampened the ardor with which a Catholic fully alive to his group spirit, and animated by its point of view, would second the interests of his Church. This view of the nature and function of the Church is central and vital in our whole system, while we live in an atmosphere which not only does not strengthen, but, on the contrary, tends to weaken belief in it.

Closely related to that view, which is widespread in our age, is another to the effect that religion is, after all, mainly ethical and not dogmatic. It is believed that men can unite on standards of conduct, can work to purify morals, and that this can be done quite apart from our forms of belief.... There is then a marked drift to develop a general ethical consciousness, a definite standard of morals and civic and social virtue, independently of men's form of belief. As a result, less and less emphasis is laid on doctrine, while more and more is laid on conduct. Surrounded as we are by that atmosphere, while we can never overrate the value, sacredness, and power of noble conduct and exalted character, we may underrate the importance of truth as truth, of doctrine as doctrine.

Thus the Catholic receives no reinforcement for his distinctive beliefs from the larger social atmosphere in which he must live. In his mind, the Church is divinely commissioned, and his relation to God involves definite beliefs, definite forms of worship, definite obedience to Church law, as well as purity of mind, elevation of character, and social service; from the larger world about him through example, conversation, newspaper, literature, lecture, magazine, comes the teaching that no Church is divinely commissioned any more than all are; service of God is mainly service of man; it makes no difference what one believes if one but act rightly. These features of our social atmosphere are lamentable from our standpoint, yet it is more profitable to seek means of defence than to complain. In no country possibly has the Church fewer legal obstacles, nowhere else will she find a more respectful hearing; nowhere else are the faithful as a body more loyal, more self-sacrificing, quicker to respond to a moral or spiritual appeal; more outspoken in defence of faith and Church. The integrity of the allegiance of American Catholics to their faith; their docility, faithfulness in worship, in devotion to the Holy See, is, to the highest degree, remarkable. And this in spite of the difficulties under which they live and the limitations to which they are subject.

But the new social forces at work on the younger generation, the wholly changed character of life and action, the dissolution of spirit and influence of small groups and local life, raise new questions day by day. In earlier days, religious bodies were more markedly individualized; group consciousness was more pronounced, the influence of group aim and spirit on the individual was greater, the religious element in life was stronger. Possibly, in those days, group consciousness was stronger in the Church, and menaces to integrity of faith were fewer. It is scarcely to be expected that the younger generations, now born into new times and influenced by other and powerful spirits, will preserve faith undimmed, loyalty undoubting, and devotion unfaltering, unless these social influences can be recognized and met.

We clothe ourselves to suit our climates. Shall not the Church clothe her children to be protected in the new atmosphere in which they are to live? The tremendous efforts made to develop a whole educational system are a thousand times justified by the conditions that confront us. If social conditions prevent natural processes from strengthening our group spirit as already described; if the atmosphere in which we live contain elements that not only do not reinforce, but even threaten our own fundamental beliefs, if the necessities of daily life and culture bring us necessarily into close relation with other points of view, and give us interests in common with those who differ fundamentally in this supreme aspect of life, it would seem that we ought to exhaust every effort to draw from all sources of group strength in forming the young....

Our school system, noble by countless sacrifices, honorable in unquestioned achievement, splendid in opportunity, and abundant in promise is one great means to work toward that development; societies, organizations for spiritual and philanthropic purposes, an active press, a growing literature, are mighty agents. The country gives the Church a fair field.... Faith, in the individual is a divine gift, obeying a special providence of God; the Church is a divine institution; but natural mental and social processes affect the Catholic in natural ways. Through association, in harmony, understanding, and co-operation, with fellow-believers, he strengthens the social reinforcements of his faith, increases concretely the authority of the Church, by stimulating his sense of loyalty, by becoming conscious of the vitality, power, and devotion in the mass of believers of which he is part; and he shapes his sympathies, emotions, habits, associations, more and more around his faith to support and corroborate it.... In this day of complex socializing, when more and more our thinking is the thinking that surrounds us, our feeling is the feeling with which we are in daily contact, our aims are largely the aims which social admirations and current valuations set up, the group consciousness of the Church should be active. The Church is the Congregation of all the faithful, not merely the teaching authority. We should then be in touch normally with that body; one in sympathy with it, reinforced by association, and stimulated by it....

Catholic World 84 (January 1907): 508–22. Printed with permission.

30. Rev. John J. Burke, C.S.P., General Secretary, National Catholic Welfare Council, Washington, D.C., "The National Catholic Welfare Council," 1920

... The Catholic Church in her great visible unity is known through all the centuries and through all the world; unity with the Holy Father Himself, as the Vicar of Christ, at the head; unity with all the bishops throughout the world governing the dioceses; unity with all the priests serving in unity of faith; unity of all the faithful, showing in their conduct, showing in their principles, the truth and the life and the purity of Christ throughout the world. And part and parcel of that unity must be the external operation, the active work of the Catholic Church in the world, for only when it is put into the word and into the act is that unity seen and testified to by other men.

Take the great Catholic Church of the United States, with its dioceses numbering over one hundred, with its people numbering about 20,000,000, with something like 10,000 women's organizations, something like 7,000 men's organizations — you all know yourselves what unity means in an organization, small as it may be. No matter what organization you may select, in that organization there must be unity of action, and in proportion as it has that unity, so will be measured its Catholic effectiveness....

When the war broke out it was seen by the bishops of the United States that unless there were harmony and organization and a national voice and representation of the Catholic cause, the Catholic cause would fail, and it is because the bishops of the United States organized the National Catholic War Council that Catholic rights were maintained and that Catholic history has been written indelibly into the history of America.

What is the National Catholic Welfare Council? It is an endeavor, without interfering with any individual [Catholic] organization, without trying to get over the boundary line of any diocese or any parish as they are, with all their power and strength, to get all of those organizations and all of the

Catholic energy to serve a common cause; to give their help whenever it may be needed to the Catholic cause throughout the country, and by their coordination and their cooperation to be such a deliberate and advisory body of all organizations that they will all be helped and be able to give the society in Missouri the benefits of the experience of a Catholic organization in New York....

The bishops looked all over the field, and the bishops organized five great departments, and... one of these is the Department of Education, that concerns itself with all matters of Catholic education, one of the greatest, most vital questions of the day, one of the questions being considered here at Washington every day, whether Congress is in session or not, where active organizations of anti-Catholics are preparing legislation that will mean the endangering, perhaps the wiping out of Catholic education.... Should we not be alive to marshall every power that we possess, that we may be able to defend ourselves, to defend Catholic rights, and to inject as far as we can into the public life of our country Catholic truth and Catholic principles?

Another department is the Department of Legislation, which will keep an account of all matters presented, not only to the National Legislature, but also, through different Catholic organizations in every state, will keep an account of every piece of legislation on religious, educational, social and moral questions that are presented to the states, so that any Catholic organization wishing to have knowledge about the standing of any matter in a legislative way may find from the legislative department, free of cost, whatever it wishes to learn.

Another department is the Department of Social Action which, as you all know far better than I do, is the most immediately important and vital question for the religious and moral welfare of ourselves, and particularly of our children....

There is the Press and Publicity Department. You know that the Catholic press of the United States is in need of help and guidance. Catholics are not interested in the Catholic press. Catholics are not today intelligently interested in matters of their faith and of their conduct, and yet Pope after Pope has said that it is in vain we build churches, in vain we build schools, that unless we have a Catholic press our work indeed will be very much in vain. The Catholic body of America today has no organ of publicity. Publish your items of news in all of your Catholic press daily and weekly and monthly, and you do not reach one-twentieth of the Catholic people. The facts are astounding, the facts are bewildering. You meet Catholics who talk, for example, or are asked to talk on the federalization of education. They do not know the first condition of things. Ask them about the present situation of sex hygiene education and the attempts to get it into our schools. These matters have been rehearsed time and again in the Catholic press, and the Catholic people of the United States know nothing about them. The Catholic people of the United States are not today intellectually fit to carry the burden that will come upon them. It is a sad condition of affairs, and yet it is absolutely true. When I speak I do not speak only as the General Secretary of the Welfare Council, but I speak as one who for years since its foundation has been one of the directors of the Catholic Press Association, and the Welfare Council has done perhaps its most effective, its most extensive work in trying to build up the Catholic press of the country. It issues every week a news sheet that you see copied in the Catholic journals of the country. We have not only a great executive staff here in Washington, but we have correspondents in Dublin, London, Paris, Berlin, and Rome, and we are extending them as our means permit.

There is the Department of Lay Organizations, consisting of men's organizations, and of women's organizations, and each of them has its council, the National Council of Catholic Laymen and the National Council of Catholic Women, and here let me say again that the purpose of that department, as the purpose of the Welfare Council, is not to interfere with any present existing organization. Coordination does not mean death, and if anybody in this Conference,[1] as some have, I know, repeats the story that the Welfare Council is to form a new organization and wipe the others out of existence, such a one tells what is positively and absolutely untrue. The Welfare Council leaves every organization with its own independent existence, with its own autonomous freedom. [No existing organization is] asked to sacrifice any right or any field of activities or any privilege that it may possess when it is asked to join the National Welfare Council. It is asked to join with all its strength, with all its power, that it, in its own power, may contribute as much as it can to Catholic unity, to Catholic activity, and to Catholic success.

Besides all this, there is the General National Committee[2] of the Welfare Council. You must understand that all of the departments are perfectly free to have their own headquarters wherever they will, but there is a General National Committee upon which sits a representative of each one of these departments, and the headquarters of that committee is in Washington. The General Secretary of that committee is myself, and upon the Executive Department devolves the coordination, the general distribution and the direction and policy of the work, and not only that, but every day practically there are questions of supreme importance to take up at the government departments, to which we must give strict attention and watchfulness. We must have representatives to go to the government departments, we must have representatives to go to national conferences, and I think the work, from what I have said to you, must at least in a small measure be quite plain. I think also from what I have said that it will be evident to you likewise that were it not for the National Catholic Welfare Council, applied to the Catholic Church as a public, living instrument in the life of America, the Church would be in a poor and pitiable way.

There is no work that does not start nationally. Here at Washington you

---

1. The National Conference of Catholic Charities, whose volunteer members were beginning to perceive the new Welfare Council as a rival.
2. That is, the executive committee.

have the beginnings of all of those movements that affect legislation, whether for ill or for good. Catholic[s] are not in politics, yet Catholic[s] have Christian principles, Catholic principles, that they will see as far as possible are imbedded in the life of America. They also will take their part, as citizens, full of courage, full of knowledge, splendid in the strength and power that the Catholic faith of the ages gives to them.

The National Council alone can prepare for the work of today, and as you look back upon it, the power of that organization will reflect upon every member of it. Your local organization today is vastly increased in power in the community, in its name, in its influence, if it can state that it is a member of the national organization, if it has affiliation with a national organization recognized by the United States Government. The moral power of it all...does it not make you thrill, does it not make you feel that we are all members of the Church of Christ, that we are all members of His mystical body, of His living love, of His living grace?

Such, in brief, is the inspiration, I think, of the National Catholic Welfare Council; such is its purpose; such its aim. And I say to you that the National Catholic Welfare Council is something that demands the soul of every Catholic in this country. You cannot work in the work of faith unless you have the spirit of love, unless you have that personal spirit of the realization of this participation in the life of God and Christ.

Proceedings of the Sixth Biennial Meeting of the National Conference of Catholic Charities (Washington, D.C.: National Conference of Catholic Charities, 1920), 65–70. Printed with permission.

31. Administrative Committee of the National Catholic Welfare Council, Statement on Federalization and Bureaucracy, 26 January 1922

1. The growth of bureaucracy in the United States is one of the most significant aftereffects of the war. This growth must be resolutely checked. Federal assistance and federal direction are in some cases beneficial and even necessary; but extreme bureaucracy is foreign to everything American. It is unconstitutional and undemocratic. It means officialism, red tape, and prodigal waste of public money. It spells hordes of so-called experts and self-perpetuating cliques of politicians to regulate every detail of daily life. It would eventually sovietize our form of government.

2. The forward-looking forces in our national life must resolutely stand against further encroachments on individual and state liberty. The press, the home, the school, and the Church have no greater enemy at the present time than the paternalistic and bureaucratic government which certain self-seeking elements are attempting to foist upon us.

Hugh J. Nolan, ed., *Pastoral Letters of the United States Catholic Bishops* (Washington, D.C.: United States Catholic Conference, 1984), 1:334. Printed with permission.

Poverty and Reform

Intellectuals and politicians of the progressive era began to address the issue of the role of the government in the social problems generated by the era of industrial growth. As discussions covered the spectrum from laissez-faire to socialism and everything in-between, Catholic thinkers began to offer their own prescriptions for social legislation and social practice based on the natural law principles of a revived Thomism. Claims about the family and the role of women anchored their arguments.

32. Rev. William Kerby, "The Poor," November 1912

We are told by social philosophers that confidence in the social order is back of all stable government, and that we are compensated for the discipline of law by the security given to our rights, the opportunity offered for our progress, and the definiteness furnished to the conditions of our civilization. It is the business of government to protect us in life, liberty, property, and to promote the conditions of our happiness. We clothe the state with the majesty of supreme human authority, with the awful sovereignty of human society, because in return it clears the path for us and surrounds us by inspiration, opportunity, and social order. And hence patriotism is a stimulus to noble action and exalted aim. Love of country and its institutions has been placed by our philosophers among the virtues sanctioned in heaven. But the poor are robbed of this inspiration, cheated of this motive, and, hence, are cynically uninterested in all that patriotism means. Not that they are political agitators. The soil where charity is found offers no hope for the seeds of revolution.

Much of the state's activity is taken up with protection of a property system which has hindered the poor from all ownership. They really, from their standpoint, lack all motive to respect it. Much of the state's activity is given over to the punishment of wrong doing, in which, unfortunately, many among the poor have experience. "The law," as the poor know and see and feel it, is the law which punishes, not the law which protects. They need protection in health against unsanitary occupations; in life against unnecessary risks in industry; against fraud of merchants and extortion of loan sharks; against their own ignorance fastened on their reluctant souls during their darkened childhood; against the breaking up of the home by labor of mothers and children; against greed of landlords and indifference of employers. They have need of protection in their right to labor and a living wage; to decent comfort and reasonable security against want. They need protection for the virtue of their daughters and the health of their babies, but they seem not to have it. These are the great overwhelming menaces which terrify them. However, the majestic state of which they are a part seems not to know it, or knowing, not to care, or caring, not to be able to give the protection which is required. Technicalities of legal procedure, sanctity of worn-out phrases like "freedom of contract," "class legislation," constitutionality of laws in defense of elementary justice, are questions of no direct concern to the poor, when involuntary idleness, preventable disease, and needless deaths are prostrating them.

Not even the hopeful beginnings of protection which we now see seem to revive zest of life, or to call back hope as the bright star in the firmament which covers them. German economists apply the term "conjunctur" to the sum of institutions, laws, customs, arrangements, and standards which surround us, and make each man's economic activity stable, fruitful, and orderly. The poor know only a "conjunctur" of neglect, oversight, uncertainty, defenselessness which make it improbable, if not impossible, that they rise. Even the rudimentary relief which government has attempted to provide for the poor in hospitals, almshouses, asylums, reformatories, has rarely won their confidence or awakened any sense of dignity in them or of gratitude. Unfortunate administration of such institutions has made them a source of horror to the gentle types among the poor, and they have often preferred starvation. Dickens wrote for other lands and times in telling us of England's care of her poor in such institutions.

Of course every political constitution fails at some point. Government is compelled to deal with the entire range of human temperament, skill, character, and sense. The fool, the idler, the criminal, the mentally and physically defective, the scholar, the social and the anti-social, those whom liberty blesses and those whom it curses, are found under every government, and they must be dealt with. The conflicting needs of these classes must be served, though it seem impossible. Institutions which favor the strong may harm the weak. Those which protect the ignorant may hamper the cultured. Those which encourage genius may crush the dull and listless. Now the institutions upon which our civilization rests have favored the strong and harmed the weak. Our modern state has failed to develop a supplementary constitution to take care of its failures, among whom we count the poor. The endeavor of the historical Church to develop a supplementary moral constitution to protect the weaker classes, to define their rights and sanctions, and to teach the strong classes natural and supernatural duties which are above and beyond constitutions, gives to the Church a role of infinite nobility in the history of the world.

The action of the state is guided not so much by principles as by definition. States have no ordinary power beyond what is defined and implied. They exist to protect our rights to life, liberty, property, and happiness. But government protects these rights only as it defines them, and not beyond. Much of the supreme effort now made to bring justice to the weaker classes, centres in the attempt to expand definitions of human rights in a way to protect these classes against the distinctive menaces to their rights. The state has fallen lamentably short in its mission because of the narrow definitions under which it operates. Morality is after all as much a question of definition as of principle. No man is cowardly if he may define cowardice. No man is dishonest if he may define honesty. No employer is unjust if he may define justice. No man is cruel if he may define cruelty. High morality depends on noble definitions.

Social justice depends on such definitions of rights and of justice as secure a broad, humane, sufficient protection to men and women and children in the peculiar conditions in which their rights to life, liberty, opportunity, property are threatened.

The state does not, will not, possibly can not, change its legal definitions of rights of man as rapidly as complex modern social conditions change the menaces to those rights. What can the poor think of the opinion of Justice Brewer, who claimed that it is a lesson which cannot be learned too soon or too thoroughly, that under this government of and by the people the means of redress of all wrongs are through the courts and ballot box. What can such words mean to the poor?

There are however grounds for hope. Determined forces are at work which promise relief. Great ideals of humanity and justice are operating throughout our civilization. Society is at work preventing industrial menaces to life and health where preventable, and forcing property interests to automatic compensation to sufferers for risks that must be faced. Knowledge of the horrible facts of massive poverty is forced daily into our higher and stronger social classes, and of itself is bringing about hopeful changes. Sciences are pointing out wiser ways and surer aims in voluntary work for prevention and relief. Lawmakers are more kindly disposed toward claims of weaker classes, which their predecessors once dismissed with impatient gesture. Charity itself, both as humane service and as the organic expression of organized supernatural faith, finds its resources multiplied, its hand strengthened, its field more clearly defined, and its efforts more heartily seconded.

The task before all of these agencies is gigantic. In some way which our collective wisdom must work out, the poor must be brought to believe in themselves, and in the benevolent mission of civilization toward them. They must be brought, through the way of definite opportunity, to the prospect of owning property necessary to decent comfort, and of securing it not at the price of health, home, education or youth, but in a way which will favor, not threaten, these blessings. Hunger, nakedness, hovels, hopelessness must be made speculative to the industrious and [*sic*] worthy among them as such things are to us. They must be touched, refined, strengthened by culture, and they must be brought by happy experience to believe in those ideals on which civilization rests, and to respond to those appeals which strengthen hand and heart for the work of life.

Although many have departed from the way that Christ points out to accomplish this, we must hope that the benevolent Providence of God may yet bring the world to this ideal of justice and peace through the accepted guidance of Him Who is the Way, the Truth and the Life. The imagination of the world is beginning to take hold of poverty as a world problem. The thousand activities now witnessed, such as insurance, pensions, legal intervention in industrial relations, improved methods in charitable institutions, scientific research into processes and tendencies of poverty, minimum wage agitation and compensation acts, pensioning of widows, and placing of orphans are organically related in a blundering and fragmentary and unsympathetic endeavor of humanity to obey its ideals. Eugenics, Criminology, Surgery, Sciences — notably Biology — Single Tax, Socialism, and related sections of human thought and action aim in varying ways at the conquest of poverty, the elimination of inferior types, the strengthening of the race, the improvement of institutions, and the establishment of justice. In all cases, these agencies ask of us faith, trust, and cooperation. There is more to be hoped for if we go back to Christ, His Law, His Ideal, and to His Philosophy to get our bearing on the problem of poverty. If we but recognize the social sin that causes it, the massive sin that grows out of it, the change of life and purification of heart that the strong classes must experience before we may hope for much, we will gradually recover the view in which alone God and grace, repentance and surrender, brotherhood and service, are seen in right relation to institutions, social reform, industrial organization, and laws.

When this view shall have been recovered, we will work in the lines of Christian perspective. We will first work with the zeal of apostles and vision of prophets to purge poverty of its sin, whether in cause or in effect. We will next labor to prevent and anticipate it, and bring to the weaker classes, which Christ loved, the heritage of hope, joy, comfort, and peace to which they have a right. The poverty that can not be headed off will then be purified and freed from all of its nameless terror.... And if there will always be poor among us, their poverty need not be the harvest of sin, the ugly outcome of ignorant selfishness, the hideous price of civilization. Freed from these horrible implications, it may yet be seen in the light of Christian Brotherhood, and once we see the poor as our brothers, we and they will forget that there are any poor among us.

Catholic World 96 (November 1912): 220–24. Printed with permission.

33. Rev. John A. Ryan, *A Living Wage: Its Ethical and Economic Aspects,* 1912

III. The Basis and Justification of Rights

... The thesis to be maintained in this volume is that the laborer's claim to a Living Wage is of the nature of a *right*. This right is personal, not merely social: that is to say, it belongs to the individual as individual, and not as member of society; it is the laborer's personal prerogative, not his share of social good; and its primary end is the welfare of the laborer, not that of society. Again, it is a natural, not a positive right; for it is born with the individual, derived from his rational nature, not conferred upon him by a positive enactment. In brief, the right to a Living Wage is individual, natural and absolute....

Man's natural rights are absolute, not in the sense that they are subject to no limitations — which would be absurd — but in the sense that their validity is not dependent on the will of anyone except the person in whom they inhere. They are absolute in existence but not in extent. Within reasonable limits their sacredness and binding force can never cease. Outside of these limits, they may in certain contingencies disappear.... The right to life is said to be absolute because no human power may licitly kill an innocent man as a mere means to the realization of any end whatever. The life of the individual person is so sacred that, as long as the right thereto has not been forfeited by the perverse conduct of the subject himself, it may not be subordinated to the welfare of any other individual or any number of individuals. Not even to preserve its own existence may the State directly and deliberately put an unoffending man to death. When, however, the individual is not innocent, when by such actions as murder or attempted murder he has forfeited his right to live, he may, of course, be rightfully executed by civil authority, or killed in self-defense by his fellow man. He may also be compelled to risk his life on behalf of his country, for that is a part of his duty; and he may with entire justice be deprived of life indirectly and incidently, as when non-combatants are unavoidably killed in a city that is besieged in time of war. Again, the right to liberty and property are not absolute in the sense that the individual may have as much of these goods as he pleases and do with them as he pleases, but inasmuch as within reasonable limits — which are always determined by the essential needs of personal development — these rights are sacred and inviolable.

With respect to their natural rights, all men are equal, because all are equal in the rational nature from which such rights are derived. By nature every man is a person, that is, a rational, self-active, independent being. Every man is rational because endowed with the faculties of reason and will. His will impels him to seek the good, the end, of his being, and his reason enables him to find and adjust means to this end....

Only in the abstract, however, are men's natural rights equal. In the concrete they are unequal, just as are the concrete natures from which they spring. This is not to say that equality of rights is an empty abstraction, without any vital meaning or force or consequences in actual life. Men are equal as regards the *number* of their natural rights. The most important of these are the rights to life, to liberty, to property, to a livelihood, to marriage, to religious worship, to intellectual and moral education. These inhere in all men without distinction of person, but they have not necessarily the same *extension*, or content, in all. Indeed, proportional justice requires that individuals endowed with different powers should possess rights that vary in degree. For example, the right to a livelihood and the right to an education will include a greater amount of the means of living and greater opportunities of self-improvement in the cases of those who have greater needs and greater capacities. But in *every* case the natural rights of the individual will embrace a certain minimum of the goods to which these rights refer, which minimum is determined by the reasonable needs of personality. The rights that any person will possess in excess of this minimum will depend upon a variety of circumstances, individual and social....

IV. The Right to Subsistence and the Right to a Decent Livelihood

... According to the argument made in the last chapter, the source of natural rights is the dignity of the human person, while their scope is determined by the person's essential needs. A man's natural rights are as many and as extensive as are the liberties, opportunities and possessions that are required for the reasonable maintenance and development of his personality. They may all be reduced to the right to a reasonable amount of external liberty of action. Some of them, for instance, the right to live and the right to marry, are original and primary, inhering in all persons of whatever condition; others are derived and secondary, occasioned and determined by the particular circumstances of particular persons. To the latter class belongs the right to a Living Wage. It is not an original and universal right; for the receiving of wages supposes that form of industrial organization known as the wage system, which has not always existed and is not essential to human welfare....

The primary natural right from which the right to a Living Wage is deduced, is the right to subsist upon the bounty of the earth. All people have given more or less definite adhesion to the truth that the earth is the common heritage of all the children of men.... Whatever objections may lie in the way of the theory of primitive communism in land, the facts at our disposal seem to indicate that scarcely any community has regarded as thieves those of its own members who seized their neighbor's goods as a last resource against starvation. This is especially true of the nations that have adopted the moral teachings of Christianity. In the early centuries of the Christian era the task of providing for the poor and needy was accepted and recognized by the bishops and secular clergy, the monasteries and other religious institutions, as an obligation of legal justice; in modern times it is most frequently discharged through the legislation known as poor laws. Underlying these various practices and institutions is the Christian conviction that every human being has not only a claim in charity, but a strict right to as much of the wealth of the community as is necessary to maintain his life.... The greatest of the theologians, St. Thomas Aquinas, maintained that the man in extreme need who had no other resource was justified in supplying his necessities from the goods of his neighbor, and that this would not, properly speaking, be theft.[1] Again, he says it is well that property should be *owned* privately, but that the *use* of it should be common, so that all persons may be sustained out of its abundance.[2] In this statement we have undoubtedly an echo and development of the saying of Aristotle that, "it is best to make property private but to have the use of it in common."[3] ...

So much for the right to subsistence, to a bare livelihood. By a *decent* livelihood is meant that amount of the necessities and comforts of life that is in keeping with the dignity of a human being. It has no precise relation to the

---

1. *Summa Theologica*, 2a. 2ae., q. 66, a. 7.
2. Ibid., a. 2.
3. *Politics*, 2.5.

conventional standard of living that may prevail within any social or industrial class, but describes rather that minimum of conditions which the average person of a given age or sex must enjoy in order to live as a human being should live. It means, in short, that smallest amount of subsistence goods which is reasonable, becoming, appropriate to the dignity of a person.... Let us say that if a man is to live a becoming life he must have the means, not merely to secure himself against death by starvation and exposure, but to maintain himself in a reasonable degree of comfort. He is to live as a man, not as an animal. He must have food, clothing and shelter. He must have opportunity to develop within reasonable limits all his faculties, physical, intellectual, moral and spiritual. The rational ground of this right is the same as that of the right to subsistence. It is the dignity and essential needs of the person. Those means and opportunities that have just been described as a decent livelihood are the minimum conditions of right and reasonable living, since without them man cannot attain to that exercise of his faculties and that development of his personality that makes his life worthy of a human being. When he is compelled to live on less than this minimum he is treated as somewhat less than a man. If it be asked, What proof can be given that a person really possess this right to a decent livelihood? the answer must be that proof in the strict sense is impossible. If it is not self-evident, none of man's natural rights are self-evident, and the dignity of personality is a delusion.... The only argument that can be adduced for the right *to live* is that the sacredness of personality is violated when one man uses the life of another as a mere means to his own welfare. Similarly a man's dignity is outraged when he is deprived of the opportunity to live a *reasonable* life, in order that some other man or men may enjoy the superfluities of life. A decent livelihood is just as truly an essential need of man, is just as absolutely demanded by his intrinsic dignity, as subsistence, or security of life and limb....

V. The Right to a Personal Living Wage

...It is the purpose of this chapter to show that the workingman's right to a decent livelihood is, in the present economic and political organization of society, the right to a Living Wage. The term "workingman" is taken to describe the adult male of average physical ability who is dependent exclusively upon the remuneration that he is paid in return for his labor. And "an individual [or 'personal'] Living Wage" means that amount of remuneration that is sufficient to maintain decently the laborer himself, without reference to his family.... It has been shown in the last chapter that, on account of his sacredness as a person, every member of a community has an abstract right to a decent livelihood, and that this right becomes concrete and actual when the material goods controlled by the community are sufficient to provide such a livelihood for all, and when the individual performs a reasonable amount of useful labor. It is assumed that the first condition is verified; and it is maintained that the second is fulfilled by the man who labors for hire during a working day of normal length. His general right to as much of the earth's fruits as will furnish a decent livelihood is clear; the correlative obligation of his fellow members of the community to appropriate and use the common bounty of nature consistently with this right, ought to be equally clear. Now, the simple and sufficient reason why this general right of the laborer takes the special form of a right to a Living Wage, is that in the present industrial organization of society, there is no other way in which the right can be realized. He cannot find a part of his livelihood outside of his wages because there are no unappropriated goods within his reach. To force him to make the attempt would be to compel him to live on less than a reasonable minimum. And the obligation of paying him this amount of wages rests upon the members of the industrial community in which he lives; for they have so appropriated the resources of nature, and so distributed the opportunities and functions of industry, that he can effectively realize his natural right of access to the goods of the earth only through the medium of wages. As long, therefore, as the present organization of industry exists, the obligation of not hindering the laborer from enjoying his right to a decent livelihood will be commuted into the obligation of paying him a Living Wage. . . .

A word will not be out of place concerning the wage-rights of women and children. According to the foregoing reasoning, it is evident that those women who are forced to provide their own sustenance have a right to what is a [personal] Living Wage for them. Since they have no other way of living but by their labor, the compensation therefore should be sufficient to enable them to live decently. Again, women doing the same work with the same degree of efficiency as men in occupations where both sexes are employed, have a right not merely to a woman's Living Wage, but to the same remuneration as their male fellow workers. Distributive justice requires that equally competent workers be rewarded equally. Moreover, when the women receive less pay than the men the latter are gradually driven out of that occupation. Unless we hold that an increase in the proportion of women workers is desirable, we must admit that social welfare would be advanced by the payment of uniform wages to both sexes for equally efficient labor.

Children of either sex who have reached the age at which they can, without detriment to themselves or society, become wage earners, but who cannot perform the work of adults, have a right to a wage sufficient to afford them a decent livelihood. They are entitled to this because their wages, generally speaking, constitute their sole source of maintenance. It must be noted that a Living Wage for children refers to their essential needs as members of a family, not to the requisites of boarding-house life, as this is not the condition in which working children are usually placed. Finally, children of either sex who perform the work of adults ought to receive the wages of adults, for the same reasons that justify the payment of men's wages to equally efficient women.[4]

---

4. In speaking of a Living Wage, whether for men, women, or children, it is assumed that they are employed during the whole of the working time of the year. Consequently, women who are obliged to devote all their attention to household duties for a considerable portion of the year,

VI. The Right to a Family Living Wage

...When Pope Leo XIII, in his encyclical, "On the Condition of Labor [1893]," declared that the remuneration of the workingman ought to be at least sufficient "to support him in reasonable and frugal comfort," a discussion immediately arose among Catholic moralists as to whether the phrase just quoted was intended to cover the conditions and requisites of family life....

Unquestionably the hypothetical wages referred to are assumed to constitute the compensation that is *normal*, but there is no explicit assertion that so much is due the laborer as a matter of *justice*. Within a few months after these words were written, a letter was addressed to the Holy See by the Archbishop of Malines, Cardinal Goosens, asking whether an employer would do wrong who paid his men a wage sufficient for personal maintenance, but inadequate to the needs of a family. Pope Leo did not himself send any official response, but referred the matter to Cardinal Zigliara, who replied that the employer in question would not violate justice, but that his action might sometimes be contrary to charity, or to natural righteousness. At present all Catholic writers on the subject hold that the employer is under moral obligation to give the workingman a wage that will maintain his family as well as himself, but they do not agree that this obligation falls under the head of justice. In other words, some of them deny that the laborer has a strict right to a family Living Wage.... The argument from the personal dignity of the laborer, however, is sound, — is, in fact, the only one that rests securely on the fundamental principles of natural justice.

For the laborer who complies in a reasonable degree with nature's universal law of work, has a natural right to at least the minimum of the material conditions of decent and reasonable living.... Now a decent and reasonable life implies the power to exercise one's primary faculties, supply one's essential needs, and develop one's personality. Self-preservation is undoubtedly the "first law of nature," but, if the experience of the race is any criterion, self-propagation is the second. At least, it is the expression of one of man's primary and strongest instincts. One of his most essential needs is the permanent love and companionship of a person of the opposite sex. The marriage state is not so imperatively necessary for right living as is security of life and a decent personal livelihood, yet it is of primary importance. The difference between these three needs is merely one of degree. All must be satisfied in the average man before he can live a reasonable and normal life. Without a religious vocation, the majority of men cannot reach a proper degree of self-development outside of the conjugal state. This is not to say that the man who has not been supernaturally called cannot be celibate and chaste — a doctrine becoming only to the foul of mind and weak of will — but it means that for the average man celibacy is not normal, and consequently cannot be taken as a measure of reasonable and natural rights. The man who is forced by poverty

---

and children who attend school, are not entitled to a Living Wage for the entire year. As we shall see, their right to a Living Wage must be secured in another way.

to accept it supports an unnatural and unjustifiable burden, and is deprived of one of the chief means of normal self-development. Hence, "the minimum of the material conditions of decent and reasonable living" comprises, for the adult male, the means of supporting a family. To this much of the world's goods he has a natural right which is valid "against the members of the industrial community in which he lives." In the case of the laborer this claim must be formulated in terms of wages. To resume: the laborer has a right to a family Living Wage because this is the only way in which he can exercise his right to the means of maintaining a family, and he has a right to these means because they are an essential condition of normal life....

It is held by some that the laborer's remuneration should vary with the size of his family, but this seems an undesirable way of measuring it. There are many reasons why the cost of rearing the family should be regarded as a unit, and the laborer's wages as a uniform rate. Then the cost of maintaining himself and wife until death and the children until they are of an age to be self-supporting, divided by his working time as an adult in full vigor, will give in terms of money the family Living Wage. Hence the laborer who is not yet married has a right to this family wage, and not merely to a remuneration that will suffice for his present needs. The difference should be reckoned as a necessary provision for marriage....

Moreover, the right to a family Living Wage belongs to every adult male laborer, whether he intends to marry or not; for rights are to be interpreted according to the average conditions of human life, and these suppose the laborer to become the head of a family. There is, too, a good social reason for treating married and unmarried alike in the matter of remuneration. If employers were morally free to pay single laborers less than a family Living Wage they would strive to engage these exclusively, and perhaps to exact a promise that they should not marry. Thus a premium would be placed upon a very undesirable kind of celibacy.

The family that it seems reasonable to take as a basis for estimating the proper remuneration of the husband and father, is that containing the average number of children found in workingmen's families. This standard is not entirely satisfactory, since it not infrequently happens that the mathematical average is exceeded in a large number (a majority sometimes) of the families of a place, but it seems to be the best that is available.... Hence it is sufficiently accurate to say that the family that ought to serve as a standard of measurement in the matter of decent remuneration for the adult male laborer, is one having four or five children.

VII. A Concrete Estimate of a Living Wage

... The following is submitted as a rough estimate of the minimum amount of goods and opportunities that will suffice for decent living and the rearing of a family:

1. Food, clothing and shelter for the laborer and his family until his children are old enough to become wage earners.

(a) The Children. It was stated in the last chapter that the average number of children found in the workingmen's families of full growth, is the only practicable standard for estimating the extent of the family's needs under this head....

Except possibly during school vacation, no child of either sex should be employed as a wage earner under the age of sixteen years. Below that age they are, as a rule, not sufficiently strong to work day after day under the direction of an employer. Besides, if they are taken out of school earlier they get less than a fair share of education, and of the industrial opportunities depending on it.

(b) The Wife. The welfare of the whole family, and that of society likewise, renders it imperative that the wife and mother should not engage in any labor except that of the household. When she works for hire she can neither care properly for her own health, rear her children aright, nor make her home what it should be for her husband, her children and herself. In the words of the Second Congress of Christian Workingmen at Rheims, "la femme devenue ouvriere n'est plus une femme."[5] Among the associations and individuals that have protested against the employment of wives and mothers, or at least of mothers, may be mentioned: the Union of Catholic Associations and Workingmen of Fribourg, Switzerland (1893); the Social Christians of Germany; the Christian Democrats of Belgium (1894); the Catholic Association of Holland (1897); the Second Congress of Christian Workingmen at Rheims (1894); the Catholic delegates to the Industrial Congress for the Protection of Workingmen at Zurich (1897); the Count de Mun; and Cardinal Manning.

(c) Food. The laborer should have food sufficient in quantity, quality and variety to maintain himself and the members of his family in a normal condition of health and vitality.

(d) Clothing. He should be able to provide himself and family with clothing adapted in quantity and quality to the reasonable requirements of comfort. In addition to being protected against the inclemency of the climate, they ought to have the means of appearing in becoming attire on "social" occasions, in school, in church, and in public gatherings....

(e) Shelter. Under this head it is sufficient to say that the dwelling occupied by the laborer and his family ought to consist of at least five rooms, and in general conform to the requirements of reasonable comfort. Three rooms (one for the parents, one for the male and one for the female children) are the minimum for sleeping accommodations, and it would seem that at least two rooms are required for all other purposes....

2. Besides the needs that are constant, actually existent, there are others that are intermittent, and still others that will be felt only in the future. The laborer's remuneration ought to be sufficiently large to enable him to provide against accidents, sickness and old age....

---

5. "The wife become wage worker is no longer a wife." Quoted in [Max] Turman's *Le Catholicisme sociale* (Paris, 1900), 55.

3. Finally, the laborer and his family have certain mental and spiritual needs, the satisfaction of which is essential to right living. The chief among them are: a moderate amount of amusement and recreation; education in the primary branches of instruction for the children; some periodical and other literature; membership in certain organizations, such as benefit societies and Labor Unions; and last, but by no means least, the means of fulfilling in a becoming manner the obligations imposed by charity and religion....

The conclusions that seem to be abundantly justified by the facts brought out in this chapter may, therefore, be stated as follows: first, anything *less* than $600 per year is *not* a Living Wage in any of the cities of the United States; second, this sum is *probably* a Living Wage in those cities of the Southern States in which fuel, clothing, food and some other items of expenditure are cheaper than in the North; third, it is *possibly* a Living Wage in the moderately sized cities of the West, North and East; and fourth, in some of the largest cities of the last-named regions, it is certainly *not* a Living Wage.

Rev. John A. Ryan, *A Living Wage: Its Ethical and Economic Aspects,* 2d ed.
(New York: Macmillan, 1912), 43–150. (Footnotes in Ryan's text.)

34. Rev. John A. Ryan, "Program of Social Reconstruction," Issued 12 February 1919 by the Administrative Committee of the National Catholic War Council

13. No attempt will be made in these pages to formulate a comprehensive scheme of reconstruction. Such an undertaking would be a waste of time as regards immediate needs and purposes, for no important group or section of the American people is ready to consider a program of this magnitude. Attention will therefore be confined to those reforms that seem to be desirable and also obtainable within a reasonable time, and to a few general principles which should become a guide to more distant developments. A statement thus circumscribed will not merely present the objects that we wish to see attained, but will also serve as an imperative call to action. It will keep before our minds the necessity for translating our faith into works. In the statements of immediate proposals we shall start, wherever possible, from those governmental agencies and legislative measures which have been to some extent in operation during the war. These come before us with the prestige of experience and should therefore receive first consideration in any program that aims to be at once practical and persuasive.

14. The first problem in the process of reconstruction is the industrial replacement of the discharged soldiers and sailors. The majority of these will undoubtedly return to their previous occupations. However, a very large number of them will either find their previous places closed to them, or will be eager to consider the possibility of more attractive employments. The most important single measure for meeting this situation that has yet been suggested is the placement of such men on farms. Several months ago Secretary

Lane recommended to Congress that returning soldiers and sailors should be given the opportunity to work at good wages upon some part of the millions upon millions of acres of arid, swamp, and cut-over timber lands, in order to prepare them for cultivation. President Wilson in his annual address to Congress endorsed the proposal....

15. The reinstatement of the soldiers and sailors in urban industries will no doubt be facilitated by the United States Employment Service. This agency has attained a fair degree of development and efficiency during the war. Unfortunately there is some danger that it will go out of existence or be greatly weakened at the end of the period of demobilization. It is the obvious duty of Congress to continue and strengthen this important institution. The problem of unemployment is with us always. Its solution requires the cooperation of many agencies, and the use of many methods; but the primary and indispensable instrument is a national system of labor exchanges, acting in harmony with State, municipal, and private employment bureaus.

16. One of the most important problems of readjustment is that created by the presence in industry of immense numbers of women who have taken the places of men during the war. Mere justice, to say nothing of chivalry, dictates that these women should not be compelled to suffer any greater loss or inconvenience than is absolutely necessary; for their services to the nation they have been second only to the services of the men whose places they were called upon to fill. One general principle is clear: No female worker should remain in any occupation that is harmful to health or morals. Women should disappear as quickly as possible from such tasks as conducting and guarding street cars, cleaning locomotives, and a great number of other activities for which conditions of life and their physique render them unfit. Another general principle is that the proportion of women in industry ought to be kept within the smallest practical limits. If we have an efficient national employment service, if a goodly number of the returned soldiers and sailors are placed on the land, and if wages and the demand for goods are kept up to the level which is easily attainable, all female workers who are displaced from the tasks that they have been performing only since the beginning of the war will be able to find suitable employments in other parts of the industrial field, or in those domestic occupations which sorely need their presence. Those women who are engaged at the same tasks as men should receive equal pay for equal amounts and qualities of work.

17. One of the most beneficial governmental organizations of the war is the National War Labor Board. Upon the basis of a few fundamental principles, unanimously adopted by the representatives of labor, capital and the public, it has prevented innumerable strikes, and raised wages to decent levels in many different industries throughout the country. Its main guiding principles have been a family living wage for all male adult laborers; recognition of the right of labor to organize and to deal with employers through its chosen representatives; and no coercion of non-union laborers by members of the union. The War Labor Board ought to be continued in existence by Congress,

and endowed with all the power for effective action that it can possess under the Federal Constitution....

18. The general level of wages attained during the war should not be lowered. In a few industries, especially some directly and peculiarly connected with the carrying on of war, wages have reached a plane upon which they cannot possibly continue for this grade of occupation. But the number of workers in this situation is an extremely small proportion of the entire wage-earning population. The overwhelming majority should not be compelled or suffered to undergo any reduction in their rates of remuneration, for two reasons: First, because the average rate of pay has not increased faster than the cost of living; second, because a considerable majority of the wage earners of the United States, both men and women, were not receiving living wages when prices began to rise in 1915....

19. Even if the great majority of workers were not in receipt of more than living wages, there are no good reasons why rates of pay should be lowered. After all, a living wage is not necessarily the full measure of justice. All the Catholic authorities on the subject explicitly declare that this is only the minimum of justice. In a country as rich as ours, there are very few cases in which it is possible to prove that the worker would be getting more than that to which he has a right if he were paid something in excess of this ethical minimum. Why then, should we assume that this is the normal share of almost the whole laboring population?...Such a policy is not only of very questionable morality, but is unsound economically. The large demand for goods which is created and maintained by high rates of wages and high purchasing power by the masses is the surest guarantee of a continuous and general operation of industrial establishments. It is the most effective instrument of prosperity for labor and capital alike....

20. Housing projects for war workers which have been completed, or almost completed by the Government of the United States, have cost some forty million dollars, and are found in eleven cities. While the Federal Government cannot continue this work in time of peace, the example and precedent that it has set, and the experience and knowledge that it has developed, should not be forthwith neglected and lost. The great cities in which congestion and other forms of bad housing are disgracefully apparent ought to take up and continue the work, at least to such an extent as will remove the worst features of a social condition that is a menace at once to industrial efficiency, civil health, good morals and religion....

24. Turning now from those agencies and laws that have been put in operation during the war to the general subject of labor legislation and problems, we are glad to note that there is no longer any serious objection urged by impartial persons against the legal minimum wage. The several States should enact laws providing for the establishment of wage rates that will be at least sufficient for the decent maintenance of a family, in the case of all male adults, and adequate to the decent individual support of female workers. In the beginning the minimum wages for male workers should suffice only for the present needs

of the family, but they should be gradually raised until they are adequate to future needs as well. That is, they should be ultimately high enough to make possible that amount of saving which is necessary to protect the worker and his family against sickness, accidents, invalidity, and old age.

25. Until this level of legal minimum wages is reached the worker stands in need of the device of insurance. The State should make comprehensive provision for insurance against illness, invalidity, unemployment, and old age. So far as possible the insurance fund should be raised by a levy on industry, as is now done in the case of accident compensation. The industry in which a man is employed should provide him with all that is necessary to meet all the needs of his entire life. Therefore, any contribution to the insurance fund from the general revenues of the State should be only slight and temporary. For the same reason no contribution should be exacted from any worker who is not getting a higher wage than is required to meet the present needs of himself and family. Those who are below that level can make such a contribution only at the expense of their present welfare. Finally, the administration of the insurance laws should be such as to interfere as little as possible with the individual freedom of the worker and his family. Any insurance scheme, or any administrative method, that tends to separate the workers into a distinct and dependent class, that offends against their domestic privacy and independence, or that threatens individual self-reliance and self-respect, should not be tolerated. The ideal to be kept in mind is a condition in which all the workers would themselves have the income and the responsibility of providing for all the needs and contingencies of life, both present and future. Hence, all forms of State insurance should be regarded as merely a lesser evil, and should be so organized and administered as to hasten the coming of the normal condition [i.e., industry-based insurance plans]....

27. The establishment and maintenance of municipal health inspection in all schools, public and private, is now pretty generally recognized as of great importance and benefit. Municipal clinics where the poorer classes could obtain the advantage of medical treatment by specialists at a reasonable cost would likewise seem to have become a necessity. A vast amount of unnecessary sickness and suffering exists among the poor and the lower middle classes because they cannot afford the advantages of any other treatment except that provided by the general practitioner. Every effort should be made to supply wage earners and their families with specialized medical care through development of group medicine. Free medical care should be given only to those who cannot afford to pay.

28. The right of labor to organize and to deal with employers through representatives has been asserted above in connection with the discussion of the War Labor Board [no. 17]. It is to be hoped that this right will never again be called in question by any considerable number of employers. In addition to this, labor ought gradually to receive greater representation in what the English group of Quaker employers have called the "industrial" part of business management — "the control of processes and machinery; nature of product;

engagement and dismissal of employees; hours of work, rates of pay, bonuses, etc.; welfare work; shop discipline; relations with trade unions...."

30. The need of industrial, or as it has come to be more generally called, vocational training, is now universally acknowledged. In the interest of the nation, as well as in that of the workers themselves, this training should be made substantially universal. While we cannot now discuss the subject in any detail, we do wish to set down two general observations. First, the vocational training should be offered in such forms and conditions as not to deprive the children of the working classes of at least the elements of a cultural education. A healthy democracy cannot tolerate a purely industrial or trade education for any class of its citizens. We do not want to have the children of the wage-earners put into a special class in which they are marked as outside the sphere of opportunities for culture. The second observation is that the system of vocational training should not operate so as to weaken in any degree our parochial schools or any other class of private schools. Indeed, the opportunities of the system should be extended to all qualified private schools on exactly the same basis as to public schools. We want neither class divisions in education nor a State monopoly of education.

31. The question of education naturally suggests the subject of child labor. Public opinion in the majority of the States of our country has set its face inflexibly against the continuous employment of children in industry before the age of sixteen years. Within a reasonably short time all of our States, except some stagnant ones, will have laws providing for this reasonable standard. The education of public opinion must continue, but inasmuch as the process is slow, the abolition of child labor in certain sections seems unlikely to be brought about by the legislatures of those States, and since the Keating-Owen Act has been declared unconstitutional, there seems to be no device by which this reproach to our country can be removed except that of taxing child labor out of existence. This method is embodied in an amendment to the Federal Revenue Bill which would impose a tax of ten percent on all goods made by children.

32. Probably the foregoing proposals comprise everything that is likely to have practical value in a program of immediate social reconstruction for America. Substantially all of these methods, laws, and recommendations have been recognized in principle by the United States during the war, or have been endorsed by important social and industrial groups and organizations. Therefore, they are objects that we can set before the people with good hope of obtaining a sympathetic and practical response....

33. Despite the practical and immediate character of the present statement, we cannot entirely neglect the question of ultimate aims and a systematic program; for other groups are busy issuing such systematic pronouncements, and we all need something of the kind as a philosophical foundation and as a satisfaction to our natural desire for comprehensive statements.

34. It seems clear that the present industrial system is destined to last for a long time in its main outlines. That is to say, private ownership of capital is

not likely to be supplanted by a collectivist organization of industry at a date sufficiently near to justify any present action based on the hypothesis of its arrival. This forecast we recognize as not only extremely probable, but as highly desirable; for, other objections apart, Socialism would mean bureaucracy, political tyranny, the helplessness of the individual as a factor in the ordering of his own life, and in general social inefficiency and decadence.

35. Nevertheless, the present system stands in grievous need of considerable modifications and improvement. Its main defects are three: Enormous inefficiency and waste in the production and distribution of commodities; insufficient incomes for the great majority of wage-earners; and unnecessarily large incomes for a small minority of privileged capitalists. Inefficiency in the production and distribution of goods would be in great measure abolished by the reforms that have been outlined in the foregoing pages....

36. Nevertheless, the full possibilities of increased production will not be realized so long as the majority of the workers remain mere wage-earners. The majority must somehow become owners, or at least in part, of the instruments of production. They can be enabled to reach this stage gradually through cooperative productive societies and copartnership arrangements. In the former, workers own and manage the industries themselves; in the latter they own a substantial part of the corporate stock and exercise a reasonable share in the management....

38. For the third evil mentioned above, excessive gains by a small minority of privileged capitalists, the main remedies are prevention of monopolistic control of commodities, adequate government regulation of such public service monopolies as will remain under private operation, and heavy taxation of incomes, excess profits and inheritances....

40. "Society," said Pope Leo XIII, "can be healed in no other way than by a return to Christian life and Christian institutions." The truth of these words is more widely perceived today than when they were written, more than twenty-seven years ago. Changes in our economic and political systems will have only partial and feeble efficiency if they be not reinforced by the Christian view of work and wealth. Neither the moderate reforms advocated in this paper, nor any other program of betterment or reconstruction will prove reasonably effective without a reform in the spirit of both labor and capital. The laborer must come to realize that he owes his employer and society an honest day's work in return for a fair wage, and that conditions cannot be substantially improved until he roots out the desire to get a maximum of return for a minimum of service. The capitalist must likewise get a new viewpoint. He needs to learn the long-forgotten truth that wealth is stewardship, that profit-making is not the basic justification of business enterprise, and that there are such things as fair profits, fair interest, and fair prices. Above and before all, he must cultivate and strengthen within his mind the truth which many of his class have begun to grasp for the first time during the present war; namely, that the laborer is a human being, not merely an instrument of production; and that the laborer's right to a decent livelihood is the first moral charge upon industry.

The employer has a right to get a reasonable living out of his business, but he has no right to interest on his investment until his employees have obtained at least living wages. This is the human and Christian, in contrast to the purely commercial and pagan, ethics of industry.

Hugh J. Nolan, ed., *Pastoral Letters of the United States Catholic Bishops* (Washington, D.C.: United States Catholic Conference, 1984), 1:255–71; also in John Tracy Ellis, ed., *Documents of American Catholic History* (Wilmington, Del.: Michael Glazier, 1987), 2:595–607. Printed with permission.

35. Pastoral Letter Issued by the Roman Catholic Hierarchy of the United States, 26 September 1919

... Secular Conditions

64. The temporal order, in the last thirty-five years has undergone radical changes. It has been affected by movements which, though checked for a time or reversed, have steadily gathered momentum. Their direction and goal are no longer matters of surmise or suspicion. Their outcome is plainly before us.

65. During the first three decades of this period, the advance of civilization was more rapid and more general than in any earlier period of equal length. The sound of progress, echoing beyond its traditional limits, aroused all the nations to a sense of their possibilities, and stirred each with an ambition to win its share in the forward movement of the world. At the same time, the idea of a human weal for whose promotion all should strive and by whose attainment all should profit, seemed to be gaining universal acceptance. If rivalry here and there gave occasion for friction or conflict, it was treated as incidental; the general desire for harmony, apparently, was nearing fulfillment.

66. Toward this end the highest tendencies in the secular order were steadily converging. A wider diffusion of knowledge provided the basis for a mutual understanding of rights and obligations. Science, while attaining more completely to the mastery of nature, placed itself more effectually at the service of man. Through its practical application, it hastened material progress, facilitated the intercourse of nation with nation, and thus lowered the natural barriers of distance and time. But it also made possible a fuller exchange of ideas, and thereby revealed to the various peoples of earth that in respect of need, aspiration, and purpose, they had more in common than generally was supposed. It helped them to see that however they differed in race, tradition, and language, in national temper and political organization, they were humanly one in the demand for freedom with equal right and opportunity.

67. As this consciousness developed in mankind at large, the example of our own country grew in meaning and influence. For a century and more, it had taught the world that men could live and prosper under free institutions. During the period in question, it has continued to receive the multitudes who came not, as in the early days, from a few countries only, but from every foreign land, to enjoy the blessings of liberty and to better their worldly condition. In making them its own, America has shown a power of assimi-

lation that is without precedent in the temporal order. With their aid it has undertaken and achieved industrial tasks on a scale unknown to former generations. The wealth thus produced has been used in generous measure to build up institutions of public utility. Education, in particular, has flourished; its importance has been more fully recognized, its problems more widely discussed, the means of giving and obtaining it more freely supplied. While its aim has been to raise the intellectual level and thereby enhance the worth of the individual, experience has shown the advantage of organized effort for the accomplishment of any purpose in which the people as a whole, or any considerable portion, has an interest. Hence the remarkable development of associations which, though invested with no authority, have become powerful enough to shape public opinion and even to affect the making of laws. If, in some instances, the power of association has been directed toward ends that were at variance with the general good and by methods which created disturbance, there has been, on the whole, a willingness to respect authority and to abide by its decisions.

68. Thus, as it appears, the whole trend of human affairs was securing the world in peace. The idea of war was farthest from the minds of the peoples. The possibility of war had ceased to be a subject for serious discussion. To adjust their disputes, the nations had set up a tribunal. The volume of seeming prosperity swelled.

Catholic War Activities

69. Once it had been decided that our country should enter the war, no words of exhortation were needed to arouse the Catholic spirit. This had been shown in every national crisis. It had stirred to eloquent expression the fathers of the Third Plenary Council [1884].

70. "We consider the establishment of our country's independence, the shaping of its liberties and laws, as a work of special providence, its framers 'building better than they knew,' the Almighty's hand guiding them.... We believe that our country's heroes were the instruments of the God of nations in establishing this home of freedom; to both the Almighty and to His instruments in the work we look with grateful reverence; and to maintain the inheritance of freedom which they have left us, should it ever — which God forbid — be imperilled, our Catholic citizens will be found to stand forward as one man, ready to pledge anew 'their lives, their fortunes, and their sacred honor.'"

71. The prediction has been fulfilled. The traditional patriotism of our Catholic people has been amply demonstrated in the day of their country's trial. And we look with pride upon the record which proves, as no mere protestation could prove, the devotion of American Catholics to the cause of American freedom.

72. To safeguard the moral and physical welfare of our Catholic soldiers and sailors, organized action was needed. The excellent work already accomplished by the Knights of Columbus pointed the way to further undertakings.

The unselfish patriotism with which our various societies combined their forces in the Catholic Young Men's Association, the enthusiasm manifested by the organizations of Catholic women, and the eagerness of our clergy to support the cause of the nation, made it imperative to unify the energies of the whole Catholic body and direct them toward the American purpose. With this end in view, the National Catholic War Council was formed by the hierarchy. Through the Committee on Special War Activities and the Knights of Columbus Committee on War Activities, the efforts of our people in various lines were coordinated and rendered more effective, both in providing for the spiritual need of all Catholics under arms and in winning our country's success. This unified action was worthy of the Catholic name....

Social Relations

120. The security of the nation and the efficiency of government for the general weal depend largely upon the standards which are adopted and the practices which are admitted, in social relations. This is characteristic of a democracy, where the makers of law are commissioned to do the will of the people. In matters pertaining to morality, legislation will not rise above the level established by the general tone and tenor of society. It is necessary, then, for the preservation of national life, that social morality, in its usage and sanction, be sound and steadfast and pure.

121. This aim can be accomplished only by reaching the sources in which life has its origin, and from which the individual character receives its initial direction. As the family is the first social group, it is also the center whose influence permeates the entire social body. And since family life takes its rise from the union of husband and wife, the sanctity of marriage and of marital relations is of prime importance for the purity of social relations....

124. It is essential, in the first place, that clean living before marriage be equally obligatory on men and women. The toleration of vicious courses in one party while the other is strictly held to the practice of virtue, may rest on convention or custom; but it is ethically false, and it is plainly at variance with the law of God, which enjoins personal purity upon each and all....

128. Where such ideals prevail, the fulfillment of marital duties occasions no hardship. Neither is there any consideration for the fraudulent prudence that would improve upon nature by defeating its obvious purpose, and would purify life by defiling its source. The selfishness which leads to race suicide with or without the pretext of bettering the species, is, in God's sight, "a detestable thing" [Gen. 38:10]. It is the crime of individuals for which, eventually, the nation must suffer. The harm which it does cannot be repaired by social service, nor offset by pretending economic or domestic advantage....

134. Of itself and under normal conditions, marital love endures through life, growing in strength as time passes and renewing itself in tenderness in the children that are its pledges. The thought of separation even by death is repugnant, and nothing less than death can weaken the bond. No sane man or

woman regards divorce as a good thing; the most that can be said in its favor is that, under given circumstances, it affords relief from intolerable evil.

135. Reluctantly, the Church permits limited divorce: the parties are allowed for certain cause to separate, though the bond continues in force and neither may contract a new marriage while the other is living. But absolute divorce which severs the bond, the Church does not and will not permit.

136. We consider the growth of the divorce evil an evidence of moral decay and a present danger to the best elements in our American life. In its causes and their revelation by process of law, in its results for those who are immediately concerned and its suggestion to the minds of the entire community, divorce is our national scandal. It not only disrupts the home of the separated parties, but it also leads others who are not yet married, to look upon the bond as a trivial circumstance. Thus, through the ease and frequency with which it is granted, divorce increases with an evil momentum until it passes the limits of decency and reduces the sexual relation to the level of animal instinct....

138. By divine ordinance, each human being becomes a member of the larger social group, and in due course enters into social relations. These are, and should be, a means of promoting good will and an occasion for the practice of many virtues, notably of justice and charity.

139. That social enjoyment is quite compatible with serious occupation and with devotion to the public good, is evident from the services rendered during the war by all classes of people, and especially by those who gave up their comfort and ease in obedience to the call of their country. Let this same spirit prevail in time of peace and set reasonable limits to the pursuit of pleasure. With the tendency to excess and the craving for excitement, there comes a willingness to encourage in social intercourse abuses that would not be tolerated in the privacy of home. For the sake of notoriety, the prescriptions of plain decency are often set aside, and even the slightest restraints of convention are disregarded. Fondness for display leads to lavish expenditure, which arouses the envy of the less fortunate classes, spurs them to a foolish imitation, and eventually brings about conflict between the rich and the poor.

140. Though many of these abuses are of short duration, their effect is nonetheless harmful: they impair the moral fiber of our people and render them unfit for liberty. The plainest lessons of history show that absorption in pleasure is fatal to free institutions. Nations which had conquered the world were unable to prevent their own ruin, once corruption had sapped their vitality. Our country has triumphed in its struggle beyond the sea; let it beware of the enemy lurking within....

143. In society as in the home, the influence of woman is potent. She rules with the power of gentleness, and, where men are chivalrous, her will is the social law. To use this power and fashion this law in such wise that the world may be better because of her presence, is a worthy ambition. But it will not be achieved by devices that arouse the coarser instincts and gratify vanity at

the expense of decency. There will be less ground to complain of the wrong inflicted on women, when women themselves maintain their true dignity....

144. The present tendency in all civilized countries is to give woman a larger share in pursuits and occupations that formerly were reserved to men. The sphere of her activity is no longer confined to the home or to her social environment; it includes the learned professions, the field of industry, and the forum of political life. Her ability to meet the hardest of human conditions has been tested by the experience of war; and the world pays tribute, rightfully, to her patriotic spirit, her courage, and her power of restoring what the havoc of war had well-nigh destroyed.

145. Those same qualities are now to undergo a different sort of trial; for women by engaging in public affairs, accept, with equal rights, an equal responsibility. So far as she may purify and elevate our political life, her use of the franchise will prove an advantage; and this will be greater if it involve no loss of the qualities in which woman excels. Such a loss would deprive her of the influence which she wields in the home, and eventually defeat the very purpose for which she has entered the public arena. The evils that result from wrong political practice must surely arouse apprehension, but what we have chiefly to fear is the growth of division that tends to breed hatred. The remedy for this lies not in the struggle of parties, but in the diffusion of good will. To reach the hearts of men and take away their bitterness, that they may live henceforth in fellowship one with another — this is woman's vocation in respect of public affairs, and the service which she by nature is best fitted to render.

Industrial Relations

146. In 1891, Pope Leo XIII published his encyclical *Rerum Novarum*, a document which shows the insight of that great pontiff into the industrial conditions of the time, and his wisdom in pointing out the principles needed for the solving of economic problems.

> That the spirit of revolutionary change which has long been disturbing the nations of the world, should have passed beyond the sphere of politics and made its influence felt in the cognate sphere of practical economics, is not surprising. The elements of the conflict now raging are unmistakable, in the vast expansion of industrial pursuits and the marvelous discoveries of science; in the changed relation between masters and workmen; in the enormous fortunes of some few individuals, and the utter poverty of the masses; in the increased self-reliance and closer mutual combination of the working classes; as also, finally, in the prevailing moral degeneracy. The momentous gravity of the state of things now obtaining fills every mind with painful apprehension; wise men are discussing it; practical men are proposing schemes; popular meetings, legislatures, and rulers of nations are all busied with it — and actually there is no question that has taken a deeper hold on the public mind.

147. How fully these statements apply to our present situation, must be clear to all who have noted the course of events during the year just elapsed. The war indeed has sharpened the issues and intensified the conflict that rages in the world of industry; but the elements, the parties, and their respective attitudes are practically unchanged. Unchanged also are the principles which must be applied, if order is to be restored and placed on such a permanent basis that our people may continue their peaceful pursuits without dread of further disturbance....

149. In the prosecution of their respective claims, the parties [labor and capital] have, apparently, disregarded the fact that the people as a whole have a prior claim. The great number of unnecessary strikes which have occurred within the last few months is evidence that justice has been widely violated as regards the rights and needs of the public. To assume that the only rights involved in an industrial dispute are those of capital and labor, is a radical error. It leads, practically, to the conclusion that at any time and for an indefinite period, even the most necessary products can be withheld from the general use until the controversy is settled. In fact, while it lasts, millions of persons are compelled to suffer hardship for want of goods and services which they require for reasonable living. The first step, therefore, toward correcting the evil is to insist that the rights of the community shall prevail, and that no individual claim conflicting with those rights shall be valid....

153. The right of labor to organize, and the great benefit to be derived from workingmen's associations, were plainly set forth by Pope Leo XIII. In this connection, we would call attention to two rights, one of employees and the other of employers, the violation of which contributes largely to the existing unrest and suffering. The first is the right of the workers to form and maintain the kind of organization that is necessary and that will be most effectual in securing their welfare. The second is the right of employers to the faithful observance by the labor unions of all contracts and agreements. The unreasonableness of denying either of these rights is too obvious to require proof or explanation.

154. A dispute that cannot be adjusted by direct negotiation between the parties concerned should always be submitted to arbitration. Neither employer nor employee may reasonably reject this method on the ground that it does not bring about perfect justice. No human institution is perfect or infallible; even our courts of law are sometimes in error. Like the law court, the tribunal of industrial arbitration provides the nearest approach to justice that is practically attainable; for the only alternative is economic force, and its decisions have no necessary relation to the decrees of justice. They show which party is economically stronger, not which is in the right.

155. The right of labor to a living wage, authoritatively and eloquently reasserted more than a quarter of a century ago by Pope Leo XIII, is happily no longer denied by any considerable number of persons. What is principally needed now is that its content should be adequately defined, and that it should be made universal in practice, through whatever means will be at once legit-

imate and effective. In particular, it is to be kept in mind that a living wage includes not merely decent maintenance for the present, but also a reasonable provision for such future needs as sickness, invalidity, and old age. Capital likewise has its rights. Among them is the right to "a fair day's work for a fair day's pay," and the right to returns which will be sufficient to stimulate thrift, saving, initiative, enterprise, and all those directive and productive energies which promote social welfare....

Education

180. The Church in our country is obliged, for the sake of principle, to maintain a system of education distinct and separate from other systems. It is supported by the voluntary contributions of Catholics who, at the same time, contribute as required by law to the maintenance of the public schools. It engages in the service of education a body of teachers who consecrate their lives to this high calling; and it prepares, without expense to the state, a considerable number of Americans to live worthily as citizens of the republic.

181. Our system is based on certain convictions that grow stronger as we observe the testing of all education, not simply by calm theoretic discussion, but by the crucial experience of recent events. It should not have required the pitiless searching of war to determine the value of any theory or system, but since that rude test has been so drastically applied and with such unmistakable results, we judge it opportune to restate the principles which serve as the basis of Catholic education.

182. *First:* The right of the child to receive education and the correlative duty of providing it, are established on the fact that man has a soul created by God and endowed with capacities which need to be developed for the good of the individual and the good of society. In its highest meaning therefore, education is a cooperation by human agencies with the Creator for the attainment of His purpose in regard to the individual who is to be educated, and in regard to the social order of which he is a member. Neither self-realization alone nor social service alone is the end of education, but rather these two in accordance with God's design, which gives to each of them its proportionate value. Hence it follows that education is essentially and inevitably a moral activity, in the sense that it undertakes to satisfy certain claims through the fulfillment of certain obligations. This is true independently of the manner and means which constitute the actual process; and it remains true, whether recognized or disregarded in educational practice, whether this practice include the teaching of morality, or exclude it, or try to maintain a neutral position.

183. *Second:* Since the child is endowed with physical, intellectual, and moral capacities, all these must be developed harmoniously. An education that quickens the intelligence and enriches the mind with knowledge, but fails to develop the will and direct it to the practice of virtue, may produce scholars, but it cannot produce good men. The exclusion of moral training from the educative process is more dangerous in proportion to the thoroughness with which the intellectual powers are developed, because it gives the impression

that morality is of little importance, and thus sends the pupil into life with a false idea which is not easily corrected.

184. *Third:* Since the duties we owe our Creator take precedence of all other duties, moral training must accord the first place to religion, that is, to the knowledge of God and His law, and must cultivate a spirit of obedience to His commands. The performance, sincere and complete, of religious duties, ensures the fulfillment of other obligations.

185. *Fourth:* Moral and religious training is most efficacious when it is joined with instruction in other kinds of knowledge. It should so permeate these that its influence will be felt in every circumstance of life, and be strengthened as the mind advances to a fuller acquaintance with nature and a riper experience with the realities of human existence.

186. *Fifth:* An education that unites intellectual, moral, and religious elements, is the best training for citizenship. It inculcates a sense of responsibility, a respect for authority, and a considerateness for the rights of others, which are the necessary foundations of civic virtue — more necessary where, as in a democracy, the citizen, enjoying a larger freedom, has a greater obligation to govern himself. We are convinced that, as religion and morality are essential to right living and to the public welfare, both should be included in the work of education.

187. There is reason to believe that this conviction is shared by a considerable number of our fellow citizens who are not of the Catholic faith. They realize that the omission of religious instruction is a defect in education and also a detriment to religion. But in their view, the home and church should give the needed training in morality and religion, leaving the school to provide only secular knowledge. Experience, however, confirms us in the belief that instead of dividing education among these several agencies each of them should, in its own measure contribute to the intellectual, moral, and religious development of the child, and by this means become helpful to all the rest....

193. As the public welfare is largely dependent upon the intelligence of the citizen, the state has a vital concern in education. This is implied in the original purpose of our government which, as set forth in the preamble to the Constitution, is "to form a more perfect union, establish justice, ensure domestic tranquility, provide for the common defense, promote the general welfare, and secure the blessings of liberty to ourselves and our posterity."

194. In accordance with these purposes, the state has a right to insist that its citizens shall be educated. It should encourage among the people such a love of learning that they will take the initiative and, without constraint, provide for the education of their children. Should they through negligence or lack of means fail to do so, the state has the right to establish schools and take every other legitimate means to safeguard its vital interests against the dangers that result from ignorance. In particular, it has both the right and the duty to exclude the teaching of doctrines which aim at the subversion of law and order and therefore at the destruction of the state itself.

195. The state is competent to do these things because its essential function

is to promote the general welfare. But on the same principle, it is bound to respect and protect the rights of the citizen and especially of the parent. So long as these rights are properly exercised, to encroach upon them is not to further the general welfare but to put it in peril. If the function of government is to protect the liberty of the citizen, and if the aim of education is to prepare the individual for the rational use of his liberty, the state cannot rightfully or consistently make education a pretext for interfering with the rights and liberties which the Creator, not the state, has conferred. Any advantage that might accrue even from a perfect system of state education, would be more than offset by the wrong which the violation of parental rights would involve.

196. In our country, government thus far has wisely refrained from placing any other than absolutely necessary restrictions upon private initiative. The result is seen in the development of our resources, the products of inventive genius, and the magnitude of our enterprises. But our most valuable resources are the minds of our children; and for their development, at least the same scope should be allowed to individual effort as is secured to our undertakings in the material order.

197. The spirit of our people is in general adverse to state monopoly, and this for the obvious reason that such an absorption of control would mean the end of freedom and initiative. The same consequence is sure to follow when the state attempts to monopolize education; and the disaster will be greater inasmuch as it will affect, not simply the worldly interests of the citizen, but also his spiritual growth and salvation.

198. With great wisdom our American Constitution provides that every citizen shall be free to follow the dictates of his conscience in the matter of religious belief and observance. While the state gives no preference or advantage to any form of religion, its own best interests require that religion as well as education should flourish and exert its wholesome influence upon the lives of the people. And since education is so powerful an agency for the preservation of religion, equal freedom should be secured to both. This is the more needful where the state refuses religious instruction any place in its schools. To compel the attendance of all children at these schools, would be practically equivalent to an invasion of the rights of conscience, in respect of those parents who believe that religion forms a necessary part of education.

199. Our Catholic schools are not established and maintained with any idea of holding our children apart from the general body and spirit of American citizenship. They are simply the concrete form in which we exercise our rights as free citizens, in conformity with the dictates of conscience. Their very existence is a great moral fact in American life. For while they aim, openly and avowedly, to preserve our Catholic faith, they offer to all our people an example of the use of freedom for the advancement of morality and religion....

Hugh J. Nolan, ed., *Pastoral Letters of the United States Catholic Bishops* (Washington, D.C.: United States Catholic Conference, 1984), 1:294–331. Printed with permission.

36. Rev. Joseph Reiner, S.J., Regent, School of Commerce and Sociology, St. Xavier's College, Cincinnati, Ohio, "A Program for Social Legislation," 1920

...I think it is a cardinal point in the Catholic program of reform as distinguished from that of the liberal school, that social legislation is an important means toward securing the natural rights of our people....

Now, despite the fact that the Catholic school, in France, in Germany, in Italy and in England, all over the world, shares this opinion, that legislation is a cardinal point in reform, we Catholics, as a body, have done very little to modify the statute books of our country. But I do honestly believe that a new day is dawning. If the large number of women in attendance at this convention is indicative of the large share that they take in Catholic social work, if their exceptionally intelligent discussion of social problems, evidencing a deep grasp of the problems and of their ramifications, of their devotion and their sacrifice and their enthusiasm, as exhibited here and as exhibited in other places, give promise of anything, I say they give promise of this, that they will use that new means [suffrage] that has been entrusted to them recently to secure that for which it is intended, namely, the enactment of laws that will protect us against exploitation, which is the cause of one-half, if not of three-fourths, of those ills that you charity workers are called upon to relieve....

It is well and good that we perform ambulance service, and I hope that the day will never come when our good Catholic people will grow remiss in performing the works of charity and in imitating the example of the Good Samaritan, but I do hope the day will come when we will more clearly see that much of this charity work is not called for, that much of it could be dispensed with, that we could devote many of our energies to other purposes if we would but safeguard our rights, our Catholic rights, by the enactment of legislation that is suggested in the bishops' program.[1]

Now I am not going to appeal to you and try to prove to you that we have an obligation in that respect. I believe that your question to me is this: "What practical suggestion have you to submit whereby we can fulfill what appears to be a plain religious and civic obligation, of seeing that these important legislative suggestions are enacted into law?" What practical methods have I to suggest? Allow me to tell you some of our experiences in Ohio during the past two years. I believe that by some examples you will understand more easily and more plainly what I might put into a more theoretical form. It so happens that the speaker [Father Reiner] was on the Board of Directors of the Consumers' League of Cincinnati, and that he on various occasions solicited the help of the Catholic organizations in the discussion of certain legislation then pending in the Ohio Legislature. Among other bills were these, a bill to prohibit night work for women, to prohibit the occupation of women in certain morally and physically hazardous employments, to regulate the oc-

---

1. See document 34 above.

cupation of children in street trades, and to extend certain laws protecting women to new occupations. Well, we soon realized that if we wished to exert our influence as Catholics, and if we wished to avoid duplication of effort and waste of energy, it would be advisable for us to form a joint legislative committee of all the organizations interested, and so, with the approval of His Grace, the Most Rev. Archbishop Moeller, of exceptionally wide social vision, such a committee was organized.

At our first meeting we resolved to continue to support the legislation that I have just referred to and to initiate legislation for a minimum wage for women workers. We adopted two principles to guide us in a general way in all our activities. The first was this, never to protest against any legislation that was designed to meet a specific need unless we could substitute something better; secondly, that we would cooperate with any and all organizations that pursued the same purpose that we have in mind. And so, following the first principle, we did not protest against prohibition, in spite of the fact that we were told that it meant the destruction of personal liberty, and in spite of the fact that we were told that three months after the enactment of prohibition the Holy Mass would automatically come to an end [for lack of sacramental wine]. And, following the second principle, we cooperated with Jew and Protestant, with infidel and heretic.

Now, after we had decided upon this minimum wage, we obtained a copy of a model law, and adapted it to the needs of Ohio. We had it printed and distributed among those we thought might be influenced. We secured the services of a legislator to introduce the bill, and then we began a very active campaign. We seized every opportunity to bring the bill to the notice of the public. We wrote letters to the editors of the papers, some of which were published, and many others found their way into the waste paper basket. We addressed Catholic audiences, practically all the councils of the Knights of Columbus and many other Catholic societies.

I should tell you here what organizations joined in the formation of this committee. We had the Holy Name Societies, we had the Cincinnati Catholic Women's Association, the Catholic Ladies of Columbia, the Cincinnati Chapter of the Knights of Columbus with a membership of approximately 10,000, we had the Catholic Knights of Ohio, the Catholic Knights of America, and others. To the foremost of these organizations we gave addresses and distributed among their membership upwards of 6,000 copies of the bishops' program....

While the Ohio Legislature was in session, a delegate from Hamilton County conducted sessions in a prominent hotel in Cincinnati, and offered an opportunity to three students to present their views in behalf of pending or proposed legislation. Of course we used that opportunity. The chairman of our committee made the principal appeal to the legislators from Hamilton County, outlining the ethical and economical foundations of minimum wage law, and answering the objections that were raised. He was followed by a Jewish social worker, by a representative of the Y.W.C.A., by a representative of the Holy Name Societies, by a representative of the Cincinnati Chapter of the Knights of Columbus, and by representatives of the other societies I have mentioned.

We also had private conferences with the legislators, and naturally had some interesting experiences. I will mention just one. One legislator told me he did not think that a priest ought to meddle in such affairs, that a priest has enough to do if he confines his activities to the sanctuary, and then we heard the surprising remark: "If you people get busy in these things, you will be introducing a new disturbing element in politics that we will have to watch when election time comes around."

Now, ladies and gentlemen, I do not feel that we, as Catholics, are ever going to amount to anything, as far as social reform is concerned, until we become a disturbing element in politics. And I do wish, and I pray, that some one will start a movement and send an appeal and clarion call throughout the length and breadth of our country, warning our Catholic women sufficiently against the wiles of the politicians who are trying to tie them up with this or that political party, someone that will beg them to maintain their political independence and cast their voice or influence with the candidate who promises to pass legislation that will respond to their ideals. If that is not followed we will have a repetition of what we have been going through during the past century. There will be an accentuation and intensification of the evils of the spoils system of our group politics.

Now, what results did we obtain? I attach most importance to the intangible and indefinite results that you cannot weigh, that you cannot measure. We awakened an interest, a permanent interest, in the social problem among Catholics, as we have been urged to do by the popes and the bishops. We introduced a lively discussion of these problems into Catholic societies. We established firm and friendly relationships between Catholic, Protestant, and Jew. These are a few of the intangible, but I think, invaluable, results of such a movement.

As for the more tangible and more definite results, I would only say that we were partly at least instrumental in having compulsory fire drills introduced in the factories in Ohio, in having certain occupations, morally and physically hazardous to women, prohibited. These were not of any far-reaching consequence, I am willing to admit. We failed in having the law prohibiting the employment of women at night passed. We did not succeed in having the bill providing for the regulation of children in street trades passed. We did not succeed in having the bill providing for a minimum wage for women workers passed. We did not expect it would be passed. We expect it is going to take several years until we succeed.

Now what have we done in the meantime? We continued to address Catholic audiences and others. We succeeded, for instance, in having the Knights of Columbus, who were assembled in state convention in Cincinnati last May, pass a resolution in favor of the minimum wage law and provide for the organization of a committee on social action in every council whose purpose it will be to support sane social legislation. We are collecting data showing just what it costs the working woman to live. For that purpose we circulated questionnaires among the students of our evening schools, and likewise among the ladies who were making a retreat at one of the academies near Cincinnati, and just before I left Cincinnati we were sending out literature to the candidates for the legislature on the minimum wage, asking them to declare their stand.

Now I would summarize the result of our efforts in this fashion: Organize in every organization that you belong to, or over which you exert any influence, a committee on social action whose main function will be the promotion of sane social legislation. With the approval of the Bishop try to establish a joint legislative committee in your city or diocese. With the advice of the Department of Social Action of the National Catholic Welfare Council, a committee by the way which renders very valuable assistance, select those laws which you think are of most pressing need and that offer promise of being enacted in the near future. Very nearly every legislative measure that was recommended in the bishops' program is incorporated in some bill that is now pending in Congress, and I wonder how many of us Catholics have ever given that matter any thought, how few of us have ever thought of urging our respective legislators to support such bills.

Cooperate with non-Catholic organizations; when possible affiliate with them; identify yourselves with them, that is as far as circumstances allow. Begin early with your campaign. Begin before the legislature is convened. Gain public opinion for your measure by the means that were outlined. See your opponents. Our big opponent was the Ohio Federation of Labor, but the chairman of our committee had a long discussion with the secretary of the federation, and finally obtained from him a promise that he would not oppose the bill if it came up. In fact, he held out hopes that he might support it. Get a prominent member who is really interested in your bill to introduce it.

The next point that I had intended to speak on is the enforcement of the laws. It is not sufficient to have measures enacted into law, but we must go a step further and see that they are enforced. We must support those public officials that do their duty by the people and who receive very little appreciation of their efforts and are frequently underpaid. We have a splendid staff on our Ohio Industrial Commission, but unfortunately, appropriations are not made to recompense these men properly, and the consequence is that we have lost a good number of the most efficient of our public servants; and, finally, secure for Catholics the benefits that much social legislation is designed to provide or secure.

Proceedings of the Sixth Biennial Meeting of the National Conference of Catholic Charities (Washington, D.C.: National Conference of Catholic Charities, 1920), 46–52. Printed with permission.

37. Helen P. McCormick, Assistant District Attorney and Chairman, Catholic Big Sisters, Brooklyn, N.Y., "Women's Interest in Social and Democratic Movements," 1920

... Our sex has been accused by some of not being able to get away from the partisan, the personal, and deal with the subject of government in the larger sense. The very exercise of the ballot, the contact with the problems of government, the realization that woman is a component part of the entire scheme of things will, without doubt, act as a great corrective. Every woman must grow socially and mentally if she devotes the thought that the good citizen should give to the question of government. As long as human nature is human nature there will be numbers of men as well as women who will assume the attitude of "let the other fellow do it," with dire results to themselves. They lack the vision to realize how closely the operation of the government functions to touch their everyday life and existence. We cannot live, breathe or have our being without coming into contact with some department of government. It naturally follows that for self-protection, if for no other reason, each citizen should express a direct say in the manner in which he is to be governed.

Years ago when to be a suffragist was to be a social pariah, a blue-stocking, a somewhat dangerous type of woman, women manifested their interest in all current movements to correct some social evil indirectly, through the vote of their husband or father or brother. Today in the United States, with twenty-seven million women possessing the presidential franchise, the opportunity for women to aid in the pressing problems of reconstruction and readjustment is infinite. Great good should come from this new element in the body politic, the woman's point of view....

Women's interest in democratic and social movements is a response to the urge of mother love, that is experienced by every normal woman, whether married or unmarried. It is a demonstration of her sense of fellowship to those in need of care or special considerations. Therefore the average woman's interest in social conditions will include those appertaining to the home, the family, and the children. This might appear at first sight to be a limited viewpoint, but upon examination we realize that it involves a large section of the social sores of the day. The home brings her into contact with the question of the high cost of living, the housing problem, etc. Children would lead to a consideration of the problems of the school system, relief and protective agencies, child labor. Industrial conditions would be of imminent concern to her as they affect her job or that of her husband....

As an articulate expression of the sentiment of large groups of working women toward the industrial problems of today the measures adopted by the First International Congress of Working Women, held in Washington in October, 1919, are of interest. The resolutions include clauses appertaining to the Eight-Hour Day and Forty-four-Hour Week, Child Labor, Maternity Insurance, Night Work, Unemployment, Hazardous Occupations, Immigration, and the Distribution of Raw Materials....

Men have, for the most part, won the shorter working day in industry by means of labor organizations. Women have been slow to unionize, and it has therefore been necessary for the state to regulate their hours of labor by legislation, in order to grant them the relief they craved. Judge Hiscock, writing the decision of the court in the case of *People v. Charles Schweinler Press*, upholding the constitutionality of state regulations of hours of labor for women employed in factories, said: "Protection of the health of women is a subject of special concern to the state. However confident a great number of people may be that in many spheres of activity, including that of the administration of government, woman is the full equal of man, no one doubts that as regards bodily strength and endurance she is the inferior, and that her health in the field of physical labor must be specially guarded by the state if it is to be preserved and if she is to continue successfully and healthfully to discharge the duties which nature has imposed upon her."

The average woman agrees and supports the working woman in her demand for the eight-hour day, the forty-four-hour week, and the prohibition of night work in industrial employment; primarily for the sake of the children that a great majority of these women will bear. Such children inevitably display in their deficiencies the unfortunate inheritance conferred upon them by physically broken-down mothers.

The principle of equal pay for equal work is so universally approved by the thinking woman that great strides in this direction have already been achieved,...[but] [t]he question of the living wage for women is still in the flux....Present economic conditions force millions of the women of this country into the industrial and business world. During the war, particularly, great numbers of women were recruited into industry to take the places left vacant by their husbands and brothers. These women rightly ask a living wage sufficient to meet their actual living expenses. They do not ask that this wage include provision for periods of unemployment, illness, or incapacity. The Minimum Wage, therefore, provides no luxuries, no rainy day fund, barely meets requirements of actual existence....

The Church has always upheld the temporal and spiritual welfare of women. The Church granted to woman her place in the sun long before the advent of the so-called modern theory of equal opportunity, irrespective of sex. But she does not subscribe to as ideal that state where millions of women, married as well as unmarried, are forced into industry to the detriment of the home. The mother should be permitted to remain in the home to safeguard the interests of the children, even if to effect this, state aid is required. No reasonable woman questions the fact that the child is the primary consideration of the state; that the very continuance of society is dependent upon him; that the child of today is the man of tomorrow. To keep the family intact — to give the child the benefit of home influences — through the use of state funds, is universally endorsed by child welfare workers. Widows' pensions have been established in a number of our States to grant this form of relief. Further expansion of this measure to cover cases involving women abandoned by their husbands, as well as those whose husbands are totally or partially incapacitated, has been recommended generally by women's organizations. This pension is not charity doled out to worthy widows, but the recognition of the value of the child as a potential factor in the development of the state itself.

Child labor, in this day and age, will not be tolerated, at least in America. First, because it is the sacred heritage of every child to enjoy the period of childhood, devoted to his mental, physical, and moral development. Secondly, because it is poor business for the country in need of stalwart citizen soldiers, and for employers in need of efficient employees physically able to meet the requirements of the work.

The question of raising the minimum entrance age into industry from fourteen to sixteen years, has been advocated by many thoughtful women. Before this becomes a reality it is necessary for all those interested to secure the enforcement of the principle of the family wage in industry. With poverty, that dread visitor, locked out from the homes of the workers, there can be no valid objection to the proposed change to sixteen years as the minimum age for entrance into the industrial world....

Woman's interest in social and democratic movements is only encompassed by those measures, principles, and plans that assure the progress, prosperity, and welfare of all the people, the nation, and the world. Her desire is to contribute something, however small and insignificant it may be, to this great work of social betterment, so that she may not have lived in vain.

Proceedings of the Sixth Biennial Meeting of the National Conference of Catholic Charities (Washington, D.C.: National Conference of Catholic Charities, 1920), 7–16. Printed with permission.

Part 3

1920–45

Introduction

The end of World War I ushered in a period of national letdown and a collective desire to slow or even reverse some of the fast-paced societal and political change of the previous epoch. Historians have interpreted the election of the McKinleyite conservative Warren G. Harding and his like-minded successor, Calvin Coolidge, as a manifestation of this conservative resurgence. Moreover, the forces of retrenchment seem to have strongly asserted themselves in the emergence of the Ku Klux Klan, the successful bid to restrict immigration, and the undercutting of much of the intent of regulatory reform of the previous era.

However, the cultural forces let loose by the tide of modernity continued to propel the nation in new directions. New technologies led the way, spurred by the rise of modern advertising. The creation of the new mass culture, typified by the popularity and widespread consumption of the automobile and the radio, had a significant effect on the shape of American life. America came into its own as a full-fledged consumer society in the 1920s — a social reality that made the Great Depression all the more intense. In many ways the good life seemed to be within the grasp of more and more Americans as a modest rise in real income boosted many into the widening middle class. The 1920s witnessed a considerable change in the role and status of women, who had only recently gotten the vote, the emergence of a noticeable youth culture, and the existence of a cadre of notorious but highly regarded artists and intellectuals who made a great deal of their disdain of American culture.

America spurned membership in the League of Nations, which Woodrow Wilson had helped to create, and in its official pronouncements and its unwillingness to cut the Gordian knot of war debts and reparations, the United States contributed substantially to subsequent European disorder and the rise of authoritarianism in Germany and elsewhere in Europe. America voluntarily downsized its military by drastic reductions in its naval strength. Nonetheless, Americans were anything but isolationist in their desire for trade, and throughout the 1920s they continued to hear news of Europe, travel abroad, and even worked with European powers to bring about a treaty which banned war as an instrument of national policy.

The prosperity of the 1920s was real but ephemeral, and because it did not extend to a wide enough segment of the general population, it was not sustainable. The collapse of the stock market in 1929 did not cause the Great Depression, but it was the starting gun for a series of bank failures and rippling economic disasters that plunged the nation into the deepest economic crisis of its history. By March 1933, one of every four Americans who could work was unemployed. Businesses and lives were ruined. Children picked their dinner out of garbage dumps in St. Louis while unpaid teachers in Chicago fainted in their classrooms for lack of food. The laissez-faire ideology that seemed so right for the prosperous 1920s was insufficient to meet the crisis. In one of the saddest ironies of his long career, President Herbert Hoover, whose humanitarian goodness had fed millions around the world, was unable and unwilling to grant handouts to people in the United States for fear that government aid would weaken their character.

Hoover was swept out of office in the Roosevelt landslide of 1932, and America ushered in a new era of government activism and energetic government. Roosevelt, a man of indeterminate ideology, had made pragmatism a political virtue. In a welter of initiatives designed to "do something" Roosevelt's New Deal attempted to regulate the industrial economy with codes of fair competition and fix farm prices through government subsidies. Roosevelt used the idled American labor force to build up the national infrastructure and imposed some long-overdue regulation on the capitalist system — if for no other reason than to save it from its own worst excesses. Roosevelt's signal accomplishment, the enactment of a program of social insurance for the unemployed and the elderly, was a watershed in American history. His support for the organization of industrial workers forged a major link between them and the Democratic Party and made them part of a larger coalition that propelled him to the White House four times and lasted long enough to ensure the election of several of his successors.

Yet Roosevelt, for all his charm and optimism, was a polarizing figure in American history and generated his share of bitter enemies on the left and right. The New Deals (there were at least two and possibly three) did not end the Great Depression, as historians are overly eager to note; rather, they created a climate of hope and an ambiance of forward movement which were indispensable to the human spirit. Whether they "worked" in a literal sense of lifting America out of high unemployment and financial malaise was to many irrelevant — they were something, anything, in an era of dust bowls, breadlines, and idle men and boys who had never known such inaction in their entire lives, and would carry the memory of it forever.

International affairs soon overwhelmed domestic concerns in the Depression decade. The rising tide of authoritarian government, which began soon after World War I in Rome, Warsaw, and Lisbon, reached its crest in Berlin in 1933. Under Hitler and his rubric of national salvation a new and aggressive Germany emerged, energized by the dictator's deft manipulation of the resentments of the past and the scapegoating of sectors of German society, communists and Jews, whom he drove from the fatherland or murdered. In eastern Asia, Japanese imperialists, imitating their Western counterparts, began to demand hegemony on the Chinese mainland for economic and cultural reasons. The rise of Germany and Japan as militant powers cast a long shadow over the late 1930s and eventually awakened self-preoccupied Americans to the reality that they could very well be alone in the world unless something were done to stop these rivals. Japan's war against China and Hitler's overt remilitarization and territorial demands gradually moved American public opinion behind a limited and then more engaged policy abroad. War erupted in Europe in September 1939, and as the summer of 1940 emerged, Britain stood alone against the German onslaught. Relations between Japan and the United States deteriorated rapidly, and Japan made the fateful decision to attempt to knock American military might off stride for enough time to secure a strong defensive perimeter around Japan's "Co-prosperity Sphere." The attack on Pearl Harbor aroused America to mobilize with a vengeance, transforming its peacetime economy in short order and supplying not only American needs but those of Russian, British, and Nationalist Chinese allies.

The homefront underwent its share of changes. Millions of armed men and women were scattered throughout the country, giving them a mobility they had never before known. Women entered the workforce in large numbers, and rationing and ideological mobilization in behalf of American democracy kept the homefront strong during the long and difficult war years. During the war, African American voices compelled a hearing when they threatened to launch an embarrassing march on Washington to protest job discrimination in government-contracted plants. The war for democracy and against Nazi racism renewed energies to push for full rights for black Americans, many of whom were fighting and working in segregated units.

Roosevelt managed to sustain a difficult and sometimes fractious American alliance with the British and the Russians. All the while each of these three major powers was scheming and working behind the scenes to advance its own postwar configuration of the world. Roosevelt played the game of power politics as well as his two rivals, and in his better moments he tried to resuscitate the dream of his old friend Wilson with the creation of the United Nations, which would try to defuse future wars. American troops fought in North Africa and Sicily and stormed the shores of Normandy and the sands of Iwo Jima and Guadalcanal. Douglas MacArthur "returned" to his beloved Philippines. Hitler and his mistress, Eva Braun, committed suicide in the Führer Bunker before vengeful Russian troops found them. Mussolini was hung upside-down with his mistress, Clara Petacci, as vitriolic Italian partisans beat and spat upon his mutilated body. The war ended in the flash of nuclear sunburst over two Japanese cities as the atomic age released its fury. A broken and divided world, full of suspicion but also ripe with hope, emerged from the ashes.

Church and Society

Catholic political strength had been growing on the local, state, and national level for many decades. Education remained a flagship issue; birth control and child labor were serious challenges for the Catholic leadership; and the anti-Catholic activities of the Ku Klux Klan in the 1920s challenged Catholics socially and politically in a number of states. Catholics debated among themselves the practicalities of their "place" in American society and politics. The real test of Catholic acceptance into the American mainstream came in 1928 during the candidacy of New York governor Al Smith.

Although Catholic organizations were often characterized as a kind of cultural ghetto, Catholics nonetheless sought to preserve and maintain their identity in American society. Building on earlier ethnic traditions, Catholics placed renewed emphasis on the education and social formation of young people – including adolescents who were now attending high school in greater and greater numbers. As they had in the past, Catholics jealously asserted the primacy of the family – not the government – to make decisions about the direction and destiny of young people. This explains in part some of the spirited resistance to a federal department of education and efforts to regulate child labor.

38. Rev. Francis J. Walsh, Mt. St. Mary's Seminary, Cincinnati, to Rt. Rev. Monsignor Edward A. Pace, Catholic University, Washington, D.C., 20 November 1920

Dear Monsignor:

I laid the matter mentioned in your communication ["the Bill on Federal control of Education and, especially, on Physical training"] before such Catholic educators in our section as I was able to reach, and also presented it to the consideration of the Archbishop of Cincinnati. Some are opposed to the whole principle of the measures proposed, and characterized it as a return to the regime of Lycurgus. Those engaged in the practical work of dealing with children were not so iconoclastic, and said that if we get our just share, preserve our moral teaching, and keep our schools free from the pestering influences of half-baked doctors and fanatical females, good results would follow. There was no unreserved approval.

Like every other educational measure, this one presents to Catholics the issue of appearing to oppose measures which may make for the general good, solely because they have an established educational system which is shut off from the financial aid afforded. Thus they are compelled to do for others what they are unable to do for themselves. On general questions of polity, such as the feasibility of National aid for the States in education, there can be no distinctly Catholic attitude, any more than on the question of the tariff. Opposition which may develop among Catholics will be on the grounds of Americanism, which they share with all their fellow-citizens, or on the ulterior basis of relief from contributing an undue amount to special institutions like schools, in whose benefits they do not participate.

A Catholic attitude as such will be based on the safeguarding of their religious interests, and indirectly, their economic interests. Religious interests require the existence and Catholic control of their schools. This control is inclusive only so far as it requires the teaching of Catholic belief and practice. Anything else the State desires they will readily adopt. It is exclusive in that it will not admit anything opposed to faith or morals, or that may in any way weaken either.

We must therefore oppose any bill whose operation would lead to such interference, or open the way for it. Further, on general economic grounds we can stand in opposition to the assumption by the government of burdens greater than it can carry, such as the effort to do in every school what is possible only here and there, or only possible by the complete devotion of parent to child which springs from paternal solicitude or motherly love in the family. Catholics are concerned with the burden placed upon them by educational measures whose intrinsic and general worth they are not inclined to question; this burden is unfair unless without sacrificing their religious interests they are enabled to share in the advantages which others will obtain. All measures for luxurious schools, special training for public school teachers, physical training limited to public schools, etc., have this defect. We have an existent, public and in many instances, free school system, erected for the attainment of genuine American ideals. If others have special ideals, they must foot their own bills; and for results achieved the government should pay all or none. This position makes it difficult for Catholics to see how they can lend help to any measure involving the expenditure of millions of public funds, a goodly share of which they must pay, unless it is made plain to them that without meeting impossible conditions, they can partake in the benefits....

In common with all our fellow citizens we are interested in the welfare of the public schools. And especially when a measure seems called for, we are anxious to see it well drawn, and of such kind that our concern for our fellow citizens and for ourselves will be best rewarded. Hence in reference to Senate Bill 3750, and H.R. 12652, the following may be advanced:

1) Physical training, as is mentioned in the Pastoral Letter of the Bishops [1919], is a part of education.

2) Certain elements of these bills go beyond physical training and reach into moral. Section 2, H.R. 12652, mentions "such desirable moral and social qualities" etc. Now moral training must be motivated; and there is no unity among our citizens on the ultimate motivation of morals, nor even on the formulation of moral principles beyond those concerned with public order.

3) Moral training is inseparable from religion; the introduction of any mere humanitarian code is offensive to revealed religion; it is the substitution of another natural religion, and this by act of Congress.

4) The provision for periodical medical examination is not clear. For it does not state whether this inspection will be compulsory; nor whether the recommendation of the examiner must be carried out under penalty. Just now the question of compulsory vaccination is agitated in the public schools of Cincinnati; certain parents refuse to abide by the ruling of the Board of Education, supported by the Board of Health. Such measures open the way to vast difficulties.

5) This bill should be limited to providing the means of physical development. If the means are provided so that all may use them, practically all will use them.

6) Only State normal schools are included in this bill (i.e., State institutions). Now does this mean State supported and controlled, or State recognized? Any normal school whose efficiency the State recognizes should share in the distribution of these national funds. The basis should be the number of students attending.

7) There is a danger lurking in the bill that the public schools will become the laboratory of faddists, — advocates of certain theories of eugenics, of divorce-at-will, of teaching problems of sex at an early age, etc. There is no specification of methods for teaching self-control, etc. Now we are opposed to the introduction into public schools of the doctrines of Lenine [sic].

8) There was a saying current in the army: "if you cannot be moral, be clean." Bathing and virtue were made synonymous. Now Doctor James Walsh says in his "Psychotherapy," p. 481, "usually the great bathing nations have been most sexually divagant [sic]." This is not an argument against cleanliness, but it is an argument against placing it before, and not next to, godliness.

9) If practical instruction in the care of the body and the principles of health are to include lectures such as were given in the army under this or some similar caption; — signs and notices such as during the war were placed in every Pullman; pictures and movies of the so-called sexually instructive character; — then it were far better that they were not so much as named among us. Such a proposal, or even the danger thereof, brings us to a moral issue on which we cannot yield.

10) That some such program is in the offing, I am led to believe by the analogy drawn from the army, and the argument from the facts revealed in the draft.

In conclusion, there is no objection to a general bill (i.e., one for all schools) which will aid in providing playgrounds, instructors in physical education by means of drills, exercises and the like. Several of my students had held positions as such instructors. Nor is their difficulty in any course involving the warning of children on the danger of diseases of various kinds. That the government should undertake the motivation of morality is impossible; hence as matters are, we should object to any investigation of the conditions among our children other than one in which we can safeguard their morals. A hygienic [*sic*] investigation of our local public and parochial schools has just been made by the local Board of Health, and with no evil consequences; in fact, benefits have resulted. The best modification perhaps that could be secured would be to include our own normal school in the reckoning for the distribution of the funds, and in their distribution afterwards.

Sincerely yours,
Francis J. Walsh

> Papers of the National Catholic Welfare Conference, Department of Education, Archives of the Catholic University of America, Washington, D.C. Printed with permission.

39. Rt. Rev. Alexander Christie, Archbishop of Oregon City, to Rev. John J. Burke, General Secretary, National Catholic Welfare Council, 13 July 1922

I am writing you upon a matter of vital and urgent importance, and one to which I beg to ask your immediate and best attention. I presume you know of the campaign that is upon us here in Oregon in the matter of our Catholic schools. In November the people will vote upon the adoption of an initiative Bill known generally as the "compulsory school law," or "the compulsory education law." The title of the measure is designedly deceptive, for we already have compulsory public school education in this State. The purpose of this Bill is to make the public school educational system an exclusive monopoly, by requiring all children between the ages of six and sixteen to attend the public schools and no others. This of course will forever close every private school in the State and destroy our whole system of Catholic parochial schools, built up by many years of labor and sacrifice and at great cost. The proposed legislation was intended to accomplish that very end, and unless we make a determined and systematic campaign against it there is every prospect of its becoming a law by the popular vote.

The Ku Klux [*sic*], aided by all other anti-Catholic influences, are behind the Bill, and in the recent Primaries they came very near to nominating their candidate for Governor; in fact there is now pending a contest by the Ku Klux candidate for a recount of the vote in order, if possible, to procure his nomination.

I am preparing to organize and prosecute the most [serious effort] to defeat the iniquitous measure at the polls. But we must have immediate and substantial aid in the way of money. It will take a large sum to properly canvass the State and present our literature and put capable speakers in the field. This is a small Catholic community in point of population, and our people are for the most part poor. The State is large in area and sparsely settled, which makes campaigning difficult and expensive. It is first necessary, if possible, to reach every voter in the State with printed and written matter covering all phases of the argument for and against the Bill, exposing its fraudulent purpose, its destructive effects, its un-American spirit, and the character of the agencies and motives that are urging it. The secular press must be furnished all the literature on our side that it will accept and publish; circulars, leaflets, pamphlets, letters and every known means of publicity must be used liberally; a general office must be equipped and maintained for the next four months, and during the last 30 days or more of the campaign public speakers must be sent to every town and city in the State.

The fight must not be lost, for it means not only our ruin here if the measure becomes a law, but its adoption will signalize a similar campaign in every other State where this propaganda of anti-Catholicism exists, which is in half the States of the Union. Oregon has been selected as the weakest link in the chain of States, and as the favorite battle-ground of radical and freak legislation. It was here that the primary election and the initiative and referendum were first adopted in the United States, and from here these innovations have spread over the whole country. It will be the same with this law to close private schools. If it carries in Oregon it will gain tremendous momentum in other States in the West, and hence the desperate effort its advocates are making to win the election, and the equal desperation with which we must oppose it.

This is the situation. It is critical, imminent and unescapable. We have a fair chance to defeat this Bill if we are furnished with proper financial aid by the other Catholics of the country, and especially if the National Welfare Council [sic] will at once send us money in a substantial amount. There is no time to be lost, for the work is large, complicated and difficult. It must be pushed promptly, persistently and with every effective means in our reach.

Please lay this matter at once before the proper authorities of the National Welfare Council, and urge upon them the absolute necessity and vital emergency of the situation.

Papers of the National Catholic Welfare Conference, Department of Education, Archives of the Catholic University of America, Washington, D.C. Printed with permission.

40. Rev. John A. Ryan, "Comments on the *Christian Constitution of States*," 1922[1]

...[T]he State, constituted as it is, is clearly bound to act up to the manifold and weighty duties linking it to God, by the public profession of religion. Nature and reason, which command every individual devoutly to worship God in holiness, because we belong to Him and must return to Him since from Him we came, bind also the civil community by a like law.... Since,

1. The relevant passage from Leo XIII's encyclical *Immortale Dei,* 1 November 1885, appears in italics below.

then, no one is allowed to be remiss in the service due to God, and since the chief duty of all men is to cling to religion in both its teaching and practice,...it is a public crime to act as though there were no God. So, too, is it a sin in the State not to have care for religion, as a something beyond its scope, or as of no practical benefit; or out of many forms of religion to adopt that one which chimes in with the fancy; for we are bound absolutely to worship God in that way which he has shown to be His will. All who rule, therefore, should hold in honor the holy name of God, and one of their chief duties must be to favor religion, to protect it, to shield it under the credit and sanction of the laws, and neither to organize nor enact any measure that may compromise its safety.... Now it cannot be difficult to find out which is the true religion, if only it be sought with an earnest and unbiassed mind; for proofs are abundant and striking. We have, for example, the fulfillment of prophecies; miracles in great number; the rapid spread of the faith in the midst of enemies and in the face of overwhelming obstacles; the witness of martyrs, and the like. From all these it is evident that the only true religion is the one established by Jesus Christ Himself, and which he committed to His Church to protect and propagate....

3. Public Profession of Religion by the State

To the present generation this is undoubtedly "a hard saying." The separation of Church and State, which obtains substantially in the majority of countries, is generally understood as forbidding the State to make "a public profession of religion." Nevertheless, the logic of Pope Leo's argument is unassailable. Men are obliged to worship God, not only as individuals, but also as organized groups. Societies have existence and functions over and above the existence and functions of their individual members. Therefore, they are dependent upon God for their corporate existence and functions, and as moral persons owe corporate obedience to His laws, formal recognition of His authority, and appropriate acts of worship. To deny these propositions is to maintain the illogical position that man owes God religious worship under only one aspect of his life, in only one department of his life....

The State cannot avoid taking an attitude toward religion. In practice that attitude will necessarily be positive, either for or against. There can be no such actual policy as impartial indifference.

This proposition receives further confirmation from the attitude of those States which refrain from any formal acceptance of religion in theory, and yet accord it some measure of recognition in practice. The policy of the United States is the most conspicuous and significant. Our Federal and State constitutions forbid the legal establishment of any form of religion, thereby ensuring the separation of Church and State, and apparently making inevitable a policy of neutrality or indifference. Nevertheless, our Federal and State governments have never adopted such a policy. Their attitude has been one of positive friendliness toward religion. Some of the manifestations and expressions of this policy are: The appointment of an annual day of public thanksgiving by the President of the United States and the Governors of the several States; the employment of chaplains to open with prayer the sessions of the National and State legislatures; the provision of chaplains for the Army and Navy; the exemption of church property from taxation; the general policy of promoting the interests of religion; and many other acts and practices, for example, the recent action of the school board in New York City in placing the school buildings at the disposal of the various denominations for the purpose of giving religious instructions.

These institutions and practices are in fact what Pope Leo calls "a public profession of religion." As compared with the degree of recognition accorded in a formal union of Church and State, they are, indeed, feeble and inconspicuous. Nevertheless, they do exemplify the principle. "The public profession of religion," is susceptible of very many forms and degrees, from the adoption, support, and toleration of only one creed, to the slight manifestations of recognition shown by countries which do not go even as far as the United States.

It is not here contended that the latter kind of attitude is normal, or desirable in the abstract. The point to be kept in mind is that the principle laid down by Pope Leo is not to be contrasted with the policy of separation of Church and State. His principle is directly and universally opposed only to a policy of specious neutrality, which in practice is always a policy of hostility. To assume that "the public profession of religion" always calls for something radically different from the arrangement obtaining in the United States is to be guilty of confused thinking and to ignore important facts of experience....

4. Attitude of the State toward the Church

But Pope Leo goes further. He declares that the State must not only "have care for religion," but recognize the *true* religion. This means the form of religion professed by the Catholic Church. It is a thoroughly logical position. If the State is under moral compulsion to profess and promote religion, it is obviously obliged to profess and promote only the religion that is true; for no individual, no group of individuals, no society, no State is justified in supporting error or in according to error the same recognition as to truth....

The principle that he is here defending has complete and unconditional application only to Catholic States. Between these and the Catholic Church the normal relation is that of formal agreement and mutual support; in other words, what is generally known as the union of Church and State....

All that is essentially comprised in the union of Church and State can be thus formulated: The State should officially recognize the Catholic religion as the religion of the commonwealth; accordingly it should invite the blessing and the ceremonial participation of the Church for certain important public functions, as the opening of legislative sessions, the erection of public buildings, etc., and delegate its officials to attend certain of the more important festival celebrations of the Church; it should recognize and sanction the laws of the Church; and it should protect the rights of the Church, and the religious as well as the other rights of the Church's members.

Does State recognition of the Catholic religion necessarily imply that no other religion should be tolerated? Much depends upon circumstances and much depends upon what is meant by toleration. Neither unbaptized persons nor those born into a non-Catholic sect, should ever be coerced into the Catholic Church. This would be fundamentally irrational, for belief depends upon the will and the will is not subject to physical compulsion. Should such persons be permitted to practice their own form of worship? If these are carried on within the family, or in such an inconspicuous manner as to be an occasion neither of scandal nor of perversion to the faithful, they may properly be tolerated by the State. At least, this is the approved Catholic doctrine concerning the religious rites of the non-baptized. Only those religious practices of unbelievers which are contrary to the natural law, such as idolatry, human sacrifice and debauchery, should be repressed. The best indication of the Church's attitude on this question is the toleration and protection accorded all through the Middle Ages to Judaism and Jewish worship by the Popes in their capacity of civil rulers of the Papal States. The same principle regarding freedom of worship seems fairly applicable to baptized persons who were born into a non-Catholic sect. For their participation in false worship does not necessarily imply a wilful affront to the true Church nor a menace to public order or social welfare....

Quite distinct from the performance of false religious worship and preaching to the members of the erring sect, is the propagation of the false doctrine among Catholics. This could become a source of injury, a positive menace, to the religious welfare of true believers. Against such an evil they have a right of protection by the Catholic State....

Superficial champions of religious liberty will promptly and indignantly denounce the foregoing propositions as the essence of intolerance. They are intolerant, but not therefore unreasonable. Error has not the same rights as truth. Since the profession and practice of error are contrary to human welfare, how can error have rights? How can the voluntary toleration of error be justified? As we have already pointed out, the men who defend the principle of toleration for all varieties of religious opinion, assume either that all religions are equally true or that the true cannot be distinguished from the false. On no other ground is it logically possible to accept the theory of indiscriminate and universal toleration....

Such in its ultimate rigor and complete implications is the Catholic position concerning the alliance that should exist between the Church and a Catholic State. While its doctrinal premises will be rejected by convinced non-Catholics, its logic cannot be denied by anyone who accepts the unity of religious truth. If there is only one true religion, and if its possession is the most important good in life for States as well as individuals, then the public profession, protection, and promotion of this religion and the legal prohibition of all direct assaults upon it, becomes one of the most obvious and fundamental duties of the State. For it is the business of the State to safeguard and promote human welfare in all departments of life....

In practice, however, the foregoing propositions have full application only to the completely Catholic State. This means a political community that is either exclusively, or almost exclusively, made up of Catholics. In the opinion of Father Pohle [a German theologian], "there is good reason to doubt if there still exists a purely Catholic State in the world." The propositions of Pope Pius IX condemning the toleration of non-Catholic sects do not now, says Father Pohle, "apply even to Spain or the South American republics, to say nothing of countries possessing a greatly mixed population." He lays down the following general rule: "When several religions have firmly established themselves and taken root in the same territory, nothing else remains for the State than either to exercise tolerance towards them all, or, as conditions exist today, to make complete religious liberty for individuals and religious bodies a principle of government."[2] Father Moulart makes substantially the same statement: "In a word, it is necessary to extend political toleration to dissenting sects which exist in virtue of a fact historically accomplished."[3]

The reasons which justify this complete religious liberty fall under two heads: First, rational expediency, inasmuch as the attempt to proscribe or hamper the peaceful activities of established religious groups would be productive of more harm than good; second, the positive provisions of religious liberty found in the constitutions of most modern States. To quote Father Pohle once more: "If religious freedom has been accepted and sworn to as a fundamental law in a constitution, the obligation to show this tolerance is binding in conscience." The principle of tolerance, he continues, cannot be disregarded even by Catholic States "without violation of oaths and loyalty, and without violent internal convulsions."[4]

But constitutions can be changed, and non-Catholic sects may decline to such a point that the political proscription of them may become feasible and expedient. What protection would they then have against a Catholic State? The latter could logically tolerate only such religious activities as were confined to the members of the dissenting group. It could not permit them to carry on general propaganda nor accord their organization certain privileges that had formerly been extended to all religious corporations, for example, exemption from taxation. While all this is very true in logic and in theory, the event of its practical realization in any State or country is so remote in time and in probability that no practical man will let it disturb his equanimity or affect his attitude toward those who differ from him in religious faith. It is true, indeed, that some zealots and bigots will continue to attack the Church because they fear that some five thousand years hence the United States may become overwhelmingly Catholic and may then restrict the freedom of non-

---

2. *Catholic Encyclopedia*, s.v. "Toleration."
3. *L'Eglise et l'etat* (Paris, 1887), 311.
4. Pohle, "Toleration."

Catholic denominations. Nevertheless, we cannot yield up the principles of eternal and unchangeable truth in order to avoid the enmity of such unreasonable persons. Moreover, it would be a futile policy; for they would not think us sincere.

Therefore, we shall continue to profess the true principles of the relations between Church and State, confident that the great majority of our fellow citizens will be sufficiently honorable to respect our devotion to truth, and sufficiently realistic to see that the danger of religious intolerance toward non-Catholics in the United States is so improbable and so far in the future that it should not occupy their time or attention....

> John A. Ryan, D.D., LL.D., and Moorhouse F. X. Millar, S.J., *The State and the Church* (New York: Macmillan, 1922), 29–39. (Footnotes in original.)

41. Cardinal William H. O'Connell [Boston] to Bishop Edmund F. Gibbons [Albany], 14 October 1924, and Reply, 21 October 1924; and Cardinal William H. O'Connell to Mrs. Thomas W. Proctor, Boston, 15 December 1924

My Dear Bishop: There have been complaints constantly coming in to me that some of the agents of the N.C.W.C. [National Catholic Welfare Conference] are sending out propaganda in favor of that nefarious and bolshevik amendment falsely labelled as Child Labor. Those named as being tied up with some of the dangerous influences at the Capital (mainly jobbers of course) are John Ryan, John Burke[1] and Mrs. Regan.[2]

How any one who knows Catholic principles and practice can have any part in this infamous proceeding is a mystery. Though it has been clear to me for some time that Ryan is making straight for trouble as slyly as he can, Burke I simply do not trust and Miss Regan is of course one of his creatures, and a rather impertinent specimen of modern social worker.

But of course the main thing is that this stuff bordering and not always even bordering on red socialism is credited to us — the hierarchy. I have openly denounced it and so have all our priests here.

Unless something is done and done quickly we shall be obliged to declare frankly that these people do not represent us or our views, but having taken the rather loose reins out of the hands of the bishops who trust them, they are drawing fast to a public condemnation.

I know my dear Bishop how far removed you are from approving all this. But may I say quite frankly that unless some check is [illegible] especially in the matter of legislation, which has been confided to your prudent and capable hands, we shall soon be facing a demand for serious explanations — and that would not be pleasant for any of us.

---

1. The general secretary of the National Catholic Welfare Conference.
2. The secretary of the National Council of Catholic Women.

My dear Bishop I love you and I have the fullest confidence in you. I entreat you to put an end to this matter by the authority vested in you by all of us. Give some clear talk to this coterie and tie their hands before they get a rapping that they will regret.

Faithfully, W. Card. O'Connell

•

Your Eminence:

Your kind letter of Oct. 14 was forwarded to me to the extreme northern part of the diocese when I was confirming last week, missed me by a day, and was returned to me in Albany. Only now I have read it and I wish to thank you for calling my attention to the so-called Child Labor Amendment and the activities in its behalf by some of our employees.

I assure you I was not aware of all this. In fact at our board meetings no mention was ever made of this subject, and nobody has ever intimated to me that any of our office personnel was working for the passage of the Amendment.

I shall write at once to Fr. Burke, Miss Regan, Bp. Muldoon (Social Action), and Bp. Schrembs (Lay Organizations) and caution them against coming out in any way in favor of the Child Labor business, and appearing to commit the N.C.W.C. to its favor. If I may suggest to your Eminence, a line from you to Bp. Schrembs and Bp. Muldoon to keep their departments free from the confrontation, would be very effective. I think I can control the department of laws and legislation. There may be danger that the Women's and Men's organization at their coming convention would adopt a resolution on the question, not realizing its full import.

Respectfully, Edmund F. Gibbons, Bishop of Albany

•

Dear Mrs. Proctor:

I have received your communication of December 12th relative to the *Child Labor Amendment* which quite recently failed of ratification on Referendum here in Massachusetts.

The Electorate of this State has in this particular instance, as often times in the past, unmistakably declared itself for the preservation of these principles of individual right and of local self-government not unwisely granted to our people by the Constitution itself.

Beneath this measure, couched as it is in apparently innocuous language, lurks a grave menace to family life, parental control and the sovereignty of the individual States. Under the guise of Child Labor regulation the individual States are asked to hand over to the Federal Government powers of a nature it never possessed before. The granting of such unlimited power would mean control of both skilled and unskilled labor performed by minors under eighteen years of age. For parental control it would substitute the will of Congress and the dicta of a centralized bureaucracy more in keeping with communism than the base-rock principles of American government.

That there is a subtile spirit abroad to overthrow the Constitution of our country no one who is in the least familiar with national affairs can reasonably call in question. One successful assault on this sacred bulwark of our rights and liberties will but serve to embolden the enemies of Constitutional government to redouble their efforts for still further conquests in their frenzied campaign of destruction. Now is the most opportune time to strike back in no unmistakable manner.

The character of the propaganda made use of by the proponents of this bill is the more dangerous because of its utter deceitfulness. The so-called *Child Labor Amendment* is a fair example of this; apparently harmless or even beneficial, but actually in its bald reality destructive of the most sacred rights both of the individual and the state. The spirit which pervades the whole movement is communistic and as such destructive of true Americanism.

Very sincerely yours, W. Cardinal O'Connell

Archives of the Archdiocese of Boston, R. G. III. G Chancellor's office: Subject Files. Printed with permission.

42. Rev. John A. Ryan, "Present Position of the Child Labor Amendment," February and March 1925

Part I

This subject has two phases: the position of the Amendment in the state legislatures and its position in public opinion. As regard the first phase, the story is soon told. The states of Arizona, Arkansas and California have ratified the Amendment, while at least sixteen have refused to ratify. By the time this article appears in print, additions will have been made to both these categories. One does not run any risk by prophesying that the Amendment will not receive favorable action from more than a dozen states during the legislative year of 1925. On the other hand, rejection of the Amendment by any state, or any number of states, does not operate to prevent favorable action by those states at some future legislative session. The Amendment remains before the states for ratification until it receives the assent of the necessary three-fourths, or until it is withdrawn by Congress, a very improbable contingency, or until it ceases to command public interest.

The status of the Amendment in public opinion is a much more complex and debatable subject. Speaking summarily, we may safely say that the general attitude of the public toward it is at present unfavorable. The principal cause of this condition is probably to be found in the fact that the opponents of the Amendment began their campaign much earlier than its advocates. From the beginning they have been better organized and have had more money at their disposal than the groups that are fighting for ratification of the Amendment. The manufacturing groups and other industrial groups have had an effective organization in most of the important states for several months. Organized groups of manufacturers and prominent individuals in these groups remain the most active, the most powerful and the most effective element in the opposition....

No legitimate reason can be advanced for condemning the activity of manufacturers any more than that of any other group of citizens, either in favor of or against the Amendment. What all honest persons have a right to criticize in this connection is the mendacious and misleading propaganda which has emanated from the opposition. Outside of war-time, it has been without parallel in this country. Neither in amount, nor in recklessness, nor in downright untrustworthiness has any propaganda for or against any other political measure equaled the propaganda against the Child Labor Amendment. The extent to which the public, even many of the more intelligent sections of the public, has credulously accepted this mass of half-truths and falsehoods, is a sad commentary on the ability of the public to protect itself against organized deceptive argumentation and publicity....

Nevertheless, it is but fair to point out that large groups in our population were predisposed to consider favorably arguments and statements against giving to the federal government the power to regulate child labor. The Prohibition Amendment, and particularly the Volstead Act, have produced so much displeasure and irritation over the extension of federal power that hundreds of thousands of our citizens have become set against any further steps along this way. They think of federal regulation of child labor as another annoying interference with their local affairs, and they visualize another horde of disagreeable enforcement agents. The Child Labor Amendment is likewise regarded unfavorably by the hundreds of thousands of persons who are opposed to federal control of education. They assume that if federalization is bad in the education of the child, it would likewise be an evil thing in the matter of his labor and employment. Both of these great groups have become prejudiced against any extension whatever of federal control or federal legislative activity....

Therefore, the propaganda against the Amendment was sown, in large part, upon a peculiarly fruitful soil....

It is satisfactory to record, however, a change for the better in this respect. The most extreme and most untruthful arguments and statements against the Amendment are now heard only infrequently. Such is the case with the assertion that the Amendment is Socialistic, or Sovietistic, that it would bring about the nationalization of children, that it would enable the federal government to control education, that it makes possible a new and very great interference with the home, and that it would automatically prevent all persons under eighteen years of age from working....

As already noted, most of the foregoing invalid and fantastic objections either originated with or received their principal publicity from powerful economic interests, whose motives in giving them currency were evidently selfish. This obvious fact should have suggested caution to all intelligent persons who were asked to accept this sort of propaganda. Nevertheless, the propaganda was taken on faith, without question, for several months, by large groups of persons who are generally accustomed to exercise discrimination which they failed to exercise in this instance....

Part II

...Not one of the difficulties and objections which we have been considering has any objective validity. Not one of them will provide any fair-minded and intelligent person with a sufficient reason for opposing the Child Labor Amendment. There is, however, an objection which has considerable merit and which to many impartial and competent persons seems adequate to justify an attitude of opposition. Whether it is really adequate, is mainly a question of alternative evils. It is the question of whether the evil of existing child labor is greater or less than the evil of increasing central control. Evidently the answer to this question depends upon subjective judgments and the antecedent attitude taken toward a political problem on the one hand and a social problem on the other. Hence, there is ample room for honest difference of opinion.

The proposed Amendment would take some power from the states and confer it upon the federal government. Other things being equal, local control is preferable to national control. This is a general proposition which is established by universal political experience. State laws are better supported than federal laws because they have the advantage of local interest and local knowledge. As a rule, the people of any state regard the laws which their legislature has enacted as more intimately their own than the laws which have been passed by a Congress, of which their representatives form but a small proportion. Again, there is a danger that state child labor laws will come to be neglected or disregarded if federal laws are placed side by side with them. The task of enforcing child labor enactments may be passed over mainly, if not entirely, to the agents of the federal government. This is but another phase of the lack of local interest and local support. Finally, federal administration of the law in a country as large as ours, easily becomes unduly expensive, difficult, and ineffective.

Such is the objection in bare outline. It is formidable, but it ought not to be confused with extravagant assertions to the effect that the Child Labor Amendment would so diminish local self-government and so enhance centralized power as to destroy the constitutional balance between the federal government and the state governments; nor with the wild assertion that the Amendment would entail the creation of a vast bureaucracy, exercising despotic power over local affairs. The amount of power which the Amendment would transfer from the states to the Congress is relatively so small and the authority of federal administrative and enforcement officers would necessarily be so restricted by any law conforming to the terms of the Amendment that these dangers will not terrify any discriminating person....

Nevertheless, the objection is sufficiently impressive to put the burden of proof upon those who contend that the Child Labor Amendment is necessary.

What is the nature of the proof? How great is the evil of child labor which the states have failed to abolish? Bearing in mind that the census figures are probably too low, since the census was taken at a time when the second federal child labor act was in effect, we note that in 1920 there were 185,337 children of 10 to 15 years of age, inclusive, employed in manufacturing and mechanical industries.... With regard to the deficiencies in the state child labor laws, it is sufficient to observe that eleven states allow children under sixteen to work from nine to eleven hours a day; that four states do not prohibit night work for children under sixteen; that some eight or nine states permit children of twelve years of age to work in stores; that thirty-five states do not adequately prohibit child labor in dangerous occupations up to the age of eighteen; that fourteen states fail to reach the sixteen year standard; and that five states have no restrictions whatever for child labor in such occupations;... and that finally in several states the laws that exist are very poorly enforced, for example, one state is said to have only one enforcement officer....

So much for the one valid objection to the Amendment, and for the facts and consideration offered in reply. My own view is that the evil is sufficiently great to justify the ratification of the Amendment. Whether a federal law should be enacted immediately after that event, may fairly be regarded as a separate question. It would be a question for Congress to consider carefully in light of all the facts. To put the matter in the most moderate terms, there is sufficient indication of the need for federal action to warrant giving to Congress the requisite power. That is the only question that is now before the American people.

Part 1 from *Catholic Charities Review* 9 (February 1925): 56–59; part 2 from *Catholic Charities Review* 9 (March 1925): 98–100. Printed with permission.

43. *Pierce v. Society of Sisters,* June 1925

These appeals are from decrees, based upon undenied allegations, which granted preliminary orders restraining appellants from threatening or attempting to enforce the Compulsory Education Act adopted November 7, 1922, under the initiative provision of her Constitution by the voters of Oregon (Jud. Code, §266). They present the same points of law; there are no controverted questions of fact. Rights said to be guaranteed by the federal Constitution were specially set up, and appropriate prayers asked for their protection.

The challenged Act, effective September 1, 1926, requires every parent, guardian or other person having control or charge or custody of a child between eight and sixteen years to send him "to a public school for the period of time a public school shall be held during the current year" in the district where the child resides; and failure to do so is declared a misdemeanor.... The manifest purpose is to compel general attendance at public schools by normal children between eight and sixteen, who have not completed the eighth grade. And without doubt enforcement of the statue would seriously impair, perhaps destroy, the profitable features of appellees' business, and greatly diminish the value of their property.

Appellee, the Society of Sisters,[1] is an Oregon corporation, organized in 1880, with power to care for orphans, educate and instruct youth, establish and maintain academies or schools, and acquire necessary real and personal property. It has long devoted its property and effort to the secular and religious education and care of children, and has acquired the valuable good-will of many parents and guardians. It conducts interdependent primary and high schools and junior colleges, and maintains orphanages for the custody and control of children between eight and sixteen. In its primary schools many children between those ages are taught the subjects usually pursued in Oregon public schools during the first eight years. Systematic religious instruction and moral training according to the tenets of the Roman Catholic Church are also regularly provided. All courses of study, both temporal and religious, contemplate continuity of training under appellee's charge; the primary schools are essential to the system and the most profitable. It owns valuable buildings, especially constructed and equipped for school purposes. The business is remunerative — the annual income from primary schools exceeds thirty thousand dollars — and the successful conduct of this requires long-time contracts with teachers and parents. The Compulsory Education Act of 1922 has already caused the withdrawal from its schools of children who would otherwise continue, and their income has steadily declined. The appellants, public officers, have proclaimed their purpose strictly to enforce the statute.

After setting out the above facts the Society's bill alleges that the enactment conflicts with the right of parents to choose schools where their children will receive appropriate mental and religious training, the right of the child to influence the parents' choice of a school, the right of schools and teachers therein to engage in a useful business or profession, and is accordingly repugnant to the Constitution and void. And, further, that unless enforcement of the measure is enjoined the corporation's business and property will suffer irreparable injury. . . .

The inevitable practical result of enforcing the Act under consideration would be destruction of appellees' primary schools, and perhaps all other private primary schools for normal children within the State of Oregon. These parties are engaged in a kind of undertaking not inherently harmful, but long regarded as useful and meritorious. Certainly there is nothing in the present records to indicate that they have failed to discharge their obligations to patrons, students, or the State. And there are no peculiar circumstances or present emergencies which demand extraordinary measures relative to primary education.

---

1. The Sisters of the Holy Names of Jesus and Mary, founded in Canada, first came to Oregon in October 1859. They were the first religious congregation of women to make a permanent settlement in Oregon.

Under the doctrine of *Meyer v. Nebraska,* 262 U.S. 390,[2] we think it entirely plain that the Act of 1922 unreasonably interferes with the liberty of parents and guardians to direct the upbringing and education of children under their control. As often heretofore pointed out, rights guaranteed by the Constitution may not be abridged by legislation which has no reasonable relation to some purpose within the competency of the State. The fundamental theory of liberty upon which all governments in this Union repose excludes any general power of the State to standardize its children by forcing them to accept instruction from public teachers only. The child is not the mere creature of the State; those who nurture him and direct his destiny have the right, coupled with the high duty, to recognize and prepare him for additional obligations. . . .

The suits were not premature. The injury to appellees was present and very real, not a mere possibility in the remote future. If no relief had been possible prior to the effective date of the Act, the injury would have become irreparable. Prevention of impending injury by unlawful action is a well recognized function of courts of equity.

The decrees below are

Affirmed.

Pierce v. Society of Sisters, 268 U.S. 510, 529–36 (1925). (Justice James C. McReynolds delivered the opinion of the Court.) Also in John Tracy Ellis, ed., *Documents of American Catholic History* (Wilmington, Del.: Michael Glazier, 1987), 2:613–16. (Footnotes in Ellis.)

44. "Alfred E. Smith's Reply to Charles C. Marshall," May 1927

. . . I summarize my creed as an American Catholic. I believe in the worship of God according to the faith and practice of the Roman Catholic Church. I recognize no power in the institutions of my Church to interfere with the operations of the Constitution of the United States or the enforcement of the law of the land. I believe in absolute freedom of conscience for all men and in equality of all churches, all sects, and all beliefs before the law as a matter of right and not as a matter of favor. I believe in the separation of Church and State and in the strict enforcement of the provisions of the Constitution that Congress shall make no law respecting an establishment of religion or prohibiting the free exercise thereof. I believe that no tribunal of any church has any power to make any decree of any force in the law of the land, other than to establish the status of its own communicants within its own church. I believe in the support of the public school as one of the cornerstones of American liberty. I believe in the right of every parent to choose whether his

---

2. The Supreme Court in *Meyer v. Nebraska* (1923) declared unconstitutional a law forbidding the teaching of any language other than English to any child below the eighth grade by any teacher in a public or private school. The court upheld the right of the plaintiff, an instructor in a Lutheran parochial school, to teach a foreign language, as well as the right of the parents to engage him to instruct their children, both as being within the liberty of the Fourteenth Amendment.

child shall be educated in the public school or in a religious school supported by those of his own faith. I believe in the principle of noninterference by this country in the internal affairs of other nations and we should stand steadfastly against any such interference by whomsoever it may be urged. And I believe in the common brotherhood of man under the common fatherhood of God.

In this spirit I join with fellow Americans of all creeds in a fervent prayer that never again in this land will any public servant be challenged because of the faith in which he has tried to walk humbly with his God.

Atlantic Monthly 39 (May 1927): 728.

Foreign Policy and International Order

The establishment of the National Catholic Welfare Conference (NCWC) provided a unified public voice for Catholics on any number of issues — but especially foreign affairs. Officials of the organization were regularly consulted by the State Department, and representations to government agencies were made through the NCWC. Official Catholic concerns over the fate of co-religionists in Mexico dominated the 1920s. In the years leading up to World War II, Catholics were bitterly divided over American intervention abroad, and these divisions erupted into public debate among highly visible clerics. Once the war was underway, Catholics overcame misgivings about an alliance with "atheistic Russia," joined the call for victory, and attempted to influence the scope and direction of the United Nations.

45. Pastoral Letter of the U.S. Hierarchy on Mexico, Feast of Our Lady of Guadalupe, 12 December 1926

1. Sympathy to those who suffer for conscience sake has never been refused by the great heart of the American people. They, almost instinctively, sense all oppression to be a destroyer of unity at home, as well as an abundant source of the misunderstandings and hatreds that divide nations and peoples and injure the cause of international amity and world peace. If then we, as American bishops, had no other reason for issuing this pastoral than to show our deep sympathy with the suffering people of Mexico in the persecution now raging against religion in that country, it would be justified; but there are other reasons, carrying even greater weight and urgency, that make of this act a duty. They are found in the fact that Mexico is our neighbor — with all the power that propinquity gives to the force of good or evil example — a republic which it was intended should be modeled on lines similar to ours, and a nation with a Christian population whose devotion to the Catholic Church makes a special call upon the charity of the faithful everywhere, but more especially upon those of the United States. . . .

We Speak in the Interests of Both Church and State

3. All the more do we feel an obligation to speak boldly and publicly on the religious persecution raging in Mexico, because the common Father of Christendom, Pius XI, Vicar of Jesus Christ, has urged the faithful of the whole world to unite with him in sympathy and prayer to God for the afflicted Church. . . .

4. Yet another and still stronger motive urges us to speak. It is that the present conflict, as one part of a war against religion in Mexico which had its inception almost a century ago, to a greater degree than any preceding it comes from an attempt at nothing less than the destruction of the divine constitution of the Church by reducing her to the status of a State-controlled schismatical body, without the right to form, train, and educate her own clergy, to have a sufficient number of them for the care of souls, and to find means for her support, to develop works in accord with her mission of charity and enlightenment, and to apply the teachings of the Gospel to the formation of a public conscience. Sad experience, as well as right reason, tells us what would follow the success of such an attempt, and what it would mean to Church as well as to state.

5. The Mexican Church thus controlled and bound, as the civil power seeks to control and bind her, nominally might be separated, but really would be a department of the political machinery of the state. Her dignities and offices would be the perquisites of politicians; her voice the changing voice of political action. She would be despised by her faithful and justly mocked by her enemies. Her bond of unity with the Church Universal would first be weakened and then snapped asunder. The Mexican government asks the Church to accept a slavery that could mean nothing today but an infection caught from evil surroundings, and tomorrow a decline into mortal sickness inevitably ending with her passing from the life of the Mexican people.

We Speak as Americans as Well as Catholics

6. To the state would come no less evil results. With the check of religious influence gone, history for her also would be repeated. She would forget her dreams of democracy and actually become despotism. Corruption would increase with power to confer ecclesiastical emoluments upon the unworthy. She would merit and receive the hatred of just men at home and the contempt of just men abroad. A "Holy Synod," doing the unholy work of despotism, would gradually absorb her strength and seize her power as a most convenient machinery of government. Whatever of good is in her ideals would be shattered on one of the oldest rocks that lie hidden in the waters of political life. . . .

8. If, then, because of the fact that the persecution in Mexico is directed against all the principles of religion, we should speak as the servants of God; if, because it is unloosed particularly against the religion of the majority of the people of Mexico, we should speak as Catholics; there are grave reasons,

too, why we have a duty to speak as Americans attached to the institutions of our country and loving them for the benefits they have conferred upon us all. The government of Mexico has, indeed, by its actions in our very midst, made it necessary that we should no longer guard silence, for it has carried its war on religion beyond its own boundaries through organized propaganda in many countries, but especially in our own.

We Consider the Mexican Government in Light of American and Christian Principles

9. Through its diplomatic and consular agents in the United States that government appeals to the American people to justify its actions. In consequence we have before us the extraordinary spectacle of a foreign government, not only filling our country with propaganda in favor of its own internal plans and policies, but even attempting to justify and defend, in our nation, laws and conduct at variance with fundamentals set down in imperishable documents by the fathers of this republic. Misinterpreting our good-natured tolerance for a neighbor still disturbed by consequences of many military upheavals, the government of Mexico has thus presumed to appeal to our fellow citizens for approval. This actually amounts to the submission of its case for judgment in a court beyond its own boundaries; pleading, not before its own citizens, who, according to its Constitution, form the only court competent to pass upon it, but before strangers who claim no jurisdiction over their neighbor's political affairs, and whose only interest in them is a desire for the well-being of the people of Mexico and their own peace in amicable mutual relations. The government of Mexico cannot, therefore, object, under such circumstances, if the case it has thus presented for judgment be considered in the light of American principles, as embodied in our fundamental laws, and in the light of Christian principles, since it appeals for the sympathy of Christians; nor, since it claims great zeal for the advancement of education, if the statements it has presented in support of its pleading be submitted to the test of history. These are the things we propose to do, so that, not only will our own citizens be fully informed of the interests at stake, but the Mexican people will not be without benefit of advocate before the court to which their rulers have actually but mistakenly appealed....

American Recognition of the Rights and Utility of Religion...

23. American laws recognize the right of the citizen to worship God "according to the dictates of his conscience," and, in order that this freedom may be assured him, religious societies are recognized as corporate legal entities having power to possess what property they need to carry out their mission. Furthermore, that mission is recognized as being, not only religious in root and trunk, but as bearing powers and fruit in works of education and social welfare. Religious societies may, therefore, own land and upon it erect such buildings as are necessary for their purposes. They may establish, own, and direct schools, colleges, universities, asylums, hospitals, and other institutions of

education and social welfare. They may, as legal entities, protect their property rights by due process of law. They may possess endowments for the benefit of these activities and receive bequests. They may have seminaries wherein their clergy are trained and educated. Over and above all this, property owned by them, when used for purposes of worship, charity, or education, almost universally with us is specially exempt from taxation; not only because it is recognized as of utility to the public welfare, but also in order to carry into effect the spirit of the national will which, expressing itself through the Continental Congress, says: "Religion, morality and knowledge, being necessary to good government and the happiness of mankind, schools and the means of education shall forever be encouraged..."[1]

24. This condition has obtained since the formation of the republic. It has worked out for the benefit of the state and of the people. No one now seriously believes that it could be changed. It has become an accepted and highly esteemed part of our national life, because it recognizes the rights of conscience, encourages private initiative in the establishing of useful agencies for learning and charity, promotes peace, contentment, and good will among citizens, encourages the enforcement of wise and good laws as well as the practice of the civic virtues, and allows to religion freedom in its own sphere for its teachings and for the cultivation of the spiritual life of the people. It has stood the test of nearly one and a half centuries, and the American people today are undoubtedly more than ever convinced of the desirability of its continuance. While with us there is no union of church and state, nevertheless there is full and frank recognition of the utility of religion to good government. Hence the American State encourages religion to make greater and greater contributions to the happiness of the people, the stability of government, and the reign of order.

Mexico's Attempt to Destroy Religion

25. In contrast with this, according to the present Constitution of Mexico no religious society may enjoy the right of corporate legal existence.[2] Officially, there are no Churches in Mexico; for a church cannot possess anything, lacks the right of petition for redress of grievances, cannot sue or be sued in the civil courts, and in general is entirely without legal standing. Clergymen are disfranchised by the fact of ordination.[3] A church cannot own the buildings in which its public worship is held.[4] It cannot possess endowments.[5] It cannot take up a collection or a subscription outside the doors of the building used for religious services. That building, however, is owned by the government, though paid for and supported by the people....

---

1. Northwest Ordinance, Art. 3.
2. Constitution of 1917, Art. 130. Law of 25 November 1926, Art. 5.
3. Constitution of 1917, Art. 37, Section III.
4. Constitution of 1917, Art. 27. Law of 25 November 1926, Art. 6.
5. Constitution of 1917, Art. 27, II. Law of 21 June 1926, Art. 21. Law of 25 November 1926, Art. 6.

26. In order to make this enactment effective, a church is not allowed to possess houses for its bishops, priests, ministers, teachers, or superintendents. Its future may not be provided for, because it cannot have a seminary in which a clergy may be trained to take places made vacant by death or incapacity....

Works of Education and Charity Destroyed

27. A church, therefore, cannot own anything, cannot provide for its expenses, cannot provide for a future clergy. A native clergy is thus made impossible, a fact which ordinarily would throw the burden of the religious care of the people upon strangers. To prevent the possibility of that happening, however, the law provides[6] that no clergyman but a native-born Mexican may officiate in any act of worship; and in consequence foreign clergy have been expelled. Thus, the law first makes it impossible for the people to have a native clergy and then impossible to have a foreign clergy; while the government keeps assuring the world of its liberality and that there is no religious persecution in Mexico...[7]

The Church and State in Mexico

48. The statement of the government of Mexico that it is now only trying to dissolve a union between Church and state, and that the Church is seeking temporal power, finds an obvious answer in the history of the Mexican nation. There has been no union of Church and state in Mexico since 1857. Even before that, however, when, in 1821, a revolutionary Mexican government desired to retain some part of the union in the ancient right of patronage, formerly enjoyed by the Spanish crown, so as to have the appointment of bishops in its hands, it was met with a refusal from the archbishop of Mexico. When the demand was made the following year, it was again rejected, this time by the whole body of the episcopate.[8]

49. The Constitution of 1857 declared the union of Church and state to be dissolved.[9] That instrument, however, recognized the Church as a legal, though separate, entity. According to the liberal doctrine then in vogue, no *legal person* was such by its own inherent right, and became so only by the grant of the state, which by a legal fiction created it. What the state makes, however, it can unmake, and this the Constitution of 1917, by a logical conclusion from a false premise, attempted to do. It recognizes[10] "no juridical personality

---

6. Law of 21 June 1926, Art. 1. Law of 25 November 1926, Art. 8. Constitution of 1917, Art. 130.

7. Plutarco Elias Calles, "The Policies of Mexico Today," *Foreign Affairs* (October 1926): 4. "In conclusion, I wish to lay stress upon the fact that a real religious problem does not exist in Mexico. I mean that there is no such thing as persecution of a religious character against religious creeds or opposition on the part of the government to the dogmas or practices of any religion."

8. Concilio III Mexicano, 569. Succeeding governments attempted to arrange for, or to assert, the right to appoint the bishops and priests, until 1857, when the Constitution declared the separation of Church and State and the policy of expropriation was adopted.

9. Art. 3.

10. Art. 130.

in the religious institutions known as churches," thus depriving them of any legal protection against the encroachment of tyrants, whose real and often expressed purpose in Mexico was, and is, not to separate the Church from the state but to subject the Church to the control of the state.[11] The Church in Mexico, on the other hand, is not asking for the union of Church and State to be restored, but for the American system of freedom of religion to be introduced. This may easily be learned from the words[12] of the Mexican bishops addressed to the legislature:

> What is it that we petition? Not tolerance, not complacency, much less privileges or favors. We demand liberty, and we demand nothing but liberty, we demand liberty for all religions.... A regime of restrictions against religion is the denial of liberty....

This Is No Appeal for Political Intervention

54. What, therefore, we have written is no call on the faithful here or elsewhere to purely human action. It is no interposition of our influence either as bishops or as citizens to reach those who possess political power anywhere on earth, and least of all in our own country, to the end that they should intervene with armed force in the internal affairs of Mexico for the protection of the Church. Our duty is done when, by telling the story, defending the truth, and emphasizing the principles, we sound a warning to Christian civilization that its foundations are again being attacked and undermined. For the rest, God will bring His will to pass in His own good time and in His own good way. Mexico will be saved for her mission whatever it may be....

Hugh J. Nolan, ed., *Pastoral Letters of the United States Catholic Bishops* (Washington, D.C.: United States Catholic Conference, 1984), 1:337–64. (Footnotes in the original.) Printed with permission.

46. "To the Spanish Hierarchy: A Statement Issued by the Catholic Bishops of the United States," 18 November 1937

1. With profound emotion we read the Pastoral letter written in your hour of sorrow to your brothers of the world. You did this gracious and invaluable service to let us know the true state of religion in your country.

2. Poignant has been our sorrow, for we could not but realize the suffering of the venerable Church of Spain to which the world is so deeply indebted for its countless contributions to everything summed up in the words "Christian culture." In the midst of great political and economic conflicts, you have been maligned before the world as though, unmindful of your great traditions and fine achievements, you had forgotten the sorry plight of peasants and workers. Clever propaganda, maliciously used by those who would promote atheism and chaos, has beclouded the real facts in the contemporary life

---

11. Law of 25 November 1926, Art. 1.
12. On 7 September 1926.

of the Church in Spain. It has sought to make prevail the notion that this Church no longer represents the very heart of the Spanish people. Human rights have been violated and the Church in Spain outrageously persecuted, not because it had forgotten the rights of the lowly and weak in human society, but because it dared even with martyr blood to stand witness to the Christian principles of a great people.

3. Tragic are the true facts of the religious persecution in Spain by men who before the world sought to appear in the role of vindicators of human rights. You tell us that ten bishops, thousands of priests and religious, and tens of thousands of laymen have been put to death, often with unspeakable cruelty, because they were active in teaching the world to promote the works of the Gospel. Your words horrify us who are wont to accept liberty of conscience and freedom of speech as an axiom.

4. Irreligion and atheism, whatever may be their changing cloak, are things with which bishops may not temporize. Pitiable indeed is the fact that many men, right-minded and honest, have fallen victims to the misshapen news which has been given the world about the Church in Spain. Worse still, some Christian leaders unwittingly have allowed themselves to be the sponsors of principles which, if given wide sway, would destroy the very last vestige of Western civilization.

5. You have spoken clearly as followers of the Prince of Peace, and your words show a realism which is not inconsistent with the high idealism that has been through the ages an outstanding characteristic of the Church in Spain. Nowhere in your gratefully appreciated Letter may honest men gather the thought that you have advocated any social philosophy which refuses to recognize the salient problems of our times. There comes to us from your Letter the assurance of the Crusaders, to promote the principles of the social encyclicals of our Holy Father.

6. As a hierarchy in a great democracy, ever alert to defend and protect for all men the fundamental principles of our American Constitution, we know from our past the sorry difficulties before the forum of world opinion which face you. To none do we yield the honor of a greater and more loyal adherence to the great democratic principles on which our government is founded. These principles are basically a thing of sound reason and wholly consonant with Christian teachings. We know full well that Your Eminences and Excellencies with your truly admirable clergy, religious, and courageous laity are laboring with a disinterestedness which compels the sympathy and support of all informed men, to inculcate the principles of social justice and charity so fully and so clearly enunciated in social encyclicals of our Holy Father. In your effort we want you to know that in common with the Catholic bishops of the world we stand beside you and thank you for your clear, calm, dignified statement on the condition of the Church in Spain....

7. We offer you our sympathy and assure you that we are deeply afflicted and moved by your tribulations. Day by day we pray with our priests, religious, and people that the land of Ferdinand and Isabella will find a solution

of its pressing problems without deserting the Christian principles which have made it great in the past. As Americans we owe you a great debt of gratitude. In our Far South, Southwest, and West there still is told the story of the heroic Spanish priests and friars who did a work which is part of our national glory. Once before, the hierarchy of Spain helped to save the Western world from the menace of Islamism. God grant that once again you may be a powerful force to stem the tide of atheism, translated into social language and disguised with diabolical ingenuity. In your sorrows and tribulations you may be comforted to know that we understand and sympathize with you. The day is dark for you but the darkness of Calvary in the history of the Church has always been followed by the light of Easter Morn.

Fraternally in the charity of Christ,
Emmet M. Walsh, Bishop of Charleston
Dennis Cardinal Dougherty, Archbishop of Philadelphia

Hugh J. Nolan, ed., *Pastoral Letters of the United States Catholic Bishops* (Washington, D.C.: United States Catholic Conference, 1984), 1:416–18. Printed with permission.

47. Address of the Most Rev. Joseph P. Hurley, Bishop of St. Augustine, 6 July 1941

I have accepted the kind invitation of Columbia Broadcasting System to speak on the subject "Papal Pronouncements and American Foreign Policy" because I consider that an address on this topic might serve some useful purpose at the present time. People with short memories are apt to forget the heroic struggle of the Popes in our day for human liberty and for human dignity just because a few Catholic publicists in America have been giving expression to views which are comforting to the Axis powers. Due to my past connection with the Papal Secretariate of State, I deem it well to say at the outset that this address is delivered without any mandate from the Holy See; that I use only documents of public record; and that I engage only my own authority....

When we were compelled to face the realities of the war in Europe, which was also potentially a war against us and all the people of Christendom, we discussed and we agreed upon a national policy and upon a Government to enforce that policy. We did that last November when we chose a President and gave him the mandate to afford all possible aid short of war to the democracies. It now appears that there has developed a conflict between these two aims, aid to the democracies on the one hand and avoidance of war on the other. Indeed from the first, it was seen that we were taking sides in the war, and that it might be difficult to avoid being involved. We knew the risk; and we took it. It was a superb policy, and statesmanlike genius presided at its conception. But as an enunciation of the American will in a war-torn world, it called for constant interpretation; it was of necessity subject to the condition which is implicit in all understandings *rebus sic stantibus,* that is to say, as long as matters remain as they are, and are not radically changed by contingency and vicissitude. If the conditions under which that policy was approved should change, then the policy must change; if those conditions change rapidly, then we must be prepared for a rapid change in the policy. What shall be our guide should such a necessity arise? I think it is abundantly clear to any one who will give it a moment's reflection. Behind our dual policy, there stands a single permanent indefeasible principle: the will and the right of our nation to live. The policy sprang from that principle; in the light of that principle it must be interpreted. Any conflict between the necessarily provisional terms of a policy must be resolved by the basic principle of national security. The question of peace or war in the last analysis is a question which can be decided only with reference to the safety of this Union.

Since then we are confronted with a conflict between aid to the allies and avoidance of war, who shall decide? Certainly not the people, for they have neither the experience, nor access to the facts, nor in many cases the understanding which are required. Nor does the Constitution demand it. The form letters and the chain telegrams and the threatened demonstration on the White House lawn are therefore quite beside the point. I have an abiding faith in government by the people; but I do not believe that questions of national security, in an epoch of crisis, should be submitted directly to them. It would be a lumbering process involving fatal delay, and fatal leakage of plans to potential enemies. Nor is the record of democratic peoples in the pre-war period such as would inspire much confidence. In France the will of the nation to live was paralyzed by the interminable acrimonious debates in press and forum; by sabotage on the left; and confusion of counsels on the right. There were elements in France as there are here, which preferred civil war to a war against a foreign foe....

To the Congress, under the Constitution, belongs the weighty responsibility of declaring war. That is clear, but I am afraid that it is not a complete answer to the practical question. For it is manifestly impossible that the day to day decisions which must be taken often in the greatest secrecy should be submitted to the Congress for discussions. Such matters are lawfully the competence of the Executive. Furthermore in times of emergency the powers of the Executive are very properly enlarged by Congress. In the very nature of the case, therefore, and with the fullest legality, important decisions of far reaching effect must be taken by the President both in his capacity as Chief Executive and in his capacity as Commander in Chief. To all practical intents, it is up to him to safeguard the interests of the nation in times of great emergency. As the Commander in Chief of our armed forces and as the one charged with the conduct of foreign affairs, he must be ready to act fast and decisively should the need arise, and it is all to the good that he is equipped by the Constitution and by Congressional enactment to do so.

In the present circumstances, we must not lose sight of the fact that the declaration of war, the constitutional prerogative of the Congress, is no longer in style; the Nazi has seen to that. We must, too, face the fact that we have already left the political and diplomatic zone, and have entered the zone of strategy. I believe this to be true not only of ourselves, but of almost every country in the world. Since the Nazi had from the first marked us as his enemy, it is well that we accept that fact, even though it has not yet pleased him to make war upon us. But his policy of limited objectives, that policy by which he betrayed and enslaved a continent, is fast approaching the point of showdown with us. *It will be folly if we do not appraise our whole relationship with the Axis powers from the standpoint of strategy.* We may not, we must not, wait for the start of hostilities before we make our dispositions. Pre-war strategy is so all-important today that wars are won or lost before they enter the shooting phase. With the example of all the countries of Europe before us, let us pray for peace but prepare for war. Even though we hope to avoid war, we must put this country, its economy, its finance, its very thinking, on a footing of preparedness for war in the shortest possible time. Any other course may be literally national suicide. Let me say immediately that I pray with all my soul that we shall never need to go to war; that our aid to our friends and our own military strength may be such as to bring about the discouragement and the defeat of the enemy of Christendom. It is not the business of a Churchman to call for war. But neither may any Churchman do anything other than encourage a Government to protect by all prudent and necessary means its sacred national interests. *A fortiori,* when the interests of religion the world over are placed in jeopardy by a ruthless persecutor of the Church of Christ. The Faith which I profess and love teaches that war is a legitimate, though extreme, instrument of a just national policy. From time to time, we Churchmen are obliged to quote the Scriptures to Governments which would encroach upon our sphere — "Render unto God the things that are God's." I believe that our Government in this awful hour may with justice say to certain Churchmen "Render unto Caesar the things that are Caesar's."

My great fear is that we will not be permitted to have the choice between war and peace; that the Nazi will not let us have peace as he did not let the nations of Europe have peace. Many qualified observers think that our only choice is when we shall enter the war. In other words, that we shall sooner or later be forced into the war by the Nazi lust for world domination. That is why this country is honeycombed with Nazi operatives, both American and foreign; that is why Central and South America are covered by a network of Nazi agents. In this view, which has much to commend it, the questions which America has to answer are three: 1) Shall we enter the war now or later? 2) Shall we enter the war on our own terms or on terms dictated by Nazi strategy? 3) Shall we enter the war with Allies or shall we bear the brunt of it alone?

If there is any merit to the foregoing considerations, born of experience and of study, it may be all boiled down to this: Since our problem is primarily a strategic one, it should be left to the Commander in Chief who alone, in constant, loyal communication with the Congress and in consultation with his military and naval advisers, is capable of bring us safely through the dangers which encompass us....

There is much talk these days of national unity. It is our imperative need. Unity of thought; unity of purpose; unity of action. May I add that we have, too, great need of the virtues of reverence and obedience? In a free people, these things must come from an inner discipline based upon conscientious conviction. If we are to be united, there is only one center around which, as a nation, we can rally: that center is Washington. If our union is to be real and effective, we must school ourselves to reverence and obey our lawful authorities, our President, in the first place, and our Congress. They personify the ideals and the will of this country. They have led us admirably in this crisis, not of their making. They are for peace — for peace as long as it is consistent with the highest interests of the nation. In the anxious hours of deliberation and decision which they, especially our President, must pass they are deserving of our deepest sympathy, of the comfort of our prayers. Patriotic men, bent on the protection of our beloved land, — I have confidence in them. I confess that I have no confidence in anyone who seeks in a time of crisis to undermine legitimate authority; who speaks disparagingly or distrustfully of our highest magistrates. I have no confidence in those who oppose the steps by which we achieved our present stage of defense; I have no confidence in those who reserve all their fault-finding for America and who praise the Nazi with faint condemnation. They may be good men; and some of them are; but be their station high or low, Americans, to whom they are giving a bad example of division, should disregard their counsels.

Among them is a small but noisy group of Catholics. We have suffered long from their tantrums. We have blushed with shame when they acted up before company as tantrum children will do in every family. Years ago they established the crank school of economics; latterly they have founded the tirade school of journalism; they are now engaged in popularizing the ostrich school of strategy. The school may change its curriculum, but the same professors hold the chairs for they are specialists in the universe of knowledge. Many Catholics are inclined to apologize for them; but I think that is unwise. They will disappear in time like those other exhibitionists — the marathon dancers and the flagpole sitters — who amused America for a while and vanished.

The American people will be wise if they turn themselves as individuals to the task of moral rearmament. The years which lie ahead will probe us with relentless fingers to find and to exploit our moral weaknesses. A democracy, above all forms of government, must find its strength in the virtue of the people; its greatest danger is decadence from within. It is my most fervent prayer that we may set ourselves with a will to the task of sanctifying ourselves, our homes and our public life, to the end that in these days of trial and reckoning we may be and remain a Christian example among the nations, a people acceptable to Almighty God.

Address delivered over the Columbia Broadcasting System Network, 6 July 1941, Washington, D.C. Hurley Papers Series II, Archives of the Diocese of St. Augustine. Printed with permission.

48. Most Rev. Francis J. L. Beckman, Archbishop of Dubuque, Iowa, "Congressmen: Be Warned!" 27 July 1941

...I am filled this evening, my dear Catholic and Christian people with an indignation akin perhaps to that which Christ the Savior demonstrated in the Temple despoiled. In the past weeks we have witnessed an unholy merger of Christianity and Communism under the guise of military necessity; we have seen what amounts to dictatorship pseudo-officially canonized by a brother cleric; we have witnessed the beginning of the end for pledges which, however well given had not truth for their backbone. "Strategy" what crimes are committed in thy name. The bland assurances of peace for the people it seems are so much honey on the lip. Step by step, my dear friends just as surely as I stand before this microphone tonight, our unhappy nation is being propelled into an honest-to-goodness "blood and tears and sweat *shooting* war!" A war not to end wars, "forsooth," but, whether we know it or not, a war to make the world and *particularly this beloved America safe for the new Bolshevism!*

I think at this time I might appropriately restate my position on this momentous issue of war or peace for the American people: From the beginning I have maintained that this war, however falsely represented, is an *economic war based on greed, a vast struggle for power* and *possessions between two diametrically opposed systems of finance.* The problem over which the warring nations have come to death-grips is simply this: "whose economy shall be dominant in Europe, ours or yours?" In short, "who is to exploit who?" The entrenched internationalists had their day; they financed the world into eternal debt and milked whole peoples, grinding them down into the dust of ignorance, poverty and abject despair. When the crimes of these vendors in human misery arose to confront them, when other nations dared to challenge their tyranny, then it was war — war in the name of democracy and a hundred other slogans — yes, even war in the name of God Almighty Himself! If it suited their purpose to call it a "holy war," that was alright too. Anything to persuade the gullible millions to go out and do the fighting and the suffering and the dying that "the system" might survive!

So today, the propaganda — smooth stuff it had to be this time for the American people were weary and disillusioned of "war to end wars." They had been fooled once and they knew it. Oh for a new slogan! Then out of the mysterious somewhere was born that supreme insult to the intelligence of our people "Aid to the Allies short of war." This was a clever bait and, anxious to aid Britain, while remaining ourselves at peace we swallowed it "hook-line-and-sinker." A few saw into the hypocrisy of this proposition but their warnings went unheeded. In no time at all "measures short of war" had become an established axiom. The foundation was laid, the course set, and whether they liked it or not the American people once again were on the spot for Britain. A few well-chosen words to mark the gravestone of our folly; a "slimy slogan" had done it again. Here is His Eminence the great William Cardinal O'Connell, dean of the American Hierarchy, on slogans: "Of all the things in the world, I think what we have to be on guard against are these slimy slogans that mean nothing. They are insults to one's intelligence. And worse than that, they are dishonest. 'Make the world safe for Democracy.' 'The war to end wars.' Oh, how slick that is. It sounds so nice, 'the war to end wars.' Of course, everybody wants to end war, so they rush in to end the war that they began. We have had wars ever since. And the worst one the world has ever known has come about since this slogan was manufactured to fool the people. 'The war to end wars.' How lovely and glib it sounds on the tongue. And the poor people; what a crime it is to deceive the poor people. What a crime! To play on their generosity of heart, and even their trust in those who govern them; to play on that, that is pretty vile. To bring about what? To bring about disunion, confusion, and little by little the loss of everything they hold dear — the loss of their own children, the loss of their possessions, the loss of their civil rights."

People! Here is a stirring indictment of deceit and a glimpse of what we may expect if as a result of our folly we get into this war unto annihilation. I reaffirm to you that the present conflict is not a "holy war," least of all a just war; but a war of one imperialism against the *other in which godlessness is incidental to all belligerents.* Neither side is interested in God so much as gold or its equivalent. And there is no crusade for Christianity or democracy afoot anywhere in the world today either, all high-sounding slogans to the contrary not-with-standing. Further, we may be sure that abroad the "four freedoms" have a phony ring. To the war-weary people of Europe this slogan is just another mask for the imperialism of the new world. Again I quote Cardinal O'Connell: "And there is one thing certain: we cannot — and we ought not try to — impose our form of government on the whole world." Why, they don't want it. If you are going to impose it on them, then you are doing an act of tyranny. I wonder if anyone really believes he could do that. If he doesn't believe it, and if he says it — I don't want to use the word. If he says what he doesn't mean, then you know what the adjective is; that is false. You can't in honesty try to deceive a whole people, much less the whole world. They know perfectly well what the American government is, and most of them, many of them, don't want it. Their traditions are all the other way. Very well; it is for them to decide, not for us. But as for our going out and trying to impose our method of life on the whole world, it is not only nonsense and impossible, but because it is utterly wrong it is tyranny.

No, my dear American friends this war is nothing more or less than a struggle to *reestablish the shattered boundaries of international finance, and other things international, in countries which have had their fill of them and do not want them anymore.* This is a struggle which if prolonged through our efforts, but for a miracle of God, may go on interminably until universal chaos and exhaustion encompasses the warring nations.

And Chaos — there is a whirlwind for you! A wind to scatter the deadly Communism like a plague through all the world! If we in this country sanction even by our silence the hatred and revenge which dwells in the high places and relentlessly, hypocritically prosecutes this war we may well fear for that super doomsday of a despair. The weight of a long and terrible war will crush and distort the human spirit, deprave and bestialize. Oh, my dear friends not death but sin is the horror of war! Maimed bodies are but an external evidence of the mangled spirit within. And the spirit of whole peoples shattered by interminable warfare will prove fertile soil for the cockle of a new type of communism. *This "new godlessness" I will call it, because it is like to be a composite of that paganism prevailing in high places* everywhere today, is something I tremble to contemplate. I pray heaven that we shall all be spared so terrible an alternative to an early "peace with justice."

But I do know that the business of this great land is the business of peace. Defense? Certainly defense — defense to the hilt, but let us not discard the moral armament of a peaceful and freedom-loving way of life pursued for the edification of all the world. The great prelate of the East advises: "Teach them (the nations) by example, yes, let them all learn to look to America as a great country, where people are contented and happy, and are working day in and day out for the welfare of their family, for the welfare of their nations, contented, honest, upright, obedient to the laws. Let them learn that. By that example, show the world what a great, big united country like this can be, united of all the different races in the world, by love of their native land, of their country whether it is their native land or not, of their nation to which we belong. — And with God's help, God, who has showered his blessings upon this country, and from whom it seems He gets very little thanks; this breadth of land from ocean to ocean, the mines, the farms, the mountains, the hills and lakes, Oh, God, what a country it is, a country to die for in defense, yes, but not to fritter away or barter out, but to preserve as it came to us from those glorious founders, whose memory ought to be our great strength and support. — That is what we mean when we say 'Defense'. Yes, all out for defense and 'then keep out of these foreign wars.' I say that, you say that. Well, Washington said it, and he was a fairly big man, one of the great men of history. And he was the one who began with the solid idea upon which this whole nation rests, or at least ought to rest."

Ought to rest, indeed! Too long in this country the American people have been led around by the nose, told what to do, robbed, kicked, and abused by the high-and-mighty masters of international finance; too long have they tolerated corruption and dishonesty in politics; too long have the Christian people of this nation remained divided on fundamental issues. Yes, I fear, that we have been nothing more than pawns in the good old game of "divide and rule." It seems we can't get together for long on any one thing, and small wonder with these past masters in the art of long division ruling the roost! It is high time that the Catholic Church in particular and all good Christian-Americans put aside their differences, unite in the common cause of Americanism and by legal means, but do it, put out these pirates who would rob and despoil our people of their very birthright, milk the nation and then go off to abuse and ridicule it for another twenty years.

And while I am at it I think this is a good time to lay an old ghost to rest. In late years it has become the fashion of much of the secular and even the Catholic press to place official interpretations on the pronouncements of clerics newly returned from abroad. Every scrap of news which might be construed as comforting to the cause of the interventionists has been hungrily seized upon and used to further divide, confuse and exploit the Catholics of the nation. Sadly enough the flagpole on the White House lawn has never lacked for clerical adornment. This is a disgraceful condition of affairs — the Catholic Church being used to further the evil ends of a privileged group! I cried out against this abuse two years ago, and with all my strength I cry out against it now. No man speaks for the Catholic Church save the Holy Father Himself, and he must of necessity remain far above all this controversy. I do not claim to speak for all the Catholic people in this country; but I am well-*advised enough to know that the overwhelming majority of our people are unalterably opposed to participation in this war.* I am prepared to risk the proof of that point; and in the wake of crumbling pledges I turn once again to the representatives of the people:

Congressmen! Be Warned! You know that the people of this nation are overwhelmingly opposed to becoming embroiled in this war. In the past many of you have voted legislation which was represented as designed to keep this country out of war. Subsequent events must have convinced you by now that the opposite appears to be true. Congressmen! The people of this nation will never forgive much less forget a negligence which permits the stealthy maneuvering of this beloved America into war either by the front or the back door. God forbid, I do not wish to speak disparagingly or distrustfully of our highest magistrates. I concur that in these anxious hours of deliberation and decision they are deserving of our deepest sympathy and the comfort of our prayers. But there are powerful figures moving in the background of this picture and powerful pressure is certainly being brought to bear upon positions of responsibility. They smack of totalitarianism, of secret counsels arriving at decisions which as I have said before will affect whole generations of the unborn — these are realities we may not ignore. Remember, the stakes are high, and a few in this country would pay almost any price for the vindication of their monstrous greed, hatred and deceit — any price, that is, in the blood and treasure of the American people. These manufactured crises and prayed for incidents bear witness to the point....

Men of the Congress: the great majority of our people look to you for earnest, speedy, patriotic action on their behalf; action which in concert with the Executive branch of our government will preserve this great nation at peace and insure against any wholesale frittering and bartering away of our vital resources. They have every hope that you will do valiantly that which needs to be done, and undone. The will of your people is and should be a vital, throbbing, prevailing thing urging you on to magnificent decisions in the name of constitutional government. So long as you loyally reflect that will we shall not lack for unity in this nation or for strong arms to defend it.

"On the question of defense we are all entirely united." Vigilant, determined, unafraid; but "the vast majority of the American people who stand for the defense of our nation also has gone on record again and again and again as being opposed to participation in foreign wars."[1] Certainly the majority millions of our Catholic people are opposed to it, to the coddling of Communists, to aid for Red Russia. In farewell tonight I would draw upon this great body of opinion, Catholic in particular, Christian in general, mutually American and unequivocally patriotic. Three times I have come to the microphone to voice the sentiments of this body—not a pleasant duty in these days of abuse. Now I charge you, Catholic and Christian citizens, to do your duty! I charge you this very hour to sit down, mothers, fathers—you who have most to lose and most to gain—make yourselves vocal to the Congress. Get out the letters and the postcards and write! Write! Write! Let both your Senators and your Congressmen know where you stand in this matter. NOW. Your right of petition implies also a sacred and a solemn obligation. It is your duty to exercise it freely, fearlessly, incessantly. In the very teeth of the slurs which have been cast upon that right I charge you to persevere. In the corridors of Congress make the welkin of petition ring today, tomorrow, and throughout all the years; for it is the sweet bell of liberty, my dear people, a deathless voice which *is* democracy.

Francis J. L. Beckman,
Archbishop of Dubuque

> Address delivered over the Columbia Broadcasting System Network, 27 July 1941.
> Beckman Papers, Archives of the Archdiocese of Dubuque, Iowa.

49. Most Rev. John T. McNicholas, Columbus Day Address, 12 October 1942

...I wish to speak briefly to you today as a Catholic bishop. In no sense do I wish to enter the arena of politics. I speak only for the church of Cincinnati.

I ask all the faithful to respect the opinions of others. There is the domain of facts and of principles. About them there can be no controversy among informed men. In this domain the Catholic church is immoveable. She will "not put light for darkness nor darkness for light." She must always insist on the existence of a personal God, on the divinity of Christ, on the divine establishment of the church. She can never compromise on these basic truths or water down unchangeable principles. In the domain of opinion there must be liberty. There is no institution in all the world that knows this domain as does the Catholic church. No teacher has ever insisted, as she insists, that there must be liberty in all matters of opinion. I beg our people, therefore, to respect the opinions of others.

I ask all to credit with sincerity those whose opinions differ from theirs. I urge them to refrain from all name calling. There has been entirely too much

---

1. Beckman is quoting William Cardinal O'Connell.

calling of names, too much determination of the motives of others. Those who differ with us in opinion do so by the right which reason gives them, and they are entitled to our respectful consideration.

I wish to say today that I speak in the name of all Catholic groups of this diocese, whatever their opinions be, about the course our country should follow. I ask all to recognize that the authority of our civil government has its source in God and that all power is from God. According to our democratic form of government and our traditional procedure, it is our duty to help to form a healthy public opinion and to make known our judgments to those who represent us in government. In our traditional freedom of speech and in our criticisms we must show both consideration and respect for those vested with civil authority.

In the name of the Catholic priesthood and of the Catholic laity of this diocese, I wish to express in a special manner our sympathy to all the occupied and oppressed countries of the world. I wish to give them the assurance that they are daily and constantly in our prayers. We beseech God that the day of the reign of tyrants shall be shortened and that the people of occupied and persecuted countries shall soon again enjoy the freedom of the sons of God.

In speaking of occupied countries, I wish to say that we consider both Germany and Russia occupied. Germany is no longer in the hands of the German people. Human tyrants are entrenched in the seats of government. They have lost every vestige of humanity and all sense of religious freedom; they are given over to the reprobate sense of practically rejecting a personal God, to whom they must answer; they are controlling the political, the religious, the economic and the war destinies of the German people. However strongly we condemn, let us not condemn the whole German people. There are in Germany millions of devout Christians who condemn religious persecution and who loath the inhumanity and brutality of Nazism. Let us pray incessantly for these people, that God may preserve them and that they may prevail and restore Germany to the place of honor that it should occupy among the nations of the world. Let us pray for the Nazis, that God may have mercy on them, soften their hearts, and enable them to appreciate the ennobling teachings of Christianity.

I wish to say frankly that I speak for the great majority of the diocese in whose veins flows the blood of German ancestors. These people rightly love the blood of their forefathers. They condemn Nazism, satanically enthroned in Germany. These people are not pro-Nazi; they are not even pro-German; they are Americans and pro-America. They have no other civil allegiance. They will abide by any decision that America makes, but they pray God daily that the decision of our Government may merit divine approval. I wish to say that it is most unjust to impute motives to those of our diocese in whose veins flows the blood of German ancestors. It is un-Christian to characterize them as a group favorable to Nazism.

Russia is also an occupied country. Its seats of government are occupied by godless, inhuman tyrants, who have tried to impose atheistic Communism not only on Russia but on all countries of the world. Their activities in our own country, even at the present moment, are shocking to the Christian sense. Because their system cannot work where there is religious freedom and where a personal God is recognized, they have endeavored to destroy all religious freedom and, in their insanity, have tried to destroy the idea of God in the minds of men and the love of God in the hearts of men. We know that where there is no religious freedom there can be no other freedom. We Americans know that the best guarantee we can have of all freedoms is our freedom of religion.

We must not be deceived by Sovietism. We know what the Russian government tried to do in Spain and what atheistic Communism has been trying to do in Mexico and in our own country. We know that the opinion-forming agencies of our country and many of the officials of our Government would have sustained the illegal atheistic, Communistic government of Spain. They would have tried to destroy the most Christian country of Europe. These same agencies and these same officials tried to have the American public accept an atheistic and Communistic Spain. They tried to glorify one of the blackest pages in all history. Let us not be deceived by Sovietism. We can never put any faith in atheistic Communism. Up to the present moment it seems almost impossible to distinguish between the Soviet government and its Communism or radicalism that is atheistic to the core.

We must not, however, identify the Russian people with the Soviet government. There are millions of poor, simple, God-fearing Russians who hate the atheistic Communism of their government and who pray incessantly for their deliverance. Our prayers are daily offered that God may have mercy on the Russian people, shorten the days of religious persecution, and restore them to peaceful prosperity.

We express our wholehearted sympathy for the persecuted Jews of the world. We assure our persecuted Jewish brethren that they are daily in our prayers. We implore the Divine Christ to deliver the chosen people of the old law from the oppression of injustice and from the bondage and murderous brutality of their persecutors. We pray that the Jews may labor for a new order in the world, which will merit divine approval.

In a moment we shall bow in adoration while the Eucharistic Christ blesses us. Let us beseech Our Divine Savior to enlighten and to strengthen all the officials of our Government that they may decide the destiny of our country according to the thoughts and plan of God. Our country faces perhaps the most crucial hour in all its history. We must pray for it as though everything depended on our prayer. We thank God sincerely that our country has not been an enemy of religion. Religious persecution is abhorrent to her and to our officials of Government. But let us admit, in all sincerity, that the majority of our citizens have been indifferent to religion.

As we pray for peace, let us realize that there can be no lasting peace founded on murderous vindictiveness or on the degradation of any group, nation or people to a state of slavery. Permanent peace can be founded only on justice and charity. The only enduring peace that will restore the world to sanity and to a sense of the dignity of human personality is the peace of Pope Pius XII.

Let us confidently pray today that in God's Providence, despite our failings and our sins, our country may be spared the chastisement of war. In our prayers, let us beseech God that we Americans may be privileged to play a major part in the restoration of a war-shattered world.

McNicholas Papers, Archives of Archdiocese of Cincinnati. Printed with permission.

50. "Victory and Peace," a Statement Issued by the Administrative Board of the National Catholic Welfare Conference, 14 November 1942

1. Our country has been forced into the most devastating war of all time. This war, which is the absorbing interest of all the world, involves unquestionably the most important moral issue of today. Some nations are united in waging war to bring about a slave world — a world that would deprive man of his divinely conferred dignity, reject human freedom, and permit no religious liberty. We are associated with the other powers in a deadly conflict against these nations to maintain a free world. This conflict of principles makes compromise impossible.

Justice of Present War

2. While war is the last means to which a nation should resort, circumstances arise when it is impossible to avoid it. At times it is the positive duty of a nation to wage war in the defense of life and right. Our country now finds itself in such circumstances.

3. Even while we meet here [in Washington], the exigencies of war have driven our armed forces into unexpected areas of conflict in Africa. Our president, in letters addressed to the rulers of all the friendly nations concerned, has given solemn assurance that the United States has no designs of permanent conquest or sordid interest. Our aim, he pledged, is to guarantee to countries under temporary occupation as well as to our own the right to live in security and peace. We bishops are confident that the pledge of our chief executive, not lightly made, faithfully mirrors the mind and conscience of the American people....

6. In the discharge of our pastoral responsibility, we are gravely concerned about the world peace of tomorrow.

7. Secularism cannot write a real and lasting peace. Its narrow vision does not encompass the whole man, it cannot evaluate the spirituality of the human soul and the supreme good of all mankind.

8. Exploitation cannot write a real and lasting peace. Where greedy and selfish expediency are made the substitutes of justice there can be no securely ordered world.

9. Totalitarianism, whether Nazi, communist or fascist, cannot write a real and lasting peace. The state that usurps total powers, by that very fact, becomes a despot to its own people and a menace to the family of nations.

Christianity and Peace

10. The Spirit of Christianity can write a real and lasting peace in justice and charity to all nations, even to those not Christian.

11. In the epochal revolution through which the world is passing, it is very necessary for us to realize that every man is our brother in Christ. All should be convinced that every man is endowed with the dignity of human personality, and that he is entitled by the laws of nature to the things necessary to sustain life in a way comfortable to human dignity. In the postwar world, the profit element of industry and commerce must be made subservient to the common good of communities and nations if we are to have a lasting peace with justice and a sense of true brotherhood of all our neighbors. The inequalities of nations and of individuals can never give to governments or to the leaders of industry or commerce a right to be unjust. They cannot, if they follow the fixed principles of morality, maintain or encourage conditions under which men cannot live according to standards befitting human personality.

12. Unfortunately, in our day we must wage a global war to secure peace. War is abnormal and necessarily brings on abnormal conditions in the life of a nation.

13. During the war crisis free men must surrender many of their liberties. We ask our people to be united and prepared to make every sacrifice which our government deems necessary for a just and enduring peace through the victory of our armed forces. We are confident that they will perform their wartime duties gladly because they know that our country has been the defender, not the destroyer, of liberties and has in the past always reestablished the full measure of peacetime freedom on the conclusion of hostilities.

Protection of Women in War Work

14. Our government has announced that the war emergency makes it necessary to employ an unprecedented number of women in industry. While we are wholeheartedly cooperating with our government in the prosecution of the war, we must, as shepherds of souls, express our grave concern about the Christian home in our beloved country in these crucial days. When mothers are engaged in industry a serious child-care problem necessarily arises. Every effort must be made to limit, as far as necessity permits, the employment of mothers in industry, particularly young mothers. Due provision in harmony with American traditions should be made for the day care of the children of working mothers. The health and moral welfare of mothers employed in industry should be thoroughly safeguarded. With a full realization of the role which women must play in winning the war and of the extreme measures that our government must take, we ask that all try to realize the dangers in-

volved, especially the moral dangers. We urge that there be a wholesome moral atmosphere wherever women are employed....

Denunciation of the Persecutions of the Jews

16. We express our deepest sympathy to our brother bishops in all countries of the world where religion is persecuted, liberty abolished, and the rights of God and of man are violated. Since the murderous assault on Poland, utterly devoid of every semblance of humanity, there has been a premeditated and systematic extermination of the people of this nation. The same satanic technique is being applied to many other peoples. We feel a deep sense of revulsion against the cruel indignities heaped upon the Jews in conquered countries and upon defenseless peoples not of our faith. We join with our brother bishops in subjugated France in a statement attributed to them:

> Deeply moved by the mass arrests and maltreatment of Jews, we cannot stifle the cry of our conscience. In the name of humanity and Christian principles our voice is raised in favor of imprescriptible rights of human nature.

We raise our voice in protest against despotic tyrants who have lost all sense of humanity by condemning thousands of innocent persons to death in subjugated countries as acts of reprisal; by placing other thousands of innocent victims in concentration camps, and by permitting unnumbered persons to die of starvation.

17. The war has brought to the fore conditions that have long been with us. The full benefits of our free institutions and the rights of our minorities must be openly acknowledged and honestly respected. We ask this acknowledgment and respect particularly for our colored fellow citizens. They should enjoy the full measure of economic opportunities and advantages which will enable them to realize their hope and ambition to join with us in preserving and expanding in changed and changing social conditions our national heritage. We fully appreciate their many native gifts and aptitudes, which, ennobled and enriched by a true Christian life, will make them a powerful influence in the establishment of a Christian social order....

Hugh J. Nolan, ed., *Pastoral Letters of the United States Catholic Bishops* (Washington, D.C.: United States Catholic Conference, 1984), 2:38–43. Printed with permission.

51. Administrative Board of the National Catholic Welfare Conference, "International Order," 16 November 1944

1. We have met the challenge of war. Shall we meet the challenge of peace? This is the question uppermost in the minds of men everywhere who in suffering and hardship have stood out against ruthless aggression. The men of our armed forces, the masses of our citizens, our leaders, all want to be true to

our heroes who have given so much, some even their lives, in this war for freedom. They want to be true, as well, to future generations on whom we have been forced to place a heavy burden as the price for their freedoms. Honestly, earnestly we want to garner from the sacrifices, hardships, and losses which have gone into this war, the full fruits of victory, in a good peace. The foremost problem in postwar planning is how to secure for ourselves and all the world a just and lasting peace.

2. Recently representatives of the United States, the United Kingdom, the Soviet Union, and China at Dumbarton Oaks formulated and presented to their governments broad tentative proposals for an international organization for "the maintenance of peace and security and the creation of conditions which make for peace." These proposals have been given to the public for full study and discussion by peoples of all countries. Our own Secretary of State has expressed the hope that leaders of our national thought and opinion will discuss them in the spirit of constructive effort.

Freedom from Hatred, Greed

3. Public opinion in our country can exert a tremendous influence in making the peace and determining the manner of international collaboration for its maintenance. If public opinion is indifferent or uninformed, we shall run the risk of a bad peace and perhaps return to the tragedy of "power politics," which in the past divided nations and sowed the seeds of war. If public opinion is alert and informed, we can have lasting peace and security. It is imperative that all our citizens recognize their responsibility in the making and maintenance of the peace. They must inform themselves on the issues and form their judgments in light of sound reason and our Christian democratic traditions. They must free themselves from hatred, from distrust, and from the spirit of mere expediency, from national greed, and from indifference to right in the use of might, and they must form their judgments on the basis of stern objective realities.

4. This war came largely from bad education. It was not brought on by primitives or unlettered peoples. The contemporary philosophy which asserts the right of aggression is the creation of scholars. Discarding moral principles and crowding God out of human life, scholars produced the monstrous philosophies which, embodied in political and social systems, enslave human reason and destroy the consciousness of innate human rights and duties. In these systems the notion of the common good is utterly distorted; it is no longer conceived as the consequence of the common enjoyment of rights and the common discharge of duties, but the creation of the caprice of a dictator or a group or a party. The gilded dreams of a new era, which these systems heralded, have proved to be a hideous nightmare. If we are to have a just and lasting peace, it must be the creation of a sane realism, which has a clear vision of the moral law, a reverent acknowledgment of God its Author, and a recognition of the oneness of the human race underlying all national distinctions.

Atlantic Charter without Equivocations

5. We have no confidence in a peace which does not carry into effect, without reservations or equivocations, the principles of the Atlantic Charter. We feel, too, that it should provide assistance for prostrate nations in reconstructing their economic, social, and political institutions. If justice is compromised, if unreasonable concessions are made to might, grievances will rankle in the bosom of aggrieved nations to endanger the peace of the world. If prostrate nations are not assisted in giving to their people fair economic opportunities, they will become the arena of civil strife and turmoil. No international organization will be able to maintain a peace which is unfair and unjust.

6. There is an international community of nations. God Himself has made the nations interdependent for their full life and growth. It is not, therefore, a question of creating an international community but of organizing it. To do this we must repudiate absolutely the tragic fallacies of "power politics" with its balance of power, spheres of influence in a system of puppet governments, and the resort to war as a means of settling international difficulties.

Might Must Yield to Law

7. After the last world war an attempt was made to organize the international community. It failed not because its objective was mistaken but because of inherent defects in its charter and more especially perhaps because the nations were not disposed to recognize their duty to work together for the common good of the world. International law must govern international relations. Might must be subordinated to law. An international institution, based on the recognition of an objective moral obligation and not on the binding force of covenant alone, is needed for the preservation of a just peace and the promotion of international cooperation for the common good of the international community. The common good of every nation is inseparably connected with the common good of the international community.

8. The international institution must be universal. It must seek to include, with due regard to basic equality of rights, all the nations, large and small, strong and weak. Its constitution must be democratic. While it is reasonable to set up a security council with limited membership, this council must not be an instrument for imperialistic domination by a few powerful nations. Before it every nation must stand on its rights and not on its power. It must not allow any nation to sit in judgment in its own case. Frankly it must recognize that for nations as well as individuals life is not static. It must, therefore, provide in its charter for the revision of treaties in the interest of justice and the common good of international community, as well as for the recognition of a people's coming of age in the family of nations.

Strong Nations Must Help the Weak Ones

9. The function of the international organization must be the maintenance of international peace and security, the promotion of international cooperation, and the adoption of common policies for the solution of common

economic, social, and other humanitarian problems. In the maintenance of peace it is reasonable that the organization have at its disposal resources for coercing outlaw nations even by military measures.

10. In fostering and promoting international cooperation it must seek to guarantee to the weak and poor nations economic opportunities which are necessary to give their peoples reasonable standards of living, and it must seek to prevent selfish monopolistic control of raw materials which are needed for the economic stability of other nations. Effective international cooperation lays definite duties on favored nations. No nation may view with unconcern conditions that permit millions of workers in any country to be without the opportunity to secure from their labor adequate family support. Nations rich in natural resources must remember that ownership of property never dispenses from the social obligations of stewardship. Nations gifted with inventive and productive genius are obligated to serve the reasonable needs of other nations. Nations should open, under effective guarantees, world lanes of commerce and world avenues of communication to all law-abiding countries. Protective national legislation for legitimate national economic interests must not impede the flow of international commerce and the right social function of international exchange.

Teeth for the World Court

11. In the international organization there should be a world court to which justiciable disputes among nations must be submitted. Its authority should not be merely advisory but strictly judicial. A condition for the right functioning of this court is the proper development and codification of international law. Competent international authority must enact into positive law the principles of the moral law in their international references, and to these will be added positive treaty provisions and the charter and legislation of the international organization....

Rights of Man

13. The international organization must never violate the rightful sovereignty of nations. Sovereignty is a right which comes from the juridical personality of a nation and which the international organization must safeguard and defend. However, national sovereignty may not be interpreted as absolving a nation from its obligations in the international community. Moreover, even within the state, national sovereignty is limited by the innate rights of men and families. Since civil authority does not confer these God-given rights, it may not violate them.

14. The ideology of a nation in its internal life is a concern of the international community. To reject this principle is tantamount to maintaining that the violation of the innate rights of men in a country by its own government has no relation to world peace. Just at this moment, in the interest of world peace, our nation is exerting itself to root out some ideologies which violate human rights in the countries we are liberating. We hold that if there is to

be a genuine and lasting world peace, the international organization should demand as a condition of membership that every nation guarantee in law and respect in fact the innate rights of men, families, and minority groups in their civil and religious life. Surely our generation should know that tyranny in any nation menaces world peace. A nation which refuses to accord to its own people the full enjoyment of innate human rights cannot be relied upon to co-operate in the international community for the maintenance of a peace which is based on the recognition of national freedom. Such a nation will pursue its own selfish international policies, while paying lip service to international cooperation.

Free Men, Free Nations

15. We have it within our power to introduce a new era, the era for which peoples have been longing through the centuries, the era in which nations will live together in justice and charity. It is a Christian hope we want to realize, the hope of a world at peace, a world of sovereign states cooperating in assuring all men the full enjoyment of their rights, a world of free men and free nations with their freedom secured under law. War may come, but if our hope is realized it will be a war of punishment meted out to outlaw nations. Through all the sufferings and sacrifices of this war we have remembered and we recall today the words of our chief executive, written at its beginning:

> We shall win this war and in victory we shall seek not vengeance but the establishment of an international order in which the spirit of Christ shall rule the hearts of men and nations.

Hugh J. Nolan, ed., *Pastoral Letters of the United States Catholic Bishops* (Washington, D.C.: United States Catholic Conference, 1984), 2:56–61. Printed with permission.

The Depression and the New Deal

The economic crisis of the 1930s elicited a renewed interest in the principles of Catholic social teaching both in the diagnosis of the reasons for the Great Depression and in the evaluation of Franklin Roosevelt's New Deal. Catholic voices were an active part of the ongoing national discussion of these issues, and, as historian Gerald Fogarty has noted, "the similarity between Catholic social teaching and New Deal legislation forged one of the closest associations between the Church and the Government since the days of Ireland and Gibbons in the 1890s."

The thrust of Catholic social thought also included moral reflection on the effects of private actions on the common good. From this vantage point Catholics joined their voices to larger discussions about population control. When the Lambeth Conference of the Church of England officially accepted the morality of artificial contraception, Pope Pius XI fired back the encyclical *Casti connubi,* denouncing the practice as contrary to the natural law. American Catholic commentators accepted papal teaching and also argued against birth control as a matter of public policy.

Meanwhile, significant efforts were made to expand and upgrade the quality of Catholic education and social provision for children. Joined by growing numbers of lay counterparts, religious women continued to supply a large majority of the dedicated workers who staffed Catholic institutions. And as the depression deepened and growing numbers of young people no longer worked at adult jobs, Catholic leaders responded with highly organized and popular Catholic youth organizations which emphasized allegiance to the church and character formation, often in the context of athletic competition.

The 1930s also saw the emergence of Dorothy Day's Catholic Worker movement. With its signature "houses of hospitality," where charity, voluntary poverty, and criticism of bourgeois culture flourished, the movement offered a radical alternative to mainstream Catholic views and challenged the government programs of the New Deal.

52. "Statement on the Economic Crisis," Issued by the Administrative Board of the National Catholic Welfare Conference for the American Bishops, 12 November 1931

1. Urged by the charity of Christ, of whose Church we are the shepherds, we seek always to extend to the multitude that spiritual food which alone sustains the life of the soul and all that the soul means to man, both here and hereafter. To the multitude we seek also to give that material food essential to the life and well-being of the individual, of the family, of all society. In this day of world-wide depression and of hardship, we voice our deep paternal sympathy for those millions of Americans of whatever creed or race, who, victims of the present industrial crisis, must rely on their more fortunate brethren for food, clothing, and shelter.

2. We urge the reading, the study, and the application to everyday business, occupational, and social life, of the encyclical of our Holy Father, Pius XI, *On the Reconstruction of the Social Order.* In keeping with the recommendations of the Holy Father, we have enlisted the services of our clergy and laity in a "crusade of charity," either in co-operation with approved relief agencies or independently of them, as varying local conditions suggest.

3. Since we are all bound together as brothers in Christ, it is our duty to insist that the wealthy are obligated in conscience to contribute for the relief of those who suffer, and the more so because the system under which they suffer has yielded wealth to others.

4. While cooperating in these private efforts, we are convinced, because of the vastness of the number suffering, that federal and state appropriations for relief in some form will become necessary.

5. Our economic system should be so improved that the laboring man, suddenly thrown out of employment, would not be deprived of sustenance during a period of severe business depression.

6. We deem it our duty also to quote the Holy Father on the relationships of armament to the present crisis:

7. "The unbridled race for armaments is on the one hand the effect of the rivalry among nations and on the other the cause of the withdrawal of enormous sums from the public wealth and hence not the smallest of contributors to the current extraordinary crisis."

8. The unemployment crisis is deep-rooted in the avarice of human nature which for a century and more has caused disorganization of the processes of production and distribution. This has run its course through unlimited individual and organized competition and is climaxed now by an ineffective economic rule. We ask a living wage for the family; a proper proportion between the wages of the different kinds of workers; an ample sufficiency for all. We ask for wages that will provide employment to the greatest extent possible; and for an equitable sharing of the goods produced so abundantly by industry.

9. And to avoid unjust and inequitable wage reductions, we ask for joint conferences of employers and their associations and labor and their unions, supplemented and assisted by government. Indeed all economic life needs such common counsel to deal with the present depression. Through such common counsel and organization, industry may proceed, animated by a sense of justice and good will to all. Thus will it care for the common good; meet the desire to solve a great problem of the present age; properly use the material resources and talents God has given us; and secure an equitable distribution of the income and wealth of our country and the world.

10. Only on these lines will the problem of how best to form a system of unemployment insurance, reserves, and old-age pensions be successfully worked out. There is dire need that our country and all its citizens bring the competence of every element, versed in the complexities of our industrial and social life, to the solution of this great crisis and the avoidance of its like in the future. There is supreme need that our country be guided and enlightened in all these things by the full teaching of Christ.

11. The present crisis should urge everyone to careful thought and courageous action. We urge Catholic organizations to study the social teaching of the Church so as to help prepare Catholics to take their full part in this great task of our times. Fidelity to the teachings of Christ and of His Church, both as individuals and as a social body, is the foundation on which sure and permanent social justice and happiness must be built. What we seek, here as elsewhere, is a fuller measure of the Kingdom of God on earth as it is in Heaven.

Hugh J. Nolan, ed., *Pastoral Letters of the United States Catholic Bishops* (Washington, D.C.: United States Catholic Conference, 1984), 1:369–70. Printed with permission.

53. Testimony before the Committee on the Judiciary, House of Representatives, United States Congress, 73d Congress, 18–19 January 1934[1]

Statement by Rev. Charles E. Coughlin of Detroit, Michigan

...Malthus was forced by public opinion to conceive the idea that, for the self-preservation of our Nation, we will advance the theory of birth control. There is the origin of Malthus of modern times, and they said, since we believe that we are incapable of raising more wheat, more lamb, more mutton, more beef, and wherewithal by which we live, let us regulate the number of children.

That is all ancient history. We have had Fulton, the inventor of the steamboat, and we have had inventor after inventor, solving facts, and that is the problem of production. Today there is no problem of production. We have more wheat than we can eat, more pigs than we can eat, more cotton than we can wear, more factories than we can utilize, turning out stockings, shoes, clothing, underwear, automobiles, and our problem is not one of production in this twentieth century. Our problem is one of distribution, one of money in the hands of the Federal Reserve banks.

We have advanced our credit, and our currency is expanded today, withdrawn tomorrow, and because of the birth control philosophy in our monetary matters, because we have refused to stand and face the problem of distribution of wealth and industry, not after the manner of socialists, but after the manner of a Washington, a Lincoln, we find ourselves in this common distress....

There was a word that came out of Corinth, "Corinthidso," look that up in your dictionary and see what it means, the first time it was used. It means, if I can translate the very thing into decent English and not offend your ears — it means to legalize birth control by other sexuality; that is the meaning of the word "sodomy," used in the Bible. To sodomize, that was the birth control before they had chemicals; Corinthidso, that was the birth-control method [before] we had our modern chemists....

There is one more problem which will be brought out in specific manner later on. This is a big country of ours, sometimes referred to as a melting pot. Are you aware of the birth rate of the various elements forming this melting pot?

I happen to be of Anglo-Saxon extraction myself, and most of you gentlemen are all Celtic. From what I know of the figures that are published, we are on our way out. There is no question of it. We who boast of our English,

---

1. The Pierce Amendment was one of several legislative proposals introduced into both the House and the Senate in the 1930s aimed at a revision of the United States Penal Code. Section 211 of the Code prohibited the use of the United States mails to send contraceptive information or articles; additional sections extended the prohibition to express companies and common carriers. The Pierce proposal was designed to exclude licensed physicians, medical schools, hospitals, and pharmacies from that prohibition.

Irish, Scotch, and Irish-Celtic-origin are going to be boasters after a while of ancient history and not of modern practice.

It is our race, the Anglo-Saxon and Celtic, I believe, more than others, who are practicing birth control today. Negroes are not practicing it like we are; the Polish people are not practicing it as we are. The Italians are not practicing it as we are. One hundred years from today, Washington will be Washingtonski, in the minds of the children to be born. We are being degenerated, and here we are advocating ways and means to uncriminalize the use of contra-conceptives and to help America forget its Anglo-Saxon origin.

How about the Negroes? The Negroes in one sense are more prolific people than are we. I heard, I believe it was Dr. Gillis, broadcasting one Sunday some figures on the advance of the Negro in the matter of begetting children. According to his figures, 100 years from now the white man of America will be an oddity. That is shocking to some of you, but go down to Texas, or to New Orleans in Louisiana, and find out for yourself. Perhaps the Negro deserves to go ahead, perhaps he does, with the advocacy among whites to curtail the birth of children, and the Negroes' outbegetting us almost 2 to 1. Some day Congress, a hundred years from now, would look back to the Seventy-third Congress and say, "Yes; they helped all of this along.... "

Statement of Dr. Joseph J. Mundell, Professor of Obstetrics,
Georgetown University, Washington, D.C.

Mr. Chairman and gentlemen, recent scientific work has shown that during the menstrual cycle in women there is a period of fertility and a period of sterility. The fertile period, during which the woman may become pregnant, lasts not longer than 9 or 10 days. This fertile period can be reckoned with almost mathematical precision. The balance of the 28-day menstrual cycle is sterile; it is not possible for a woman to become pregnant during this time. Abundant clinical experience is being collected to substantiate and confirm these observations.

Granting that there are women with grave kidney, heart, and lung diseases in whom pregnancy would jeopardize their lives, we now have available scientific medical devices that will definitely safeguard them against pregnancy. Furthermore, mechanical and chemical contraceptive contrivances are hazardous, because if indulged in continually over long periods they undoubtedly will result in chronic or acute inflammation of the pelvic organs, which may result in chronic invalidism, and over long periods is conducive to the development of cancer.

For these reasons I urge that there is no need for such legislation as is proposed here.

Statement of Dr. John A. Ryan, Professor of Industrial Ethics,
Catholic University of America

Those who advocate the bill which we are discussing here obviously have reasons for so doing, but I notice that there has been a shift in the emphasis in their argument from the individual to social grounds. At most hearings previously, the plight of the individual, the individual mother, and the individual family was stressed, and the necessity therefore of bringing contraceptive methods and information to such a person.

But this year it seems that the emphasis is upon social considerations. It is asserted that the bill is necessary, and the information which it provides for should be available in order to prevent an increase in the children of destitute parents, because the burden of destitution among children is very great, and this would be one method of lessening that burden upon society.

I shall have a word or two to say about the efficacy and the justice of that proposal a little later, but first I want to call attention to another social consideration which seems to be entirely ignored by the advocates of this bill. That is the consideration which is involved in the fact — it is notorious to everyone who takes an intelligent interest in this subject of population — of our declining birthrate....I don't think there is any doubt that, in the mind of any observer, the main cause for the decline in birthrate is the use of those methods which are advocated and which are to be provided for in this bill....

Father Coughlin I believe said yesterday the Anglo-Saxons won't be here after a while. He and I are the same kind of Anglo-Saxons as Schneider the butcher, Levinski the clothier, or O'Leary the contractor; at any rate we won't be here very long....I venture to predict that there will be no material increase in the population of any except a few of the largest cities from now on. So what is going to happen to the real-estate business? What is going to happen to the construction industry?...

The steel industry, I venture, will never again in our lifetime reach the point it reached in 1929. Where is it going to find the market? Automobiles? Yes; they will be fairly constant. Railroads? No more, except a few for replacement. Office buildings, and big buildings generally, will not be there for them. So I believe we will have to bid good-bye to steel as an index to business activity....

If I may take a minute or two to summarize the situation with reference to this bill, you are asked to pass this bill in order to make birth-control knowledge available to the poor so they will have fewer children, and the drain on our relief through the Government agencies will be smaller; in return for the relief they have had, they owe the Government the duty of restricting their families.

I protest against that theory. That is Toryism. That is the belief that society, which means we, the more fortunate classes, and the rich classes, have a right to determine all policies, and we will put on them the burden of lessening their families....This line of argument tends to divert the people from the real causes of maladjustment, and these are failures on the part of society.

Finally, as regards the problem of recovery, the idea that this bill will have any effect on recovery, I think, is fantastic. If we are not well on the way to recovery from this depression by the time any considerable number of children could be born, after the enactment of this bill, then we better get ready for something else in the social order, or a social revolution. That is utterly irrelevant to the whole question. We simply cannot — those who believe as I do — subscribe to the idea that the poor are to be made responsible for their plight, and instead of getting justice from the Government and a more rational social order, they are to be required to reduce their numbers. I repeat that is Toryism.

The Position of National Catholic Alumni Federation and Its Associates

In order that the position which we take against this bill may be clear, we herewith state our reasons for opposition. We do not rest upon the teaching of our church, which has been uniformly and unalterably opposed to the theory of birth control through contraceptive methods.... The objection of our church will be presented by others. We have no authority to speak on behalf of the Catholic Church. That is strictly the province of the hierarchy of the church. We, however, are speaking as Catholic gentlemen and as American citizens.

We intend in this memorandum to oppose the birth-control movement and, in particular, this bill (1) because it is un-American and in direct violation of the principles of social justice, which is the underlying theme of the whole of the administration's social program; (2) because it is subversive of public morals and a violation of the natural law; and (3) because the medical profession is opposed to it.

By reason of the foregoing the permission of the dissemination of literature under the guise of the education of doctors and nurses, etc., is wrong and therefore this bill should be defeated.

Point I: Social Justice and Not Birth Control Is the Solution of the Deplorable Condition of the Poor in This Country: Harry L. Hopkins, Federal Emergency Relief Administrator, said on January 12, 1934, that there were 5,500,00 children on relief in 1933. The birth-control advocate argues that if the poor practiced birth control they would not now be in their present state. The argument apparently is that had the present bill been enacted in one of the past seven Republican congresses there would have been no depression. A little levity is wholesome even in so important and so sacred a subject as the deprivation of life of the future generations. However, we are unable to ascribe this argument of the advocates of this bill to their sense of humor....

Point II: Birth Control Is Subversive of Public Morals and a Violation of the Natural Law: We postulate in this argument...the natural law, and by this we do not mean any preachings of any church.... Blackstone recognized it when he said: "As man depends absolutely on his Maker in all things, it is necessary that he should in all things conform to his Maker's will. This will of the Maker is called the law of nature. When God created man and endowed him with free will to conduct himself in all parts of life, He laid down immutable laws of human nature. These are eternal immutable laws of good and evil which he has enabled reason to discover for the conduct of human actions. This law of nature is binding all over the globe, in all countries, at all times; no human laws are of any validity if contrary to this."

Proceeding with our argument, we state without fear of contradiction that if we permit the use of contraceptives and allow the dissemination of this literature we are opening the door to the destruction of the cornerstone of society — the family. The advocates of this bill argue that this information is necessary to enable married persons to "space children so that they will arrive when wanted and when the parents are financially able to provide for them." They totally disregard the fact if it is made easy for married persons to obtain this information, that it is just as easy for unmarried persons to obtain it. What, then, becomes of the sanction which nature has imposed upon man? What, then, is to discourage and prevent the evil practice of fornication?... There is no doubt that the natural law and the Author of nature forbid and condemn the practice of contraceptive birth control.

Statement of Mrs. Margaret Sanger

Mr. Chairman and Gentlemen of the Committee, it must be rather confusing to you to hear so many statements, misstatements, overlapping of evidence, as has been given to you in the past 2 days. We have had the introduction of the amendment, but I want to tell you that in approving this bill about a year ago, I believed that those who opposed it, especially the Catholic organizations, should be interviewed, and that it would be a good thing to submit this bill to them and to see just where we could get together on the bill....

[I]t may seem there has been a great deal of warfare practiced between the people who oppose the bill and we who propose it, and that the people who have come here to oppose this bill are at the north pole and we are at the south pole; but I beg to inform you that is not true.

There is a book that has recently been published by the Latz Foundation called "The Rhythm of Sterility and Fertility in Women." This has been published with "ecclesiastical approval," and this has been recommended by all of the Catholic societies and Catholic publications.... To me it is a very dangerous thing to put out a book like that, when the physicians and the scientists of the country do not by any means agree that there is a safe period for all women, as Dr. Willson has suggested to you.

Now it comes down to a safe device or a safe period, and that is just about where both sides are now. I can read to you out of this book, "Rhythm," answers to everything that has been said here. Out of this book comes answers, and I will take up your time to read at least some of them. It states here that Catholic doctors are not in agreement as to the serious physical consequences of contraception, and the answer is that they are by no means in agreement on this, and I would want you to understand, they agree that the consequence of over-child bearing and the consequences of prolific child-bearing are to a certain extent a greater cause for worry and anxiety than the other point of contraception....

Father Coughlin also said it is our duty to increase and multiply, and he quoted the Bible, and he said that today, "we, believing as Catholics that marriage was invented by God for the primary purpose of propagating children." This was rather humorous to me, that he, a celibate, never knowing the joys of fatherhood, could come here and tell us to increase and multiply. It seems to me if that is the word of God, certainly he should be on the job....

In our clinic, where many Catholic women come, we have all due respect for them, and all due respect for everyone who has an opinion, whether religious or moral. We know that this bill is not mandatory, it is not asking those opposed to do anything different than they do today. It is permissive legislation that we are asking for.

There are about twenty or twenty-one million Catholics in the country, and there are about a hundred million other people who are not Catholics. It seems to me there is no reason why any one group should impose their will upon the rest of the country, whether it is their moral or religious or their political ideas.

I think you should know, as we have found, that women who come to our clinics average just about equal. We have had 35,000 women in one clinic in New York City, and there are over 150 clinics throughout the country and every one of them reports the same thing, that about one third are Catholic, one third Protestant, and one third Jews, so that they run about even.

I myself had the most pathetic cases of Catholic women torn by their loyalty to the church and their desires to control the size of the family. They have exactly the same problems every other woman has, except it is a greater hardship on them not to be able to have religious sanction of the thing they feel they should do....

This law as we find it, affects the United States mail and common carriers. Someone asked about a physician prescribing by mail. No physician would prescribe by mail, but a physician needs to get proper information of newer means and methods, he needs to exchange with other physicians, clinics, laboratories, and so forth, through the United States mails. As it is now, as one of our physicians testified yesterday, the medical publishers do not want to jeopardize their liberty under such conditions of the law. This book here, "Rhythm," is going through the mails, not by right, but by privilege, and it gives illegal information just as any book I might write on preventing conception....

Mr. Healey [Rep. Arthur D. Healey of Massachusetts, member of the judiciary committee]: You don't mean to leave the impression with this committee that the opposition to the passage of this law is confined to Catholics?

Mrs. Sanger: I think the organized opposition is.... There is no organized opposition except from the Catholic Church. A small group of Lutherans have opposed it, and they are the only groups we have any record of....

Committee on the Judiciary, House of Representatives, United States Congress, 73d Congress, Hatton W. Sumners, Chair, 18–19 January 1934. Hearings on H.R. 5978 introduced by Rep. Walter M. Pierce, (R) Oregon.

54. Social Action Department of the National Catholic Welfare Conference, *Organized Social Justice: An Economic Program for the United States Applying Pius XI's Great Encyclical on Social Life* (131 Signers), 1935

Now that the NRA [National Recovery Administration] is destroyed, a new and better way must be found to abolish the principal injustices that afflict our economic life. This is the first thing needed. The second and more fundamental is to create an economic order which will enable men to do justice readily and in some degree automatically. Without justice we cannot have either industrial recovery or lasting prosperity....

Necessity of Intervention by Government

In 1933 many of the masters of industry professed to be persuaded that the country could never and should never go back to the old economic regime. Now that their fears of economic collapse have been dissipated or mitigated by the recent improvement in business conditions, the most powerful industrialists are clamoring for "a return to unlimited competition and *laissez faire.*" In 1931, Pope Pius XI declared that, "The whole economic life has become hard, cruel and relentless in ghastly measure." Industrialists who desire a return to the regime are, without realizing it, equally cruel; for they would defeat recovery, make unemployment chronic and indefinitely postpone the coming of social justice.

Government is by right and duty more than policeman. It should see to it that the laws and institutions and the whole character and administration of the country shall be such as of themselves will bring public well-being and prosperity. It should protect the poor, and wageworkers generally, because of their great weakness. Social legislation of a sweeping sort is in its province. The social obligations of ownership it should define and enforce. It should help to establish the form of personal ownership which will best meet the common good, and set up public ownership or control of those industries which cannot safely be left in private hands.

In the United States all these and many other social and industrial obligations of public authority will have to be performed mainly by the federal government. Since industry is national in scope and effects, it cannot be adequately regulated except by national action and legislation. Unfortunately, this fact is not grasped by all of those who believe in adequate regulation. Some of them desire and hope that the thing can be done by the forty-eight States.

As a matter of fact, the constitutional power of the States to fix wages, hours or prices, or to enact any of the other important regulations of the NRA is so uncertain that it is not worth serious consideration. In half a dozen or more decisions, the Supreme Court has indicated that most State legislation of this character would violate the due process clause of the Fourteenth Amendment to the Constitution. Even if States had the requisite constitutional authority, they would be unable to agree upon uniform legislative measures for our nation-wide industries and our nation-wide competition. Hence the only alternative to a constitutional amendment enabling Congress to set up standards of industrial and social justice, is no standards at all. Pope Pius XI called for a just regulation of industry by public authority, but the only public authority competent to do this in our political system is the federal government. Those, therefore, who oppose an amendment to the Constitution which would confer this power upon Congress are, either wittingly or unwittingly, demanding the continuation of the old order — *laissez faire*, individualism, liberalism and unlimited competition....

Limitations upon Intervention by Government

Yet to think of the economic welfare of the people in terms of government only is fatal. The amount of government regulation would have to be progressively increased. Even so, it would not be adequate. Let us consider a few of the most important regulations which have been enacted or are likely to be enacted in the United States.

Social insurance is good; it fills out the living wage and cushions our insecurity; but it assumes that the underlying insecurity and injustice are to be otherwise cared for. Regulation of farm production and special taxes to assure parity of farm prices with other prices have been, it seems, necessary; but underproduction when so many are poor and taxation devices to assure parity are the heroic measures of an unjust society. Low credit for farmers and governmental inauguration of a new kind of homesteading by establishing farmers in land ownership at low interest rates is good; but the production, marketing and credit system will require more and more assistance for them from government. Special governmental commissions or bureaus for the regulation of output, prices, wages, hours and collective bargaining are apparently necessary in certain industries; but this implies an endless battle of government with industries which are not organized for service either of the community or their own workers....

As things go, the government would have to keep on tinkering. The totalitarian State, fascist or collectivist, would sooner or later come upon us from around the corner where now it lurks....

Organization by Occupational Groups

If the regime of individualism and *laissez faire* is bankrupt (as it surely is) and if no amount of government regulation can bring about an adequate or just economic order, where shall we find a satisfactory solution? In some form of collectivism (either Socialism or Communism) is the answer given by many of our intellectuals. They reject as futile any program of regulation. They completely overlook the middle ground between individualism and collectivism. This attitude is inexcusable for two reasons: first, because it ignores the proposals for reconstructing the social order set forth by Pope Pius XI; second, because it minimizes or misrepresents the important achievement of the industrial codes under the NRA.

The essence of the Pope's program is a system of occupational groups. In each industry the occupational groups should include all interested parties: labor as well as capital; employees as well as employers. Employers and labor and the other subdivisions of other occupations would keep their rights of separate assemblage and vote inside the occupational groups and their right of separate organizations.... The occupational groups would seek to modify competition by maintaining standards of fairness with regard to wages, hours, prices and business practices; to avoid private industrial dictatorship by enabling labor to share in all industrial policies and decisions, and to exclude political or bureaucratic industrial dictatorship by keeping the immediate and day to day control in the hand of agents of production. They would be prevented from injuring the consumer or the common good by governmental action, "directing, watching, stimulating and restraining, as circumstances suggest or necessity demands...."

Some persons who are sympathetic with an occupational group organization have been confused by references to the Medieval Guilds. The resemblances are, indeed, considerable, but so are the differences. In striving to understand the structure and function of occupational groups it is much more helpful to compare them with institutions within our own experience: the trade associations, the code authorities and the codes of fair practice which functioned under the NRA. If employees had been represented (adequately, of course) in the associations which drew up the NRA industrial code and in the "authorities" which administered the code provisions, the NRA and its institutions would have been fairly comparable with the proposed occupational groups. Had the NRA been permitted to continue, it could readily have developed into the kind of industrial order recommended by the Holy Father.

Three other modifications of the NRA structure are needed for an adequate and just economic order. (a) Economic self-government should be extended to farmers and to the professions. (b) A council or federation should be formed, of all the organized industries and professions, to handle their relations to one another and to the whole community. (c) Government should have the power not only to prevent wrong but to be a positive agent in promoting the common welfare....

A right economic order is a partnership for the common good between government — federal, State and city — and the self-governing, democratically organized membership of the industries, of farming, of trade and of the professions. In the proper functioning of economic life the immediate responsibility rests upon the people, so organized in their industries and professions and in the federation of their organizations as to be able to fulfill their responsibility....

Conclusion

Many Catholics who believe that we need a new economic order are discouraged over the prospects for an occupational group system. It will not be adopted, they fear, within one hundred years. Nevertheless, it is the only arrangement that will hold America safe from Fascism or Communism. Faced with these alternatives, how can any zealous and intelligent Catholic justify himself in yielding to discouragement or following a course of aloofness and inaction?

Moreover, the establishment of the economic order described in the foregoing pages need not be unusually difficult nor postponed to the indefinite future. If the NRA had not been destroyed it could have been developed and transformed into an occupational group system within ten years. It can be reestablished through a constitutional amendment within five years. Here is a work that ought to stir the emotions and enlist the energies of all genuine believers in social justice. To sit by with folded hands or to heed the selfish and misleading propaganda of the servitors of plutocracy, is to commit apostasy from Catholic social principles and treason against America.

Not the least of the virtues of the economic order set forth in this pamphlet is its fundamental democracy. Men would be able to order their own economic lives. They would not be regimented by plutocratic or proletarian or political dictators. The intrinsic and indestructible dignity of the individual would be safeguarded against submergence in and subordination to the mass. The significance of the human person as a child of God and a brother of Christ would obtain, for the first time since the Middle Ages, effective recognition in economic institutions. The sacredness of personality has never been formally recognized in the maxims of historical capitalism. It is frankly rejected in the philosophy of Communism. It is treated as an exploded theory by most of our intellectuals. In the occupational group system it would again become a vital element in American thought and life....

Published by Paulist Press, New York, 1935; reprinted in Aaron Abell, *American Catholic Thought on Social Questions* (Indianapolis: Bobbs-Merrill, 1968), 378–93. Printed with permission.

55. Conference of Religious, National Conference of Catholic Charities; Chair, Sister Katharine, O.S.B., College of St. Scholastica, Duluth, Minnesota, "Catholic Programs of Child Care among Racial Groups," 1935

Rev. Francis J. Gilligan, S.T.D., St. Paul Seminary, St. Paul, Minnesota, "The Catholic Social Worker and the American Race Problem"

...Prominent among the chronic social disorders which persistently are flaring forth and disturbing the peaceful development of the nation is the American race problem. Approximately one-tenth of our population is colored. Toward those eleven million colored the white populace entertain a prejudicial attitude varying from slight aversion to intense hatred. In every state of the Union the Negro is treated differently from the white man. Even in the North the only employment usually open to him is that of menial service, and in periods of depression even those jobs are seized by the white group. Quite generally hotels, restaurants, private schools, hospitals, and even churches are closed to them. Not infrequently the mere attempt of a Negro to purchase a home in a white residential section occasions a racial disturbance involving rioting, property damage, and even loss of life.

Is there a Catholic attitude towards the American race problem? Are there certain phases of the problem about which Catholic social workers and Catholic sociologists should entertain strong convictions? Is the Catholic sociologist able to offer any leadership to the serious Americans who are seeking a solution to this problem?...

In the past in this conference and other Catholic assemblies, many earnest words have been spoken about the ruthless violations of natural rights of individuals here and in other countries. Now, according to the Catholic position, the fountainhead in which those natural rights have their source and justification is the end of man. Each individual was created to glorify God subjectively, by adoration and objectively, by a good life spent in the proportionate development of all his faculties. Because of that obligation to glorify God the Eternal Creator has bestowed upon each individual inviolable moral powers as means towards the attainment of that end. Those means are natural rights.

If that fundamental doctrine is applied to the American race problem, we must concede that the natural rights of the Negro are identical in number and sacredness to the rights of white persons. No matter how strong the prejudice or how persistently through our history the Negro may have been regarded merely as a hewer of wood and a drawer of water, his natural rights must be respected as those of the white man. Natural rights are rooted not upon membership in one nation or upon membership in the white race, but upon the sacredness which the individual enjoys because of his eternal destiny. The Negro must be considered human first and racial afterwards.

In any discussion about rights allowance, indeed, must be made for the differences and inequalities which exist among men. Yet there is a minimum of goods which all men both white and black need and upon which they have a claim. That minimum includes the right to life and the right to liberty. It involves in return for honest labor, the right to remuneration sufficient to maintain the worker and his family in health and comfort. It involves the right to reasonable opportunities for recreation and education. It involves the opportunity to seek a home in an environment which is conducive to wholesome moral living. To all of those rights every Negro has a claim. To deny him less is to degrade him, to treat him less than a man.

As Catholics, then, we must condemn vigorously such practices as peonage, lynching, illegal restrictions upon liberty, and such drastic differentials in wage scales that the Negro is unable to supply his family with the essentials for respectable and decent living. And in order that our protest may not be merely verbal, we should cooperate positively with the agencies which are working constructively for the protection of those elementary rights....

In theory the majority of Americans would concede to the Negro the basic rights enumerated above. Yet in practice many white persons would insist that the Negro must ever be content to occupy a menial position at least when he enters the common national life in which white people participate. Only in the Negro ghetto may the Negro own and operate a business, practice medicine and aspire to cultural leadership. And actually every effort of the Negro to enter the common life of the nation on a status other than that of a servant is vigorously resisted. In factories and stores many employers are reluctant to hire Negroes. And if an exceptional employer is disposed to unlock the racial door he is threatened by his white employees. Towards that attitude and practice is there a definite Catholic attitude?

Catholic moralists teach that in addition to the minimum, men have some rights to other goods and privileges, such as, to seek employment in a variety of business, to seek promotion, to seek higher remuneration, to seek higher education, to be free from unfair and unreasonable restrictions when pursuing other legitimate goods. The basis and measures of the right to more goods than the minimum are the peculiar needs, capacities, and abilities of the individual. Catholic moralists vindicate such rights because the arbitrary denial of all opportunity and progress, renders men bitter and destroys the contentment which is necessary to reasonable human living. In harmony with this opinion of moralists is the moral sentiment of Americans who regard as evil any system in which goods above the minimum and positions of trust in the economic and commercial life are distributed solely upon the basis of nationality or family associations.

If these principles are applied to the American race problem it would seem to follow that the Negro has a claim to goods and positions above the minimum in our economic and commercial life, proportionate to his ability and efforts. These principles would seem to imply that any attempt at least in the northern states, to bar a Negro from an office or factory solely because of his color is a violation of a natural right — it is an act of injustice.

The only serious objections which may be raised against these assertions must be founded upon one of two assumptions: either all Negroes are inferior to whites, or, the Negro ghetto offers complete economic and cultural opportunities.

It is true that there is decidedly a greater proportion of whites who are educated and refined. Yet it is also true that at the present time some Negroes are decidedly superior to the average white person. It is also conformable to the truth to say that at the present time there is no conclusive scientific proof that the Negro is essentially inferior to the white man. The Negro applicant for a position then must be judged on his merits and not arbitrarily rejected because of his color.

The assumption about the adequacy of the Negro ghetto is also unfounded. It is just as impossible to isolate one section of the city as it is impossible to separate a living hand from a living body. The commercial and industrial life of the city flows back and forth through every section of the city as blood flows through the veins and arteries of the human body. We Catholics would strongly denounce as a violation of natural rights any practice which would deny employment to Catholics in all stores except those patronized by Catholics, or any practice which would limit Catholic attendance at schools and institutions to a Catholic neighborhood. Our own sense of justice in that regard suggests the natural moral quality of the policy advocated for the Negro. As Catholics then it appears that we are committed to a policy of opening wider and wider to the deserving Negro the door to the nation's economic and cultural life.

Not infrequently well-intentioned white persons have been induced to gather for the discussion of the Christian attitude towards the race problem. But invariably just as the meeting was progressing the terrifying spectre of possible intermarriage would appear. Usually the mere mention of the word was sufficient to disrupt the meeting and send the members scurrying to their homes where they vowed the problem to be insoluble.

But Catholics do not usually believe in ghosts. Since this is a Catholic meeting, it should be advantageous to force the dark spectre out into the wholesome atmosphere of Catholic association and to examine it in the pure light of Catholic thought.

In the first place, an obvious observation which has been consistently ignored must be made, namely, that the overwhelming majority of white people to do not care to marry Negroes. Likewise the overwhelming majority of Negroes do not wish to marry white persons. Moreover, because of the virility of race prejudice, for several centuries to come it is unlikely that any considerable number of either group would care to marry outside their own race. So the fear of intermarriage is much like a ghost. It lacks substance and form.

More seriously the contention may be advanced that the entrance of Negroes into the commercial, industrial, and cultural life of the nation will lead necessarily to intermarriage, and that as a protection against intermarriage all forms of discrimination and segregation are justifiable. That contention is not true. Contacts between young people working together in offices or factories or attending the same school do not lead necessarily to marriages. In New York City marriages between Jews and Gentiles are rare although they intermingle in offices and commercial life. Contacts leading to marriage are formed only where young people may meet together socially, such as in one another's homes or in private gatherings of certain groups. Such gatherings are personal and private. To such gatherings Negroes have no desire to go, neither have they the right. Separation of the races in such gatherings can be defended as a means of preventing interracial marriages. Separation in offices, factories and schools cannot be justified as a necessary protection against interracial marriages. In conclusion the observation may be made that interracial marriages at the present time are not desirable, not because of any biological reason, but because of the high degree of probability that the marriage would be a failure.

Some attention, too, should here be given to the fact that the source of many of the evils besetting the Negro is the thoughtless acceptance and the repetition of unverified and disparaging rumors about Negroes. Seldom in the history of mankind has any group been more widely misrepresented, misunderstood and handicapped by popular rumors than the American colored group. The basis of much of the prejudice which blocks the progress of the colored group, especially in the North, is the constantly repeated assertions that all Negroes are lazy, or ignorant, or immoral. Sufficient evidence can be presented to indicate that Negroes when placed in an industrial system, labor as energetically as white men. From numerous sources may be gathered testimony that many Catholic Negroes live chastely despite a physical environment which drastically thwarts the development of Christian home life. The ever increasing number of American Negroes who are making valuable contributions to literature and science disproves the assertions that the colored are necessarily unintelligent. To state that all Negroes are bent upon attacking white women is arrant nonsense.

The practice indulged in by white individuals of repeating carelessly those statements is morally wrong. The human mind was created for the reception of truth and the organs of speech for its conveyance. Probably because such statements are made carelessly and uttered thoughtlessly they seldom in themselves constitute a serious moral offense. Nevertheless each white person is under a serious obligation to strive to correct such an evil tendency just as he is under obligation to correct any other bad habit, for the colored group suffer drastically as a consequence. And those who are accustomed to advocate violence in the solution of race problems may well meditate upon the conclusion of the Chicago Race Commission: "The moral responsibility for race rioting does not rest upon hoodlums alone, but also upon all citizens black and white who sanction force or violence in interracial relations or who do not condemn and combat the spirit of racial hatred thus expressed."

Throughout this paper an effort has been made to suggest some correlations between Christian principles and the American race problem. The realization is keenly entertained that some dissenting criticism will arise. But the hope is treasured that this attempt will lead to discussion, and the discussion will lead to the formulation of a statement of a Catholic attitude on the race problem. Catholic students of social problems and Catholic social workers in their readings and group discussions encounter the problem constantly. To them the Catholic laity look for guidance and leadership. To them our fellow citizens of different faiths may well voice a challenge asking what light Catholic philosophy offers. It is hoped that a Catholic group will not be content to hold aloft a mirror-like statement which merely reflects existing conditions. Rather, taking a stand upon the firm principles of Catholic doctrine and relying upon the grace of Christ, may the Catholic students of social problems courageously hold before all Americans the strong light of a Catholic attitude, which will point the path to ultimate cooperation and harmony in all racial problems.

Catechist Margaret Campbell, Society of Missionary Catechists, Victory-Noll, Huntington, Indiana, "Catholic Care of Mexican Children"

...The true character of Mexicans is little known to the average American. Mexicans are naturally docile, pleasant, courteous, and sensitive. They are more apt to be grieved or deeply disappointed in a person, than to be revengeful. They quickly sense the superior attitude of another, and they deeply resent it. It deadens and discourages them, and prevents them from giving confidence. It is a superior attitude on the part of many social workers and teachers which so commonly hinders their work with the Mexicans.

Parental authority and family ties are still strong. These poor, mostly illiterate, parents have the greatest desire to give their children the better things in life. We find they are willing to make extreme sacrifices for whatever they think is best for their children.

The housing of Mexican families is anything but conducive to health, happiness or high morale. In the Calumet Steel District they pay high rent for the worst kind of basement or attic room in the slums. A whole family lives in one room. On the Texas cotton ranches we find them existing in abandoned stables, sheds, garages, places usually considered unfit for domestic animals. Occasionally a ranch owner provides one-room shacks. In the California cotton and vegetable camps we find some families in small one or two-room houses, but many have only a tent, or, what is worse, a sort of tepee made of old burlap bags, cardboard boxes and newspapers. In Mexican settlements within the limits of cities there are single lots rented at high rates to as many families as can manage to crowd on with their little shacks of discarded lumber, boxwood, or airweed. The more families on the lot the better returns in rent. No provision is made for sewage disposal.

When an attempt was made to improve such conditions in the Imperial Valley the help of city officers was sought, but it was found that some of those officials owned lots in the Mexican district. Their only response was to advise that birth control literature be spread among the Mexicans....

The circumstances of the average Mexican family plainly show the need for Catholic care.

Their physical handicap must be considered. The infant death rate is appalling. Comparing the Mexican infant mortality rates with that of other races in California, we see that it is almost three times as high as that of Japanese, and about twice as high as that of Negroes....

The public school systems in the Southwest usually segregate the Mexicans from the so-called Americans. Naturally the Mexicans do not get teachers who are considered the best. Unless a teacher takes a real interest in Mexicans she cannot successfully work with them. On the other hand, American and Mexican Communists are taking keen interest in our Mexican youth....

Having considered the immediate needs of the children let us give a brief account of what we are doing for them.

We help the body in order to help the soul. Hence we have organized mothers' clubs, dispensaries, clinics. We give the mothers simple instructions in Spanish on caring for themselves, their infants, home and family. We find them eager to learn and most willing to cooperate. With charity fund donations, donations from educational departments of cereal, milk and baby food, and other like helps, we are able to give some of these children a fair start in life.

Physicians, the majority non-Catholics, are giving us their unstinted cooperation, and their services gratis. Where there is no free hospitalization for Mexicans we sometimes have to beg the money to pay hospital bills. We have cases of communicable diseases, physical handicaps of every kind, requiring specialists' attention which is being charitably applied, bringing rehabilitation to these little ones.

In prevention of epidemics, especially to be feared in the overcrowded Mexican quarters, the health authorities turn to us to get the Mexicans to submit to immunization and use disease preventives. For our humble Mexicans seem to think that whatever the "Madrecitas," "Little Mothers," advise is safe.

The Mexican parents want their children to get at least a fair education, to be able to speak and read and write English. They feel that is their only chance for future economic and social betterment. We Americans little appreciate that attitude on the part of the Mexicans. Nor do we realize their disappointment in being in inferior schools.

When we opened a mission in Lubbock, Texas, seven years ago, there was in the Mexican district within the city limits, a very small one-room school which could not well accommodate more than 25 children. There were nearly 200 children of school age. Within easy walking distance across the tracks were two modern grade schools. Saying nothing of our American ideals, the laws of our land would not keep those Mexican children out of the graded school. The majority of them were born in our States. Their parents were taxpayers. But public opinion, race prejudice, confined them to the little shack with a Spanish-speaking apostate for teacher. The children disliked school in spite of the teacher's beguiling efforts to win them to the Baptist sect. Most of them played hooky several days a week. Parents were loathe to insist on their children attending that school. We encouraged the parents to send them, and to work and pray for a better school and teachers. We used all our influence with the children and I believe they sometimes thought we were acting as truant officers.

As there was not the slightest possibility of getting a Catholic school, we sought the Board of Education and pleaded for a better public school. With the exception of one member, the Board was strongly against Catholics and Mexicans. We struggled on and prayed. The good Padre in charge of the Mexicans took a vital interest in the situation and used his influence with authorities, thus paving the way for bettering the school.

At the close of the second year we got the President of the Kiwanis, a District Judge, interested. Through his influence a modern two-room school was put up in the Mexican district and two better teachers engaged. But two months after that school was opened the enrollment had so increased that it was necessary to rent the Methodist church and hire another teacher.

We conduct Christian Doctrine classes for public school children after school hours during the week, and on Saturday and Sunday. Many of the teachers and school authorities cooperate with us. They tell us that there is a marked improvement in children attending Catholic instructions. Sometimes we are permitted to conduct our classes in the public school buildings, but ordinarily we have to resort to shacks, old dance halls, shops, fields, roadsides and ditch banks....

Through clubs, sodalities, and scout troops we are trying to supplement the meager Catholic training of poor underprivileged Mexican youth, and to provide recreational and social programs. We try to preserve the best of the Mexican tradition and culture, while at the same time encouraging the adoption of true American customs.

For the thousands of Mexican, and Mexican-American children in the United States, not counting the millions battling an obscene, socialistic education in Old Mexico, there is but one hope — Catholic care. Poor, neglected, downtrodden, and defenseless, though the Mexicans are, they are our people, and as such have a right to our sympathetic interest and protection....

Mother Teresa, O. Carm., Corpus Christi Carmel, Kearney, Nebraska, "Catholic Care of Mexican Children in the North Platte Valley"

Before speaking of our work with the Mexican children in the North Platte Valley, may I give you a few details of the living conditions of their parents, which will give you an idea, not only of the difficulties in the way of practising their religion, but of their existing at all.

The Mexicans of the Grand Island Diocese are employed almost entirely in the beet-fields. The farmers engage them to weed, hoe, thin, and block the beets in their growing stage. The average Mexican family takes care of from 20 to 30 acres during the season, and this means laborious work from early morning until sun-down. There are no machines — all is done by hand. The pay they are supposed to receive, averages $13 per acre for the entire season. I say "supposed," because in many cases the Mexican is defrauded of even that meagre sum. Very often the family begins the year's work in a penniless condition. Since they must have food at least, the farmer makes an agreement with a local grocer by which he supplies the Mexican with all that he needs, at the farmer's expense. In consideration of this convenience, the grocer charges considerably more than the market prices, perhaps 30 to 50 per cent more. Mexican families are usually large, and by the end of the beet-season when the grocery bill is deducted from wages, there is very little, if anything, left. How is the family going to exist, be clothed or have the barest necessities of life during the remaining six months of the year?

Last year, Federal relief answered the question, but I understand that it is to be discontinued this fall. There is practically no other employment available to Mexicans in this part of the country. As to their housing conditions — they are deplorable. The owners of the sugar factories have put up what are commonly called "shacks" for their use. In most cases, these shacks consist of one room divided by a partition or only a sheet. If there is sickness — and there is plenty of it most winters — there is absolutely no way of isolating, and there are certainly no comforts or conveniences for the sick.

It is when the Mexicans begin to come into these shacks from the ranches in the late fall that our work with them begins. It is impossible to give them any religious instruction when they are on the ranches, as the whole family down to the little children, work out among the beets.

We begin by taking a census in six towns of the North Platte Valley: Scottsbluff, Minatare and Bayard to the east, and Mitchell, Morrill and Lyman to the west. The Mexicans number roughly 800 on either side, east or west. Lack of employment has driven many representative Mexican families back to Mexico, but accessions from the neighboring states leave the actual number of families on each mission about the same. However, it is necessary to take a census each year, in order to discover the new-comers.

In this way, the Sisters are enabled to find out how many children ought to be at catechism classes, and how many have not yet made their First Holy Communion. The census taken, classes begin. Each town has two lessons a week, with extra lessons given in the convent to adults, or to those who are backward, and who live near enough to come more often to us. They are taught to go to Confession in Spanish and in English. The Sisters visit every family, especially where trouble, sickness, or death has entered, and however crowded the room, men, women and children will promptly go down on their knees to join in the prayers the Sisters send up to the Father of Mercy....

On Sundays, the priest resident at Scottsbluff goes to say Mass at two of the three churches in his towns, taking two Sisters with him. Mass is followed by catechism classes, or "Doctrina" as they call it; in Spanish for the little ones, but in English for the older children who attend the public school. In Bayard and Minatare, Americans and Mexicans join quite happily in the same classes. In Scottsbluff and Bayard, they have fine choirs singing both Latin and Spanish hymns and high Mass, often with stringed instruments....

Our Sisters also visit the hospitals and bring rosaries and Spanish prayerbooks for the use of the Mexican patients. The work goes on steadily until the month of May, when the Mexicans begin preparing once more to go out on the ranches. Then great preparations are made for the children preparing to receive their First Holy Communion....

The priest and Sisters have much difficulty in combating the influence of certain so-called "welfare workers," who think to "civilize" the Mexican, they must turn him from his faith. These agents work side by side with our people in the fields, and live with them as members of the colony, gradually instilling into their minds false ideas about their faith and winning them over by means of material gifts. Gradually some of their beautiful Catholic customs are given up. They begin to feel ashamed of their family altars, without which, before the coming of these workers, no Mexican home was complete....

Sister Mary Martina, O.P., Maryknoll Home for Japanese Children,
Los Angeles, California, "The Care and Training of the Oriental Child"

Possibly only a relatively small number of us are acquainted with the Church's
work for the Oriental in our country. The Oriental population in the United
States is restricted mostly to the west coast centering in and near the larger
cities there, Los Angeles, San Francisco, Sacramento, Seattle, and several others
to a lesser degree. The bulk of our Japanese population is to be found in and
around the city of Los Angeles. Catholic work for these people in the Diocese
of Los Angeles and San Diego has been committed to the care of the Sisters
from Maryknoll.

Some 25,000 Japanese reside in the city of Los Angeles and perhaps as many
more are to be found in the rural parts of the diocese. These form Maryknoll's
field of labor in the Southwest. In past years comparatively few Japanese
children found their way into child-caring institutions. This is at least partially explained by the traditional family system in vogue among the Japanese
whereby a child of needy parents was passed on to relatives in better circumstances, whether they resided in this country or in Japan. At the present time,
due largely to the depression, more Japanese children are finding their way
into institutions such as our own Home. Strangely enough, but few of them
are real orphans; the majority are children whose parents are suffering from
tuberculosis and hence are unable to care for them. The Japanese physique
seems to have little resistance to this dread disease, statistics indicating that
they have a four-fold greater susceptibility to it than people of other nation-
alities. Broken families, which furnish so great a percentage of the children in
our American child-caring institutions, send few children to Japanese Homes.

The children who do come to us, however, are left with us more unreservedly than are those of other racial groups. While our responsibility thus
becomes greater and more extended, at the same time we enjoy the compensat-
ing feature of increased freedom in dealing with them. As a result, practically
all our children manifest a desire to become Catholics after being with us for
a few years, in spite of the fact that nearly all of them are children of Buddhist
or Shinto parents.

Realizing the influence of home life on the whole development of a child's
nature, we try to create a home-like atmosphere for our youngsters. The children are permitted to do many of the things that they ordinarily do in their
own homes. Experiments in the culinary arts, the delight of adolescents, are
freely permitted for the older group. And the boys enjoy it as much as do the
girls. Birthday parties, every tot's supreme joy, are the "homiest" of affairs.

At the same time we strive to prepare these children to meet the obligations
and solve the problems that will inevitably present themselves in later life.
Our children receive their formal education at the St. Francis Xavier School,
which is conducted by our Sisters. This school is attended by about four hundred Japanese children, daily brought in busses from all parts of the city. The
course given in the school is a thoroughly Catholic one from kindergarten

through the eighth grade. Besides the full English curriculum, the pupils receive daily instruction from Japanese teachers in their native tongue. This is essential, inasmuch as the only openings with any chance for advancement, available to the "Nisei" or second generation Japanese, are those in which a knowledge of their own language is required. And I might add that it is not a language that can be learned in a short time or by any abbreviated course. It takes continuous study and practice, and plenty of that.

During the past several years hundreds of Japanese children have been educated in this school. Through them, we feel, have been sent into the heart of a pagan world the first principles of Christian society. Uncounted numbers of these pupils have returned to their native land, not all as baptized Catholics, but all of them impregnated with highly Christian ideals. We feel justified in thinking that the friendly relations between our pagan and Christian brethren, not only on our own western coast but also in Japan, have been advanced in appreciable measure through the mediation of this school and its graduates....

In our section of the country there is a regrettable prejudice against the Japanese people, but we whose privilege it is to know them more intimately find them truly admirable. Our work brings us constantly into the section of the city known as "Little Tokio," a typical Japanese settlement. Here we have an opportunity of observing the splendid characteristics of the people, their courtesy, their courage in the face of difficulty and sorrow, their eagerness to be of service to others, their unfailing gratitude for the least favor or kindness. And so it is only natural that we should desire to make them better known and more appreciated.

It may be surprising to many that it is the pagan Japanese of Los Angeles who are making our school work among them possible. The Home, of course, receives help from the Catholic Welfare Bureau and the local Community Chest, but for the school and the various works connected with it, we depend on the generosity and self-sacrificing efforts of these good people. The knowledge of what we are endeavoring to do for their children is becoming more widespread among them. We frequently receive calls from Japanese business men asking for our young people to fill responsible positions in their offices, stating as their reason that those trained in our Catholic schools are trustworthy, honest, and assume responsibility well. This is a gratifying assurance that the training being given in the Home and in the school is appreciated by our pagan people who recognize in our children something that they do not find in other groups. Very often, too, it is the curiosity to know just what this "something" is, that leads the adults to a study of the Catholic doctrine, and conversions frequently result....

Of late years there has occurred quite a noticeable stiffening of Japanese feeling along racial lines, due partly to the increasingly important role being taken by the mother country in international affairs. The older generation seems to be making a last determined effort to reclaim its American offspring for its own traditions. The movement receives considerable strength from increased Buddhist and Shinto activity conducted largely on patriotic lines. It has become a considerable threat now that proselytizing efforts have been successfully extended to include elements of the Caucasian population. A Mr. Goldwater, duly accredited Buddhist Bonze, possibly Jewish originally, is able to muster an audience of some 200 whites when he conducts the services in the Buddhist temple in "Little Tokio," not far from our own school.

We are inclined to view this development with some fear when we realized that so many of our countrymen practice no religion and yet are possessed of the natural religious sense which may find in Buddhism at least a palliative or an opiate capable of satisfying this normal religious craving. The doctrines of Buddhism have been made more accessible recently by the preparation of a Buddhist scripture text. Its ritual is little short of magnificent and its appeal to the religious sentiments, though superficial in the main, is quite powerful.

Our work in Los Angeles, though restricted to a small proportion of the total population, acquires a new importance when viewed as a possible bulwark to the spread of Buddhism among our own people. We like to think of it not only in this wise, but also as a potent factor in the conversion of Japan itself.

The harvest of Oriental souls is great. But conversion from paganism necessitates a complete revolutionizing of the individual's philosophy of life. We realize that this requires God's grace, as faith is indeed a gift. We ask, therefore, that you, who have the glory of God at heart, help us by your prayerful support. We feel confident, then, that in God's own good time we may look forward to an abundant reaping of this precious harvest of Oriental souls.

Proceedings of the Twenty-First Annual Meeting of the National Conference of Catholic Charities (Washington, D.C.: National Conference of Catholic Charities, 1935), 303–25. Printed with permission.

56. Rose J. McHugh, Chief, Administrative Surveys Division, Bureau of Public Assistance, Social Security Board, Washington, D.C., "Functions of Catholic Charities in Assisting People to Obtain Their Rights under the New Governmental Programs," 1939

It is not within the competence of one person nor the scope of any one paper to deal adequately with the subject matter encompassed in this spacious title, nor is it a simple matter to select for examination and comment the areas of it which lie most closely to the interests of this audience. The organization of the program for this meeting implies emphasis on the services to individuals which the new governmental programs provide. Limitations on the scope of this paper obviously are imposed by the technical aspects of many of the programs, notably those of health, employment, child welfare, housing, and assistance to persons in need.

The assistance programs administered under the Social Security Act, though only a small segment of the vast field of government activity carried on as service to individuals, touch definitely upon the welfare activities of local communities. The daily experience and responsibilities of social workers in Catholic agencies open new areas of interest and arouse questions on relationships between Catholic or other private social agencies and the public agencies administering governmental programs. For the purpose of this discussion, however, I shall limit my subject to the assistance programs and give passing consideration to the insurance programs administered under the Social Security Act.

It is important, I believe, in order to relate this paper to something tangible, to restate some basic principles of social and individual welfare. They are, briefly, that rights are not established by governmental agencies; that man by his nature has inalienable rights; and that rights cannot be exercised unless known.

The Social Security Act provides for financial assistance from the federal treasury to the states for the support and extension of services in the fields of health; vocational rehabilitation; social insurance for aged and unemployed workers; and for assistance payments to the needy aged, the needy blind, and dependent children. The recipients of the benefits of the insurance programs contribute financially to the benefits they receive;[1] the recipients of old-age assistance, aid to dependent children, and aid to the blind do not. As part of our inheritance from the English Poor Laws the idea still persists that contributory programs are based on individual rights and that non-contributory programs, such as public assistance, are not.

You are aware that this has never been the Catholic position. The right to subsistence is a primary natural right from which the right to a living wage is deduced. This was the doctrine of the early Fathers of the Church; of Basil, Ambrose, and St. Thomas Aquinas. Within our own time, but as long ago as 1906, Dr. John A. Ryan defined the Christian doctrine in these words: "...every human being has not only a claim in charity, but a strict right to as much of the wealth of the community as is necessary to maintain his life."[2] He further defines the right of subsistence as the right of man "to maintain himself in a reasonable degree of comfort..." and to have "the opportunity to develop within reasonable limits all his faculties, physical, intellectual, moral, and spiritual." He reminds us that this is the doctrine of all moral theologians; the encyclicals of Leo XIII and Pius XI have reaffirmed it specifically. Said Pius XI, "If however private resources do not suffice, it is the duty of the public authority to supply for the insufficient forces of individual effort, particularly on a matter which is of such importance to the common weal, touching as it does the maintenance of the family and married people...."[3]

Why is it that Catholic teaching on these grave problems is so little known and accepted? The "destitute" do not know their rights. Not all of us know

---

1. Employees contributed to the unemployment compensation program in only seven states in June; in the other forty-four jurisdictions they do not contribute.

2. Rev. John A. Ryan, *A Living Wage: Its Ethical and Economic Aspects* (New York: Macmillan, 1906).

3. Encyclical on Christian Marriage.

and acknowledge the rights of our brothers in need. And this, I believe, is a primary function of Catholic Charities — to make known the Catholic teaching on the right to subsistence and the right to a living wage.

It is accepted that the Social Security Act marks progress in defining and promoting these basic rights and in providing the means by which millions of individuals who previously were unable to exercise their rights now do so. And this gives us courage to face the tasks ahead, for we are still far from a goal where "subsistence" as used in the definitions quoted is a reality. I mention some mileposts. Since 1935, when the Social Security Act went into effect, all states, the District of Columbia, Alaska, and Hawaii have passed unemployment compensation laws; the last two states began paying benefits in July, 1939. In these 51 jurisdictions the old-age insurance program is in operation, though benefits, except the lump-sum payments to relatives of deceased wage earners and to persons who have attained the age of 65, will not be paid until 1940. More than $43,000,000 in job-insurance benefits were paid to unemployed workers during June, 1939, and lump-sum payments of a little more than a million and a half dollars were made to claimants of old-age insurance benefits. The old-age assistance program is in operation in the 51 jurisdictions, but the aid to the blind and aid to dependent children programs are administered in only 42. In June of this year there were 1,847,856 recipients of old-age assistance who received $35,887,421 in assistance payments; 44,457 recipients of aid to the blind received $1,029,002; and 718,414 children in 297,557 families were given assistance amounting to $9,255,641; but not all persons eligible under the act were receiving assistance payments. On June 30, applications were pending for 246,478 old-age assistance applicants, 5,556 for applicants for aid to the blind, and 65,606 for families (including 152,872 children) who had made application for aid to dependent children.

Information on the operations of the insurance programs has been widely distributed. The technical aspects of their administration are complicated, but it is generally known that benefits for aged and unemployed workers are paid; and the conditions under which benefits are payable have been publicized extensively, and with clarity. Up to July 1 [1939] more than 44,700,000 workers had been registered and given "account numbers" by means of which their identity and their claims to insurance payments may be established. There are local field offices distributed throughout the states, the District of Columbia, and the territories of Alaska and Hawaii for the administration of old-age insurance. Instances of individuals who are unaware of the benefits under the insurance programs to which they are entitled or whose claims are not satisfactorily adjusted will undoubtedly come to the attention of Catholic and other agencies from time to time. These individuals present relatively simple problems to non-governmental social agencies, since in most instances they may be referred to the agencies administering the programs. There are, however, broad social questions with respect to these services that are matters of concern to social agencies and to all citizens. The programs must be protected by legislation, by adequate appropriation, by administrative integrity and competence.

To each and all of these aspects of the administration of the insurances, the private social agencies must be alert, and they must be prepared to exercise leadership which good citizenship dictates as necessary in pertinent situations.

Similarly, it is the responsibility of all citizens and Catholic agencies to promote measures that will insure economical and efficient administration of the assistance programs. Many of our social principles are confused at present by pressures from economic interests. The protection of economic resources and of tax funds is vitally important, and wisdom in the expenditure of public monies for assistance is basic to the protection of individual rights.

The Social Security Act provides for federal matching of assistance payments made to individuals by the state according to plans submitted by the state agency, and for the administration or supervision of the plan by a single state agency operating in all political subdivisions. It was the intent of Congress that these provisions would enable the state to establish administrative measures by which applicants and recipients would be assured equitable treatment throughout the state. It was also its intent that responsibility for administration would rest with the state agency and that through federal-state relationships the appropriate administrative measures to effect this would be established.

In each of the titles determining grants to states for old-age assistance, aid to dependent children and aid to the blind, a clause provides for, under the state plan, the granting to any individual whose claim for assistance is denied, "an opportunity for a fair hearing before such state agency." The Social Security Board has interpreted this clause and the word "claim" to mean that inherent in the right to a fair hearing is also a right to apply. It has counseled the state agencies accordingly in negotiations with them on the plans they have submitted to the board for approval. For the person whose application has been denied, and for the recipient whose assistance payment has been unreasonably restricted or canceled, the right to a fair hearing implies that the administrative policies and procedures of the agency must be such that upon application from him the decision will be reviewed by an administrative unit or agent other than the one responsible for the original decision. It implies that this right will have been explained to him by the agency, that the definitions of eligibility under the state and federal laws, in respect to which his claim for assistance is determined, will have been set forth in terms he clearly understands, that he shall be informed of the means he may use in making his appeal, and that he shall, if he so desires, be represented by counsel at the hearing. The rules and regulations of the state agency for the administration of assistance are therefore reviewed by the board as to their compatibility with this provision of the Social Security Act.

The right to apply is not specifically defined in the act, but the logic of the interpretation by the Social Security Board that this is inherent in the right to a fair hearing is obvious. The several rules and regulations of the agency safeguard this right when they are based on sound administrative policies and procedures.

"The right to a fair hearing" has a new and unfamiliar appearance in social work practice. It has not been clearly understood by the state agencies nor by the public generally. Compliance with this section of the Social Security Act has presented to the agencies some problems of administration that have been difficult but are not unmanageable. The fundamental right of the individual to the maintenance of his own integrity, his right, and his duty to share responsibility for decisions with agencies which have the power to affect his welfare is protected in the law. The social rights of the individual which are fundamental in our concept of government in the United States, so far as I know, have not been written into law previously in terms of the right to assistance. May it not be a function of Catholic agencies, therefore, to accept civic responsibility for the interpretation and broadcasting of the legal right of the applicant for assistance to a fair hearing?

The Social Security Act breaks completely with the Elizabethan laws of poor relief. In the protection to individual integrity which it gives to applicants and recipients there is not only hope of a nearer approach to social justice for the destitute but there is, I am inclined to believe, a heavy measure of responsibility placed upon Catholics particularly to see that this doctrine of rights which is so completely their own becomes a living reality. Unqualified acceptance of the theory is not the answer however. The public agency is dependent upon legislative support. The community needs to understand the law, its social and economic implications. It needs facts about administrative practices and procedures that prejudice may not arise against this new definition of measures under which public assistance is to be granted.

There are practical considerations for Catholic agencies assisting persons to obtain their rights under the new governmental programs that arise from the present stage of development of these programs, and from situations which involve serious threats to their integrity and continuation. I shall refer briefly to only three of these. They are familiar to you and there is tangible evidence of the need of community concern for them. They are the situations with respect to the inadequacies of general relief throughout the country, the inequities of the categorical assistance programs, and the uneven development of the programs both within and between the states.

Responsibility for relief has not been accepted uniformly by states and localities. While federal funds have been made available to states for the assistance of specified groups of persons, there are still vast numbers of unemployed and unemployable persons whose necessitous circumstances do not constitute eligibility for assistance within the technical and legal definitions of the Social Security Act. Restrictions in law and practice by local units leave an unknown number of persons in need of the essentials of existence. The concentration of funds and of interests on categorical groups has tended to restrict state funds for expenditures to the areas where federal matching is available. State funds are not always sufficient, or if sufficient, not always available for the support of a general relief program. Generally it is true that state appropriations for assistance represent new and marked increases in state expenditures, but much remains to be done by the community and the fiscal officers of the state so that allocation of available funds will be commensurate with needs and sound social planning.

Legislative and social resources, as well as social attitudes developed for the care of the needy which may have been adequate for the conditions under which they were established, continue to restrict thinking and practice in communities where social conditions are greatly modified and in which the conditions which prevent thousands of persons from obtaining assistance are far more numerous and complicated than those of earlier times. Migratory persons and families are restricted in the exercise of their rights to subsistence and a living wage by processes that involve financial adequacy of assistance programs, barriers between state and local governmental units, the economic aspects of seasonal labor, the movement of labor from its established residence in search of more lucrative fields, and the attitude of the public toward the migrant. The normal resistance of human nature to the acceptance of the stranger is not the basis of that state of public opinion, which expresses itself in discriminatory legislation and practice. The Social Security Act does not require residence as a condition of eligibility for public assistance. A state plan may not be approved by the Social Security Board, however, if it requires as a condition of eligibility for old-age assistance or aid to the blind a residence of more than five out of nine years, or one year's continuous residence, or for aid to dependent children a residence requirement of more than one year. It is the policy of the board to recommend to states that persons be cared for wherever practical in places where they wish to dwell.

Prejudice against any group of persons which tends to curtail their rights is subversive to our system of government. Is it not the function of Catholic Charities to bear witness to the rights of disadvantaged groups, to their sufferings which result from inequitable administration of assistance, and by study, research and negotiation to promote the development of a sound social policy? Deliberation on the legal aspects of the problem, the availability of funds, the precedents for social action historically established in the state, and the sources of propaganda must be implemented with constructive and stable leadership in the community.

Inequities in the assistance programs are strikingly obvious. It has already been mentioned that old-age assistance is the only program in operation in the 51 jurisdictions and that only 42 extend aid to needy blind and dependent children. These inequities are illustrated further in a comparison of the number per 1,000 in the aged population with the number per 1,000 in the estimated population under 16 years of age who received assistance in June, 1939. In the aged group 232 per 1,000 estimated population 65 years of age and over received assistance payments while only one-tenth as many children, or 24 per 1,000 estimated population under 16 years of age were given aid. In this same month obligations incurred for payments to aged recipients amounted to more than 35 million dollars; and approximately nine million dollars were paid for aid to dependent children. This overemphasis on old-age assistance has militated against the reasonable development of the aid to dependent children program. It is also clear that there are vast numbers of children in the families receiving general relief whose needs are not adequately met by that program. Measures to meet the needs of children in whatever circumstances they are living must be provided, if adequacy is to be approached. The unnecessary differences with respect to financing and assistance standards in the old-age assistance and aid to dependent children programs as between states create inequities and prevent the application of sound administrative standards. Likewise, similar discrepancies exist in administrative standards on state and local levels. A more reasonable distribution of responsibility for financing and administration between federal, state, and local units involves important questions of public policy which require research and call for responsible leadership to direct deliberations and decisions. Administration of the programs on sound financial and social policies, free from political influences, by persons of competence and integrity are no longer questions of theory or controversy.

May I say in conclusion that the technical questions of administration in these programs must remain primarily the responsibility of the administering agencies, that I believe it is the function of Catholic agencies and of the community generally to accept responsibility for the development of informed public opinion that will be dedicated to the support of sound financial and socially desirable administration. The Catholic agency alert to its opportunity will be a resource for counsel and reference to applicants or recipients of assistance who may be unable to interpret their true circumstances, and it will be of assistance to them in situations where unreasonable requirements for the determination of eligibility may exist. It will always be peculiarly the function of Catholic agencies to interpret the Catholic doctrine of human rights in terms of reality to the minds of those not of the Faith, so that its reasonableness may appeal to all men and become an accepted principle for the equitable and uniform administration of public assistance in our country founded for the preservation of human rights.

> *Proceedings of the Twenty-Fifth Meeting of the National Conference of Catholic Charities* (Washington, D.C.: National Conference of Catholic Charities, 1939), 240–48. (Footnotes in original.) Printed with permission.

57. Dorothy Day, *House of Hospitality,* 1939

... We have never faltered in our conviction during these six years of work[1] that hospices such as our Houses of Hospitality are a vital necessity in times like these.

We do not deny that the State is bound for the sake of the common good, to take care of the unemployed and the unemployable by relief and lodging houses and work projects. Pope Pius XI pointed that out very clearly. He lamented that so much money was spent in increased armaments that should

---

1. The Catholic Worker movement began in 1933.

be spent on the poor. He urged the "press and the pulpit throughout the world" to fight the increase of armaments....

No, we are not denying the obligations of the State. But we do claim that we must never cease to emphasize personal responsibility. When our brother asks for bread, we cannot say, "Go be thou filled." We cannot send him from agency to agency. We must care for him ourselves as much as possible.

And we claim that as Catholics we have not sufficiently cared for our own. We have not used the material, let alone the spiritual resources at our disposal. We have not drawn upon our tremendous reserves of material and spiritual wealth. We have scarcely known or recognized that we possessed them.

Approximately twenty-five million Catholics in the United States! It would be interesting to know how many of them are on relief, trusting to State aid. If we took care of our own, and relieved the government of this immense responsibility, how conditions would be transformed! Then indeed people would say "See how they love one another." Then indeed we would be "bearing one another's burdens." But of course, we would not be limiting our care only to our own. We would inevitably be caring also for others....

Our work in the labor fields takes place not only in the Houses of Hospitality. To reach the organized and the great mass of unorganized workers we have had to go out on the streets, to the public squares, to the factories, waterfronts and picket lines.

The hardships of the migratory worker and the sweatshop worker are even greater than those who are on the bread lines and in the lodging houses. They are the family men and women who are trying to care for others. They are those who are seeing their dear ones go without essentials in the way of medical care and food, who are seeing their children grow up to find no employment awaiting them.

Here is a brief review of some of the labor issues we have dealt with during the past six years:...

Again and again we have helped workers on strike regardless of all talk as to whether the strike was just or unjust. We have done this for two reasons: first, it is never wrong to perform the Works of Mercy; secondly, because in time of industrial warfare it is easy to get in touch with the workers by meetings and by widespread distribution of literature. It is a time when the workers are thinking and struggling; they are enduring hardships and making sacrifices, they are in a receptive frame of mind.

The first number of the paper[2] came out in May 1933. In that issue we featured a story of the Negro labor on the levees in the South which was being exploited by the War Department. We also wrote about women and children in industry and the widespread layoffs of men.

In the second issue we took up the farmers' strike in the West and wages and hours of restaurant workers. In the third issue, child labor in the textile industry, as well as a two-page synopsis of labor struggles during the month.

---

2. *The Catholic Worker.*

In the fourth issue we had front page stories on the coal strike and the milk strike. In these first issues of the paper there were also stories on the race issue and the condition of the Negro in industry and in professional work. In the sixth issue of the paper we were already combating anti-Semitism. In the same issue we showed up some profit-sharing plans of industrialists as a further move to exploit child labor.

By the second year, our circulation had jumped from 2,500 to 35,000 copies, and our readers included workers and students throughout the country. In the second year, 1934, the seaman's strike on the West coast, the strike of the rural workers in the onion fields, a silk workers' strike in New Jersey, the textile strike, took up many columns in the paper. In New York City we helped Orbach's department store workers in their mass picketing, and called upon our readers not to patronize a store where such wages and long hours prevailed. We helped to defeat an injunction — one of the chief weapons of the employer to break strikes — which was handed down against the picketers. Our participation in this strike and in the National Biscuit Company strike cost us many readers. Our circulation was by now 65,000, but many church and school groups cancelled their orders because of the pressure of employers' groups. There were 3,000 on strike in the National Biscuit Company factory on 14th Street, and every day there were mass picket lines and scuffles with the police.

In the March 1935 issue there was printed a speech in regard to the Child Labor amendment.... Our endorsement of the Child Labor amendment also cost us many subscribers, as a majority of Catholics were opposed to it, for fear of government interference in the education of our youth. But in spite of consistent opposition (which, as we have always pointed out, is very good for the clarification of thought), our circulation rose to 100,000 at the beginning of the third year.

When the Borden Milk Company the next year attempted to foist a company union on their workers, the editors took up their cause and called public attention to the unethical conduct of the employers. We called attention to the intimidation of Borden drivers by gangsters and thugs, and urged our readers not to use Borden's milk while unfair conditions prevailed. As a result of the story we ran, the employers attacked *The Catholic Worker* in paid advertisements in the [Catholic] *Brooklyn Tablet* and the *Catholic News*. This dispute also cost us some thousands of subscribers.

A few months later the spring strike of 1936 started among the seamen on the East coast. Because we had moved into our larger headquarters on Mott Street we were able to house about fifty of the seamen during the strike. In the fall strike, we not only housed some of them, but also fed thousands of them daily in the store we opened on Tenth Avenue, which we kept going for about four months. At that time we printed our "Stand on Strikes" which has been widely circulated in pamphlet form among labor unions throughout the country.

By publicity and moral support, we encouraged the organization of the steel industry when the C.I.O. began its activities. In the same year, our workers assisted the marble workers' strike in Vermont, the fishermen in Boston, the sharecroppers in Arkansas, the auto workers in Detroit. We covered the sit-down strike in Michigan, and the five and ten cent store strike in New York, the steel strike in Chicago. We also helped in the organization drive of the stockyards in Chicago.

That was the tragic year when ten workers were killed and scores more wounded in the Memorial Day massacre. One of our staff had a friend killed in that tragic episode. Our workers in Chicago had been helping in the soup kitchens and marching on the picket lines as well as distributing literature.

Many of these strikes I covered personally, in order to get a complete report to our readers, and also to speak to the workers at their meetings. I was one of the few newspaper reporters allowed into the Flint Fisher Body plant to visit the hundreds of sit-down strikers who had been in the plant for forty days. By this time we had groups of Catholic Workers in many big industrial centers throughout the country.

In the labor field the Pittsburgh group was most prominent, headed as it was by Fathers Rice and Hensler. They were the first priests to go out on the picket line and on sound trucks at street corners. Their example led many other priests to become active in the labor field.

The Lowell textile strike was interesting from several angles. When our workers began to distribute *The Catholic Worker* to the strikers and the public, and to start a food kitchen, the officials of the town telephoned the Chancery Office in Boston to find out if we were all right and were assured that we could go ahead. (On the other hand, we know of an occasion when a speaking engagement at a church in Jersey City was cancelled because of Mayor Hague's opposition to the paper.) The local paper proclaimed in their headlines that the entrance of *The Catholic Worker* into the Lowell strike marked the turning point in the conflict and led to prompt negotiations between the workers and the employers. . . .

In the past six years we have had many interviews with Catholic industrialists and many of them were not too cheering. Not wishing to increase class war attitudes, we did not publish many of them.

During these past years, former Governor Murphy's stand in the auto strikes, and Sheriff Boyle's and Mayor Michael Sewak's stand in the steel strike in Johnstown were highlights. By moral force rather than by armed force, these men prevented violence and bloodshed and stood out not only against the industrialists but against a campaign of public vilification and condemnation. Because they resolutely refused to use armed guards against the workers, and insisted upon arbitration — because they upheld human rights above property rights — they were termed spineless and yellow-livered, not only by atheistic capitalists but by many of their fellow-Catholics. Their courage and leadership in public life have been an inspiration to others and a message of hope to the workers. May God raise up other men like them. . . .

Dorothy Day, *House of Hospitality* (New York: Sheed and Ward, 1939), 257–66. Printed by permission.

58. Edward Roberts Moore, *Roman Collar*, 1948

...Several times I have mentioned that this was my first visit to Chicago in connection with the CYO. Perhaps I may close the chapter with a brief account of my second. One happy result of the initial trip had been the establishment of a very cordial relationship between our two organizations.[1] Out of this came the plan for a great inter-city boxing show at Wrigley Field, Chicago. It seemed like a good idea on all counts. We needed more publicity; a big inter-city contest would give it to us. Our kids would be, and were, crazy about it: a trip to another city, names in the paper, glory before their fellows. And, confidentially, we at headquarters, where you have to pay the bills, thought the plan had its points too: expenses and a good share of the profits of a jammed Wrigley Field. The arrangements were made. We alerted all our parish centers, had them pick candidates for the team. We held preliminaries and made final selections. We engaged a special trainer, selected a priest to go along as chaplain, bought all new uniforms and snappy CYO capes for boxers, trainers, seconds. We secured transportation, housing quarters, training space. In the meantime from Chicago were coming newspapers by the crate, filled with accounts of the approaching donnybrook. Their boys' pictures, our boys' pictures, life histories of all concerned, speeches by the Bishop, great meetings at CYO headquarters. The White Sox and the Cubs had good teams that year, but there was hardly room on the Chicago Sports pages for box scores; it was all of the coming CYO show. Plans were made for a mass reception, a parade through the streets, a civic holiday. It was *something!* Our team went on a few days ahead, with Reggie Townsend, one of our board members, as official convoy. The rest of us were to follow. When the train pulled into the Chicago station at 9:30 A.M. of a Tuesday morning, Reggie heard a band playing, and reflected idly as he snapped his bag shut that there must be some visiting potentate on board. It never occurred to him that "Hail to the Chief" was in his honor. The train ground to a stop and Reggie checked his team; he didn't want to leave his light-heavy asleep in his berth and have to go looking for him later out in the train yards. "Mr. Townsend," he heard his name called. It was the Bishop, both hands outstretched in welcome. Reggie was taken completely by surprise; he had had no expectation of being greeted at the station by the Bishop himself. But he hadn't seen anything yet! The amenities having been exchanged, the Bishop requested Reggie to gather his troupe together and line them up on the station platform. "We have a little ceremony arranged," he said. Unprepared for anything of the sort, Reggie was a bit flustered, but finally got his boys and their mentors out and more or less in order. Then the fun began. The Bishop, who had previously left the car and rejoined his own group, stepped up and presented Chicago's Mayor and other important city officials. Then, "The National Anthem, gentlemen, if you please," he said. Everyone stood at attention while the band

---

1. The New York and Chicago CYOs.

played the thrilling air. The platform and as far as Reggie could see, the whole station, was jammed with people. Other travellers from points East stopped to see what was going on; they couldn't have gotten through the crowd anyway. Then his Honor the Mayor: "Mr. Townsend, on this auspicious occasion it is my privilege...welcome...all that we can do for you...the Keys of our City." Reggie, by now catching his breath, "I am overwhelmed" (he still hadn't seen anything!) "by the magnitude of this reception—its warmth...its spontaneity...its graciousness; we thank you...." They were off: down the platform, into big limousines, another great crowd in the street, cheers. Then tearing through downtown traffic, a whole flock of motorcycle police clearing the way; the South Shore Country Club. Breakfast, with more speeches of welcome; sightseeing, lunch on the North Side, more sightseeing (no rest; they don't seem to need it in Chicago), dinner then the *piece de resistance* in Jackson Park. Reggie had never seen so many people at one time. "A hundred thousand," said the Bishop. Even the police conceded fifty thousand. Bigger and better speeches this time, a half-dozen bands, fire-works, a "Pageant of Youth"; Reggie completely dizzy. "I never have been able to remember what I said when my turn came," he declares to this day. "But it didn't seem to matter for everybody cheered anyway."

Dan[2] and I joined the show the next day. With us was Gene Tunney, of our board, who had broken into a vacation at the beautiful Webb Estate on Lake Champlain to make the trip. In passing, let me pay tribute to Gene. Our CYO over the years has asked a good deal of him; he always produces. I have never known anyone even remotely in his position to be more consistently generous and gracious. Jewish Benny Leonard was with us, too, that greatest competitor of all time in his class, and a worthy associate of Gene's when it came to lending his aid and prestige to any good work. Benny was then and always one of the best friends our CYO ever had. So Dan and I came well fortified, but Chicago had done a great job too: practically every living ring great of the present or the past had been gathered for the occasion. From the moment of our arrival we were on a merry-go-round: rushed from breakfasts to luncheons to formal dinners, making speeches at them all. Broadcasting on the drop of a hat over nation-wide hook-ups. Flash appearances at mass meetings; posing for motion pictures and stills, a preview at Wrigley Field, with both teams staging an afternoon rehearsal and the temperature at 100 degrees Fahrenheit. A midnight reception for us at our hotel. Rest? Who ever heard of such a thing? A waste of time—heaven knows we were not given a chance to waste much!

The next night the big show. And what a show! Every seat occupied; milling thousands unable to get in; the whole city agog. More pell-mell rushing through streamer-lined streets, sirens screaming. Dignitaries of Church and State and civic life; silk hats and shirt sleeves. Introductions in the ring. The Governor of the State; the Mayor again. Gene Tunney shaking hands with

---

2. Dan Higgins, another New York CYO board member.

Joe Louis; old Battling Nelson shadow boxing. Dan and I posing with the Bishop. Officials bustling around; the fighters nervous, as well they might be. Being ushered down to ring-side seats; radio announcers going from one to another of us with hand mikes: "Father Moore, tell the people of the nation, for from coast to coast they are listening in, how you are enjoying your visit in Chicago, what you think of the Chicago CYO, how you like our Bishop." "Mr. Higgins, you know the fight game. You were a National Amateur champ yourself once. Tell the folks back home what you think of their boy's chances tonight." "Mr. Tunney, how about telling us tonight the real story of the long count? It was right in that ring, you know."

Lights out in the arena, glaring in the ring; fighters, seconds, officials climbing over the ropes. Announcement of the first bout, the warning bell — and the Fights Are ON!!!

Three hours later and they are over. Guess who won? But was all good clean fun. Next day, all the shouting over, exhausted but relaxed, back on the train, on the way home. The profits? I nearly forgot. Big-scale promotion costs a lot, you know. The Bishop sent Mrs. Higgins a huge bunch of American Beauty roses. Dan thought they came from Reggie Townsend and returned him a pineapple. Ultimately, we did indeed get a check, but nothing like what we had expected. Perhaps this was one of those occasions when a little *less* promotion! We decided not to promote a return engagement in New York. It would have been an anti-climax anyway, and further, we didn't think we would survive it.

Edward Roberts Moore, *Roman Collar* (New York: Macmillan, 1948), 150–55.

Part 4

1945 to the Present

Introduction

The end of World War II was an important watershed in American life. The new configuration of world politics created by the Allied victory over the Axis set into motion an extended period of tensions between the United States and the Soviet Union called the Cold War. On any number of fronts, these two superpowers confronted each other directly and through their surrogates to secure economic, military, and geopolitical hegemony. From time to time, the animosities would erupt in hot war in such places as Korea and Vietnam. The stakes involved in these periodic confrontations escalated dramatically with the onset of the nuclear age and the proliferation of weapons of mass destruction as well as the technology to deliver them to the population centers of the enemy. The world lived under the very real shadow of nuclear annihilation.

The fear of communist hegemony abroad was in part created by the domestic politics of the post-Roosevelt presidencies. Leaders of both political parties attempted to use the fear of communist infiltration for their own political advantage. Ultimately, the Republican Party, out of favor and lacking dominance since the Great Depression, gained the upper hand in the quest to ferret out and punish traitors in the land. The second red scare, usually associated with the worst excesses of Joseph Raymond McCarthy, was also fanned by lesser political figures, popular entertainers, zealous law enforcement officials, state legislatures, and even clergymen. The culture and climate of Cold War America provided at least one of the meridians of life for the nation until the collapse of the Soviet Union in 1989.

Yet even with the heightened international and domestic tensions, the United States embarked on a period of unparalleled prosperity and economic dominance presided over by the beaming and benign Dwight D. Eisenhower. In part, this was made possible by continued government involvement in the economic and social affairs of the nation. American citizens moved in large numbers into colleges and universities, aided in part by the generous provisions of the G.I. Bill of 1944. The good life of independent home ownership was brought within the reach of many through generous federal subsidies of housing. Suburbia grew dramatically and with it automobile ownership, also made possible through generous government support of the automotive industry. This prosperity made it possible for Americans to reproduce in record numbers, thereby creating new industries geared around children. The 1950s emerged as a period of mass consumerism, saw the rise of youth culture, and witnessed the development of one of the most powerful mediums of all time, television. Although the era seemed in nostalgic retrospect to be one of peace and stability, a powerful and not-so-subtle transformation of American culture took place in the 1950s which, as journalist David Halberstam has noted, had a direct link with the more tumultuous decade of the 1960s.

A new presidency was the leitmotiv of a new era as forty-three-year-old John Fitzgerald Kennedy raised his hand to take the oath of office in January 1961. Whatever doubts were later sown about his personal morality, JFK represented boldness, youth, and "vigah" in the popular mind. America continued its Cold War policies, skirting dangerously close to the dreaded nuclear exchange during the Cuban Missile Crisis in the fall of 1962. Kennedy's tragic assassination in November 1963 left a deep scar on American life and psyche. His capable successor, Lyndon B. Johnson, actually accomplished a great deal more in terms of significant legislation. However, Johnson lacked the "charisma" of his flashy predecessor and ultimately found himself caught up in the maelstrom of antiwar protest and radical activism.

Civil rights, the demand of black Americans for full civil rights within America — especially in the Jim Crow South but also in the hyper-segregated cities of the North — was an issue as old as the republic. The rising tide of public awareness and revulsion at the overt discrimination visited on African Americans in the South was accelerated by the flickering television images which brought the horrors of racism into the living rooms of millions of Americans who watched peaceful protestors being mauled by attack dogs, knocked to the ground by power hoses, and set upon by brutish hooligans. The television also introduced the American people to the gospel rhythms of Martin Luther King's oratory and created the political moment to enact legislation which reactivated the promises of the Fourteenth and Fifteenth Amendments. King's leadership of the civil rights movement was undone by assassination in April 1968, and he was replaced by more militant voices. Nonetheless, the civil rights movement did more than set into motion a legal process that freed black people from the effects of segregation and discrimination — it infused a whole new rights consciousness into the American mainstream. Moreover, it brought about a rejuvenated pride in self-identity that propelled "liberation" movements among other minority groups, such as gays and lesbians, and among American women.

The Cold War reached a turning point during the American involvement in Vietnam. The mobilization of American forces in 1965 seemed to promise quick results and an end to communist aggression. However, the tenacity of the North Vietnamese, who were determined to expel the Yankee invader and his puppet regime from their soil, punctured the myth of American invincibility. When communist fighters advanced within feet of the American embassy in Saigon during the February 1968 Tet offensive, American patience with the conflict wore thin and in increasing numbers ordinary citizens joined scores of young people in the streets of America to demand American withdrawal. Serious polarization among Americans over the Vietnam debacle shattered the Cold War consensus in foreign policy. No longer were American presidents given carte blanche to commit American military forces abroad for lengthy periods of time. Even with the end of the war in Vietnam, there were still new challenges — this time from the oil-producing states of the Middle East, which nearly brought the industrialized nations of the world to their knees when they decided to sharply escalate the price of crude oil and strategically hold back the amount sold on the open market. The culture of abundance in America was dealt a serious blow by the gasoline lines, brown-outs, and efforts to make energy savings the "moral equivalent of war." While these measures may have reminded an older generation of the rationing of World War II, they befuddled middle-class baby boomers who had not known serious deprivation.

As America moved into the 1970s, a political and cultural backlash set in against the "excesses" of the 1960s. Although the forces of technological change and cultural modernization continued to have an impact on American life, many people began to yearn for the "simplicity" of the 1950s. Conservative politics had been catalyzed by the candidacies of Alabama's governor George C. Wallace, but the Republican Party came to be the primary repository of American social conservatives. Taking a page from the book of the militants of the 1960s, social conservatives learned the skills of communication and mobilization and packaged their message in a way that reassured and resonated with many middle-class Americans in all regions of the country. The economic and foreign policy missteps of President Jimmy Carter's administration provided an opening for this growing movement, closely aligned with a resurgent evangelical Protestant base, and led to the 1980 election of an old movie actor, Ronald Reagan, who could easily and genially articulate the message.

Reagan attempted to revivify the unifying energies of the Cold War with imprecations about the "evil empire" and built up the peace-time military to all-time heights, including the enhancement of America's nuclear capability. He also waged unrelenting warfare on leftist insurgencies in Central America. Domestically, he attempted to dramatically scale back the scope and influence of the federal government. He pushed through Congress massive tax cuts and floated ambitious plans to reduce and even eliminate a number of government programs. These proposals encountered stiff opposition from vocal constituent groups, and as a result Reagan was compelled to fund them and his military build up by running the largest budget deficits in U.S. history. The Reagan years of the 1980s witnessed a conservative intellectual and social renaissance that percolated through every sector of American society. Toward the end of his presidency and at the beginning of that of his successor, George Bush, the fall of the communist empire took place, affirming the aspirations of those who had supported Reagan's hard-line and sometimes saber-rattling diplomacy toward the Soviet Union and once again providing a new climate in which to work out geopolitical realities.

Every structure of American life underwent dramatic change. Family life was dramatically altered by important changes in the meaning of marriage and the enactment of laws to make divorce easier and less socially oner- ous. Economic realities altered earlier patterns of the working male and the stay-at-home woman. Single parents and latch-key children became the pattern not the exception. The realities of fast-paced technological change af- fected every aspect of American life. Instant communication became possible through improved telecommunication systems. The advent of the personal computer created the Information Superhighway, which Americans are still navigating. Medical technology brought promises of new hope for age-old af- flictions — from cancer to impotence — and also buoyed those who confronted the scourge of AIDS. Reproductive technologies changed the sexual mores of the country as John Rock's birth control pill became a common household pharmaceutical and abortion became a legal practice.

In ways faster than their minds or the consciences could absorb, the people of the United States entered a period of dynamic change.

Church and Society

This set of documents reveals the many ways in which American Catholics have reflected on the relationship of their faith to the values and institutions of American life. The statement of the Administrative Board of the National Catholic Welfare Conference (NCWC) reflects a residual defensiveness to- ward American culture with its worries about secularism. John Tracy Ellis's letter to a fictional bishop gave him the opportunity to explain the interac- tion of American culture with Catholic belief and how it ought to impact the "leadership style" of American prelates. Joseph Bernardin's statement on American civil religion, set against the backdrop of the celebrations of the American bicentennial, to some extent amplifies the message of the 1952 statement of the NCWC — that religious values must play a role in shaping national policies. Margaret O'Brien Steinfels suggests that "a crisis of plausibility" has erupted in the public life of the church in the wake of Vatican II.

59. Administrative Board, National Catholic Welfare Conference, "Religion, Our Most Vital National Asset: A Statement by the Bishops of the United States," 16 November 1952

...Man's Need of Religion

4. Man, as an individual, needs religion. He needs it for many reasons. He needs it because he is a creature of God, entirely dependent on his Creator, and hence must acknowledge his obligation of adoration and love. He needs it

to give meaning to his present existence; for without religion this life, with its disappointments, its uncertainty, its cruelty and its suffering, becomes

> "but a walking shadow, a poor player that struts and frets his hour upon the stage and then is heard no more,...a tale told by an idiot full of sound and fury, signifying nothing." (Macbeth V, v, 17)

Again, a man needs religion to give him that sense of responsibility which prevents human existence from becoming a wilderness of warring passions and aimless strivings. He needs religion because, apart from God, man is lonely and he can never find in himself or in the institutions which bear his image the means to fill up that void of loneliness which is in the human heart. Man needs religion because he is weak, and in his weakness he must have access to the source of all strength. Man needs religion because without the hope that religion alone can give, he cannot rise above that pessimism, that sense of despair, which threatens to engulf the whole of our civilization. Man needs religion because he has an impelling need to worship, and if he does not worship God he will direct his worship to base objects that will pervert his mind and heart.

Religion, a Fundamental Need of Society

5. Religion, necessary to individual man, is necessary also to human society. From the very beginning the family, the primary unit of society, has been intimately dependent on religion, and from it has drawn its unity, its stability, and its holiness. Apart from its divine origin and sanction, parental authority, upon which the family is founded, becomes but an arbitrary application of force to be superseded by any stronger power. Where religion has grown weak the family has shown a corresponding tendency to disintegrate. When religion remains strong, it stands as a protective armor, safeguarding both individual and family. Unique as a compelling ideal is the Holy Family of Nazareth with the striking lessons of love and obedience it teaches. More than the knowledge of all the abstract principles of ethics and sociology, the example of this perfect fulfillment of God's plan has through the Christian tradition strengthened and protected the primary unit of society.

6. Nor is the civic community less dependent on religion. Men are indeed forced by the conditions of human nature to unite and cooperate in the fulfillment of their common needs. But union and cooperation can continue to exist among free men only when justice and charity, universal in their binding force because imposed by God Himself, are embodied in law. While civic authority may have its immediate source in the consent of the governed, that authority must be recognized as coming ultimately from Him upon Whom all men depend. Unless religion with its binding force in justice and charity supplies the foundation of the law and authority, there remains only human convention or brute force as the unifying element in society. In the last analysis there is no society of free men without the creative and sustaining force of religion. Civic society received its most effective support from Him Who taught us to render to Caesar the things that are Caesar's and to God the things that are God's.

7. Nor is religion less important to the complex modern state than to the more primitive social structure. In the measure the state has excluded religion, it has shown a tendency to become an instrument of tyranny. The irreligious state sets itself up in the place of God, substituting its own arbitrary dictates for the decrees of eternal Wisdom. It demands an absolute loyalty such as can be claimed only by Truth itself, and it has no effective deterrent from violating its solemn treaties and from waging unjust and aggressive wars. Since religion is what contemporary tyrannies are attempting first to shackle and then to destroy, one can rightly conclude that it is the one thing most necessary for the preservation of free nations.

8. Religion then is of the utmost importance to society in all its aspects and in all its stages of development. It is like the rays of the sun, bringing the light of God's wisdom and grace into man's whole social life. It lights up and purifies the city of man and turns it into the city of God. Without these sustaining influences, the city of man is gradually overrun by a Mayan-like jungle of human passions, in whose rank undergrowth of greed and cruelty and every other vice man lives his life in terror — and in the end perishes.

Religious Influences in American Traditions

9. All society, particularly our own, is intimately dependent on religion. In the beginning of our own nation, at the very time when the revolutionary movement on the continent of Europe was planning to destroy all influence of religion on public life, it is a remarkable fact that our founding fathers based their own revolutionary action on the rights inherent in man as a creature of God, and placed their trust in His divine providence. The concept of man, which they set forth in the Declaration of Independence and on which they based the Constitution and our Bill of Rights, is essentially a religious concept — a concept inherited from Christian tradition. Human equality stems from the fact that all men have been created by God and equally endowed by Him with rights rooted in human nature itself. Against any other background, human equality has no meaning. Freedom, too, is essentially bound up with the religious concept of man. In any context that separates man from the creative and sustaining hand of God, there can be no freedom. The same is true of all man's inalienable rights. The enjoyment of such rights is safe only in a society which acknowledges the supreme and omnipotent God. The whole idea of government, dedicated to the welfare of the human person in the common good and subject to God's eternal law, is derived form the religious concepts of man and society which our founders inherited from their Christian tradition.

10. The founders of this country were deeply conscious of this debt to religion. The long deliberations to which they submitted the First Amendment to the Constitution and the many revisions it underwent before adoption bear witness to the important place religion occupied in the minds of the first Congress. Certainly it was not their purpose to eliminate the influence of religion on public life. On the contrary it was their intention to guarantee to religion

its essential freedom. In a country of divided religious allegiance, the federal government was indeed prohibited from setting up any established religion; but it was also prohibited from interfering in any way with any religious institution or with the freedom of the individual in the practice of the religion of his conscientious choice. That nothing other than this was intended, that the Federal Government was not prevented from encouraging and even aiding religion, so long as no particular form of religion should be established by the state, is clear not only from the wording of the First Amendment but also from the fact that from the beginning, under the Constitution and its amendments, many practices have flourished which have continued to give great help to religion.

11. Apart from the record of deliberation and the wording of the First Amendment itself, there is abundant evidence that this carefully thought out solution was not indicative of indifference and still less of hostility to religion. Both the Northwest and Southwest Ordinances, passed by the very men who were responsible for the amendment, speak of religion and morality as "necessary for good government and the happiness of mankind." And even more pointed are the words used by our first president in his Farewell Address:

> "Of all the dispositions and habits which lead to political prosperity, religion and morality are indispensable supports. . . . Reason and experience both forbid us to expect that national morality can prevail in exclusion of religious principle."

12. Such were the prevailing convictions of the founders of this country. Such, too, were the traditions which have in large measure determined the course of its development. No one has better expressed American traditions or has contributed more to their development than Abraham Lincoln. Eight times during the term of his presidency he issued proclamations of thanksgiving and of days of prayer and fasting which strongly emphasize this nation's need of religion. The proclamation of March 30, 1863 seems even more pertinent today than it was at the time it was issued.

> "We have been the recipients of the choicest bounties of Heaven; we have been preserved, these many years, in peace and prosperity . . . but we have forgotten God. We have forgotten the gracious hand which preserved us in peace, and multiplied and enriched and strengthened us; and we have vainly imagined, in the deceitfulness of our hearts, that all these blessings were produced by some superior wisdom and virtue of our own. Intoxicated with unbroken success, we have become too self-sufficient to feel the necessity of redeeming and preserving grace, too proud to pray to the God that made us."

The Threat of Secularism

13. These words of Lincoln not only recall to us our national traditions relative to the importance of religion; they also remind us of the constant

temptation for this country to turn away from God and to become immersed in material pursuits. In our own day widespread yielding to this temptation has given rise to an even greater danger — the way of life we call secularism. Those who follow this way of life distort and blot out our religious traditions, and seek to remove all influence of religion from public life. Their main efforts are centered on the divorce of religion from education. Their strategy seems to be: first to secularize completely the public school and then to claim for it a total monopoly of education.

14. To teach moral and spiritual values divorced from religion and based solely on social convention, as these men claim to do, is not enough. Unless man's conscience is enlightened by the knowledge of principles that express God's law, there can be no firm and lasting morality. Without religion, morality becomes simply a matter of individual taste, of public opinion or majority vote. The moral law must derive its validity and its binding force from the truths of religion. Without religious education, moral education is impossible.

15. In criticizing this secularist trend in education, let it not be said that we are enemies of public education. We recognize that the state has a legitimate and even necessary concern with education. But if religion is important to good citizenship — and that is the burden of our national tradition — then the state must give recognition to its importance in public education. The state, therefore, has the duty to help parents fulfill their task of religious instruction and training. When the state fails in this help, when it makes the task more difficult and even penalizes parents who try to fulfill this duty according to conscience, by depriving their children of their right under our Federal Constitution to auxiliary services, this can only be regarded as an utterly unfair and short-sighted policy....

Hugh J. Nolan, ed., *Pastoral Letters of the United States Catholic Bishops* (Washington, D.C.: United States Catholic Conference, 1984), 2:149–57. Printed with permission.

60. John Tracy Ellis, "Letter to a Bishop," 9 November 1972

The Canon Law Society of America met in Seattle October 23–26 [1972] to consider the theme "Participative Leadership and Shared Responsibility in the Church." In the opening address, noted historian Msgr. John Tracy Ellis... presented his views in the form of a letter to a nonexistent, newly appointed bishop to the fictional See of New Haven.

The Most Reverend James J. Farrell
Box 210
New Haven, Connecticut 06520

My dear Jim:

Little did we think that day in September, 1934, when we met for the first time as next door neighbors on the second floor of the Sulpician Seminary in Washington that the time would come when you would be the ordinary of a new diocese in a heavily urban area of your native state. Nor would I have thought that in light of the numerous and vexing problems that face you in this revolutionary age, you would have felt this historian classmate located thousands of miles away on the Pacific Coast, had something to offer by way of practical advice and counsel in the execution of the formidable task that lies before you.

In responding to your request I do so with real assurance on at least one point, namely, that the request was sincerely motivated, and that the openness and honesty of our relationship of years ago has not in the meantime dimmed, nor has it changed by your being named a bishop. Knowing you as I do, therefore, I feel certain you wish me to reply with utter candor, in the way that I used to reply now and then to another dear bishop friend, Paul Hallinan of Atlanta, that being the only way that men like Paul and yourself recognize as having validity or value. I shall answer you in the spirit that I think was Saint Paul's when he told his converts at Corinth that having been entrusted with this work, there would, as he said, be "no weakening on our part," to which he then added, "we will have none of the reticence of those who are ashamed, no deceitfulness or watering down the word of God; but the way we commend ourselves to every human being with a conscience is by stating the truth openly in the sight of God."[1] The vision of any one of us is at best severely limited, but insofar as I see the truth, I shall state it.

Obviously, your principal concern is now and must remain the evolving situation within the ecclesiastical framework that constitutes your diocese. Yet the Diocese of New Haven cannot exist of itself; it is a part of larger entities, the universal Church and the United States of America, to mention only two, both of which in these early 1970's are engulfed in the most profoundly revolutionary movement humankind has witnessed since the French Revolution tore apart the fabric of western society nearly 200 years ago. Just as once the Bastille had been stormed and the Reign of Terror had loosed its senseless fury, there was no returning to the relative calm of the eighteenth-century aristocratic regimes, so there is not now, nor will there be again, a return in the civil order to the comparatively placid era before our world was overtaken by what Walter Lippmann has described as "the revolution no one understands."[2] Nor will the ecclesiastical order see restored in your lifetime and, perhaps, in the lifetime of your successor, the Catholic Church's seemingly impregnable strength and security of the period before Vatican Council II.

It would be entirely unreal, therefore, in my judgment, to imagine that any phenomenon in contemporary society suggests a surcease to the constant whirl of changing social forces as you and I know them, ceaselessly accelerated as they have been, and will continue to be, by further scientific discoveries and the mounting speed and tension of the technological age in which we live. If

---

1. 2 Cor. 4:1–4.
2. San Francisco *Sunday Examiner and Chronicle*, 9 June 1968, 3.

many in middle age and beyond have not reconciled themselves to this rather uncomfortable fact, it is, nonetheless, a reality that every discernible sign indicates will endure, a reality that is exemplified, to name but a single feature of our hour in time, in the communications media that have accustomed the young to take for granted an instant culture in which they wish to share.

In other words, Jim, as I see it, you are called to live out your years as an ordinary in the midst of the kind of change and ferment that future historians of this late twentieth century will characterize as revolutionary, even though that revolution will not parallel in every detail the revolutions that have gone before it. This, I think, is a fundamental promise that should inform the thinking of every bishop as he strives to direct his course into the uncertain future in a way that will redound to the spiritual and temporal welfare of the people of God among whom he works. I can well imagine that you may have grown weary of hearing that you received your assignment in order to serve and not be served. At the risk of taxing your patience, however, I am going to quote two sentences from the ritual now used in an episcopal ordination. They read as follows:

> The title of bishop derives not from his rank but from his duty, and it is the part of a bishop to serve rather than to rule. Such is the counsel of the Master that the most important should behave as if he were the least, and the leader as if he were the one who serves.[3]

As native-born Americans you and I know the predominant traits of the people whose citizenship we are proud to own. Our national ethos embodies many splendid qualities that others have long admired, for example, the unparalleled generosity with which the United States has shared its bountiful riches with those less favored over all the globe. If we are realistic we will likewise candidly admit our national defects, one of the most striking of which is as well described by the old biblical word "mammon" as by any other term, with all the evils implied by Jesus when in the Sermon on the Mount he bluntly told that privileged congregation, "You cannot be the slave of God and of money."[4] Judged at the bar of history, Americans as a nation have countless good deeds that weigh in the scales to their credit; but we would be less than honest were we to disguise the fact that same history reveals a national mania for money that has too often swept everything before it. Thoughtful people are agreed that not infrequently the keenest insight one can gain about oneself is to learn how others see one. In this regard the most discerning foreign visitors to our country have been all but unanimous in detecting this prevailing characteristic in Americans. Let me cite for you a passage from what is by virtual universal agreement regarded as the most penetrating analysis of a foreign visitor ever written on our national life and customs, a commentary

---

3. *Provisional Text of the Roman Pontifical for the Ordination of Deacons, Priests, and Bishops* (Washington: National Conference of Catholic Bishops, 1969), 25.
4. Matt. 6:24.

that while it bared our ills was, nonetheless, diffused with warmth and even affection for our people. After a prolonged visit to this country over 140 years ago Alexis de Tocqueville wrote of the arbitrary way in which Americans classified human vices, and he declared:

> There are certain propensities which appear censurable to the general reason and the universal conscience of mankind, but which happen to agree with the peculiar and temporary wants of the American community: these propensities are lightly reproved, sometimes even encouraged; for instance, the love of wealth and the secondary propensities connected with it may be more particularly cited. To clear, to till, and to transform the vast uninhabited continent which is his domain, the American requires the daily support of an energetic passion; that passion can only be the love of wealth; the passion for wealth is therefore not reprobated in America, and, provided it does not go beyond the bounds assigned to it for public security, it is held in honor. The American lauds as a noble and praiseworthy ambition what our own forefathers in the Middle Ages stigmatized as servile cupidity....[5]

I can picture you saying as you read, "What has all this got to do with me?" Because you are an American among Americans it has everything to do with the image that you create, not only among your own priests, religious and laity, but, too, in the minds of the observant non-Catholics among whom you dwell. Whether they are Catholics, Protestants, or Jews only a very few will ever have the chance to watch you as you commune *solus cum sole* with God in your private chapel, although now and then they will have the occasion to observe your prayerful postures at liturgical functions.

Figuratively speaking, however, everybody in the Diocese of New Haven will see you and hear about you in what may be called your public life. And as you go about they will comment on the kind of car you drive, on the neighborhood in which you live, on the brand of clothes you wear, and on the place and form of recreation and amusement you choose to patronize. In brief, the external features of your daily living will count for or against you, and people will take your measure as a churchman who has, or has not, suc-

---

5. Alexis de Tocqueville, *Democracy in America*, ed. Phillips Bradley (New York: Alfred A. Knopf, 1953), 2:236. Both before and after de Tocqueville one meets the same kind of comment, for example, in a report written in 1818 by the French-born Sulpician Ambrose Marechal, third Archbishop of Baltimore, who stated, "Among the principal vices of the Americans are the desire for unlimited riches, which seems to have seized the minds of all, and the vice of drunkenness among laborers and the lower classes" ("Archbishop Marechal's Report to the Propaganda, October 16, 1818," in *Documents of American Catholic History*, ed. John Tracy Ellis [Chicago: Henry Regnery Company, 1967], 1:208). Sixty years after de Tocqueville another famous commentator from abroad noted the same phenomenon when James Bryce remarked, "The fault which Americans are most frequently accused of is the worship of wealth" (*The American Commonwealth*, 3d ed. rev. [New York: Macmillan, 1895], 2:749). Bryce, however, was at pains to state that he found this defect no more offensive among Americans than among others, for example, the acceptance of English society of persons of great wealth who might lack any other qualifications to recommend them.

cumbed to the multiple and varied lures of the affluent society and whether, for example, a weakness in that respect has betrayed you into driving a Cadillac or a Lincoln, or whether through an exercise of restraint a Chevrolet or a Ford is found sufficient for your needs.

Indeed, even the crassest hedonists in town will take notice of you in their cynical way if they find you living in the city's most fashionable section, next door, for example, to a mansion that sold for $425,000, as I was told some time ago of one of your fellow bishops or, perhaps, in an area so exclusive that a fee has to be paid for the people to drive by your residence, as is true of another of your rank.

Curiously, some of these same hedonists of whom I spoke — and they do have influence that you can hardly afford to ignore — while more frequently than not, they are oblivious to most basic questions within the Catholic community, will have somehow become aware of the simple style of living adopted by bishops in distant places like Madison where the bishop lives in two rooms in the diocesan seminary or Spokane, Boise, and Helena whose simplicity of life is much admired. In their mocking manner your see city's hedonists, and others as well, will wonder aloud should they find you living at striking variance to these your brother prelates. Your life style, to use a somewhat fatigued term, is, then, a major matter, for you can scarcely expect that people will believe you or take you seriously should your episcopal exhortations emanate from the best appointed office in the block, if you hold membership in the city's most elite golf club, and if it should become known, as such things have a way of doing, that your clothes carry the Brooks Brothers label.

Should this strike you as an exaggerated emphasis, remember, Jim, that for many Americans these are the norms by which values are largely reckoned, and that even among the most mundane there often lingers at least a faint recollection from their remote religious training that externals of this kind are incongruous in one who has been known on occasion to refer to those at his ecclesiastical level as successors of the apostles.

In a word, the American instinct is to judge you, as they judge others, by the external and material elements in your conduct. Neither the worldling nor the devout, of course, would experience any moral uplift should it become known that you are an alcoholic or that you keep a mistress. Yet when all the evidence were to have been gathered and weighed for or against you, their censure, I honestly believe, would be less severe for these manifestations of human weakness than it would were you to indulge in a display of affluence and luxury. In their typical American way of assessing virtually everything in monetary terms, there would probably also be those prone to comment that this style of life touches them personally since it is their money, not your own, that you were spending. If the stress has seemed here to be on the more mundane of your laity, I should add that it is not meant to imply that the same line of thought, *mutatis mutandis,* would not suggest itself to the more religiously inclined among your people, even if they should be less articulate in saying so.

Of late a far keener sensitivity about the uses to which money is put has become commonplace with the well nigh universal stress on the needs of the Third World, and the obligation for those who have to assist those who have not. As we both likewise know, great fortunes in the United States are no longer the prerogative of those with proper Wasp credentials, for Catholic millionaires now number in the hundreds. Many of the latter, alas, have ceased to be practicing Catholics in the traditional sense, but they have not formally withdrawn from the Church, and even if they had, they are still the object of divine love and, therefore, remain an object of love for you and me as well. As I have said, some of these people though now far distant from their early religious instruction and practice, still dimly recall that long ago the One whom you are called to represent in their midst, addressing John the Baptist's followers, asked who it was they had gone out to the wilderness to see, "a man wearing fine clothes," as he put it. He answered his own question when he said, "Oh no, those who wear fine clothes are to be found in palaces." And lest any doubt should linger in his listeners' minds about what he thought of his austere precursor, he declared, "I tell you solemnly, of all the children born of women, a greater than John the Baptist has never been seen...."[6] If the New Testament contains a more signal compliment from the Son of God to one of his contemporaries, I do not know it....

> *Origins* 2, no. 20 (9 November 1972): 317, 319, 323–31; also in John Tracy Ellis, ed., *Documents of American Catholic History* (Wilmington, Del.: Michael Glazier, 1987). (Footnotes in Ellis.) Printed with permission of the estate of John Tracy Ellis.

61. Archbishop Joseph Bernardin, "Civil Religion in the United States," 8 June 1975[1]

National reassessment is a popular pastime in this summer of our discontent. The double shock of Watergate and Vietnam, and the stimulus of the bicentennial, lead many Americans to ponder seriously our national values and commitments, as well as our fidelity in living up to them. It is healthy and essential that we do so. Uncertainty and confusion of purpose have characterized many aspects of our national life in recent years. If the current period of reassessment leads to a renewal of principled consensus, it will perform a valuable service.

This reassessment must be a corporate enterprise, involving all responsible sectors of our society. I wish today to contribute to this dialogue from the perspective of the religious tradition in America — a tradition which embodies insights and values essential to our well-being as a nation. The religious tradition is not the only voice to be heard in this dialogue, but it is a voice which must be heard, because it has things to tell us which are of profound importance for our national life.

---

6. Matt. 11:7–11.

1. This address was delivered at Miami University, Oxford, Ohio, 8 June 1975. Archbishop Bernardin was the president of the National Conference of Catholic Bishops at the time.

Even as I say this I am aware, as you are, that organized religion does not play precisely the same role in national life today that it has played at times in the past. There are many evidences of this. A recent poll of opinion leaders, conducted by *U.S. News and World Report,* gave organized religion low grades among the institutions which influence our society. Churches ranked just ahead of motion pictures — although it is to our credit that we achieved this without benefit of popcorn.

There are those who believe that because the role of organized religion has changed, religion itself has therefore diminished in importance as a social institution. I do not believe that this is precisely the case. It may very well be true that the churches today do not have the same direct, immediate impact on society that they have had at other times in our history. Yet they do have a real impact, exerted primarily through their formative influence on the values and attitudes of those who are their members. Because this is difficult to quantify, it is easy to overlook. Our fondness for what is measurable — for what can be reduced to statistics or charted on graphs — should not blind us to the powerful part that ideas and symbols, including the ideas and symbols of religion, play in the lives of individuals and nations. On this profound level, not easily accessible to polls and instruments of empirical investigation, religion has always had, and continues to have, its most significant impact on national life.

Along with this, however, it is necessary to acknowledge a certain diminution in the role of organized religion in our country in recent decades and a corresponding increase in the role played by another phenomenon to which the name "civil religion" has been given. One need not accept in all particulars the elaborate parallels worked out by some between traditional religion and civil religion in order to recognize the basic truth of what they are saying. Public life must necessarily be organized around a system of value-laden symbols, and in a pluralistic and increasingly secularized country such as our own, it is natural that a significant part of this role should be played by figures, institutions and events of a broadly "political" character. To the degree that civil religion helps to give continuity, coherence and purposefulness to our public life, it serves an essential purpose.

Nevertheless it is possible for abuses to be perpetrated under the cloak of civil religion. This happens when its symbols are manipulated — by the misguided or the unscrupulous — in order to conceal unworthy motives and vicious politics. It is at this point that we become painfully conscious of the fact that civil religion, while necessary, is also radically inadequate. Without awareness that our nation stands under higher judgment, the judgment embodied in the ideas and symbols of theistic religion, the tradition of civil religion is positively dangerous.

I confess to a certain anxiety that, perhaps through inadvertence rather than intent, this kind of manipulation of the symbols of our civil religion may become a debilitating part of our observance of the bicentennial. Appreciation of the heritage we enjoy as Americans should not conceal failures of moral sensitivity in our national life, in both the past and the present. Nor should avowed commitment to American principles be used as an excuse for breast-beating and unrelieved castigation of our past and present, as if the two hundred years of our life as a nation had witnessed nothing except an unrelieved series of betrayals of national ideals. Our past and our present, like the past and present of any nation, present a canvas of contrasting light and shadow, virtue juxtaposed with vice. We should not gloss over our failings, but neither should we fail to celebrate our achievements.

I wish to mention in particular three areas in which the symbols of our civil religion are perhaps particularly susceptible to manipulation and abuse, calling for judgment and correction by the higher values of theistic religion.

One is the tendency to think of America and Americans as enjoying a kind of privileged moral superiority by comparison with other nations and peoples. At various times in American history, this notion — that we are a new chosen people — has led us to indulge ourselves in such abuses as racism and nativism. Perhaps something of the same tendency surfaced, momentarily at least, in the hostile reactions of some toward the Southeast Asian refugees. Granted the very real, practical difficulties we face in attempting to provide homes and jobs for these people in the midst of a recession, the fact remains that there were overtones of a hysterical self-righteousness and more than a tinge of racial bias in early criticisms of the refugees. In particular, I deplore the response of some public figures and opinion leaders who, often through the use of code language, seemed to appeal to the bigotry which is part of the dark side of the American character, rather than to the generosity which is equally a part of that character.

A second area which should be of deep concern to all of us is our national fondness for violence. The Minuteman, the frontiersman, the cowboy, the GI are mythic figures of our civil religion — rightfully so. Yet the values and virtues they symbolize — self-reliance, courage, devotion to duty — are sometimes given less prominence than the brutal notion that they were men who, when the chips were down, knew how to settle problems with a gun. This idea is deep-rooted and persistent in American life. Popular culture consistently panders to our addiction to violence. The statistics on gun ownership, legal and illegal, by private citizens in the United States are truly staggering — as, for that matter, are the statistics of violent crime committed with these same weapons. After years of debate, we seem no more able to divest ourselves of handguns than to cure the common cold. Is it because the legal and constitutional issues are really so complex? Or is it also because of what the gun and its relationship to violence symbolize for us on some darker level of the national psyche?

Similarly, at various times in our history, our international relationships have too often seemed to be based on the assumption that violence is a cure-all. I do not question the proposition that, in this very imperfect world, it may sometimes be necessary for a nation, as for an individual, to resort to force in order to vindicate certain rights. Yet if we have learned nothing else from the experience of Vietnam, we should have learned that violence is not the answer to every problem and that winning minds and hearts is not ultimately accomplished by guns, bombs and napalm. We must be prepared as a nation to respond intelligently to challenges on the level of ideas and ideologies, values and commitments. We cannot rely exclusively on military power, however necessary it may be, to promote our valid national interests and serve our national purposes.

A third area of concern involves the ambivalence of our attitudes toward relationships with other nations. Much of our history has been marked by the predominance of one or the other of two extremes — on the one hand, a sometimes messianic commitment to "manifest destiny" or some equivalent thereof; on the other hand, isolationism, aloofness and withdrawal from international involvements, almost as if these would be a source of moral contamination to us. Yet side by side with these attitudes, America's international record also reflects great generosity and a proper sense of commitment to our real duties in the world. Let us hope that, as the post-Vietnam reassessment of our international role proceeds, this aspect of our tradition will be emphasized. Our foreign policies in the years ahead should properly be defined in terms of interdependence and our obligation, in view of our national power and wealth, to play a truly exemplary role on the world scene.

We cannot, however, simply take it for granted that what is best in our tradition will prevail during this present period of re-study and reassessment. On the contrary, the confusion and uncertainty manifest in many areas of national life today create the conditions in which manipulation of the symbols of civil religion is all too easy and all too possible. At such a moment we should be particularly wary of the danger of demagoguery — whether of the left or the right — which would cloak itself in the symbols of civil religion in order to appeal to our selfishness and baser instincts.

Rational, principled discourse, not demagoguery, is an urgent national need today. In particular we must be respectful of what all responsible groups have to contribute to the ongoing national dialogue. It would be tragic if the building of a new national consensus in fact degenerated into a version of the tyranny of the majority, in which hard sayings — including those spoken by persons addressing national issues from the perspective of the religious tradition — were shouted down and denied a hearing. We have heard much, even from our Supreme Court, about the evils of religious "divisiveness." But it would be a far greater evil if any responsible group, including persons of religious commitment, were denied an effective opportunity to address public issues because of the fancied danger of "divisiveness."

As I have suggested, civil religion by itself is not capable of supplying the principles and values necessary for determining the course of public policy in our nation. The symbols of civil religion are an important part of our tradition, but they must be animated by the principles of other value systems. It is at this point, I believe, that our religious tradition properly comes into play.

I do not mean to suggest that in the last analysis religion should dictate public policy. This would be both impossible and unacceptable. But religion does provide a normative system of values against which our behavior as individuals and our corporate behavior as a society should be measured. To use an old-fashioned word, this is a question of conscience — and conscience, formed by religious values and commitments, is an essential part of our lives both as individuals and as a nation.

Describing and putting into practice the proper relationship of the religious tradition to national life is not a simple matter in times like ours — times marked by the secularization of society, by religious and ideological pluralism, and by controversy and confusion over church-state questions. It is essential, however, that there be a rich, deep relationship marked by vitality and healthy interaction. Important as civil religion may be, it does not and cannot substitute in national life for the contribution of authentic religious values and commitments. In this time of national reassessment in particular, the nation would risk being rudderless — or, even worse, being propelled into false choices and dangerous courses — if it were to rely solely on the symbols of civil religion, symbols too easily manipulated for unworthy purposes. It is my hope and also my expectation that, in the present and the future, as in the past, our nation will draw inspiration and purpose from the abiding insights of our religious tradition.

Origins 5, no. 18 (31 July 1975): 113, 115–17.

62. Margaret O'Brien Steinfels, "The Church and Its Public Life," 10 June 1989[1]

...This lectureship has as its general purpose the examination...of religion and its implications for public life in the United States. In place of religion in general, however, I am going to talk about our religion, Roman Catholicism, and by the deft insertion of the pronoun "its," I have shifted our attention from American public life to the church's own public life.

Let me be clear: The church's public life is quintessentially expressed in our gathering for worship in the Sunday Eucharistic celebration. This is any Catholic's most common experience of the public life of the church. But, except peripherally, that is not what I am talking about. My topic rather is the public life constituted by what we Catholics do to one another when we are not at Sunday Mass; what we say not to God but to each other: the conversation, sometimes political, sometimes cultural, sometimes intellectual, sometimes poetic and impassioned, that we carry on there, and the ethos — the disposition, attitude, turn of phrase, focus of attention — the habits of mind and heart distinctive to our public life....

This public life has changed a great deal since John XXIII's inspiration in 1959 when he declared there was to be an ecumenical council. His inspiration has carried us a long way. At times it has been a bit like Monty Python's

---

1. This is the 1989 John Courtney Murray Forum Lecture, delivered 18 May 1989, at Fordham University School of Law. Steinfels is the editor of *Commonweal* magazine.

Flying Circus: the visual jokes converging at the margins almost out of sight at the edge of the screen; vast contradictions accommodated; the logical and the irrational companionably ascending in the balloon while the parents, the police and the priests clamor from the ground.

But the running, jumping start of the past 27 years looks as though it may end not in a start but a falter. Vatican II was a turning point in the church's history. The transition that has followed has created new understandings of the church and new confusions about it. But what must be a matter of serious concern — and what I am looking at tonight — is that one of the possibilities of transition periods is for the transition not to take place. It is possible to reach a turning point in history and not to turn....

Certainly the present moment, when the whole direction of the past quarter century seems to be at stake, is not lacking in analyses, as one intramural Catholic crisis succeeds another. My own particular concern, however, is not one or several of these attention-grabbing events but a quiet, continuing underground crisis, not a heart attack but a kind of seeping hemorrhage; not a crisis of heresy or of free speech but nonetheless a crisis of truth. It is a crisis, I want to argue, of plausibility, of credibility, and — speaking as an editor and writer — a crisis of language....

[The issue of the relationship of the church and the world] touches the very heart of what was accomplished at Vatican II. The council achieved, or so it was thought, a decisive shift in the church's understanding of its stance toward the world. "The joy and hope, the grief and anguish of men of our time, especially of those who are poor or afflicted in any way, are the joy and hope, the grief and anguish of the followers of Christ as well. Nothing that is genuinely human fails to find an echo in their hearts." The change was not signaled in "The Pastoral Constitution on the Church in the Modern World" alone. It was found in the council's attitude toward religious freedom, toward other branches of Christianity, toward other world religions. It was shown in the council's recognition that the church, too, was part of the movement and sometimes even the drift of history. The council, or so it was thought, put an end to the easy recourse of condemning the world as an excuse for the church to hide out in its many thick-walled fortresses — philosophical, political, ascetic, intellectual and even territorial, fortresses left over from those days when the papal states were defended as being as critical to papal authority — and as theologically well-grounded — as *Humanae vitae* is today.

Yet the church/world dichotomy keeps popping up like some manic jack-in-the-box, punctuating the discussions at the 1985 extraordinary synod, the working paper for the synod on the laity, the recent meetings of the American archbishops and Vatican officials, and numerous church documents. It reemerges in both conservative and radical rejections of political complexity and compromise. On both sides of the church/world relationship, the language grows steadily more implausible. Of the world we are told that it is a sinkhole of materialism, individualism, consumerism, or collectivism (depending on your economic system), and relativism. Now American culture, to start at home, has its problems — no news to readers of *Commonweal* and *America* — but to hear the Curia and our archbishops in Rome, one would think it on the verge of unredeemable depravity. Frankly I think our archbishops chose to avoid uncomfortable disagreements with their Vatican confreres by badmouthing the party that wasn't there to defend itself.

But maybe it is true, as some claim, that Vatican II was too optimistic, too liberal if you will, about the world. It did not, of course, reject all tension and conflict. In proclaiming a solidarity with all that is "genuinely human," it implied an opposition to the falsely human or the genuinely inhuman. To remain in solidarity with all men and women, even those we might want to ignore and forget, the poor, the suffering, the excluded, requires us to oppose the forces that impoverish, burden and exclude them. It is arguable, at least, that the council underestimated the degree to which the genuinely inhuman already dominates us as individuals and societies. But the council extended the same benefit of the doubt to the church....

If the council's tendency to deemphasize the harsher aspects of the world's record is now being corrected with a vengeance, its parallel tendency to deemphasize the harsher aspects of the church's record is being pursued with an equal vengeance. It is here that the plausibility crisis looms even larger. As we are all supposed to know, the church has always taught what it teaches now: about race, about women, about slavery, about economic justice, about human rights, about torture, about who is and who is not saved. Individuals may and do err, of course, and need to repent. But magically the church need not repent: not in Germany or Spain or Austria in the 1930s and 1940s; not for the "Syllabus of Errors," or the Crusades, or the burning of heretics or the long history of spiritual and physical cruelty inflicted on poor sinners out of thoughtlessness and arrogance.

One reason that the dichotomy between church and world keeps popping up is our failure as a church to formally acknowledge these sins and errors, to do penance for them, to learn from them. If the dark, monochromatic image of the world projected in this dichotomy does not match the many-hued and subtly shaded world most lay people know, the image of innocent church has even less chance of passing the plausibility test.

Behind the revival of the sinless church/sinful world dichotomy is a failure of nerve. We do not trust the spirit to guide us in a free and open conversation with each other. Instead of a church that viewed its surroundings as an object of conquest, the council gave us a church that approached its surroundings in an attitude of dialogue. Key Catholic leaders have been frightened by the inability of the postconciliar church to reverse the rising tide of secularization in Western Europe and by the coincidence of the anti-traditionalist turmoil of the 1960s. These leaders appear to be convinced that a dialogical stance will lead to accommodation, assimilation and further secularization. Dialogue requires the lowering of barriers and the search for a common ground, but the lowering of barriers is now increasingly feared as the abandonment of all distinctions. Common ground is feared as so much quicksand.

No one should feel stubbornly obliged to defend every postconciliar development carried out under the impulse of a new dialogue with the world. But we cannot avoid the choice of our fundamental attitude toward the world. We have to decide whether the experience of a decade and a half in Western Europe should be pivotal for a universal church. We must ask ourselves whether that experience stands as a judgment on a few years of dialogical Catholicism or on 175 years of fortress Catholicism....

No one can say with complete certainty — not even an editor — what is the prudent and wise, pastoral and Christian response to our crisis. I realize we are not all in equal jeopardy in this regard; bishops and archbishops may be summoned for interrogation, priests may be threatened with loss of their teaching authority or their priestly faculties, religious may be threatened with silencing and dismissed from their communities. Nonetheless, there is a price to pay. A church that lived through Vatican II and then backs away from it may end up more badly wounded than if the council had never occurred. The church itself has taught us too much about the necessity of reform and the demands of human dignity to expect a return to the preconciliar model of patient submission with the pious hope of future rehabilitation.

My own concern is that in mapping our course and choosing our words we may misgauge the gravity of the moment and underestimate the price already being paid in the currency of demoralization, rancor and loss of faith, all because words and deeds have parted company. What we need are words that do not veil intentions but disclose realities. What we need are candor and courage.

America 160 (10 June 1989): 550–58. Printed with permission.

Communism

The breakup of the wartime alliance with the Soviet Union precipitated the long and bitter Cold War. American Catholics had long been suspicious of any alliance with atheistic Russia and had noted time and again the anti-religious policies of communist-dominated regimes. As geopolitical realities reconfigured the world into American and Soviet blocs, American Catholics raised their voices once again to decry the harsh repression of Catholicism behind the Iron Curtain and strongly supported the efforts of the United States to contain the communist menace. They also shared and indeed contributed to the growing concern over internal communist subversion in some of the critical institutions of American life. Because these concerns came to be expressed in the career of the era's leading foe of communism, Roman Catholic Joseph McCarthy, many saw his activities as a positive sign of Catholicism's contribution to American ideological strength. Others, such as Bishop Bernard Sheil, dissented and distanced themselves from McCarthy's methods.

63. Diocesan Confidential Questionnaire on Communism, Commissioned by the National Catholic Welfare Conference with Responses from the Diocese of St. Augustine, Florida, 1945

Section 1: Public Attitudes

1. *In your diocese, what is the current state of public opinion in regard to communism? Has Soviet military success influenced general thinking on communism?*

Generally speaking, public opinion seems to prescind entirely from the question of communism. The average person seems to view Russia as unquestionably our greatest friend, militarily, but along with this great admiration there goes a sort of "suspended judgement" about a lot of questions involving Russia which formerly were uppermost in the mind of the average American. Among these questions is communism. For the present the public has conveniently put this question aside without answering it.

2. *What is the reaction in your diocese to communist political maneuverings in Europe?*

As far as I can determine, this "suspended judgement" is the prevailing attitude to these questions also. People still remember the double-crosses which Russia and Stalin indulged in in the past. The insincerity of the Communist "turnabout" is still lingering in the back of the average Floridian's head.

3. *What was the general reaction to the charges of communism leveled during the recent political campaign? Is there a fear of communist influence in regard to the Political Action Committee of the C.I.O.?*

Business interests generally looked with concern upon the New Deal and seemed to have accepted sincerely some of the charges of communism leveled at the New Deal candidates. The public at large was unimpressed by the charges and quite in favor of the New Deal men. The P.A.C. was not very active in this state as the results of the election were evident.

4. *Is there a fear of communism as a factor in the labor movement?*

Yes, in so far as the labor movement is greatly a product of the north, but a sort of "can't happen here" attitude pervades the general thinking. Even among men who are very well acquainted with the labor movement in this state, there does not seem to be any fear that it can happen here. For this reason, I feel that it would be extremely easy for communists to gain influential positions virtually unnoticed if they maintained a cautious and non-provocative approach.

5. *Does the public understand that communists, through their organizational ability and other techniques, can have an influence beyond their numbers? What groups in your diocese are attempting to teach this lesson?*

Definitely no! On this point more than on any other there is need for concern in this state. Florida does not have that same healthy fear of communism which some sections of the East have. I know of no other organization which is attempting to teach this lesson other than the Church and the Diocesan newspaper.

Section II: Communist Strength

6. *If Communism has any foothold in your Diocese, would you kindly list the cities where it is strongest. If possible, estimate the number of members, sympathizers, and followers.*

Miami, Jacksonville, Tampa, Orlando.

However, all of these are very small factions. According to a reliable estimate made by the district head of the F.B.I., there are not more than 200 really good members of the Communist party in the state. Ordinarily now, the party goes under the name of the Florida Press and Educational Association.

There is a sizeable following among the "pinks" of the colleges. The University of Florida, the University of Miami, and Rollins College all have their share of professors of the liberal turn of mind, who constitute a danger to the young men and women whom they teach. These college "pinks," for the most part are men of purely materialistic outlook, persons who don't believe in God and who are satisfied to cooperate with anything and anybody who will offer some material advancement to the poor or underprivileged. There are several of these persons who are notable for their cooperation with the Communist front organizations. Included in this group are: Prof. A. J. Hanna, Mrs. Angela P. Campbell, both of Rollins College; Prof. William Carlton, Prof. Rembert Wallace Patrick, of the University of Florida; Prof. Charles Doren Tharpe of the University of Miami. Some of these persons have been in close association with persons who are avowedly Communists.

7. *Would you list the names and positions of its locally or nationally prominent officers, followers, and sympathizers? If possible, also list the national origin, racial or cultural background of these communist-minded persons. If any are apostate Catholic, please note the fact.*

Charles N. Smolikoff, Miami: Regional Director of the C.I.O. He is of Russian descent. Studied at Columbia University and is a very capable person. He has some success in organizing the small shipyards in the Miami area and also the Pan-American Airways workers for the C.I.O.

Rev. Joseph Barth, Miami: Unitarian Minister, at present running for City Commissioner in Miami. He is an apostate Catholic and in fact, according to his wife, once studied for the priesthood. He studied at Creighton Univ. After leaving the Church, he obtained a degree of Bachelor of Divinity at the University of Chicago. He has for some time been associated with some of the radical elements among the colored in Miami and especially among the youth.

Mrs. Ramona Sawyer Barth, Miami: wife of Rev. Joseph Barth: Executive Secretary of the Miami Council of American-Soviet Friendship; lecturer, Mrs. Barth studied at Tufts College and at the University of Chicago, where she received a degree of Bachelor of Divinity.

Bertha Howe, Orlando:

Mr. _____ Trainor, Jacksonville:

The above names were given to me by the F.B.I.

Henning Heldt, Miami: Columnist for the Miami Herald, writes on Gov't and politics; labor. Very well acquainted with the labor movement; he is especially well acquainted with the labor situation in and around Miami. He seems, in some ways, to me at least, to follow the Communist line. He was at one time an official in the Writers Guild, is a close friend of Michael Quill, etc.

Prof. J. J. Hanna, Winter Park: Professor of History at Rollins College

Prof. William Carlton, Gainesville: Professor of History at the University of Florida. He is now lecturing extensively throughout the State on Russia.

Prof. Rembert Wallace Patrick, Gainsville: Associate Prof. of Social Sciences, Univ. of Fla.

Mrs. Angela P. Campbell, Winter Park: Prof. of Spanish at Rollins College. Spanish by birth. Was very active on the Loyalist side during the Spanish Civil War.

Philip S. May, Jacksonville: Head of the Board of Controls of the University of Florida.

Margaret Rawlings, Gainesville: Novelist, of *The Yearling* fame.

Norman Silverman, Gainesville, Chicago: Student at the University of Florida; since has left the University. A Jew. Tried to organize the American Youth for Democracy on the Campus. A group of students, led by a Catholic and under the guidance of the Catholic Chaplain attacked the AYD in the University paper and succeeded in getting the faculty to force the local branch to disavow all connection with the parent organization.

Dr. Karl G. Knoche, Jacksonville: Russian born. Dentist. Chairman of the Local Council of Am-Soviet Friendship. Is a thorough philosophical Communist. His wife was at one time the head of the Communist party in Jax [Jacksonville].

Mrs. Karl G. Knoche, Jacksonville: Was at one time the local head of the Communist Party. She studied in one of the Communist leadership schools in New York. Claims no longer to be a member of the party.

Samuel Kipnis, Jacksonville: President of the National Container Corp. A Russian born Jew. Has many Communistic ideas and sponsored at his own expense showing of a Communist film.

8. *What specific communist activities are in the forefront in your diocese? Papers, schools, subsidiary and front organizations are particularly worth noting.*

The Council of American-Soviet Friendship in this state is a communist front. It has local councils in Miami, Tampa and Jacksonville. It is at present sponsoring extensive lecture programs by prominent Communists — Rose Mauer, Rowena Meyer, are included

The Southern Negro Youth Congress, Miami

Florida Press and Educational Association — Jacksonville, Miami, Tampa, Orlando

The Floridian — a cheap newspaper published in St. Petersburg

9. *Please describe communist influence on local labor, indicating the specific titles, local numbers and membership figures of unions controlled or strongly influenced. In each case, note if possible, the evidence of control or influence. What is the position of city and state industrial union councils?*

Miami: Industrial Union of Marine and Shipbuilding Workers of America (C.I.O.) At present it has between 2000 and 2500 members, including the workers at the Pan-American Airways. They were organized by Charles N. Smolikoff. However, practically all of these so far organized are in industries that will all but vanish after the war.

The local Transport Union (C.I.O.) Roy Whitman and his wife, whom I suspect of being fellow travelers, but I have no facts to substantiate the suspicion, are the organizers. He is a graduate of Columbia. I was unable to obtain membership figures.

Jacksonville: Industrial Union of Marine and Shipbuilding Workers of America (C.I.O.) This union has succeeded in organizing only the Merrill-Stevens Shipbuilding Company, a repair yard, employing about 2500 to 3000 workers, nearly half of whom are negroes.

The local Painters Union of the A.F.L. has had some communist influence in it in the past.

Orlando: Food, Tobacco, Agricultural and Allied Workers of America (F.T.A.) A C.I.O. affiliate. Has succeeded in organizing a few of the citrus processing plants in central Florida. Its organizer, Miss Anne Mathews, is suspected of being communistic, but I have no facts to substantiate it.

Tampa: All the shipyards in Tampa are 100% A.F.L. organized and seem to have had remarkably little trouble.

Remark: Generally speaking, communism is not likely to have much appeal to the white shipyard workers of Florida. Whatever else may be said of them, they seem to be loyally American in every way.

10. *Was the Political Action Committee of the C.I.O. in your diocese communist-controlled or influenced on the local or state level? If so, please indicate reasons for this belief, cities affected, and the influence PAC had upon the vote.*

The PAC was not a factor in this state during the election. The outcome of the elections was clear and any large outlay of funds would have been wasted. The PAC did, however, spend some money in and around Miami: Charles N. Smolikoff, regional director of the C.I.O. was in charge of this fund.

11. *Is there any evidence of communist activity among Negro groups? Please give names and details.*

Yes, there is some evidence, but it does not appear on the surface to be of great consequence. Generally speaking, I don't think that it is sizeable, the better communist leaders working among the negroes in the South are careful not to cause any outbursts of racial feeling. They seem to follow the line of indoctrinating their charges while still insisting that they continue to act as good Southern Darkies. The reasons are obvious.

However, radicalism is not apt to have a very great appeal to the southern negro. The average southern colored man makes his living working for the southern white man; there are at present no other avenues for economic advancement open to him, nor are any others visible. Radicalism tends to disturb the only certainty which he has and for this reason will probably be unpopular.

Jacksonville: There is a Communist party (Fla. Press and Educational Association) among the colored in this city, but I have not been able to determine the size of its membership or its influence. No one among the whites seems to know. There is a great amount of suspicion on the part of the whites that there is a large communist movement among the colored in that city. This is understandable when one recalls the fact that the population is almost 50% colored. The headquarters for the communist party is on Broad Street. I was unable to discover a local branch of the American Youth for Democracy, but there probably is one.

Miami: There is a local branch of the Communist party (Fla. Press and Educ. Ass'n) and a local branch of the AYD. The local branch of the Southern Negro Youth Congress seems to have replaced the AYD. Both of these organizations seem to be small and the latter is composed mostly of high school boys and girls. The Rev. Joseph Barth and his wife Ramona Sawyer Barth (whites) are very active among the negro radical groups.

Tampa: The colored group in this city seems to be a conservative group, with some good leaders. There was some agitation in the past by the local longshoremen's Union, but nothing of recent date.

Orlando: There has for some time been good cooperation between the whites and colored. The inter-racial committee in Orlando in the past has been a good one; boy scout and youth leaders also among the whites have worked in close cooperation with the colored leaders.

Wages in the fruit and vegetable industries have for some time been excellent; naturally the negro workers have been satisfied. As a matter of fact the employers are confronted with a problem in trying to get the negroes to work for a full week. There has been no attempt as yet to organize the field workers in these industries. The Citrus interests are satisfied that there won't be for some time.

The large group of migratory negro laborers which have been brought into the State from the Bahamas and Jamaica are no problem principally because their wages are excellent but also because of the nature of their contracts whereby troublemakers can quickly and finally be sent back to their homes.

The F.T.A. (C.I.O. affiliate) is attempting to organize the workers in the processing and canning plants but without marked success to date. The organizer in the Central Florida area is Anne Mathews (white), a very capable person. I do not know whether or not she has any communistic tendencies. The Citrus industries have succeeded in preventing much organization by a sort of vigilante system which may cause some trouble in the future.

12. *Is there a local branch of the American Youth for Democracy? If possible, please indicate approximate membership and list prominent names.*

There is only one branch that I know of, that is at the University of Florida and it is supposed to be divorced from the parent organization. At present it is quite unpopular on the Campus anyway. The Miami branch which did exist not many months ago, and may still exist, seems to have given way to the Southern Negro Youth Congress.

13. *Is there evidence of Communistic influence among the foreign-born? Is the International Workers Order a factor in your diocese?*

At present I would say there is very little. In years past (during the Spanish Civil War) there was a great deal of communistic activity in Tampa among the Cubans. There are about 25,000 Cubans in that city. Of late there doesn't seem to have been much red activity. In Miami, a small, inconsequential Hungarian organization, the Hungarian-American Cultural League (250 members) has been Communistically inclined. There are about 1500 Hungarian-Americans in the Miami area.

14. *Is there any indication that federal government officials in your diocese are sympathetic to communism? Please list name, position and reason for inclusion.*

None that I know of, except, perhaps, Senator Claude Pepper, who has his name on some of the front organizations honor rolls.

15. *Please give details of any other radical organizations in your diocese, or groups working to foster irreligion, anti-clericalism or immorality.*

I know of none. This state has witnessed almost a complete dying out of organized anti-Catholicism since the last war.

16. *Would you have any suggestions for programs or techniques on a local, diocesan, state or national level which would be effective in combating communism and establishing a positive counterprogram? Would you kindly describe any local activities of this nature, indicating briefly their nature and the names of their principal leaders?*

In my opinion, the chief danger to the country is from the material-mindedness of our leaders who can see no danger in cooperating with the communists so long as there is some little material advantage to be gained for the people. This is particularly true of labor leaders. They will tell you that they will use anything and anybody that will help them sell their idea to the workers. The CIO does in fact use and distribute communist propaganda for this purpose. Perhaps the time has now come for advocating some national legislation limiting the power and circumscribing the activity of the Unions.

Hurley Papers, Series II, Box 41, Archives of the Diocese of St. Augustine. Printed with permission.

64. Administrative Board, National Catholic Welfare Conference, "Persecution behind the Iron Curtain," 22 April 1952

1. Reports of the banishment of Bishop Hlouch from his episcopal see in Czechoslovakia centers our attention once more to the sad plight of the Catholic Church in that country. It is a notorious fact that Archbishop Beran of Prague has been held under house arrest for the past several years and has been subjected to countless indignities at the hands of the Communist government. In these prelates we are witnessing a repetition of the atrocities already visited upon Archbishop Stepinac and the other heroic Bishop of Yugoslavia, also upon Cardinal Mindszenty and Archbishop Josef Groesz of Hungary.

2. In view of the new wave of terror which is being visited upon the Church in Czechoslovakia, we the members of the Administrative Board of the National Catholic Welfare Conference, assembled in our regular semi-annual meeting, express our deep sympathy for the archbishop, bishops, priests, and laity of Czechoslovakia. We pray that God may support them in their suffering and strengthen them in their resistance to the forces of evil.

3. Even more terrible has been the fate of the Church in Romania, where the entire hierarchy has been liquidated; in Lithuania, whose bishops, priests and laity were among the first to feel the full lash of the new terror; in Albania, whose smaller number of Catholics has tended to obscure the greatness of the sufferings endured. If in Poland, the woes of the Church have been less dramatic, equally persistent and far more insidious have been the means used to win the people from their spiritual allegiance.

4. Our present sympathies, however, go out particularly to our fellow Catholics in China. There seventy-seven bishops and vicars-general have been imprisoned or are under arrest or have been expelled or otherwise gravely impeded in the exercise of their office. Twelve among these are Americans. There are actually seven American bishops or vicars-general in prison. The overall number of Catholic missionaries known to be in prison is twenty-one. Almost 4,000 Catholic foreign missionaries have been expelled or forced out since the Communists have taken over China. The number of foreign Catholic missionaries in prison at the present time is almost one hundred fifty; more than two hundred Chinese priests have suffered the same fate. The number of Catholic priests and religious who have been killed by the Chinese Reds or who have died as the result of maltreatment is at least one hundred. Three bishops have died in Communist prisons.

5. Every week that passes greatly adds to the number of those who are called upon to suffer for their faith in Communist countries. We may well ask whether any decade in history has been richer in martyrdom than our own.

6. In view of the sufferings to which all men of religious belief have been subjected, we beseech our fellow citizens to renew their prayer for all, Catholics and non-Catholics alike, who bear the heavy burden of tyranny and are persecuted under a system of government which is the acknowledged enemy of all those decencies which have been the special blessing of our own country.

Hugh J. Nolan, ed., *Pastoral Letters of the United States Catholic Bishops* (Washington, D.C.: United States Catholic Conference, 1984), 2:107. Printed with permission.

65. Bishop Bernard J. Sheil, Address to the UAW-CIO International Education Conference, Chicago, 9 April 1954

I would like to talk about a subject we hear a lot of these days — anti-Communism. Note that I said *anti*-Communism. I think it is necessary that we give a little thought to just what form anti-Communism should take at this point in America's history. That all decent Americans are against Communism, I should think, would go without saying. That we are opposed to Communism, both as individuals and as a nation — and why — hardly needs explanation. I know that I could stand here and tell you what you already know. I could tell you that Communism is morally evil because it is militantly, viciously, one might even say *diabolically* set against God and man. I could tell you that Communism deprives men and women of life, liberty and the pursuit of happiness. I could detail the bloody history of Communism as it operates in every land where it has taken hold. I could repeat the story of Communist treason in the United States. I could outline the well known attempts of the communists to infiltrate into our great national institutions. In a word, I could match the oratory so familiar to all of us. Or, I could try to. But what purpose would be served in going over all that we know to be so bitterly true? The problem is no longer one of alerting people to the danger of Communism. We are all aware of that danger. The problem we are facing is what do we do about it. The unsolved problem, in other words, is what constitutes effective anti-Communism. More than that, what kind of anti-Communism is moral? What kind of anti-Communism is proper in a freedom-loving country like ours? The three go together, in my mind. If anti-Communism is immoral, it is not effective. You cannot effectively fight immorality with *more* immorality. If anti-Communism flouts the principles of democracy and freedom, it is not in the long run effective. You cannot effectively fight tyranny with tyranny. And if anti-Communism is not effective, it is so much sound and fury, signifying nothing.

It is not enough to say that someone is anti-Communist to win my support. It has been said that patriotism is the scoundrel's last refuge. In this day and age anti-Communism is sometimes the scoundrel's last refuge. As I remember, one of the noisiest anti-Communists of recent history was a man named Adolf Hitler. He was not wrong because he was anti-Communist. He was wrong because he was *immorally* anti-Communist; he countered Communist tyranny with a tyranny of his own. And inevitably, Herr Hitler was a dismal failure as an anti-Communist. Half of his own Germany now lives under communism and half of Europe lives in Communist slavery. Would this be true, I wonder, if Hitler had been *morally* anti-Communist? If Hitler had fought Communist tyranny with democratic freedom, the world we live in — I am persuaded — would be quite different today. And I venture to say there would be less, not more Communism in it than there is.

No Hitler has risen in America, and I must say that I think it is nonsense when foreign reporters and journalists describe us as living in a kind of Hitlerian reign of terror. We are still free, and we will remain free — let's have no doubts about that. But, it seems to me that *now*, while we are free, is the time to cry out against the phoney anti-Communism that mocks our way of life, flouts our traditions and democratic procedures and our sense of fair play, feeds on the meat of suspicion and grows great on the dissension among Americans which it cynically creates and keeps alive by a mad pursuit of headlines.

How much more of this are we going to tolerate before we remember that we are proud Americans, with values of our own? If we throw those values away — and I am referring to our traditions of innocent-until-proved-guilty, I am referring to our concern for *means* as well as ends, I am referring to our trust in our basic institutions — then we will be left with our anti-Communism, but very little else. An America where the accused is guilty until he is proved innocent, where means don't matter but only ends, an America which has lost faith in the integrity of the government, the Army, the schools, the churches, the labor unions, press, and most of all an America whose citizens have lost faith in each other — *such* an America would not need to bother about being anti-Communist; it would have nothing to lose. Such an America would have nothing to recommend it to freedom-loving men — nothing at all, not even the shining image of its victorious junior Senator from Wisconsin....

In my book, if a man is truly anti-Communist, he is concerned with meeting the challenge of Communism on every level. He is interested first of all, in seeing to it that conditions here and abroad are such that they don't provide a fertile breeding ground for Communism. He is interested in such matters as seeing to it that people get enough to eat, have decent homes, are able to raise their children in dignity. His scope is broad. He is interested in measures to share the wealth of "have" nations with the have-nots. He is interested in breaking down the barriers that separate people — national barriers, religious barriers, class barriers. He is interested in making a better place of his own little corner of the world and of doing all he can to see that others are not in want. I judge an anti-Communist — the real thing, not the cops-and-robbers version — by how well he does these things. If he happens to be a legislator, I look at his record. I see how he voted on measures, to make freedom a reality and not merely an aspiration in the lives of his own fellow citizens and of the poor of the world. By this standard, a number of famous anti-Communists, I'm sorry to say, simply don't measure up....

On the question of internal subversion, I judge an anti-Communist according to how well he does the very difficult job of seeking out subversives, clearly identifying them and removing them from critical positions. I take it that a genuine anti-Communist is one who despises the covert methods of the Communists. I take it that the genuine anti-Communist is one who above all believes in the democratic procedures and is willing to stand by them, even in the face of great temptations to lose one's temper and to lose one's faith in the methods of free men. I judge an anti-Communist by how well he fulfills all these responsibilities in a difficult, delicate job. In a word, on this score I judge an anti-Communist according to how well he succeeds in doing what he is supposed to be doing — not according to how many headlines he makes. I judge him according to how well he clarifies the difference between treason and non-conformity — not according to how well he blurs the distinction. I judge him according to how many innocent people he has helped prove innocent and how many guilty people he has proved guilty. I do not admire him as an anti-Communist according to how many guilty and innocent both leave his courtroom without his having made clear and convincing just what their status is but only fogging the issues and the reputation of innocent and guilty alike.

As you can see, I take a pretty dim view of some noisy anti-Communists — one in particular, the junior Senator from Wisconsin. I do not take a dim view of them because they are anti-Communists, but because they are such pitifully ineffective anti-Communists. I hate to see anti-Communism identified with this kind of playing-for-the-grandstand.

Now I want to make clear that what I have said is my personal opinion. I am not speaking for the Catholic Church but only for myself, a citizen. Other Catholics may take a more kindly view of the public career of the junior senator from Wisconsin and of the effect he is having on the nation. That certainly is their privilege, as it is my privilege to speak as I have. Other Catholics may agree or disagree with the judgment I have reached. On political matters such as these, a Catholic's statement — even a bishop's — bears no more authority than whatever he can bring to it as a citizen and public figure. I know that there are many in my Church who do not agree with me on this. So be it. Time will tell which of us is right.

But although the Church takes no position, and will not, on such a matter of public controversy, the Church does take a position on lies, calumny, the absence of charity and calculated deceit. These things are wrong — even if they are mistakenly thought of as means to a good end. They are morally evil and to call them good or to act as if they were permissible under certain circumstances is itself a monstrous perversion of morality. They are not justified by any cause — least of all by the cause of anti-Communism, which should unite rather than divide all of us in these difficult times.

Joseph McCarthy Papers, Archives of Marquette University, Milwaukee.

66. Rev. Fulton J. Sheen, "Foreign Policies and the Missions," 1954

The two major foreign policies of the world which seek to bring other nations under their ambit are those of (1) The United States [and] (2) The Soviets. Unlike either is the third influence: The Missions.

(1) The Foreign Policy of the United States

American foreign policy has largely been directed to a concentration of a *defense* against Communism with Europe as the bastion of that defense. The nations of Western Europe have been invited by the United States to accept its military aid and to become perimeters of defense against the Soviet assault on the world. The strength and the failure of American foreign policy has to a large extent fluctuated with the acceptance or the rejection of its plan of European Defense. As the European nations fail for one reason or another to co-operate with the program of the United States, the latter turns toward the army of its former enemy, Germany, to arm it against the Soviets. The important point is that the foreign policy of the United States sees Europe as the best defense against Communism.

(2) The Foreign Policy of the Soviets

The United States concentrates on *defense;* the Soviets on *offense.* But the Soviet thinking has completely altered concerning the nature of this offense.

The first stage represented by the philosophy of Marx and Engels applied dialectical materialism to world affairs. The revolution which would produce Communism, it was predicted, would take place in a highly capitalistic or advanced industrial country. Marx said that just as there were dialectics in matter so that it produced its own motion without the need of God, so there was a dialectic in all capitalistic productions: capitalism would eventually increase the mass of the exploited; this, in its turn, would produce the Communist revolution or the "expropriation of the expropriators." Stalin himself once boasted that this immanent law of economic determinism enabled the Soviets to foresee the course of history.

But it happened that history did not follow Communist theory. First of all, instead of the rich growing richer and the poor becoming poorer, there arose in highly developed countries a large middle class; the class lines between capital and labor, instead of becoming more rigid, became more loose; the most highly industrialized country of the world, namely, the United States failed to produce a Communist proletariat; and finally the development of technology, the spread of popular government, and social reforms completely disproved the Communist expectation that the revolution would come first in the so-called capitalistic countries. Marx, himself was so convinced of his own theory that he completely discounted Russia as a nation that would one day become Communist, simply because it completely lacked industrialization and, therefore, the raw material for the unfolding of the immanent law of dialectical materialism.

Marx ignored the revolutionary struggle in the so-called economically underdeveloped areas of the world. But now there has been such a shift in Communist thinking that Russia is expecting the world revolution, not in the area where Marx expected it, but rather in the so-called backward areas of the earth. Lenin himself seized power in one of the least developed countries of Europe, and it is very likely that, if it had been highly industrialized, he would never have seized power. Furthermore only in underdeveloped countries has Communist revolution been successful. Since Communism has not developed the way Marx expected it, namely in the highly industrialized nations, the Soviets are now concentrating on the underdeveloped countries of the world; hence the spread of Communism in Korea, Indo-China, Malaya, Indonesia, Burma, India, Iran, Guatemala, and the present terrific concentration on Africa. Poor Marx would turn over in his grave if he saw how his theory of revolution failed to operate in capitalistic countries. But his followers were wise enough to scrap the theory for the fact that the more vulnerable areas of the world for Communism are the underdeveloped.

Even Lenin himself at times was wrong about revolution in capitalistic countries. He argued that the less advanced peoples of the world or the underdeveloped areas would increasingly become the tools of capitalistic exploitation. When Karl Kautsky argued that capitalistic imperialism was not a necessary phase of capitalism, Lenin severely criticized him. In 1947, Eugene Varga, the Soviet economist was disciplined by the Soviets for saying that some underdeveloped areas may be breaking away from capitalistic domination. Facts proved that Varga was right. There has been a drop of about four hundred million people under colonialism in the last few decades. India and Pakistan have become fully free from Great Britain; Indonesia is free from the Dutch; Britain's African colonies are taking steps toward self-rule, and France is in danger at the present time of losing or giving up an area in Africa equivalent in size to the United States. Kautsky and Varga are now recognized to be right. But since capitalism does not necessarily produce the exploitation of the underdeveloped areas, the Soviets were realistic enough to know that it is to those areas that they must go in order to establish world revolution.

Despite the error that Lenin made concerning Kautsky, he did see that the masses of people in the underdeveloped areas were the potential allies of the Communists, as he wrote:

> In the colonial countries, millions and hundreds of millions, in fact the overwhelming majority of the population of the globe, are now coming forward as independent, active, revolutionary factors. It is perfectly clear that in the impending battles in the world revolution, the movement of the majority of the population of the globe, which at first is directed toward national liberation, will turn against capitalism and imperialism and will, perhaps, play a much more revolutionary part than we expect.

The Communist policy in the Far East has been to transform its society by skipping the phase of capitalism which Marx said was absolutely essential for the development of Communism. Now the Soviets see that in the underdeveloped areas it is possible to seize power through propaganda against "capitalistic and imperialistic" nations and then exploit the resources of them in the manner in which it accuses capitalism.

There is no point in elaborating in detailed fashion the shift in Communist policy. What is important is to note the vast divergence between the foreign policy of the United States and the foreign policy of the Soviets. The United States concentrates its *defense* against Communism in Europe; the Soviets, on the contrary, concentrate their *offense* against Europe and the United States in the underdeveloped countries of the world. As Lenin once said: "The shortest route to Paris is through Peiping."

The Missions

The missionaries with their roots in Western Christian civilization have this in common with the Soviets: they, too, concentrate on the East and the underdeveloped areas of the world. One hundred thousand missionaries are presently fulfilling the Divine mandate to what foreign policy makers of the world call the underdeveloped areas, but which, to the missionaries, are the yet un-Christ-ed areas. The East to the missionaries is like a great giant that is being aroused from sleep by the Western nations. There is an appointed time for every nation and it could well be that we are witnessing what Spengler called "The Decline of the West." The moment has now come for the curtain to roll up on the East. The prohibition to Paul not to pass into Asia has now been rescinded by the Holy Spirit!

The missionaries and the Communists are meeting head-on in the underdeveloped areas of the world. To anyone interested in the missions, it would seem that the Soviet foreign policy is wiser than the foreign policy of the United States, and that if the United States had concentrated on the underdeveloped areas of the world instead of on Europe, there would have been less danger of Soviet Imperialism. While the United States was building up defenses in Europe, the Communists were on the *offensive* in the East. So were the missionaries, but for a totally different purpose; the Soviets to crucify human personality, the missionaries to crucify egotism to make room for the Spirit and the unfolding of personality.

Communism knows that it cannot tyrannize man except through the destruction of the spirit — hence the denial of the soul and God in its philosophy of dialectical materialism. The missionaries, on the contrary, know that wherever God is exiled, man is tyrannized; hence the basis of their teaching is that man is endowed with inalienable rights by God, and therefore, has powers transcendent to any State. Since man did not receive his rights and his liberties from the State, no State or tyrant can ever take them away. A second point of conflict is that the Soviets utilize individuals in any area as a means to an end. Persons are like grapes who have their life squeezed out of them in order to produce the wine of totalitarianism. The missionaries, on the contrary, believing in the sacredness of personality, insist that as soon as possible a native clergy must be established, for under no circumstances must the people be made subservient to any other nation or power. This explains the zeal of the missionaries to develop a native clergy and a native hierarchy.

The conflict of the Missions and Communism in any part of the East, for example, Korea, Indo-China and China is a cameo of the world-situation. The real problem today is not the conflict of democracy and totalitarianism, for a democracy with a loss of morality and belief could vote itself out of a democracy into a totalitarianism. The real struggle is between two contrary philosophies of life: one submerging man to the collectivity, the other elevating man to spiritual solidarity in Christ. The center of the stage is occupied

by the Communists and the missionaries because both concentrate on the underdeveloped areas. The foreign policy of the United States is off-stage and
off-center because it thinks primarily of defense in Europe but not among the
socially disinherited peoples of the East. The violent persecution of the missionaries by Communists is an evidence of how much Communism knows
them to be their real enemy; before man can be tyrannized, God and the
soul must be exiled. The struggle is unequal because the Communists use the
sword while the missionaries must drink the Cup — the Cup which the Heavenly Father giveth them to drink. As Simone Weil has said: "He who takes
not the sword will perish on the Cross." The missionaries cannot use Peter's
sword against Communist hordes; therefore they must take the Cross and become "witnesses" or martyrs. But in heaven's scales their Cross will outweigh
Soviet swords.

Russia will never be stopped in Europe; it could overrun Europe in four
days including England and its Atlee. What a tragedy that the Western World
did not foresee Russia's move toward world domination! Emil Montaigne writing at the close of the eighteenth century warned: "One day and in conditions
that *will be fearful* for Europe, are we not likely to see Russia taking up her
schemes for world domination and invasion." A few years earlier Donoso
Cortes announced, "the coming of a great anti-Christian empire, that would
be the colossal empire of the demagogue, an empire governed by a plebian of
Satanic grandeur, the man of sin."

Carnot on the 17th of June, 1868, addressed the Legislative Assembly, "If
Russia were someday to realize her dream of invading the whole Slav world,
she would lie against Europe with such weight that Europe would be reduced to a subordinate position...and it would not be the Slav element that
would predominate, it would be the Muscovite element; and the civilization
of Asia, with Moscow to lead it, would be triumphing over the civilization
of Europe."

A missionary in a Chinese cell being brain-washed by a Chinese Communist offers a better miniature of the world situation than the representatives
of the nine European powers agreeing to arm Germany. Europe will not save
either America or the world. But the faith will save it and particularly the
faith in underdeveloped areas of the world. If we may look into the future,
Ruandi-Urundi and Nigeria will be the two parts of the underdeveloped areas
where Communists will be the least successful. Only those who know the
Missions well will know the reasons for this statement. The missionaries and
the Soviets are already colliding in the underdeveloped areas. It is a pity our
foreign policy and Point IV program did not utilize them and aid them in
their social works. It is still not too late!

Worldmission 5, no. 4 (winter 1954): 387–92.

Race

The civil rights movement and the progress of racial relations in the United States are defining features of postwar American life. The Catholic public response to these issues was polarized. Episcopal statements, such as those sampled here, drew on the principles of natural law ideology and Catholic social teaching to condemn racism, and Roman Catholic prelates used the weight of their office to mandate an end to segregation in Catholic schools and institutions. Roman Catholic priests, religious, and laity participated in many of the public demonstrations that marked the rise of the civil rights movement. However, other Catholics, whose voices are also included here, did not accept racial integration of cities and neighborhoods and at times actively resisted such endeavors.

67. Rev. Daniel M. Cantwell, "Postscript on the Cicero Riot: A Turning Point in Race Relations Might Have Been Reached in Chicago with the Frank Display of Bigotry," 14 September 1951[1]

Had Harvey Clark and his family succeeded in moving into the Cicero, Illinois apartment he had rented in July, he would have been the first Negro resident of the town. By now the story of the riot and the violence in Cicero has gone round the world.

The damage to the building has been variously estimated from $20,000 to $50,000. The building stands uninhabitable. The Clarks are still without a place to live. The 19 families who formerly lived in the building are gone. For them too the riot was a tragedy. They were willing to live in the same building with the Clarks. Organized violence decreed otherwise.

In retrospect there are mysteries about the incident. There was, for instance, the criminal negligence of the police. Neither the Cicero chief of police, nor the Sheriff of Cook County, nor the local officials of Cicero showed any disposition to use techniques which have been developed for controlling riots. Riots are no longer excusable.

Moreover, on the Wednesday night the destruction took place a lawyer who identified himself as living a block and a half from the building was allowed by the police to address the mob. He told the people there were no legal and peaceful means for keeping "niggers" out, that they had to take the law into their own hands, that they must give this family and any other Negro family thinking of moving in a lesson not to be forgotten. The police standing by were conveniently deaf, as they were blind when the destruction began.

Possibly, too, there was criminal conspiracy. Many of the families living in the building had moved out during the day. Who had forewarned them? Apparently the riot was organized and planned. And did the police know of

---

1. Rev. Daniel M. Cantwell, of the archdiocese of Chicago, was chaplain of the Catholic Labor Alliance when this article was published.

the plan? There are rumors that someone has so testified before the grand jury hearings now in progress. At any rate the open hostility of the police to the Clarks prior to the move-in is a matter of record. No semblance of equal protection under the law was given the Clarks.

Finally there was the moral vacuum which became apparent in the days following the riot. The vacuum grew, I think, not merely because only a comparatively few religious leaders spoke up, but because when they spoke what they said was, for the most part, incomplete, cautious, negative. They said nothing about discrimination, nothing about the denial of brotherly love. On the part of Catholics there was none of the spirit of the policy laid down by Cardinal Stritch to govern the Catholic institutions of the diocese, a policy which allows no discrimination in the life of the Church and which Catholics should feel it is their duty to carry over into civic and community life.

There were some exceptions. The clearest and most far-reaching moral pronouncement came from a group of laymen, residents of Cicero-Berwyn and the adjacent suburbs. They did more than protest the violence. They came to grips with the central moral issue — compulsory racial segregation.

In an open letter they asked their neighbors whether people who love God could consistently go along with a social policy which condemned their fellow-men to indignities and injustices. The letter was picked up by the Catholic and secular press and was, I would judge, read by close to six million people.

"Attempts are made," they wrote, "to justify segregation by saying that it produces peace and harmony by keeping separate, people who would otherwise be in conflict. This ignores the fact that separation itself is a principal cause of conflict... since it fosters those traits in both the majority and minority groups that lead to conflict...."

From close to the scene came some other moral protests. In at least one of the neighboring churches the priests spoke forthrightly on the riot. I know the same was done in at least three churches in Chicago....

Cicero could mark a turning point in race relations in Chicago. That hardly seemed possible the week of the riot. Something close to despair over Cicero weighed on lots of stalwart people. Many people said that it was a thoroughly corrupt community, that the residents had no moral or civic pride, or they would long since have done something about the gambling, the syndicates, the political machine.

As a matter of fact, the community is rare where the small home owners have a greater pride in the neighborhood than prevails in Cicero. The town is an enviable picture of order and peace. Czech housewives are second to none in the care of their homes. Fathers and mothers there are as close to the syndicates as the rank and file of Chicago used to be to Al Capone.

Cicero is by no means thoroughly bad. Indeed, what has gone wrong in Cicero is something good. The home-making virtues of these people have been oversown by cockle, by national exclusiveness, by middle-class materialism, by the drying up of human compassion and sympathy for other families in need. They have acquired homes, but then made them the golden calf to be worshipped and possessed at all costs. They have arrived at middle-class suburban Utopia. The story of Dives repeats itself. The Scripture does not say that Dives was a very rich man. He was a man who had his spirit in his riches; he didn't like his spirit disturbed by anything as low-class as a beggar. He doesn't today like to be disturbed by anything as obviously "low-class" as brown skin. It runs down Utopia.

There are many signs that the Cicero incident has stirred an unprecedented revulsion against racial conflict and racial segregation. Individuals have acted.... There is the beginning of group action too. The group of Catholics who issued the "Dear Neighbor" letter have organized themselves into a west suburban unit of the Catholic Interracial Council. And an effort is under way to create a broad coordinating citizens' council in the western suburbs — working against discrimination and cooperating with the Illinois Interracial Commission.

What must be developed now is a long-range educational effort. Its form is becoming clear. First of all it must be broad-scale. Cicero has given the final answer, I hope, to the contention that there is no use talking about the racial problem in church or school because we have no problem when there are no Negroes there. There were no Negroes in Cicero, either. There was hatred and prejudice which had never been challenged. By July, 1951 it was too late. Silence is no cure. Cicero may be repeated elsewhere. Negroes will not remain in the ghetto.

The indoctrination should begin with something positively Christian. It is not enough to decry events like the Cicero riot merely because the Communists use them as propaganda against us in Europe and Asia. The question is not what do the Communists think of Cicero, but what does Christ think about Cicero.

Christ pictures the good neighbor as the man who bridged over in action the gap which separated Jews from Samaritans in His own day. The good neighbor took the man in trouble not to an inn for the Jews, but to his own inn. Then he footed the bill. He lost money; his good neighborliness cost him something. This good neighbor resisted the social pressure against fraternization, put himself to inconvenience, and paid a price financially.

Christ cited this as a case of love in action. There is no other proof of our Christianity comparable to it. "By this shall all men know that you are My disciples, that you have love one for another."

But good will is not enough. Intelligence must be enlisted in the fight against the ghetto. The ghetto will not go till more white people are helped to understand how bad life is there for parents. And until some effort is made to unravel clichés about property values and what happens to them when a Negro moves into a neighborhood. The first problem would require a long article.

About property values, the most obvious thing is that few people really know anything about them, and few people really mean what they say about them. Few realize that Negroes do own and take care of property when given the chance. They do have beautiful apartment buildings when not exploited. There is evidence available for any honest person in Chicago and other large cities of the country.

Few people know that the conservative National Association of Real Estate Boards and honest real estate men here in Chicago have admitted that a Negro tenant will take care of property as well as any tenant on the same economic level. There will be some exceptions, of course. But there will also be some Negroes who will do a better job than whites.

The Association also maintains that a Negro home buyer carries through to completion the purchase of his home as reliably as a white buyer of the same wage status. In some cases, even better. White persons will say that property values have always gone down when Negroes move into a neighborhood. They don't really mean that. Actually the most valuable rental properties in Chicago, the properties providing the most lucrative return, are the apartment houses in the crowded ghetto on the South Side....

Interracial marriage, too, must be discussed if we are going to educate ourselves away from maintaining the ghetto. By and large we have been enforcing a hush-hush policy about it. Such a policy is not removing an irrational fear. Actually, Negroes by and large are not interested in interracial marriages. Moreover, segregation has not prevented interracial "marriage," of a type we don't like to talk about, where the aggressor has not been the Negro man.

The Church has not condemned interracial marriage. In a sense, she too is not interested. She is concerned that couples know what they are going into, in any marriage, and that they enter the marriage freely.... Interracial marriage in itself is not a moral problem. I have known interracial marriages that give every evidence of coming as close to the Christian ideal as any that I have ever seen. Interracial injustice *is* a moral problem. An irrational fear about interracial marriage should not distract us from our goal or move us toward condoning injustice.... But the problem before us is not marriage, interracial or otherwise. The problem is seeking the Kingdom of God and His justice, and then all things else will take care of themselves in time.

Commonweal 54 (14 September 1951): 543–45. Printed with permission.

68. Administrative Board, National Catholic Welfare Conference, "Discrimination and Christian Conscience," 14 November 1958

...Progress Made

5. Our nation now stands divided by the problem of compulsory segregation of the races and the opposing demand for racial justice. No region of our land is immune from strife and division resulting from this problem. In one area, the key issue may concern the schools. In another it may be conflicts over housing. Job discrimination may be the focal point in still other sectors. But all these issues have one main point in common. They reflect the deter-

mination of our Negro people, and we hope the overwhelming majority of our white citizens, to see that our colored citizens obtain their full rights as given to them by God, the Creator of all, and guaranteed by the democratic traditions of our nation. There are many facets to the problems raised by the quest for racial justice. There are issues of law, of history, of economics, and of sociology. There are questions of procedure and technique. There are conflicts in cultures. Volumes have been written on each of these phases. Their importance we do not deny. But the time has come, in our considered and prayerful judgment, to cut through the maze of secondary or less essential issues and to come to the heart of the problem.

The Question Is Moral and Religious

6. The heart of the race question is moral and religious. It concerns the rights of man and our attitude toward our fellow man. If our attitude is governed by the great Christian law of love of neighbor and respect for his rights, then we can work out harmoniously the techniques for making legal, educational, economic, and social adjustments. But if our hearts are poisoned by hatred, or even by indifference toward the welfare and rights of our fellow men, then our nation faces a grave internal crisis....

8. Our Christian faith is of its nature universal. It knows not the distinctions of race, color, or nationhood. The missionaries of the Church have spread throughout the world, visiting with equal impartiality nations such as China and India, whose ancient cultures antedate the coming of the Savior, and the primitive tribes of the Americas. The love of Christ, and the love of the Christian, knows no bounds. In the words of Pope Pius XII, addressed to American Negro publishers twelve years ago, "All men are brothered in Jesus Christ; for He, though God, became also man, became a member of the human family, a brother of all" (May 27, 1946)....

10. From these solemn truths, there follow certain conclusions vital for a proper approach to the problems that trouble us today. First, we must repeat the principle — embodied in our Declaration of Independence — that all men are equal in the sight of God. By equal we mean that they are created by God and redeemed by His Divine Son, that they are bound by His Law, and that God desires them as His friends in the eternity of Heaven. This fact confers upon all men human dignity and human rights....

Enforced Segregation

14. The question then arises: can enforced segregation be reconciled with the Christian view of our fellow man? In our judgment it cannot, and this for two fundamental reasons.

15. (1) Legal segregation, or any form of compulsory segregation, in itself and by its very nature imposes a stigma of inferiority upon the segregated people. Even if the now obsolete Court doctrine of "separate but equal" had been carried out to the fullest extent, so that all public and semipublic facilities were in fact equal, there is nonetheless the judgment that an entire race, by

the sole fact of race and regardless of individual qualities, is not fit to associate on equal terms with members of another race. We cannot reconcile such a judgment with the Christian view of man's nature and rights. Here again it is appropriate to cite the language of Pope Pius XII:

> God did not create a human family made up of segregated, dissociated, mutually independent members. No; He would have them all united by the bond of total love of Him and consequent self-dedication to assisting each other to maintain that bond intact (September 7, 1956).

16. (2) It is a matter of historical fact that segregation in our country has led to oppressive conditions and the denial of basic human rights for the Negro. This is evident in the fundamental fields of education, job opportunity, and housing. Flowing from these areas of neglect and discrimination are problems of health and the sordid train of evils so often associated with the consequent slum conditions. Surely Pope Pius XII must have had these conditions in mind when he said just two months ago:

> It is only too well known, alas, to what excesses pride of race and racial hate can lead. The Church has always been energetically opposed to attempts of genocide or practices arising from what is called the "color bar" (September 5, 1958)....

Hugh J. Nolan, ed., *Pastoral Letters of the United States Catholic Bishops* (Washington, D.C.: United States Catholic Conference, 1984), 2:201–6. Printed with permission.

69. Cardinal Albert Meyer, "The Mantle of Leadership," Resurrection Parish, Chicago, Illinois, 21 September 1960

...As we turn our glance from the world scene to that which is closer to us at home, we see that the internal migration of our population is bringing Negroes to other northern cities as well as to our own for fuller opportunities and for a fuller enjoyment of basic human rights. The Church blesses and encourages such aspirations and is anxious that all of the children of God should attain their full stature.

It is our conviction that the missionary endeavor to evangelize the Negro people in our big cities will be the most necessary, and the most fruitful apostolate of the Church in urban America in our century. The evidence of the massive change in our own city of Chicago, presented here today, underscores the urgency of even more intensified efforts to evangelize the Negro in our Archdiocese. We do not believe that we overstate the need for an untiring missionary zeal when we call upon every "changing parish" to become a "mission center" — reaching out to embrace all newcomers within its confines.

In stressing the urgency of a zealous missionary effort in our Archdiocese, we must caution, however, against regarding the Negro solely as an object of conversion. We must never lose sight of his needs as a human being, his deliberate desire to be accepted with dignity into the fabric of society generally, as well as into the Church. His place in the Catholic community of the Archdiocese must be made secure by moral recognition, and by adequate and timely practical measures....

In our day, however, the demands of the Negro apostolate in Chicago have over-reached even the most zealous efforts of our priests, both religious and diocesan, who have been engaged in it. The Archdiocese itself now has a large commitment to this work, in terms of priests and parish facilities. The pastoral care, the evangelization, of the Negro in our city is becoming more and more an apostolate of the entire clergy of the Archdiocese.

This development represents something new for a good many diocesan priests. We have learned today of the great number of our parishes that have gone through a substantial change in the past decade. The prediction was advanced, too, that we will continue to see significant changes in the years ahead. In our mind, this increasing involvement of the diocesan priests in the Negro apostolate, together with those parishes of our Religious where the same changes are taking place, implies certain important considerations. I would like to single out these three:

First of all, it is required that our clergy generally, both diocesan and religious, become more knowledgeable about the Negro people. Too often our Catholic laity have opinions about the Negro that are ill-informed. Their views are frequently distorted by an unthinking acceptance of myths and stereotypes. In this urgent matter of understanding between the races, however, it is the responsibility of the priest to form public opinion rather than to follow it. Certainly no priest would offer encouragement to anti-Negro sentiment, nor would he at any time be identified with the anti-Negro activities of any group in his community.

In the second place, we must give consideration to those of our parishes in "changing neighborhoods." It would appear that two things are of paramount importance in this situation: on the one hand, to avoid any spirit of "defeat," and on the other, to develop a parish program that is apostolic....

In this connection, I would encourage our pastors to work out the problems of community change on a community-wide basis and to join together with other parishes and other groups, bearing in mind that change and tensions are not just a Catholic problem. I recommend to you the work of the Organization for the Southwest Community and that of the parishes who are members of this group. There is much to be learned from the hard-won experience of pastors in this area.

A third consideration follows from these first two. We need to stress a broader familiarity with the methods and techniques which have proven effective in the Negro convert apostolate. Unfortunately, the record of transition in the parishes of the Archdiocese over the past decade has not been one of general success. We do not believe that each newly-changing parish represents so different or unique a problem that the experience of a score of its predecessors is without value. On the contrary, we would recommend strongly the importance of a regular exchange of ideas and experiences among the clergy of the parishes engaged in the Negro apostolate....

There are converts to be won to interracial justice in every parish of the Archdiocese. Honesty compels us to admit that racial prejudice has deep roots and is spread everywhere. Realism compels us to admit that Negroes may appear in any parish of the city or suburbs tomorrow. The priest must be in the vanguard of true priestly leadership, not in a condemnatory manner, but in the manner of the Gospel itself, "to persuade and teach...."

The virtue of justice requires that we assume the mantle of leadership to insure that all our Catholics of the Negro race are integrated into the complete life of the Church. This obviously means that every Catholic child of the Negro race, whether his parents be Catholic or not, have as free access to our schools as any other Catholic child on all levels of our academic training, elementary and secondary, as well as the higher levels.

This acceptance of Catholic children of the Negro race is based on the same policy which guides the acceptance of other Catholic children, whether in the schools of territorial or non-territorial parishes. In other words, pastors of territorial parishes as well as pastors of non-territorial parishes will accept these children — the pastors of territorial parishes for all Catholic children whose parents are domiciled within the parish boundaries, and pastors of non-territorial parishes in the same manner in which de facto they accept Catholic children who otherwise do not qualify because of the special language or national background which serves as the basis of the non-territorial parish. If it should be necessary for a pastor to have a further explanation of these points, I shall always be happy to discuss particular cases with him. It follows from what has been said that Catholic Negro boys and girls should be accepted in our Catholic high schools....

When we speak of the complete life of the Church, we are, of course, not restricting our attention to our schools. We are thinking of accepted and wholehearted membership in the entire life of the parish, in our fraternal and parish organizations, in our hospitals, in the life of the community, — without distinctions or restrictions based solely on the accidental facts of race or color, or, for that matter, national backgrounds.

The principles enunciated above apply to all these areas, and we are confident that our fraternal organizations, our medical staffs, and other administrators, will also assume the mantle of leadership, and, in the words of the Supreme Court decision, "with due and deliberate speed," effectively apply these principles to the several areas indicated. As pastors, chaplains, and priests serving all our people, we can do much to inspire and encourage that leadership, and I sincerely hope that our priests will do so.

In this whole matter of justice, we do not deem it necessary to spell out by specific statute the implications and applications already inherent in the clear teaching and practice of the Church and of the Archdiocese in these practical areas of civic and religious life. Neither should it be necessary to call attention to the well-known and well-publicized decisions of the highest courts of our land in the whole realm of civil rights. Both our duty as responsible citizens and leaders in our civic communities, as well as our duty as religious shepherds of souls demand that we be in the vanguard of responsible leadership in the practical defense of these rights. Let us not forget the obvious truth that we priests, in the words of Cardinal Suhard, have one face turned toward eternity, and another toward the world. Our schools, our fraternal and parish organizations, our hospitals, our whole parish plants serve the public interest of the civic community as well as the eternal interest of souls. Both viewpoints prompt us to pray with the psalmist: "May your priests be clothed with justice" (Ps. 131)....

> "The Negro and the Catholic Church," Meyer Papers, Archives of the Archdiocese of Chicago.

70. National Conference of Catholic Bishops, "Statement on National Race Crisis," 25 April 1968

1. In 1958, the Catholic bishops of the United States issued a statement on *Discrimination and the Christian Conscience*. In it they condemned racism in all its forms....

2. The bishops pointed out that full and equal justice must be given to all citizens, specifically those who are Negro. They urged that the religious community "seize the mantle of leadership from the agitator and the racist." They further pleaded: "It is vital that we must act now and act decisively."

3. The religious bodies of the United States did act in the years that followed. The 1963 National Conference on Religion and Race became a landmark of ecumenical social action. There is reassuring evidence that the ensuing religious involvement contributed greatly to the passage of national civil-rights legislation in 1964 and 1965.

4. Now — ten years later — it is evident that we did not do enough; we have much more to do. When the National Advisory Commission on Civil Disorders concluded last month that white racism was a key factor in creating and maintaining the explosive ghettoes of our cities, it became clear that we had failed to change the attitudes of many believers.

Needs

5. Despite ten years of religious, civic, and governmental action, millions of our fellow Americans continue to be deprived of adequate education, job opportunity, housing, medical care, and welfare assistance, making it difficult, perhaps even impossible, for them to develop and maintain a sense of human dignity.

6. Catholics, like the rest of American society, must recognize their responsibility for allowing these conditions to persist. It would be futile to deny what the Commission on Civil Disorders has told America — a white segregationist mentality is largely responsible for the present crisis....

The Unfinished Business of the Catholic Community

10. There are certain tasks which we must acknowledge remain the unfinished business of the Catholic religious community. First among these is the total eradication of any elements of discrimination in our parishes, schools, hospitals, homes for the aged, and similar institutions. Second, there is the Christian duty to use our resources responsibly and generously in view of the urgent needs of the poor.

11. Other tasks may be performed better by a united front of the religious community. Here we pledge our continued cooperation with the National Council of Churches, the Synagogue Council of America, and with other religious groups. Effective action is demanded of us all in the midst of this crisis in American life.

12. It is to this task that the statement issued on April 14 by the spokesmen for the major religious traditions of the United States addressed itself when it called for: (1) coordinated efforts on the part of the American religious community to raise the substantial funds needed for the implementation of local programs; (2) continuing interfaith efforts to push for the enactment of critically needed legislation in the fields of employment, housing, health, and welfare which comprise what the late Martin Luther King, Jr., called the "Poor Man's Bill of Rights."

13. Within our own communion, we hereby direct the various departments, offices, and bureaus of the United States Catholic Conference, in collaboration with other interested Catholic organizations, to set up an Urban Task Force to coordinate all Catholic activities and to relate them to those of others working for the common goal of society, based on truth, justice, and love.

14. It is essential that similar programs be established within the Church on the provincial, diocesan, and local levels throughout the land....

21. We owe special attention to the following areas:

Education

22. Education is a basic need in our society, yet the schooling available to the poor is pitifully inadequate. We cannot break the vicious cycle of poverty producing poverty unless we achieve a breakthrough in our educational system. Quality education for the poor, and especially for minorities who are traditionally victims of discrimination, is a moral imperative if we are to give millions a realistic chance to achieve basic human dignity. Catholic school systems, at all levels, must redouble their efforts in the face of changing social patterns and despite their own multiple problems, to meet the current social crisis. The crisis is of a magnitude and peril far transcending any which the Church in America or the nation has previously confronted.

Job Opportunity

23. Job opportunity is also essential to insuring self-respect and stable family life. We urge American business, the industrial community, management

and labor, to put every possible initiative, resource, and know-how into the fight against the problem of minority unemployment. But, if the private sector of the economy is unable to provide work for the unemployed members of the minority groups — particularly, at the moment, young Negroes — then it becomes the duty of government to intervene....

Housing

24. Lack of decent housing adds pathetically to the burdens of millions of American families. Living conditions in many cities and rural communities are themselves an obstacle to wholesome family life. Housing segregation inevitably becomes an added barrier to employment, particularly as job opportunities open in the suburbs and decline in the cities. The problem is two-fold: removing the barriers of segregation for those who prefer and can afford suburban living, and providing low-cost housing in cities for those who cannot afford decent housing at the prevailing prices....

Welfare Assistance

25. Finally, there is need for welfare assistance which respects dignity and privacy, for those who cannot secure adequate employment. The so-called "Man in the House" rule is a national scandal. It is absolutely intolerable that families are being broken up by its application. Every possible care should be taken that public or private assistance always be provided under conditions that respect the dignity of the person and the integrity of the families assisted. It is hoped that Catholic social services will lead the struggle for adequate and compassionate aid for those in need....

Hugh J. Nolan, ed., *Pastoral Letters of the United States Catholic Bishops* (Washington, D.C.: United States Catholic Conference, 1984), 3:156–60. Printed with permission.

War and Peace

The postwar era was a time of relative peace and prosperity for America, but also of numerous challenges on the international front. The antagonisms fostered by the Cold War occasionally erupted into hot wars, especially in Asia, which had witnessed the "fall" of China to Marxism in 1949. Although both the Korean and Vietnam conflicts were linked to these larger geopolitical realities, Catholics reacted to these two military actions in significantly different ways. They tended to support American intervention in Korea and initially supported American intervention in Vietnam, which was governed by the fervent Roman Catholic Ngo Diem. However, Catholic opposition to the war in Vietnam flared dramatically with the escalation of antiwar sentiment in 1965.

Since the experience of opposing the Vietnam War, Catholic leaders have occasionally dissented from the foreign policy initiatives of the U.S. government. One important instance is in the matter of nuclear stockpiling and the morality of atomic warfare. Under papal direction, American Catholics also took time to consider the impact of nuclear weaponry on traditional notions of a "just war." Other voices as well were raised against U.S. policies in Central America.

71. "Taking a Stand," 7 July 1950

The invasion of South Korea dashed the hopes of all those who have felt that Soviet Russia had at last entered on a period of consolidation of her vast territorial gains of the past five years. There is to be no breathing spell. For whatever reason the USSR is driven on implacably in her conquest of the world.

A stake in South Korea is far more than the disposition of the "dagger pointed at Japan." In fact that embattled peninsula has been considered (if not declared) outside the perimeter of our Pacific defenses. Nor has this technically backward and politically feeble ward of the United Nations figured as a strong military bastion.

But in transforming the cold war into a hot war the Russians have challenged the security of the threatened peoples of Southeast Asia and all other sectors of the globe. The strategic Near East is involved here. Also in Western Europe tangible progress toward unity and strength has been contending with a strong popular sentiment for neutrality, which would be terrifically enforced if the United States, our allies and the United Nations had contented themselves with ineffectual protests about Korea.

So that whatever may be known of the terrain on which the United States has decided to make a stand or the comparative strength of the forces at our disposal in the area, politically Mr. Truman's second historic decision was almost inevitable. To let Korea go would be to encourage sorties against the other weak spots adjacent to Soviet territory and spur on Soviet aggressiveness and enslavement.

If the fighting can be localized and the North Koreans turned back, it will give a tremendous boost to the morale of the whole non-Soviet world. It will mark the turning point of the whole cold war. If American and other aid to the South Koreans is insufficient or too belated, even then Mr. Truman's decision to intervene with ships and planes will tend to stiffen resistance elsewhere.

But even supposing that all goes for the best: that support of the South Koreans by the United States and other nations succeeds in throwing back the invaders and that Formosa, the Philippines and Indo-China are subsequently strengthened to the point of discouraging attack, even then our vigil will not be ended. For Soviet Russia has now so plainly revealed her hand as to convince even the most stubborn or lethargic doubter.

The failure of a major skirmish and the shifting of comparative military strength would not alter the objectives of the Kremlin men.

Until the Russian threat to human freedom has subsided, those outside the Soviet orbit cannot flag for an instant. Unhappily effective resistance seems to require the most painful sort of regimentation throughout the United States. There seems to be no other way for us to marshal forces equal to this task.

But more than that, what we need is the spirit of resistance. We must no longer acquiesce in the fate of the millions in the satellite countries, of those at forced labor in uranium mines and Siberian forests, of men who because of their heroic manifestation of their personal beliefs suffer the terror of the concentration camp. All such victims we must determine to set free. Somehow or other we must emulate those Christians of earlier centuries who substituted themselves for the galley slaves chained to labor for the Turk.

If we can get away from our present servitude to material comfort and develop such a spirit, the task of proving to the world our devotion to human freedom would become comparatively easy. Our unalterable opposition to injustice would take active form. Our unwillingness to luxuriate in plenty while two-thirds of our fellow-men struggle for the barest livelihood would result in actions that would endear the people of the United States to men and women the world over.

Such are the abiding implications of the Soviet world challenge. For although the USSR can no longer count on internal uprisings and now has resorted to naked aggression from without, the Kremlin can still count on the disaffection and confusion of the multitudes who feel that they have little to defend.

That is what the determination of the Russians — as revealed by the attack on South Korea — should bring home to the people of the United States.

Commonweal 52 (7 July 1950): 307–8. Printed with permission.

72. "Questions Raised by the Korean War," September 1950

Like a nightmare we hoped was over, war has come back to rob us of our blood and our peace and our treasure. It seems so little time ago we were reading the same kind of headlines, scanning the same kind of casualty lists, studying the same kind of arrow-marked maps. So little time, and now the nightmare is upon us again, and we know not how or when or where it will stop. In the long weeks of the Korea conflict, America as a nation has risen magnificently in a cause that is just if ever a cause was just. As a nation we have not counted the cost but have resolutely poured men and materials into the desperate fight against cold-blooded aggression. As a nation we are willing to pay more in taxes; if necessary, to knuckle down to rationing and control over wages and prices and profits. We are willing to mobilize our manpower, give to our country those lost years out of a man's lifetime, the years spent in military service. For some, the giving has already included life itself. And the same demand will be made of too many others before the nightmare is over.

America has indeed risen generously and magnificently in the defense of justice and freedom. But the citizens of this land are not dolts. They are not automatons to be pushed around without asking any questions. Official Washington would do well to give some of the answers and give them soon. For as the numbers of wounded and dead Americans grow, as the undreamed of unpreparedness of our military establishment becomes increasingly more apparent, as the evidences of shocking ineptness in our State and Defense departments accumulate, there is bound to arise a groundswell of popular indignation that will be as towering in its wrath as the national debt is in its needless magnitude.

Who was the architect of our Far Eastern policy which lost us China and lead [sic] us unprepared into the Korean mess? Is that person or persons still free to tinker with the present abruptly changed policy we were forced to adopt? Who is to blame for our woeful intelligence performance, or, if our intelligence was good, who sat on the information and bungled the interpretation? The only friendly force in the Far East today is Chiang Kai-shek. Whose is the hand that would restrict MacArthur in working with him? Whose the hand that would muzzle even yet any official mouth bold enough to speak candidly and assert that we must stand with Chiang as against Red China?

Who are the military planners responsible for our neglect of tanks and transport planes, of tactical and naval aviation? Whose idea is it to keep the frightening gravity of our weakness in national defense from the people until after November?

And why did we so long listen to Russia at Lake Success accuse us of starting the Korean war while our delegates only frantically denied it? Who kept them from hurling the lie back in their teeth by indicting Russian aggression loudly enough for all of Asia to hear? Who is instructing our delegates to smart in idle wrath instead of challenging Russia's right to sit in the U.N. without standing trial for her many crimes of aggression? Why must we be eternally afraid to point the finger at the culprit guilty of all the human misery and turmoil the world suffers?

The American people have a right to know the answers to these questions. Not because we need a scapegoat. We have a right to know that the misguided and misguiding policy makers are no longer able to lead us to ruin. Americans are dying right now. The nation is militarily weak in the face of world-wide peril. Those responsible should be booted from power, and booted quickly. We cannot risk further blundering and mischief at their hands.

Sign 30 (September 1950): 9–10.

73. Rev. Philip Berrigan, S.S.J., "Vietnam and America's Conscience," October 1965

It has been said, with considerable truth, that the American conscience is dulled and silent on the issue of the morality of war, and that this state of affairs is largely traceable to our condonation of American savagery in the closing years of World War II, the anti-Communist conditioning of the Cold War years, the failure of the post-war world to conform to our idea of what it should be, and our feverish attempt to plan the next pleasure and secure the next luxury in the face of the twenty-five per cent of our population that is poor at home and the sixty per cent abroad. Moreover, and this fact alone is cause for shame and guilt, the Christian Church has been one of the staunchest allies of nationalism and the armor of weaponry and militarism that nationalism demands, of imperception and witch-hunting with regard to Communism, of international isolationism, of the trivia and baubles of bourgeois existence. As a consequence, the American hierarchy has not pronounced one word of moral analysis of our conduct in Vietnam, or in the Cold War generally, and our moral theologians have more prudently concerned themselves with the by now "safe" premises of racial justice or defense of the mind of Pius XII on contraception. Gordon Zahn believes that our position has already reached the measure of default of the German Church under Hitler, and that our inaction is far less defensible, since in order to speak out against the immorality of Hitler's aggressive wars, the German Church would have had to confront a totalitarian regime, and we do not. It may well be that the American people have gone beyond the point of no return in the question of arms, and that if peace is won, it will be won not as something right and Christian, but as a simple condition for survival. . . .

An incontestable case can be made that our country's contribution to the Cold War and to the shameful actions in Vietnam is immoral in Christian terms. I do not advance this as personal opinion, nor do I say that it is so because I hold it. I say rather that the whole weight of the Gospels and early Christian tradition advances this contention in the most objective terms, that preponderant world opinion supports it, and that the very words of the Pope himself state most emphatically that war, as we wage it today and as we are preparing to wage it on an ever-increasing scale, is immoral. In commenting on the Pope's encyclical *Mense Maio, Civilta Cattolica*, the Jesuit weekly published in Rome, has said that modern nations no longer have the right to wage war. Moreover, our position in Vietnam is one of fundamental outlawry. . . .

In the case of Vietnam, we have not even declared war, first, because we don't know what country to declare war against, and second, because we know that any declaration of war against North Vietnam or China would be ridiculed overwhelmingly by world judgment. Our support of the Saigon government, which is in reality no government at all; our bombing of the industries of a nation against which we have no grievance and against which we have not declared war; our testing of horribly inhumane weapons and increasing commitment of troops to a combat role; our plans to bomb the dikes of North Vietnam, an act that would inundate the land and drown tens and perhaps hundreds of thousands of people — the whole rising tide of savagery and ruin that we have provoked and that we now sustain — these things not only contradict the Gospel and render fidelity to it a mockery, they also violate the whole theory of the just war. If one does not accept the discipleship of truth and love that the Gospel clearly enunciates, one must then at least believe in a rigid application of the just-war theory. Yet neither approach can justify the present American policy in Vietnam or in the Cold War. If, on the other hand, we believe in neither (and the consensus that the President claims to have would seem to indicate that most Christians in this country believe in neither), then we become collaborators in the present savagery and are guilty of genocide by intention, since in practice the majority of Christians in this country have made possible, whether by default or by active support, everything we are now doing or intend to do....

By their nature, and because of their enormous destructive capacity, nuclear weapons cannot be considered as anything else but offensive weapons, which can vaporize non-combatants, open cities, and neutrals, in the process contaminating the atmosphere, water, and vegetation....

It can be argued that tactical nuclear weapons could be restricted in their employment, but once they are used, it is safe to surmise that the provocation they represent would be met by massive and even megatonic retaliation. At that point, there would be no reason for not meeting fire with fire, on both sides. We are only slightly aware now, it seems to me, that a psychology of violence has been slowly amassing in the world for nearly thirty years, and that the whole range of atrocity from Pearl Harbor, Coventry, Rotterdam, Buchenwald, Dachau, Hamburg, Dresden, Tokyo, Hiroshima, and Nagasaki, during World War II, and more recently in the Congo, the Dominican Republic, and Vietnam, has conditioned us to the most awful kinds of violence, and made us quite complacent about its reality as long as we are not directly involved. Furthermore, we do not understand that the barbarity of such violence and our accommodation to it does not leave us uninvolved, but rather brutalized as long as we remain inert in its presence or approve of it in any way. It is no accident that Americans today no longer recoil from accounts of atrocities in Vietnam or from President Johnson's admission that things in Southeast Asia must get worse before they get better, "worse" meaning the frightful pyramiding of all that war connotes, while "better" means — what? The "better" has been awaited in Vietnam for ten years, our leaders competing with each other in a variety of promises as naive as they were unfounded. The fact is that total war (and the war in Southeast Asia is total except that we have not used nuclear weapons) leaves nothing or no one better....

The only international agreement that could possibly justify our action in Southeast Asia was the Geneva Conference of 1954. Against the wishes of Secretary Dulles, that Conference called for a united Vietnam in two years by national plebiscite. We refused to sign the agreement but promised to honor its terms. Within seven months we had broken our word by beginning to organize and train the South Vietnamese Army. In 1956, we again broke our word by refusing to hold the Geneva-ordered elections. Ho Chi Minh, with patience that goes largely uncredited, waited until 1958 before calling for guerrilla action in the South, and from that time on our position has grown increasingly disastrous. We have never admitted that the war is a civil war, because this would be tantamount to admitting that we have no right there, that no recognized government invited us in, that we are opposing an international agreement, and that the increasing scale of our aggression has been punishing a popular uprising....

In short, we will not admit that we were wrong in 1954, that we have been wrong in the interim, and that we are wrong today. The Defense Department insists that we must have nearly two hundred thousand American troops in South Vietnam by the end of the year, and in our simple-mindedly vicious way, we expect to recoup the losses of eleven years of stupidity and brutality by stepping up the pace of stupidity and brutality. It would be enough cause for grief if it were only ourselves who were involved, but modern war does not work that way. And so we continue to ravage a country already devastated by twenty-five years of outside aggression, and in the process, we are inexorably drawing the nations of the world into the ultimate folly of World War III....

Catholic Worker 32 (October 1965): 2, 6.

74. Cardinal Lawrence Shehan, "The Overriding Moral Issues of Modern Warfare," Pastoral Letter to the Archdiocese of Baltimore, 28 June 1966[1]

Dearly Beloved in Christ:

The approach of our national Independence Day provides me with an opportune occasion for suggesting some line of thought about the patriotic duties of an American Catholic in the present hour. My desire to do so is intensified by the fact that I have just returned from Rome where, on the feastday of his patron saint, I heard our Holy Father itemize his various and unwearying efforts for world peace during the past year.

Pope Paul made specific mention of Vietnam where, in ever increasing numbers, our fellow Americans and fellow human beings are fighting, suffering and dying. He called it a land "tormented by conflict and by struggles that make it suffer greatly and seem to have no end." He also spoke of the "worsening of the situation and the terrible prospect of a possible extension of the conflict."

Our Holy Father, of course, has been speaking and acting in harmony with the somber and urgent words of the Second Vatican Council on the unique dangers of war and warlike attitudes in the nuclear age. It is no secret that the immensely complicated situation in Vietnam is a source of grave concern to the whole world and also a subject of acute controversy, not only in our own country but throughout the world.

In the remarks which follow, I intend only the modest purpose of recalling

---

1. This letter was issued one day before the beginning of U.S. bombing of Hanoi and Haiphong.

some of the pertinent principles formulated by the Vatican Council concerning modern warfare. It devolves on each Catholic citizen in every country to weigh political situations in terms of such principles and to exert whatever moral and civic influences seem dictated by his conscience.

Christians of equal sincerity and equal devotion to the Gospel may honorably differ in their conclusions, especially when the problems are gigantic and important facts are themselves a matter of dispute. But certainly no Catholic who claims to find in the living teaching of the Church a source of moral guidance can be indifferent to his duty to care about the overriding moral issues of modern warfare, as well as his duty to know and to follow the pronouncements of the Church on the moral limitations even of lawful self-defense.

Because America is militarily the strongest nation in the world, because her policies can influence literally every human being on earth and because numerically Catholics are the largest organized religious body in the United States, American Catholics have a particularly grave and binding obligation to follow the lead of the Church and to exert their share of moral influence on the councils of government.

Let it first be said that the Vatican Council recognized the legitimate role of patriotism: "Citizens should develop a generous and loyal devotion to their country, but without any narrowing of mind. In other words, they should always look simultaneously to the welfare of the whole human family, which is tied together by the manifold bonds linking races, peoples and nations" (The Church in the Modern World, n. 75)....

Though this approval of patriotism is qualified, the Council did not rule out...a country's right to legitimate self-defense: "As long as the danger of war remains and there is no competent and sufficiently powerful authority at the international level, governments cannot be denied the right to legitimate defense once every means of peaceful settlement has been exhausted" (The Church in the Modern World, n. 79). Neither did the Council rule out what love of neighbor itself might demand, namely that one nation help another in its struggle against aggression.

The work of self-defense is normally carried out by the military personnel of a nation. Speaking of such, the Council affirmed that "those who are pledged to the service of their country as members of its armed forces should regard themselves as agents of security and freedom on behalf of their people. As long as they fulfill this role properly, they are making a genuine contribution to the establishment of peace" (The Church in the Modern World, n. 79).

Surely it is not blindly nationalistic for us to believe that most of the American servicemen involved in the Vietnam conflict are not acting and do not wish to act against their consciences. Hence, their valor is in itself worthy of praise, and their spirit of sacrifice worthy of more intense imitation on the part of their fellow citizens who are spared the perils and rigors of the battlefield.

At the same time, especially since modern warfare bears within it the seeds of global holocaust, the viewpoint of the sincere conscientious objector merits careful consideration: "It seems right that laws make humane provisions for the case of those who for reasons of conscience refuse to bear arms provided, however, that they accept some other form of service to the human community" (The Church in the Modern World, n. 79).

In particular, the Council gave its "unequivocal and unhesitating condemnation" to "any act of war aimed indiscriminately at the destruction of entire cities or of extensive areas along with their population" (The Church in the Modern World, n. 79). It is clear how contrary to Catholic teaching are some of the suggestions occasionally made about the degree and kind of violence our nation should inflict on its enemies. The Council emphasized what modern popes have repeatedly affirmed — that all is not permissible even in a presumably lawful war of self-defense.

Because citizens who enjoy representative government are especially answerable for the decisions of their leaders, these citizens have a moral right to know, insofar as national security permits, the truth about government decisions and operations which implicate the general public: "There exists within human society a right to information about affairs which affect men individually or collectively, and according to the circumstances of each" (The Instruments of Social Communication, n. 5).

This right entails a corresponding duty of the citizenry to seek out the facts about government policy, especially in time of war, when human beings suffer injury and death in the name of one's own country. The Vatican Council was not speaking only of government leaders when it insisted: "The men of our time must realize that they will have to give a somber reckoning for their deeds of war, for the course of the future will depend largely on the decisions they make today" (The Church in the Modern World, n. 80).

It is difficult for a nation to wage war with restraint and to nourish sentiments of peace at the same time. This is true particularly when its own casualties begin to mount and the conflict threatens to grow in duration and intensity. In such circumstances, those who argue against restraint and against keeping a nation's war-making acts within moral bounds are likely to win an ever greater hearing. Within our nation it seems that such harsh voices are growing stronger and are attempting to pressure our leaders into decisions which the Christian conscience could not endorse.

If we are to resist such lethal appeals to our understandable impatience, we must constantly recall that only on moral grounds can our cause in Vietnam be just. If our means become immoral, our cause will have been betrayed. Let us also avoid the narrowness of supposing that all the vice and bad will lie on one side of any major conflict and that all the virtue and good will lie on the other.

Assuming our cause in Vietnam is just, our duties to mankind as a whole forbid us to indulge in passions of hatred and aggression. Indeed, viewing the world as a whole, the Council insisted: "Those who mold public opinions should regard as their most weighty task the effort to instruct all in fresh sentiments of peace" (The Church in the Modern World, n. 82).

Even though our hands are embattled, then, our hearts must remain steadfastly peace-loving. Otherwise, at the peril of an escalation which could end in mutual annihilation, we may fail to be responsive to the possibilities of reasonable and honorable negotiations.

That our president has earnestly sought such negotiations in the past, we do not doubt. That he and our other national leaders would gladly enter into such negotiations now we firmly believe. All of us have the duty to beg God fervently that he in his wisdom may quickly provide the occasion of such negotiations, and that they will be fruitful in lasting justice and peace.

Catholic World 203 (September 1966): 365–67.

75. William V. Shannon, "The Case for the War," 8 December 1967

Although I am in disagreement with *Commonweal*'s editorial position on the Vietnam war, I respect that position because of its honest, unequivocal nature. The editors believe that the war's moral costs exceed any possible gain and therefore advocate U.S. withdrawal. They recognize that withdrawal will mean a political defeat for this country in Vietnam and probably for its allies throughout Southeast Asia, but they are willing to accept that fact.

Because of this straightforward position, no time need be wasted on intermediate issues such as bombing passes, peace signals, coalition governments in Saigon, or Ho Chi Minh as an Asian Tito. A defeat is a defeat, and let's get it over with.

This same uncompromising attitude characterizes two recent anti-war statements, one issued by a group called RESIST and the other by 27 Catholic intellectuals.

My own view is that the many justifications for our military effort in Vietnam are not self-contradictory but rather complementary and interrelated.

First, the great issue in the world today is freedom vs. tyranny. Second, the United States is the principal defender of freedom. Since the idea of freedom is much broader and more significant than the particular selfish interests of the national society that currently defends that idea, it is easy for critics to juxtapose them and play one off against the other. There is not and cannot always be a perfect one-to-one correlation between human freedom and American national interests, but desire to promote human freedom informs and ennobles American foreign policy and, broadly speaking, what strengthens American influence strengthens freedom.

Since many readers do *not* regard that as axiomatic, let me remind them that if the United States had not interposed first its economic and then its military strength in Western Europe in the late 1940s, then West Berlin would not be a free city and the French and Italian Communists would probably have seized power, establishing in France and Italy the same drab tyrannies that now prevail in Poland and Czechoslovakia. If the United States had not defeated Japan in World War II, then all of Asia from Korea to the borders of India would be under the control of a ruthless Japanese military dictatorship. Such personal freedom and national independence as exist in Asia are largely due to American intervention from 1941 to 1945. Those gains were defended by American blood and sacrifice in Korea from 1950 to 1953 against an attack by North Korea backed by China and Russia. They are being defended today in Vietnam against an attack by North Vietnam backed by China and Russia.

Underlying the arguments of the peace advocates is the assumption that if the United States abandoned the "folly" of its intervention in Vietnam, there would be peace in the world. Vietnam, however, is only one episode in a worldwide political struggle that has been going on for decades and will continue for decades. The source of this struggle is the ideological effort of Russia and China to appear as the vanguard of world revolution. Traditional national interests sometimes reinforce this ideological drive. Thus, ideology and interest are both involved in the Russian effort to obtain military bases and a sphere of interest in the Middle East by arming the Arabs. But, for Russia, only ideology explains its support of Cuba and North Vietnam, both of which are economic burdens and irrelevant to Russia's national interests. As long as Russia and China — not to mention the aggressive ideological pretensions of Cuba — keep pushing outward, there cannot be peace in the world.

This brings us to the question of means. It is permissible to spread ideology by peaceful politics, foreign aid, propaganda and diplomacy. If this is all that the ideological cold war amounted to, both sides could enjoy "competitive coexistence." But the Communists, relying upon the mystique of revolution to confer legitimacy, have no scruples about using force. The United States, as the chief organizer and defender of the free world, cannot permit freedom to be nibbled to death by "wars of national liberation."

Many who criticize the deployment of American power in Vietnam and elsewhere around the globe have a double standard on the use of force. The Communists can use force to keep a country within their system as the Russians did in Hungary. They can use it to extend their system as the Chinese did in Tibet. They can use force to blackmail, intimidate and subvert from the Berlin blockade to Vietnam. But if the United States uses force to block these aggressive moves, then it is denounced for intervening in other people's affairs or accused of illusions of omnipotence or ridiculed for trying to be the world's policeman. We should instead be grateful that America has the power to defend freedom and the will to use that power.

I am not impressed by the argument that the U.S. ought not to intervene in Vietnam because what is really going on is a social revolution which cannot be stopped by force of arms. Communist revolutions are not more inevitable or desirable than the Fascist upheavals of 30 years ago which were once thought to be the "wave of the future." These social revolutions, these brutal shortcuts to modernization, bring more misery than material gain to their victims. The peasants get cheated out of their land, the workers get sweated, and the intellectuals lose their freedom. Cuba in 1959 and Russia in 1917 only needed a liberal reform; instead, in the name of revolution, they have suffered an unending totalitarian ordeal. Ho Chi Minh is just one more murderous tyrant shuffling his bloody way across the stage of history.

The nationalist argument has greater weight. Insofar as the Communists in Vietnam have had a political success, it is by capturing the role of spokesmen for Vietnamese aspirations and picturing Americans as successors to the colonial French. But the willingness of five million South Vietnamese to vote in the recent elections indicates that the Saigon Government is acquiring political legitimacy. Pope Paul has spoken of the importance of people being "the artisans of their own destiny." The difficulty is that the armed, terrorist Communist minority will not permit the ordinary South Vietnamese to be artisans of their own destiny. As a result, the South Vietnamese will either be subjugated by the Communists or protected by the Americans. It is not the ideal choice, but it is the only choice.

I think it is important to fight it out in Vietnam if only to learn how to counter Communist guerrilla and terror tactics. If they are not countered successfully in Vietnam, the Communists are sure to try them elsewhere in Southeast Asia and in Latin America.

But I must end on a note of pessimism. I do not think either the American government or the American people are prepared to stay the course in Vietnam in the only way which I regard as sensible. The war has to be won on the ground, in South Vietnam, and over a long period of time, perhaps seven to ten years. But instead we have turned the war into the kind of war we are used to winning. We are hoping to win by air power and fire power rather than by slow, small-scale infantry actions.

I am opposed to the bombing of North Vietnam not only because it is morally indiscriminate — that is true of almost all bombing — but also because it is militarily ineffective. The strategic bombing surveys of Germany and Japan after World War II showed conclusively how quickly bomb damage can be repaired. If that was true of highly industrialized nations, it is even more relevant for North Vietnam which has relatively little industry and which is accustomed to primitive means of transport. Moreover, bombing of the North is needlessly provocative of Communist China. I am also opposed to the spraying of chemicals in either North or South Vietnam because it poisons the atmosphere and the food chain for an indeterminate length of time.

The American government, however, has become obsessed by the need to find a quick solution. The American people, notoriously impatient, are wearying of a war to which there can be no early end. If we had the patience, we could probably wear down the Communists in a smaller, slower, less mechanized war while gradually refining and improving our political warfare techniques at the village level. Lacking that patience, we are likely to meet defeat in Vietnam and in the other Vietnams that may come in "the third world."

Commonweal 87 (8 December 1967): 326–27. Printed with permission.

76. "The War, Patriotism, and Extremism," 20 September 1972

Nine U.S. Trappist abbots have called on the United States to "re-evaluate its strategies and tactics in Indochina to assure their morality and humanity." In their statement, released September 20, the abbots noted that it is not ordinarily the role of a Trappist to raise his voice publicly. But, they added, the situation in Indochina is no ordinary one. The text of the abbots' statement is below. The signers were Abbots: John Eudes Bamberger, Abbey of the Genesee, Piffard, N.Y.; Edward Mc-Corkell, Holy Cross Abbey, Berryville, Va.; Thomas Aquinas Keating, St. Joseph's Abbey, Spencer, Mass.; David Wechter, New Melleray Abbey, Dubuque, Iowa; Michael Abdo, St. Benedict's Monastery, Snowmass, Conn.; Benedict Griesemer, Guadalupe Abbey, Lafayette, Ore.; Robert Matter, Assumption Abbey, Ava, Mo.; Thomas X. Davis, New Clairvaux Abbey, Vina, Cal.; and Anthony Chassagne, Mepkin Abbey, Moncks Corner, S.C.

Nine Trappist Abbots

The call of the monk into the "desert" of his monastic solitude includes a call to silence — a silence in which he listens to and attempts to interpret the Word of God. It is not, ordinarily, the role of the monk to raise his voice in the public forum.

The present situation, however, is no ordinary one. Our country continues to be embroiled in a war in Indochina that becomes daily more costly in terms of public morality, human dignity and human life itself. Without minimizing the alleged atrocities of North Vietnamese troops and the Vietcong reported in the press, we believe our government should re-evaluate its strategies and tactics in Indochina to assure their morality and humanity.

We ask our government to make every effort to negotiate a speedy cease-fire in Vietnam and to pose only such conditions as are essential to our legitimate and stated aims in its demands for peace. These stated aims are to prevent the imposition of an undesired form of government upon the South Vietnamese people, and to protect the people who have supported the present government from reprisals.

We wish to repeat and make our own the words of Pope Paul VI, spoken on July 9, 1972: "We make ours the voice of a population driven to exhaustion by massacre and calamity. We cry out...to beseech those who can and who ought to discuss and deliberate: enough!"

We invite all men to respond to Christ's invitation to be peacemakers, and we ask our fellow citizens to join us in prayer and in fasting to beg our Father in heaven for his great gift of true peace. We are confident that such united prayer will bring to our country and our leaders the courage and wisdom necessary to achieve what many years of war and untold suffering have failed to produce: peace.

Abbot McCaffrey, O.S.B.

Just a few days prior to the above statement by nine Trappist abbots, another American abbot spoke out on topics related to the war and patriotism. This time (Sept. 16) it was a Benedictine, Abbot Edmund McCaffrey of Belmont Abbey in North Carolina. In a homily before 3,000 persons gathered at the National Shrine of the Immaculate Conception in Washington, D.C., for a God Day rally, the abbot deplored what he called Berriganism[1] and said that a retreat from international obligations could be a retreat from the law of charity....

There are forces today in the Church and in the nation that are harmful to the unity of peoples, that work against reconciliation, and that are harmful to world order and stability. These forces weaken the Church and the nation. Sometimes they speak in the name of the Church, but we must dispel this myth as they are speaking only as individuals.

Representatives of these forces thrive on discord, their vision is myopic, they are endowed with an overabundance of pride and self-righteousness. They substitute the individual good for the common good. One of the heresies of the modern time is the substitution of the individual good for the common good of society. Representatives of these forces are a scandal to the Church and yet much of what they do and say is under the guise of good and in the search for peace and justice. One does not question their motives in seeking peace, but one must condemn many of the means.

Berriganism is such a force. It is wrong because it subverts the common good. It is wrong because it is disobedient and scandalous. It is wrong because it is Machiavellian insofar as it frequently adopts the principle that the end justifies the means. Many of their followers certainly are not Machiavellian, but they are Neroian (as in Nero). The sad thing is that they do not know that they fiddle, nor do they know that Rome burns. They are misguided.

Berriganism is wrong because it seeks peace without the firm foundation of justice and truth. Pope John XXIII in his beautiful encyclical *Pacem in Terris* clearly indicated that peace is a product of justice and truth. Berriganism can only lead to social disorder and religious disaster because it misinterprets political realities and because it is founded on arrogance.

We must seek after justice. We must actively pursue it. In our pursuit of justice and peace all Americans must avoid extremes. America cannot afford extremes on the left and the right. We cannot afford self-appointed minute men or vigilantes on the right, nor can we afford Berrigan brigands on the left who burn legitimate government records and interfere with legitimate governmental functions. The true patriot is balanced. He is sensitive to the common good. He seeks after the law of God and here respects the objective moral order. He does not seek to create this order.

---

1. A reference to the antiwar activism of priest-brothers Daniel and Philip Berrigan.

We must return to judicial and legal norms based on the law of nature and of God. Our yardstick must not be based on numbers or on the behavioral sciences. Sociology is not theology. Sociology is not law. When sociological jurisprudence replaces objective moral legal norms we will have social and moral chaos. When sociological jurisprudence dominates the life of America, as it threatens to do today, freedom becomes license and the hideous crime of abortion and the cult of permissiveness finds legal and social acceptability. Unfortunately today, permissiveness and license have become a standard because the law of God, the common good and prudence have been extinguished.

Origins 2, no. 14 (28 September 1972): 219, 221, 229. Printed with permission.

77. Archbishop John Roach, Statement on the Murders of Catholics in El Salvador, 5 December 1980

On Dec[ember] 4, [1980], the bodies of four U.S. women — three nuns and one laywoman — were found buried in shallow graves in El Salvador. The murders of the four women led to an immediate cutoff of U.S. aid to El Salvador pending a full investigation.

The assassination of Archbishop [Oscar] Romero in March of this year has dramatized to Christians, as few other events could, the inherent risk faced today by those who would be faithful to the Gospel of Jesus Christ. The pastoral task of accompanying the people, especially the poor and oppressed, in their daily suffering and struggle, has made the church of El Salvador a vibrant symbol to all the world.

In these last days the price of such fidelity has brought death and destruction of unprecedented proportions to the Christian community of El Salvador.

One week ago, as we in this country gathered in our homes and churches to give thanks to God for his bounty, armed men invaded the Jesuit high school in El Salvador where some two dozen people were meeting peacefully. Within 24 hours the bodies of six of them, including most of the top leadership of the opposition movement, were found, marked by signs of savage torture.

Soon after their bodies were brought to the metropolitan cathedral where many came to mourn their slain leaders, the church was rocked by an explosion that destroyed parts of the building and wounded several.

No sooner had their funeral ended yesterday when we learned of the disappearance of four American women, all missioned to El Salvador. Maryknoll Sisters Ita Ford and Maura Clark had been met at the international airport on Tuesday evening by Ursuline Sister Dorothy Kazel and lay volunteer Jean Donovan, both of the Cleveland mission team. Their burned-out microbus was found abandoned along the highway near the airport. And just today we have received confirmation that all four have been killed.

This campaign of violence against the poor and those who side with the poor is an abomination that cries to heaven. People of good will everywhere must now more than ever make their own the anguished cry of Archbishop Romero's last public homily: "In the name of God and in the name of that suffering people whose cries, each day more insistently, reach to the very heavens, I ask, I beg, I command in the name of God, stop the repression!"

Let those who govern in El Salvador fulfill the elementary duty of any government claiming legitimacy, namely, bring under true control its own military and security forces and end the bloody repression against the church and the popular movements.

Let those who are responsible for the policy of the United States toward El Salvador, those now in office and those about to assume office, make unmistakably clear to all the revulsion of the American people at the sickening spiral of violence affecting the Salvadoran people. Cessation of all assistance to repressive security forces and a clear affirmation of our perduring commitment to human rights are measures available to our political leaders; let such measures be taken now.

The church in the United States shares the grief of the families, the religious communities and the dioceses from which the four dedicated and valiant women came. We share the grief of all in El Salvador whose loved ones have been so brutally taken from them. And we pray, during this time of waiting for the Lord's coming, that the hour of justice, peace and healing will come soon to El Salvador.

> "Murders of U.S. Women Protested: Statement on the Murders of Catholics in El Salvador," *Origins* 10, no. 27 (18 December 1980): 417, 419. Printed with permission of Archbishop Roach.

78. National Conference of Catholic Bishops, *The Challenge of Peace: God's Promise and Our Response,* 3 May 1983

As bishops in the United States, assessing the concrete circumstances of our society, we have made a number of observations and recommendations in the process of applying moral principles to specific policy choices.

A. On the Use of Nuclear Weapons

1. Counter Population Use: Under no circumstances may nuclear weapons or other instruments of mass slaughter be used for the purpose of destroying population centers or other predominantly civilian targets. Retaliatory action which would indiscriminately and disproportionately take many wholly innocent lives, lives of people who are in no way responsible for reckless actions of their government, must also be condemned.

2. The Initiation of Nuclear War: We do not perceive any situation in which the deliberate initiation of nuclear war, on however restricted a scale, can be morally justified. Non-nuclear attacks by another state must be resisted by other than nuclear means. Therefore, a serious moral obligation exists to develop non-nuclear defensive strategies as rapidly as possible. In this letter we urge NATO to move rapidly toward the adoption of a "no first use" policy, but we recognize this will take time to implement and will require the development of an adequate alternative defense posture.

3. *Limited Nuclear War:* Our examination of the various arguments on this question makes us highly skeptical about the real meaning of "limited." One of the criteria of the just-war teaching is that there must be a reasonable hope of success in bringing about justice and peace. We must ask whether such a reasonable hope can exist once nuclear weapons have been exchanged. The burden of proof rests on those who assert that meaningful limitation is possible. In our view the first imperative is to prevent any use of nuclear weapons and we hope that leaders will resist the notion that nuclear conflict can be limited, contained, or won in any traditional sense.

B. On Deterrence

In concert with the evaluation provided by Pope John Paul II, we have arrived at a strictly conditional moral acceptance of deterrence. In this letter we have outlined criteria and recommendations which indicate the meaning of conditional acceptance of deterrence policy. We cannot consider such a policy adequate as a long-term basis for peace.

C. On Promoting Peace

1. We support immediate, bilateral verifiable agreements to halt the testing, production, and deployment of new nuclear weapons systems. This recommendation is not to be identified with any specific political initiative.

2. We support efforts to achieve deep cuts in the arsenals of both superpowers; efforts should concentrate first on systems which threaten the retaliatory forces of either major power.

3. We support early and successful conclusion of negotiations of a comprehensive test-ban treaty.

4. We urge new efforts to prevent the spread of nuclear weapons in the world and to control the conventional arms race, particularly the conventional arms-trade.

5. We support, in an increasingly interdependent world, political and economic policies designed to protect human dignity and to promote the human rights of every person, especially the least among us. In this regard, we call for the establishment of some form of global authority adequate to the needs of the international common good. . . .

In concluding . . . we respond to two key questions often asked about this pastoral letter.

Why do we address these matters fraught with such complexity, controversy and passion? We speak as pastors, not politicians. We are teachers, not technicians. We cannot avoid our responsibility to lift up the moral dimensions of other choices before our world and nation. The nuclear age is an era of moral as well as physical danger. We are the first generation since Genesis with the power to threaten the created order. We cannot remain silent in the face of such danger. Why do we address these issues? We are simply trying to live up to the call of Jesus to be peacemakers in our own time and situation.

What are we saying? Fundamentally, we are saying that the decisions about nuclear weapons are among the most pressing moral questions of our age. While these decisions have obvious military and political aspects, they involve fundamental moral choices. In simple terms, we are saying that good ends (defending one's country, protecting freedom, etc.) cannot justify immoral means (the use of weapons that kill indiscriminately and threaten whole societies). We fear that our world and nation are headed in the wrong direction. More weapons with greater destructive potential are produced every day. More and more nations are seeking to become nuclear powers. In our quest for more and more security, we fear we are actually becoming less and less secure.

In the words of our Holy Father, we need a "moral about face." The whole world must summon the moral courage and technical means to say no to nuclear conflict; no to weapons of mass destruction; no to an arms race which robs the poor and the vulnerable; and no to the moral danger of a nuclear age which places before humankind indefensible choices of constant terror or surrender. We are called to be peacemakers, not by some movement of the moment, but by our Lord Jesus. The content and context of our peacemaking is set not by some political agenda or ideological program, but by the teaching of the Church....

Published by the United States Catholic Conference, Washington, D.C., 1983. Printed with permission.

Education

One of the continuing battlegrounds between Catholics and American society was over the question of parochial schools. Noisy disputes broke out over various Supreme Court decisions that more narrowly defined the expenditure of public funds for virtually any aspect of private schools. Efforts in Congress to allot Catholic schools money on a per-pupil basis also engendered much controversy — at one point pitting Cardinal Francis Spellman against Eleanor Roosevelt. While public funding of private collegiate education was approved without argument, continued efforts to extend the benefit of federal money to other private schools always aroused rancorous public debate. Catholics vigorously defended their schools and in California mobilized politically to have them exempted from taxation.

Catholic voices continued to reaffirm both the significance of parochial schools as an important element in promoting American values such as freedom and effective citizenship and the overall academic excellence of those schools — despite the lack of public funds.

79. Administrative Board, National Catholic Welfare Conference, "The Child: Citizen of Two Worlds," 17 November 1950

I. A Sense of God

1. In the present grim international struggle, the American people have resolutely championed the cause of human freedom. We have committed ourselves to oppose relentlessly the aggressions of those who deny to man his God-given rights and who aim to enslave all mankind under the rules of godless materialism. The responsibilities which we have thereby assumed are both grave and continuing. They deserve conscientious consideration.

2. It is of primary importance for our people to realize that human freedom derives from the spiritual nature of man and can flourish only when things of the spirit are held in reverence. Our present principles of action need to be evaluated in the light of that truth. But we must go even further. Small comfort to be successful today if tomorrow the world finds us unworthy of the trust reposed in us. We need, therefore, to examine carefully what spiritual direction we are giving to our children to prepare them to fulfill their future moral responsibilities to God and to their fellow man.

3. In recent decades, striking advances have been made in meeting the child's physical, emotional, and social needs; but his moral and religious needs have not been met with the same solicitude and understanding. As a result, many of our children betray confusion and insecurity because these unmet needs are fundamental to the harmonious development of their whole nature.

4. The child must be seen whole and entire. He must be seen as a citizen of two worlds. He belongs to this world surely, but his first and highest allegiance is to the Kingdom of God. From his earliest years he must be taught that his chief significance comes from the fact that he is created by God and is destined for life with God in eternity.

5. The child's prospects for fulfilling this great hope which God has reposed in him must be viewed realistically. He will come to maturity in a society where social, moral, intellectual, and spiritual values are everywhere disintegrating. In such a society, he will urgently need the integrating force of religion as taught by Christ. Such a force will give him a complete and rational meaning for his existence.

6. First of all, it will arouse in him a consciousness of God and of eternity. His vision will be opened out upon a supernatural world revealed by faith which differs from the world of nature his senses reveal. Thus he will discover a higher life than this daily one and a brighter world than he sees. Second, it will give him a continuing purpose in life, for it will teach him that he was made to know, love, and serve God in this world as the condition for meriting eternal happiness. Third, it will induce in him a deep sense of responsibility for those rights and obligations he possesses by reason of his citizenship in Heaven as well as on earth. Finally, religion will challenge him to sanctify

whatever walk of life he chooses and to seek and accept the will of God in whatever way it may be manifested. Thus, as a principle of integration, religion will help the children to develop a *sense of God*, a *sense of direction*, a *sense of responsibility*, and a *sense of mission*.

7. The child is not complete in himself. He will find his completion only in life with God; and that life must begin here upon earth. Parents, therefore, should make early provision for their child's growth in God. This is not something to be postponed for nurture by school authorities. It must begin in the home through simple and prayerful practices. Morning and evening prayers, grace before and after meals, the family rosary, the saying of a short prayer each time the striking clock marks the passage of another hour nearer eternity, the reverential making of the sign of the cross, the inculcation of respect for the crucifix and other religious objects — all these practices which should be encouraged in the religious formation of the child. No one can doubt that there is a readiness on his part to receive such formation, and if parents are remiss in giving it they will lose a splendid opportunity to develop in their child that habitual awareness of God which is vital to his full growth.

8. Only two courses are open to the child: either he will be God-centered or self-centered. He is made and destined for God, but he bears in his nature the lingering effects of original sin which incline him to seek the satisfaction of every selfish whim. To correct this bend in his will so that God, rather than self, will occupy the center of his life is one of the most challenging tasks facing parents.

9. In meeting this challenge, let parents make use of the strong, supernatural motivation which can be drawn from the life of Christ. Let them encourage the imitation of Him, particularly in His obedience, patience, and thoughtfulness of others; and let them foster the emulation of that spirit of unselfish giving so characteristic of Christ. This can be done in many practical ways, particularly through providing the child with frequent opportunities for making acts of self-denial in the home. If he is taught to deny his selfish whims for the sake of Christ, he will not only discover a supernatural motive for his actions, but he will learn to give God that central place in his affections which God must occupy if the child is to come to his full spiritual stature.

10. Little point would be served in intensifying the child's awareness of God during his preschool years, if later his schooling were to rob him of that. The child's education during school years should be of a piece with his education at home. Catholic parents, clearly grasping this essential truth, have undergone great sacrifice and enormous expense to establish and maintain schools which will continue and enlarge the spiritual development of the child that was begun at home. In doing this, parents have acted within their competence, because it is they, and not the state, who possess the primary right to educate. This natural right of parents is one which has ever been recognized

in our American traditions. As recently as 1944, the highest court in our land confirmed it in these words:

> It is cardinal with us that the custody, care and nurture of the child *reside first in the parents* whose primary function and freedom include preparation for obligations the state can neither supply nor hinder.

11. In helping parents to exercise this right, the Church stands ready at hand with all her material and spiritual resources. At infancy she initiates the child into the life of grace and for the rest of his days she stands by his side ready to minister to his needs. She recognizes his preeminent need for God and she meets it by providing Catholic schools for each stage of his educational development. She does this in virtue of the sublime teaching office conferred on her by Jesus Christ.

12. When it is impossible for parents to take advantage of the God-centered education which Catholic schools offer, they have a grave obligation to provide for their child's religious instruction in some other way. At least they must see that their children attend catechism classes and vacation schools and receive the benefit of other activities of the Confraternity of Christian Doctrine.

13. Nor should the state, which has demonstrated a genuine interest in so many aspects of the child's welfare, be indifferent to the inherent value of religious instruction and training for the child attending tax-supported schools. The continuance and well-being of a state based on democratic principles require that it show a lively concern for moral principles and practices which are firmly grounded only in religion. For the child who is not receiving thorough religious education, the state should look with favor on released-time programs for his religious instruction.

14. Many important services have been rendered by the governmental agencies to the child who has been deprived of the care and support of his parents by death, illness, or misfortune. However, it is a source of growing concern to us that in certain parts of our country there is a trend to regard this whole field of foster care as falling within the exclusive province of governmental authorities. It surely lies within their province to set up and enforce legitimate minimum standards of care for the dependent child; but the responsibility for his care should not be entirely assumed by them. There is a definite place in America for the voluntary agencies of mercy — particularly those operating under religious auspices, which are equipped to safeguard and develop the religious life of the dependent child. Certainly the child bereft of the immediate care of his parents is entitled to those opportunities for a religious upbringing which his parents were obligated to give him. These opportunities can be best supplied by an agency operating under religious auspices. . . .

Hugh J. Nolan, ed., *Pastoral Letters of the United States Catholic Bishops* (Washington, D.C.: United States Catholic Conference, 1984), 2:97–105. Printed with permission.

80. Administrative Board, National Catholic Welfare Conference, "Private and Church-Related Schools in American Education," 20 November 1955

1. Freedom under God is America's dearest treasure. Its roots lie deep in her Christian heritage, and its germ is the concept of man's personal responsibility to his Creator for his temporal and eternal salvation. Here in America freedom has flowered in an ordered democracy, which guarantees to her citizens the widest latitude of individual expression within the framework of commonly held principles of justice, decency, and law.

Schools Must Teach Freedom

2. To preserve freedom America must teach freedom. It is in the schools of the nation, preeminently, that this educative process is carried on. It is in the classroom that the principles underlying our Christian concept of human liberty must be defined and inculcated, if future generations are to appreciate, defend, and preserve it. But that this be done, it is an absolutely necessary condition that the schools of America should themselves be guaranteed their rightful freedom to teach truth.

3. Historically and actually our nation has been blessed with educational freedom. Her school system is not a closed, unitary creation of the state, a servile instrument of governmental monopoly, but one which embraces, together with the state-supported schools, a whole enormous cluster of private and church-related schools, including many of the most honored names in the entire educational world, and devoted to the education of many millions of the nation's youth.

4. That these private and church-related schools serve a minority in America, by sheer numerical computation, is a purely incidental factor, and it is plainly unrealistic thinking to discount their importance on that score. Indeed, it is unrealistic to belittle in any way the schools in which more than five million young Americans are currently receiving their education. These schools, emphatically, are an integral part of the American educational system. And so long as our nation is faithful to her principles of justice and due process of law, these schools will remain a permanent part of that system.

Private Schools Produced the First Leaders

5. It is not without significance that the private and church-related schools were the first in the field of American education. For well-nigh two centuries, during our colonial and early national periods, they occupied that field alone. It was from such schools, as from fruitful seed-beds, that there came the guiding intellectual and moral impulses which led to the definition and establishment of American freedom, no less than the leadership which launched the young republic on her career in history. The familiar pride of a Daniel Webster in his alma mater, which was both private and church-related, is echoed by countless other Americans in all walks of life and at all stages of

our growth. And it is demonstrably a faulty interpretation of the mind of such a liberal theorist as Thomas Jefferson which would present him as champion of a monopolistic state system of education.

6. As Catholics, our memory is stirred by the recollection of the valiant efforts of our religious founders in this country to provide, out of their slender resources, for the educational needs of their people. We think of young John Carroll, destined to be our first bishop, conning his lessons at Bohemia Manor, in colonial Maryland. The torch he grasped there was to be carried by myriad hands to enkindle brighter fires from end to end of our expanding nation. It is with honest pride that we survey the development of Catholic education in America, so intimately a part of her cultural growth, so deeply intertwined with the traditions and aspirations of her people. The Catholic school has matured with the Church, a joint product of the foresight of the Bishops and the enlightened generosity of her faithful. It is no foreign importation, no alien growth, but a sturdy native plant, a conspicuous example of a common religious impulse working under the favorable conditions of our republic.

Accomplishment of Public Schools

7. The rise and vigorous expansion of the American educational system is cited, correctly, as one of the major achievements of Western civilization. During the past hundred years, in particular, general education, sponsored by states and communities, religious groups and private bodies, has come very near to the goal of providing adequate educational opportunities for every American. It would be blind prejudice which would refuse to acknowledge, in this connection, the tremendous accomplishment of the public educational agencies. Whatever uneasiness may or must be felt on the score of educational theory and philosophy as illustrated in large areas of American teaching, the plain physical fact of the school system is a matter for unanimous congratulation. This, at least in part, is what freedom has achieved.

8. But if the unparalleled growth of the schools supported by public funds is a mighty tribute to America's zeal for learning and her ambition to build an intelligent democratic society, no less astonishing has been the growth and accomplishment of the private and church-related schools during the same relative period. In candor, it deserves to be said that their record affords an even more impressive example of the American spirit at work, for it has been brought about not by the advantage of public funds nor by the spur of legislative mandate, but by the free cooperation of those convinced of their importance and necessity. It is, incidentally, wholly erroneous to conceive that these schools represent a diminishing force in the American educational system. Their growth today, proportionately, equals where it does not actually exceed that of schools maintained by public authority.

9. Let this be fully understood: Private and church-related schools in America exist not by sufferance but by right. The right is implicit in the whole concept of American freedom and immunity from totalitarian oppression and in the constitutional framework of our federal government and of the sev-

eral states. Under attack it has been rendered explicit by the decision of the Supreme Court of the United States in the celebrated Oregon School Case. Thus far, happily, the right of the parent to educate the child has not been successfully challenged in any American court. The country agrees that this right is basic to the definition of freedom. Be that education provided by the state-supported school, the private school, or the church-affiliated school, the choice of the parent is decisive. If the state has a concurrent right to decree a minimal education for its citizens, as a vital necessity in a modern democratic society, that right does not extend to an arbitrary designation of the school or the educational agency. It is, rather, a general right, limited by the primary right of the parent to exercise his choice according to his best wisdom and his conscience. Indeed, it is worth remarking that while the state may usefully engage in the business of education, as demonstrated in our national experience, it has no authority either to monopolize the field or to arrogate to itself exclusive privileges and powers. The state, by definition, is not itself primarily an educative agency.

10. The right of the parent to attend to the child's education is, moreover, antecedent to any human law or institution. It is vested in his very nature and is demanded as a fulfillment of his actual parenthood. In this it reflects the inviolability of the human person and his freedom under God. It is indeed a right which must be exercised in accordance with sound reason and consistently with the just demands of society, but it remains fundamentally intact in the parents' keeping. It is a manifestation of the law of nature in concrete action. So it is that private and religious education in America rests upon the law of nature as well as upon the law of the land. . . .

12. It is dangerous thinking to suppose that the existence of the private school is an infringement upon the domain of the school supported by public funds. The private school is a concrete demonstration of the fact that education is not a monopoly of public authority. It should be added, moreover, that the private school provides a saving and challenging variety in the total system, beneficial to the whole and manifestly fruitful in its effects. Those who would seek to abolish the private school would not only sin against justice, they would destroy something very precious in American life.

13. Neither is the church-related school a limitation on the right of the state to insure an educated citizenry. It exists not only to fulfill the function of education in our democratic society, but specifically to educate the Christian for his dual citizenship in time and eternity. It exists to teach not only the content of the accepted curriculum, but that which the tax-supported school under present conditions may not teach, namely, positive religion. Other nations, with varying success, have attempted general educational systems in which provision is made for religious instruction in separate church-related schools. Practical considerations, in view of wide religious differences, almost from the outset prevented the American tax-supported schools from following this pattern. There are those now, even among public school educators, who regret the development, involving, as it has, the risk of religious indif-

ferentism and secularism. The solution of the problem is indeed difficult. The alternative, so far as the religious bodies who believe education essential to their mission are concerned, is the school under religious auspices....

18. Church-related schools reflect nothing so clearly as that American spirit which demands unity in the essentials of citizenship while defending to the death those things in which the citizen is guaranteed his freedom.

19. What, then, is the place of the private and church-related schools in America? Their place is one dictated by nothing more than justice and equity, and accorded the recognition of their worth. They have, we repeat, full right to be considered and dealt with as components of the American educational system. They protest against the kind of thinking that would reduce them to a secondary level, and against unfair and discriminatory treatment which would, in effect, write them off as less wholly dedicated to the public welfare than the state-supported schools. The students of these schools have the right to benefit from those measures, grants, or aids, which are manifestly designed for the health, safety, and welfare of American youth, irrespective of the school attended....

> Hugh J. Nolan, ed., *Pastoral Letters of the United States Catholic Bishops* (Washington, D.C.: United States Catholic Conference, 1984), 2:179–84. Printed with permission.

81. Washington Archdiocesan Catholic Lawyers' Committee on Equal Educational Rights, "Freedom of Choice in Education," 7, 14, and 21 April 1961

The Congress is now considering legislation to authorize a program of Federal assistance for education costing $2,300,000,000 over a three-year period. This proposed legislation, as presently drawn, is supported by the National Administration as a means of bringing about "the maximum development of every young American's capacity." (Statement by President Kennedy.)[1] It would give money grants to public elementary and secondary schools but would deny such grants to private and church-related elementary and secondary schools.

This proposed legislation has engendered national concern and has been the subject of intense debate, as many see in it the possible ultimate doom of parochial and private elementary and secondary education and a frustration of the very purpose attributed to this legislation, namely that of providing "rich dividends in the years ahead — in increased economic growth, in enlightened citizens, in national excellence." (Statement by President Kennedy.)[2] While Catholics have always held steadfastly to the upholding of the Constitution, and still do, nevertheless it is the position of Catholic parents, the Catholic hierarchy and many others that it is contrary to principles of social justice, equal treatment and nondiscrimination to provide money grants to public schools

---

1. Text of President Kennedy's special message to Congress on education, *New York Times*, 21 February 1961.
2. Ibid.

but to withhold such grants from private and parochial schools and that such unjust treatment and discrimination is contrary to the best interests of our national existence.

No criticism is raised to the giving of Federal aid to education. It is the position of Catholics that the granting or withholding of Federal aid is a political and economic decision to be made by the citizens of our country acting within the structure of our representative form of Government. But it is further the Catholic position, once Congress decides that Federal aid is necessary, that there should be full equality of treatment with respect to all children whether they be enrolled in public, private or church-related schools....

This is a matter of high principle. The parochial schools of this country are discharging a public service. They provide an educational program which fully satisfies present governmental standards for competence. The state and all the citizens thereof benefit from this educational effort. If massive Federal expenditures are to be made from the tax collections of all the people, this aid should not go only to a select segment, however large, of the population. To the extent that parochial schools provide a recognized and accredited secular education they are entitled to equal treatment.

A child in a parochial school deserves the same opportunity to achieve excellence (the national purpose, as stated by President Kennedy) as his public school neighbor. A physics laboratory, provided by Federal funds, does not teach the tenets of any religious faith. It is equally suitable for instruction whether it be located in a public or parochial school. Any other judgment erroneously assumes that the government may expect to achieve the excellence of its future citizens only in the public schools.

If it is wrong in principle to so discriminate against the private and parochial school children of this country, then any proposed legislation which seeks to effectuate this discrimination would be wrong. It is upon this high ground that Catholic parents and the hierarchy have determined to oppose any aid program which seeks to deprive Catholic children of their opportunities for future intellectual development....

The principle argument raised against the Catholic position is a constitutional one. Our opponents say it clearly violates the First Amendment and breaches the wall of separation between church and state. The question is largely one of the means to be employed. Catholic lawyers together with distinguished non-Catholic constitutional scholars like Professor Corwin[3] of Princeton and Professor Sutherland[4] of Harvard feel that equitable treatment can be afforded the parents of parochial school children without offending the Constitution.

It is helpful to recall the language of the First Amendment.[5] It does not say

---

3. Edward S. Corwin (1878–1963) retired in 1946 after holding the McCormick professorship of jurisprudence at Princeton University since 1918.

4. Arthur E. Sutherland (1902–73) was professor of law at Harvard from 1950 to 1973.

5. Made applicable to the states by the Fourteenth Amendment. Cf. *Everson v. Board of Education*, 330 U.S. 1 (1946).

that there should be an absolute wall of separation between church and state. It says, in relevant part:

"Congress shall make no law respecting an establishment of religion, or prohibiting the free exercise thereof."

These words had a clearly defined purpose to the framers of the Constitution. The word "establishment" possessed an historical significance now lost to many interpreters of the Constitution. It referred to the practice in England and many European countries of establishing a state religion to which all citizens were required to take an oath of allegiance and to support by contributions or taxes. Many American colonies, notably Virginia and Massachusetts Bay, followed this tradition in their early years. Yet to escape these burdens of conscience many colonists had originally come to America and it was to avoid this practice that the language of the First Amendment was framed. There was to be no national church. Persons were to follow the dictates of their conscience. The language of the First Amendment was framed as a *means* to preserve individual freedom of conscience. The latter was the *end* intended, not the secularization of society.

However, there has been engrafted by the Supreme Court upon the words of the First Amendment a phrase taken from the writings of Thomas Jefferson — "a wall of separation between church and state." That this does not mean a wall, high and impenetrable, is clear from the majority opinion of Mr. Justice Douglas[6] in *Zorach* v. *Clauson,* 343 U.S. 306, 312 (1952):

The First Amendment, however, does not say that in every and all respects there shall be a separation of Church and State. Rather, it studiously defines the manner, the specific ways, in which there shall be no concert or union or dependency one on the other. That is the common sense of the matter. Otherwise the state and religion would be aliens to each other — hostile, suspicious, and even unfriendly.

Mr. Justice Reed[7] in his brilliant dissent in *McCollum* v. *Board of Education,* 333 U.S. 203, 238 (1948) has suggested that the court should return to the language of the Amendment and interpret that rather than Jefferson's phrase. Whatever the merits of that suggestion, it is clear that the meaning of the metaphor has gotten so confused that many people cannot distinguish the metaphor from the principles involved.

The First Amendment means simply that the Government may not *actively* and *directly* support any religion. Accordingly, any legislation which is intended to favor directly a particular religion is forbidden. The words of emphasis are "actively" and "directly." Legislation which has an incidental and secondary effect upon religious activity is not forbidden. Legislation which

---

6. William O. Douglas (1898–1980) was an associate justice of the United States Supreme Court from 1939 to 1975.

7. Stanley F. Reed (1884–1980) retired in 1957 after having served for nineteen years as an associate justice of the United States Supreme Court.

accords religious persons the same benefits afforded the public generally is not forbidden.

These principles are clear from the decided cases and from our American traditions. This is what we demand, as Catholic parents, from Government — constitutionally permissible treatment which attempts to equalize our burden with those of our non-Catholic neighbors. . . .

Catholic Standard (Washington), 7, 14, and 21 April 1961; also in John Tracy Ellis, ed., *Documents of American Catholic History* (Wilmington, Del.: Michael Glazier, 1987), 2:655–58. (Footnotes in Ellis.) Printed with permission of the estate of John Tracy Ellis.

Social Questions

In the years after World War II, the shape and scope of Catholic social teaching have changed. Earlier commentators like John A. Ryan called for increased government activism to ameliorate the worst dislocations of economic life. Moreover, the economic and social status of Catholics in the United States was comparatively modest. Catholics were largely to be found in the working classes and among the ranks of recent immigrants. All of this changed dramatically during the Great Depression and the postwar period. Active government intervention in American economic and social life became a fact of life in the United States and assisted many into middle-class status. The rising affluence of American Catholics conditioned their response to the social teaching of the church, providing a wider spectrum of public opinion on the ordering of national economic and social affairs.

One of Catholicism's signal contributions to the public weal has been its network of schools, social welfare centers, and hospitals. The provision of these human services has been one of the most important elements of its public identity.

After World War II, health-care issues became a concern of the federal government in a new way. The Hill-Burton Act of 1949 provided needed federal funds for hospital construction, and government support for health-care research and development increased dramatically. The passage of Medicare and Medicaid in 1964 added health care to the growing list of entitlements to the American population. The heavy human and financial investment of the American Catholic community in hospitals and the steady professionalization of health care are reflected in these documents. Church leaders were quick to seize on the notion advanced by liberal politicians that health care is a right and have supported government initiatives in this regard.

Official Catholic voices turned their attention to those who did not share the ever-widening circle of affluence generated by postwar conditions. Catholic leaders approved of President Johnson's War on Poverty, and Catholic charitable activity dealt extensively with the phenomenon of homelessness that afflicted American cities during the 1980s. A formal and nuanced response to the economic policies of President Ronald Reagan occupied the energies of the American hierarchy, but even before their letter was officially released after the 1984 elections, Catholic laypersons offered a formal rebuttal to certain aspects of the bishops' document — especially the notion of "economic rights."

82. Robert D. Cross, "Catholic Charities," 1962[1]

When James Cardinal Gibbons, archbishop of Baltimore, presented a paper to the World's Parliament of Religions, convened in Chicago in 1893, on "The Needs of Humanity Supplied by the Catholic Religion," he insisted that the Church's strongest claim to the sympathetic interest of outsiders was its "wonderful system of organized benevolence." The Church, he said, had always been mindful of its duty to see "in every human creature a child of God, and brother or sister of Christ." It had been wholly natural, therefore, for American Catholics, just because they were Catholics, to build the hospitals, asylums, protectories, and orphanages that could then be seen in nearly every American city.

Gibbons failed to realize, however, that the range of institutions he rightly admired had no precise counterpart outside the United States and Canada. Christ's command to love one another had no doubt been revered by all Catholics, everywhere, at all times, but only in America had the result been a proliferation of charitable institutions built and maintained and supervised by the faithful. Only in America had need for charity been combined with a strong popular conviction that most human hardship could be alleviated if men would only act constructively, with a political system willing to help the Church to respond in its chosen ways, and with a society that preferred to consign charitable work to denominational hands....

The American Church today, as compared with the Church in contemporary Europe or the American Church of the 1880s, seems confidently activist, optimistically unwilling to accept the inevitability of most human suffering. There are always Catholics who insist that society needs saints more than social crusaders and that those ministering to the unfortunate should do so not to save but to be saved. Thus, the incomparable Peter Maurin of the Catholic Worker movement can, in fine disregard for all social justifications of charity, say to the Bowery derelict, "You give me the chance to practice Christian charity. You are an ambassador of Christ. Thank you."

Other Catholics, out of deeply bourgeois faith in the self-sufficiency of the individual, and from lingering suspicion of the motives of social workers, Catholic and non-Catholic, write saturnine letters to the Brooklyn *Tablet* about

---

1. When this article was published, Robert D. Cross was associate professor of history at Columbia University and the author of *The Emergence of Liberal Catholicism in America* (1958). This issue of the *Atlantic Monthly* was devoted to the topic "The Roman Catholic Church in America."

"do-gooders" and "bleeding hearts." But for each Catholic Worker or rugged individualist, there are dozens of Catholics today who insist that only organized charity can begin to cope with the bewildering variety of charitable needs. No observer, certainly, who has studied the annual reports of the Catholic Charities of the archdiocese of New York or watched on television the recent Catholic Charities show, in which Francis Cardinal Spellman and a number of professional entertainers joined efforts to appeal for funds, can believe that the Church today is willing to rely primarily on spontaneous impulse for its charity work. Efficiency, rationality, concerted planning are the watchwords....

Catholic charities today make use of both the volunteer and the paid worker, the amateur and the professional, and with much less sense of lurking irreconcilability than nagged at both sides during the years when the "new charity" was first bruited. This is partly because government has assumed responsibility for making most direct financial grants to the needy; Catholics are thereby freed from the old worry that limited funds were being squandered by improvident priests and laymen.

Atlantic Monthly 210, no. 2 (August 1962): 100–114.

83. Bishop Walter Sullivan, Address to the Committee for National Health Insurance, 12 September 1975[1]

I am here with you this afternoon not as an official representative of a national or church organization; I cannot claim to speak for the American Catholic bishops or for the Catholic population. Rather, I am here with you this afternoon as a concerned pastor and as a religious leader. I am the Catholic bishop of a newly-aligned diocese of 37,000 square miles in the state of Virginia. Not the Virginia that can be seen in the sprawling suburbs across the Potomac, but the other four-fifths of our state, from the farmlands of the eastern shore to the coal regions of central Appalachia.

From my travels and ministry in the different parts of our diocese, I can put very human faces with all the dimensions of the current crisis in our health care system — the migrant farm workers of our eastern shore, the black lung miner of Appalachia, the trapped share-cropper of southside Virginia, the despondent unemployed and the fearful marginally employed of our central cities. But I know that you, too, have names and faces to go with the problems and injustices we have heard described this afternoon.

There is no need for me to elaborate further the crisis in obtaining adequate health care today for the poor, for the oppressed and even for the middle-class. There is no need for me to elaborate further on the vast inequities in the quality of health care received by different segments of our society. We each

---

1. The Committee for National Health Insurance was a group representing some labor interests and lobbying for the Health Security Bill, introduced by Senator Edward Kennedy and Representative Al Corman (D-Cal.). Bishop Sullivan was a member of the committee and a member of the Health Affairs Committee of the U.S. Catholic Conference.

bring with us a high degree of personal concern for people and a long history within each of our denominations of institutional care for the sick.

Nevertheless, I think we will agree that today's crisis in health care is related to great inequities in our socio-economic system. We recognize that those most in need of health care and unable to obtain it continue to face many *structural* injustices. These problems are so vast that we cannot make an adequate response simply with greater pastoral care nor with more health care personnel and facilities. Rather we must confront the underlying issues in the political area — where the decisions are made that affect our socio-economic system.

Just as church men and women have long been active in providing direct care for the sick, we must now become equally active in advocating the political change that will make adequate health care a reality for all our people.

If we believe that the right to health care is implied in the very right to life itself, then we must act to create the structures that will guarantee and protect this right. We must advocate legislative change.

- That will make health care *financially* accessible to all people by guaranteeing payment for health care services without co-insurance, deductibles, and high premiums;

- That will make health care *physically* accessible to all our people by encouraging a more equitable distribution of personnel and facilities;

- That will provide people with a sense of involvement and self-determination in the health care system by having broad citizen participation on all levels of planning and policy development;

- That will make *all* forms of health care accessible to people, most especially forms of diagnostic and preventive care which can eliminate future suffering and great cost;

- That will provide the same caliber and quality of health care services for all people regardless of their economic or social status.

The above goals must be more than just part of "the great American dream," ideals which are never translated into reality. Many of us will agree that necessary changes can only be brought about by a significant program of national health insurance. I am convinced that we have a responsibility as religious leaders to do all in our power to insure that such a program be as just and equitable as possible.

For this reason, we must analyze and evaluate the numerous legislative proposals that have been introduced in the present Congress. In evaluating such legislative proposals, the churches should always advocate the concerns and interests of the voiceless, the oppressed, the least powerful of our society. Physicians and health care professionals have concerns and interests regarding proposed legislation: they can, they will, they do voice those concerns and make themselves heard. Insurance corporations have concerns and interests regarding pending legislation: they can, they will, they do voice those concerns and make themselves heard. It is our role as religious leaders to raise up the concerns and interests of those who have so few to speak on their behalf.

So I come today — and hopefully we all come — to learn and to share our concerns for all people, especially for those most in need. I hope that we come with a sense of real urgency, ready to deal with the complexities and ambiguities involved in the issue of national health insurance so that our religious denominations might ultimately exert strong religious leadership in this area.

Many of us come to this discussion from religious traditions with a long history of concern for the sick through our own institutional expressions of health care delivery. Of these we are justifiably proud and concerned. We must work hard and seriously to insure a smooth harmony between the coming of a national health insurance program and the continued role of churches and other voluntary agencies in the delivery of health care.

We come with many concerns and questions from our unique position as members of the religious community. We are concerned about health care coverage for those residents who are not citizens of our country. We are concerned about safeguards for voluntary hospitals which do not receive many forms of governmental aid. We are concerned about safeguarding the conscientious objection of health care professionals and institutions to certain medical practices such as abortion and euthanasia. These are serious questions and concerns. These concerns should add to the urgency and importance of this discussion; they must *not* make us hesitate to become involved and to exert clear moral leadership.

We come here today at the invitation of the Committee for National Health Insurance to consider specifically our support for the Health Security Act. This bill has been drafted by politicians, not by gods. It is not a work of perfection. There is need for discussion and clarification regarding some of the concerns that I have just mentioned. Nonetheless, it appears to me that the Health Security Act, compared to other legislative proposals that have been submitted, is the best basis for a socially just system of national health insurance for our country. No other bill provides as *much* coverage for as *many* people in as *equitable* a fashion as the Health Security Act.

It is my hope that we will live up to our responsibility as religious leaders to study, discuss and evaluate the legislative proposals for national health insurance. We believe that health care is a right; if we fail to witness to that belief clearly and strongly in the political arena — where that right can be made real and can be protected — then we have failed to act responsibly as religious men and women and as moral leaders in our time. As we begin the celebration of our nation's Bicentennial, the religious community must continually call our nation towards its ideal of "liberty and justice for all." It is in this context that we are challenged to raise the issue of national health insurance before our people and to exert the leadership which is expected of us.

Origins 5, no. 15 (2 October 1975): 233–34. Published with permission of Bishop Sullivan.

84. National Conference of Catholic Bishops, Statement on the Housing Crisis, 20 November 1975

I. Introduction

The United States is in the midst of a severe housing crisis. This is a broader, more pervasive and more complicated phenomenon than the customary photographs of urban slums and rural shacks indicate. It involves more people, more neighborhoods and communities than was thought to be the case even a few years ago. It touches millions of poor families who live in inhuman conditions, but it also involves many middle-income families whose ability to provide themselves with decent housing is being painfully tested.

Rising costs of shelter, maintenance and utilities — as well as high interest rates and regressive property taxes — are forcing many families to live in inadequate housing or do without other basic essentials. Other low- and middle-income families have been confined to neighborhoods without adequate services, minimal safety or necessary community life....

II. Housing: A Pastoral Imperative for the Church

In the face of this cruel and discouraging condition, we, the bishops of the United States, cannot remain silent. The reality of this housing crisis provides a challenge to our country as we approach the bicentennial.

In the past 200 years our nation, with the abundant blessing of God, has overcome many other complex problems and has provided a standard of living previously unknown to the world.

We are not so naive as to believe that there are easy solutions to this crisis. The housing crisis is overwhelming. It touches facets of our economic, political and social life that are extremely complicated. Any attempt to solve these intricate problems can given rise to petty self-interest and alarming divisions.

Addressing ourselves to our own people and to the whole country, we plead with all, in both the private and the public sector, to confront our housing crisis with the courage, conviction and talent that have brought about our greatest achievements in the past.

As preachers of the gospel, we proclaim the message of Jesus Christ who identified himself with the needs of the least of the brethren. The second great commandment is to love our neighbor.

We cannot deny the crying needs for decent housing experienced by the least of the brethren in our society. Effective love of neighbor involves concern for his or her living conditions.

We begin with the recognition that decent housing is a right. Our Catholic tradition, eloquently expressed by Pope John XXIII and Pope Paul VI, insists that shelter is one of the basic rights of the human person.[1] The Second Vatican Council has said with great directness: "There must be made available

---

1. Pope John XXIII, *Peace on Earth* (April 1963), 11; Pope Paul VI, *A Call to Action* (May 1971), 11–12.

to all men everything necessary for leading a life truly human, such as food, clothing and shelter...."[2]

As teachers, pastors and leaders, we have the responsibility to articulate the principles and values that govern the church's concern for housing. We believe that each individual possesses an inherent dignity and priceless worth because he or she is created in the image and likeness of God. We also believe each person should have the opportunity to grow and develop his or her potential to the fullest extent possible.

Human dignity and development are threatened whenever social and economic forces imprison or degrade people. We call on Catholics and all citizens to join us in working against these debilitating forces.

In particular, we take this opportunity to reflect on the consequences of poor housing. The physical and social environment play an important role in forming and influencing the lives of people. We cannot ignore the terrible impact of degrading and indecent living conditions on people's perception of themselves and their future. The protection of the human dignity of every person and the right to a decent home require both individual action and structural policies and practices.

Our faith teaches us that "the earth is the Lord's" (Psalm 24) and that wealth and private property are held in trust for others. We are trustees of God's creation, and as good stewards we are required to exercise that trust for the common good and benefit of our brothers and sisters.

The role of those who own land or other wealth is one of stewardship. While the church has traditionally recognized the right to private property, that right is always subject to certain limitations. As the Second Vatican Council pointed out:

> "God intended the earth and all that it contains for the use of every human being and people.... Whatever the forms of ownership may be, as adapted to the legitimate institutions of people according to diverse and changeable circumstances, attention must always be paid to the universal purpose for which created goods are meant. In using them, therefore, a man should regard his lawful possessions not merely as his own but also as common property in the sense that they should accrue to the benefit not only of himself but of others."[3]

This teaching is central to a discussion of the ethical and moral dimensions of the housing crisis. It imposes major responsibilities on those whose land and shelter resources or skills might help society guarantee the right to a decent home. This concept of stewardship must be reflected in our concern and action on housing. It must be practiced not only by individuals, but also by institutions.

---

2. Pastoral Constitution on the Church in the Modern World (December 1965), 26.
3. Ibid., 69.

The church must give witness to this trusteeship in the use of its own property and resources. Just as individual property holders are bound by this principle, so it must be reflected in public policy at each level of government.

Our concern is not simply for houses or programs but for the people who inhabit these dwellings or are affected by these programs. These include families whose attempts to create a stable and wholesome family life are inhibited by inadequate living conditions; people and parish communities in neighborhoods without the housing services or community life which foster love and Christian service; the many elderly whose meager incomes are consumed by housing maintenance costs, utility bills and property taxes; and countless young families who lack the resources to acquire decent housing....

Origins 5, no. 24 (4 December 1975): 375–76. Printed with permission.

85. Archbishop John Quinn, "Health Ministry in a Pluralist Nation," Address to the Catholic Hospital Association, 4 June 1979[1]

There are two great issues confronting Catholic health facilities today. The first lies in the area of social justice. The second in the area of medical-moral issues.

Our ability to deal with the enormous complexities of both depends to a large extent on the recognition that both converge at a single point. The human person, the dignity of the human person, is the basic principle of all Catholic social teaching, as it is of Catholic medical ethics.

It is not surprising, then, that a key document of the council, *Gaudium et Spes* ("The Church in the Modern World"), states that the fundamental role of the church in society is to be the sign and the safeguard of the transcendent dignity of the human person. And most recently Pope John Paul II has made this the theme of his first encyclical, *Redemptor Hominis.* Consciously building on the conciliar teaching, the pope called the whole church to the vision of the human person as the "primary and fundamental way for the church."

This is a statement of moral truth: It affirms the defense of human dignity as a preeminent task for the church in its teaching and its social witness. But it is also a religious truth because for the church the human person must always be understood through the key of divine revelation and consequently in the light of a destiny which surpasses the limits of this world. For the church the understanding of the dignity of the human person cannot be confined within the narrow limits of any merely human ideology or philosophical system, and above all it cannot be understood in terms of a purely materialistic or atheistic philosophical or political system. The church, then, has an altogether unique

---

1. Archbishop Quinn was president of the National Conference of Catholic Bishops at the time of this address. The Catholic Hospital Association was in the process of changing its name to the Catholic Health Association when Quinn delivered this address. He uses the older form in the body of the speech. See Christopher J. Kauffman, *Ministry and Meaning: A Religious History of Catholic Health Care in the United States* (New York: Crossroad, 1995), 303.

understanding of the human person and it is ultimately rooted in the person of Christ.

Conviction about the dignity of the human person leads to other moral affirmations. The logic of the argument is simple, but its implications are manifold. To protect human dignity, Catholic social teaching affirms the existence of a spectrum of rights and responsibilities which each person possesses precisely and solely because he or she is human.

The timeliness of this affirmation is evident before the grave and spreading tendency toward the reification of the human person, reducing the human person to the level of a thing, a pawn of economic or political interests, a commodity, a unit of production. The transcendence of the human person is also violated when reduced to a mere instrument for the purposes of scientific or medical progress. In an age increasingly influenced by this attitude, it is important to remember that each life is not only equal in dignity, but that that dignity is in turn the title giving each person a clearly defined range of inviolable rights. Among the basic moral claims to be made in the name of human dignity Pope John XXIII specifically included the right to health care.

But human rights and human dignity are not simply abstractions or mere theory. They exist and are protected in a social context. A Catholic view of anthropology is radically social. The person requires the social setting of family, civic community and church to grow and develop and to fulfill the divinely given purpose of human existence. And because the social setting of our life in its political, economic, legal, cultural and religious dimensions is directly linked to our dignity, the way a society is organized is a moral question of the first order. And so if health care is a right rooted in human dignity, then the structure of the health care system is not merely a question of politics, economics or bureaucracy: It is a moral question — there is an imperative that the right be satisfied.

1. Health Care and Social Justice

Although the very definition of what we mean by health is still publicly debated, there is growing agreement that access to a defined range of basic medical services is not a privilege but a right. The need of the moment, then, is to express our conviction by sharing in the public debate which will translate rights claims into realistic policy. As you are aware, the U.S. Catholic Conference, along with the Catholic Hospital Association and the National Conference of Catholic Charities, has been in the health care dialogue for the past several years. It is our intention at the USCC to continue and intensify our participation in that dialogue.

A particular aspect of the problem as it confronts us today is the tension between privately sponsored health care and government supervision and intervention in the health care area.

Almost all proposals for reform of the health care system accept an increasing role for public funding and recognize a correlative degree of increased government participation in the system. At the same time, Catholic health care facilities, like other private institutions, are justly concerned about the growing intrusion of government through the excessive use of its regulatory power. It is understandable, then, that there is considerable disagreement about the levels of funding and the kind of public participation which is needed.

In his masterful encyclical *Pacem in Terris*, Pope John XXIII sketches out a framework within which we can come to grips with this problem. First of all, he noted that modern life is characterized by increasing interdependence. And this is both a cause and an effect of increasing state intervention in the life of society. This phenomenon by which the state becomes a part of almost every significant aspect of social life the pope called "the process of socialization."

Balancing the principle of socialization the pope articulates another principle, the principle of subsidiarity. The primary purpose of this principle has been to argue for a pluralistic approach to social organization, affirming the legitimacy of a variety of actors in the social process and endorsing state intervention only when it has been demonstrated that other agencies and organizations cannot secure what is required for the common good.

Consequently, the principle of subsidiarity does not rule out state action in the various spheres of society. On the contrary, the state has a moral character and cannot stand by passively when the basic needs of the person remain unfulfilled. And so, while Pope John has not resolved our problem, he has provided a framework or moral principle which we must use creatively in the public debate about health care and human dignity.

2. Health Care: The Medical-Moral Issues

As in the area of health care, so in the area of medical-moral questions the church has a rich tradition of ethical wisdom.

And here we face two kinds of problems. First, there are the old questions which have qualitatively new dimensions, questions such as medical transplants or care of the terminally ill, for instance. These exist in a new setting today, one transformed by new possibilities which in turn create new problems.

The traditional moral calculus provides some help in assessing these issues but it does not of itself deal with all the dimensions of the contemporary medical scene.

Second, there are new questions which have never been considered in any previous generation; the problems of fetal experimentation and *in vitro* fertilization fit into this category. In dealing with these new questions, it is not that we lack moral wisdom from the past to assess them, but the practical moral decisions they force us to confront as issues of both personal and public morality have never faced past generations.

But underlying both the old and the new question is the essential moral question of the technological age: In a time when we can do almost anything, what should we do? This is the challenge a proliferating technology offers to our moral and religious vision, and Pope John Paul II has described this impact of technology on human dignity as the central drama of our time. Each time we expand our capacity to act through technological innovation, we expand our range of moral choice and are confronted with the need to make a moral decision.

The most difficult moral choices, however, arise at the point where the social justice questions and the medical-moral questions intersect.

For example, Catholic social teaching maintains that health care is a right and is necessary for the protection and promotion of human dignity. In a modern industrial society this implies the necessity of a significant degree of state intervention to achieve this right for each person.

At the same time, expanding state intervention means greater specification by law and policy of the kinds of health care which should be provided at public expense and the range of health services which are to be available in institutions receiving public funding. This degree of intervention appears problematic when we consider the state of medical-moral debate in the United States today. This very strength and clarity of our Catholic moral teaching mean that we hold quite explicit positions on some of the most controverted questions of the day: abortion, fetal experimentation, euthanasia, contraception and sterilization.

And so we come to the question, "How are we to relate our social justice objectives and our medical-moral concerns in a coherent policy?"

We must first face this question among ourselves within the church. We must be clear where we stand on each of the specific issues and, as Catholic institutions giving a Catholic witness in a pluralistic society, we must stand with the magisterium of the church. It is also important to look ahead and determine how we will stand when the specific issues become part of a general policy of health care.

Our Catholic tradition is rich in resources enabling us to address both aspects of the problem, but we need more systematic consideration of how to use our resources in shaping a coherent and consistent moral policy in conformity with the church's moral teaching.

This formulation of a coherent policy within Catholic institutions is a precondition for the ultimate test of shaping health policy. It is necessary to project our conception of policy into the wider public debate of a pluralistic society. And we must remember that a truly pluralistic society is not one in which there can be only private and individual differences, but one in which there can be varieties of institutions and policies as well. But even in a pluralistic setting it is necessary to formulate some public policy regarding the moral dilemmas of modern medicine.

Pope Paul VI called the church to the evangelization of cultures. He said: "For the church it is a question not only of preaching the Gospel in ever wider geographic areas or to ever greater numbers of people, but also of affecting and even upsetting through the power of the Gospel, people's criteria of judgment, their values, points of interest, lines of thought, sources of inspiration and models of life.... What matters is to evangelize human culture and cultures."

How we project our twin concerns of social justice and medical ethics in courageous and unambiguous fidelity to the teaching of the church is the test of our ability to evangelize our culture. There can be no question that it is our right and our obligation to preserve *space* within which our religious and moral values may be affirmed and may govern the functioning of our institutions. But the task is not purely defensive. We should always see the pluralistic dialogue and the public debate about social justice and health care as an opportunity to evangelize: to articulate a vision and argue a case in the name of human dignity revealed by God in all its transcendent beauty.

Origins 9, no. 7 (5 July 1979): 104–5. Printed with permission of Archbishop Quinn.

86. Bishop Joseph M. Sullivan, "Budget Cuts and Human Lives: The Harsh Reality of the Economic System: Testimony before the House Committee on the Budget," 22 February 1982

I am Bishop Joseph Sullivan of Brooklyn, N.Y. I am pleased to appear before you on behalf of the U.S. Catholic Conference, which is the national social action arm of the Roman Catholic bishops, and on behalf of the National Conference of Catholic Charities, which represents the largest network of voluntary providers of social services in this nation.

These two institutions bring to your discussion two important resources: 1) a rich heritage of social teaching on human rights; and 2) a wide range of direct experiences in providing for the needs of the poor in this country. From this perspective I would like to suggest two points for your consideration: 1) that the impact of last year's budget cuts has already been so severe that voluntary agencies have nowhere near the capacity to take up the slack; and 2) that, consistent with the Catholic Church's social teaching, we strongly believe that when other social institutions are unable to do so the government has the responsibility to ensure that the basic needs of all the citizens are met. Therefore, we believe that additional entitlement cuts proposed for fiscal year 1983 should be rejected....

As the budget was being debated last year, we were assured repeatedly that it would not be balanced on the backs of the needy, that a "safety net" would be maintained and that the budget cuts would streamline social programs by improving efficiency and eliminating the non-needy. While my own work at Catholic Charities suggests that last year's cuts have not produced a more efficient system, I believe the more important question to be addressed is: What has been the impact on the poor? The news is not good....

The Impact of Last Year's Budget Cuts

What we have heard from across the country — from individual bishops, from Catholic Charities agencies, from inner-city pastors, from organizers of self-help programs for the poor, from volunteers who are running soup lines, food pantries and emergency shelters — is essentially the same message: The cuts in entitlement programs have hurt the poor severely.

Some people are going without the bare minimum required for a decent standard of living. In many states the full impact of last year's cuts has not yet been felt. It will take until later this spring and summer for all the changes to have their complete impact. In many cases the resources of the states are already pressed to the limits in their ability to cushion the blow of federal cuts.

The National Conference of Catholic Charities has asked its member agencies and institutions (some 750 around the country) to complete an impact survey on the effects of the fiscal year 1982 budget on their programs and services, on the number of clients served and on the numbers of new community-service programs initiated. This survey is not yet complete or compiled, but we would be happy to furnish its results to the task force, if you wish. Even now, however, without all the final data, we know a lot about the impact of the budget cuts. We know because the people affected by the budget cuts show up on the doorsteps of thousands of Catholic parishes across the country. They show up at hundreds of Catholic Charities agencies and institutions and at untold numbers of other church-sponsored programs for the poor.

Before the National Conference of Catholic Charities finalized its impact survey, we did a phone survey of nine agencies of varying size and in different geographical regions. In each case the level of services is being reduced significantly because of federal and state retrenchment. In only one case has the state moved to make up the difference represented by the federal cuts. In each case Catholic Charities budgets have been reduced — by amounts ranging from a low of $50,000 in a small agency which had little in the way of purchase of services or direct contracts, to more than $1.7 million in a moderately sized agency. All agencies report a large increase in volunteers working in their programs and also a heavy increase in the number of people coming for emergency assistance, housing, food and a variety of services.

Despite the budget cuts, the overall level of activity has increased in these agencies. How long they can sustain such increases is not clear. While it is true that during the past several recessions Catholic Charities nationwide has gone into deficit, this situation cannot be sustained forever.

Allow me to cite several examples from individual dioceses that have felt the effects of the budget cuts. Here in the Archdiocese of Washington requests for emergency financial assistance have doubled and tripled at Catholic Charities offices and the lines at soup kitchens are longer than ever before. For the first time we are seeing in these lines not only the chronically destitute but many new faces — for example, the recently unemployed, the working mother who has lost AFDC benefits. At one parish hundreds of people wait in line for a meager 60 cents to help them through one more day. The parishes and volunteers who provide these services say that the demands on their limited resources have been staggering this past year.

In the Archdiocese of Detroit, Archbishop Szoka reports that nearly every Catholic social service agency has reported an increase of at least 100 percent in requests for material assistance. For example, at an emergency food center run by the Capuchin Fathers in the archdiocese, demand has doubled since last year. Close to 1,000 people are being served there every day....

One final example from the Archdiocese of St. Paul-Minneapolis. A woman there, knowing of the lack of adequate shelter for the homeless, left a stack of blankets in an unlocked car overnight. The next morning she found six adults sleeping inside, huddled together against the cold.

I could go on with a long litany of examples, but the message would be the same — the poor are paying a terrible price as a result of last year's budget cuts.

I have listened carefully to the suggestion that the voluntary sector and the churches in particular can and should take up the slack caused by the budget cuts. For example, in New York recently, President Reagan said: "If every church and synagogue in the United States would average adopting 10 poor families...we could eliminate all government welfare in this country, federal, state and local."

Role of Government

This suggestion, that private charity can increase sufficiently to make key entitlement and social programs unnecessary, ignores both reality and history. Even a preliminary examination of the dollars and resources involved makes it obvious that the voluntary sector cannot replace major government programs.

If we consider only the $35 billion–$40 billion in federal cuts that were approved last year, it is clear that the gap cannot be filled either by the churches or by the entire voluntary sector. In fact, for several reasons the voluntary sector is more hard pressed now than before the cuts. A preliminary study by the Urban Institute indicated that the cuts will mean an estimated loss of more than $27 billion of federal revenue to the voluntary sector during a three-year period. In addition, a similar study by the Urban Institute indicates that the tax cuts that were approved will create a disincentive to give to charitable causes, resulting in a further loss of revenue, despite the passage of the charitable contributions legislation last year. And, finally, the increase in demand for services and emergency assistance has been so great since the budget cuts took effect, that they threaten to overwhelm the resources of many human needs programs in the voluntary sector....

In the end the churches and the voluntary sector as a whole cannot be expected to fill the growing gap created by the budget cuts. While the religious community has been and will continue to serve those in need, our efforts should not be viewed as a basis for the government's abdication of its own responsibility. The churches cannot by their charity be mufflers of the harsh injustices imposed by an unresponsive government. The return of soup lines and the dramatic increase in the demands for emergency food assistance and financial aid should not be interpreted as signs of success for the "new voluntarism." They are instead sad symbols of a retreat by government from a fundamental responsibility.

This brings me to the core of the message that I would like to leave with you this morning. That message has to do with basic human rights and the role of government in guaranteeing that these rights are protected. The Catholic Church has a long tradition of social teaching on human rights. I believe it is directly relevant to the subject of entitlements before this task force. Allow me briefly to summarize that teaching.

The dignity of the human person is one of the key elements in all of Catholic social teaching. Made in the image of God, the human person is endowed with a special dignity. This dignity generates obligations, which in turn point to basic human rights. These rights are universal and arise from the very nature of the human person. In his encyclical, *Pacem in Terris,* Pope John XXIII listed some of these rights:

"Every person has the right to life, to bodily integrity and to the means which are suitable for the proper development of life; these are primarily food, clothing, shelter, rest, medical care, and finally the necessary social services."

We believe that these rights are a kind of base line — a set of minimum conditions of material well-being which must be met if human dignity is to be protected. The Catholic Church fully recognizes the significance of classifying these basic necessities as rights. For rights are not matters of privilege or choice. Rights are functions of duties. They imply an obligation on the part of society, and ultimately this responsibility rests on the government. When, through the normal workings of the economy and the social system, the basic material needs of citizens are not met, the government has the responsibility to intervene. It has a duty to protect the fundamental rights of all by seeing to it that no one goes without adequate income, food, shelter, health care, etc. By no means does the church include all desirable material goods in the category of human rights. On the contrary, we consider as rights only those necessities required for a basic level of human decency — those essentials without which basic human development and human dignity are impossible.

The harsh reality of America's present economic system is that, without substantial and effective government intervention, people will go hungry; families will be homeless; mothers and children will be without basic health care. In theory one might hope that the government would not have to be the direct provider of these services; in reality, however, given the best efforts of the private sector, government must bear a large share of the burden. In short, the powers of government must be used in a constructive way, directly as well as indirectly, to guarantee a minimum level of decency for all Americans.

Some have challenged the very notion of entitlements and have said that people are not entitled to any services. Our Catholic tradition, as I have said, implies something quite different. Human dignity generates moral obligations. These in turn undergird true human rights. We believe that all people have a right, an entitlement, to the basic necessities of life. When these basic needs go unmet, the government has the ultimate responsibility to intervene.

Seen from this perspective, the cuts in entitlement programs proposed for fiscal year 1983 are intolerable. Particularly in the case of food stamps, AFDC, and Medicaid, the cuts constitute a denial of the most basic needs for thousands of Americans. They are in this sense detrimental to human dignity. They represent a partial abandonment of one of the most fundamental roles that government is called to perform.

The enactment of AFDC, food stamps, Medicaid and other entitlement programs, were important national achievements. They represented our progress as a society in recognizing new roles and responsibilities for government. We see that when mothers and children were dislocated because of economic forces beyond their control, when people were hungry or unemployed through no fault of their own, then it was to the benefit of our society as a whole for the government to provide the basic entitlements. We are a more secure nation, a more humane society, as a result of these government initiatives. Now, in a time of increased economic pressures, there must be no abandonment of the government's responsibility, no retreat from the social progress that has marked our history in the past 50 years. . . .

Allow me to offer from our Catholic tradition a principle which I hope and pray will be a moral criterion that will govern the actions of the Budget Committee and the entire Congress in the months ahead. That principle is as follows: The poor have a right to have their minimum needs met before the less basic desires and wants of others are fulfilled. I submit that this moral principle should take precedence over the purely political and economic factors which are inherent in the budget debate. The nation's current economic and budgetary problems are obviously very serious. They will require difficult choices. But these problems can and must be solved without punishing the poor, without violating their rights to basic necessities. In the Christian tradition, how we treat the poor is seen as a measure of our religious faith. I believe it is also a measure of our health as a nation and our wisdom as a people. . . .

> *Origins* 11, no. 40 (18 March 1982): 629, 631–33. Printed with permission of Bishop Sullivan.

87. Michael Novak, "The Two Catholic Letters on the U.S. Economy," 1985[1]

Now that the flurry of early discussion has passed, it's time to evaluate the pastoral letter of the Catholic bishops on the U.S. economy more coolly, and with it the lay letter issued by thirty-one Catholic laypersons headed by William E. Simon.

---

1. This is a response to the first draft of the bishops' pastoral letter on the economy (1984). The final version, *A Pastoral Message: Economic Justice for All*, was issued by the National Conference of Catholic Bishops in November 1986 after considerable revision. See document 88, below, for excerpts from the final text.

The bishops' letter has four parts. First, the bishops give a sound justification for their concern about the effects of economic life on the religious life of persons and families.

Second, they give a biblical justification for Christian concern about the poor most of all.

Third, they set forth at some length a new interpretation of the last one hundred years of Catholic social thought, distilling it into several useful (but theologically debatable) guiding principles.

Finally, in the longest part of their letter, they select several specific areas and make quite specific recommendations on poverty and welfare, employment, cooperative social planning, and foreign aid. This last part, especially the short section on poverty, received most of the early public attention.

In some ways, the press may have been misled by the short press summary the bishops attached to their draft, which, much more than the draft itself, stressed highly political state-oriented analyses and state solutions.

The bishops are not alone in wanting to help the poor. Since 1962, when John F. Kennedy launched the extensive welfare reform that was to lead to "the Great Society," the people of the United States have become nearly thirty times more generous in governmental aid to the poor (cash and in-kind), on an annual basis. The problem is, the design of these expenditures seems to be causing extensive damage to poor families, as shown in startling figures for illegitimacy, single-parent households, and the rapidly growing number of children affected thereby.

You don't have to be a Catholic to wish to help the poor. John Stuart Mill observed a century ago that the measure of a good society is how well it helps its weakest members. But actually helping the poor is quite different from merely wanting to help. The argument today concerns the effectiveness of programs, not simply their good intentions. The ideas offered by the bishops are, mainly, old ideas, some of which have failed in the past. In principle, most Americans believe in helping the poor; in practice, many both left and right are uneasy about the methods so far used.

Insofar as the poor or the unemployed can be helped by jobs, economic activism is by far a better agent of change than political activism. The bishops recognize this. Yet they actually have very little advice for economic activists — workers, entrepreneurs, managers, finance officers, and the like. Their letter often approaches practical problems in the light of what the state can or should do. This is a disappointment.

The lay letter, issued just before the bishops' letter (and not in criticism of it, but as a complement) by William E. Simon, myself, and twenty-nine other Catholic laypersons, suggests that Catholic laypersons in suburban parishes, skilled in entrepreneurship, should be invited to put personal efforts into helping Catholics in poor parishes to teach such skills and help local economic activists get businesses started. In poor neighborhoods, there is invariably a lot of work to be done and a lot of unemployed labor — *some* catalyst is needed to put these two factors together creatively.

Taking a Stand on Specifics

The entire last part of the bishops' letter reads rather more like a party platform than does the parallel part in the lay letter. The lay group brought the argument down to specifics, and then mentioned a wide range of specific programs, but without endorsing any. The religious point is to show how the moral principles apply to concrete approaches, but without foreclosing the question about which specific approaches will actually work. Two persons sharing common moral ideals might well disagree about which practical courses of action will best achieve them. The bishops' draft took the risk of being more partisan.

In fact, U.S. Catholics include rádicals and conservatives, moderates and liberals. All devout Catholics do not and need not agree on specific political programs.

As the press has widely noted, the bishops' document leans to the left of [Walter] Mondale; *Newsweek* called it "God as Social Democrat." Is it right to divide the church along political lines? Should not the bishops stand above all factions? No moderate or conservative critic had a chance to read the bishops' draft before it appeared, in order to warn the bishops away from needlessly inflammatory language.

For example, the bishops used the slogan that Tom Hayden and Jane Fonda have chosen to describe their agenda: "economic democracy." They repeat the slogan of the sixties: "Participation in the decisions which shape our lives." The full implications of these slogans seem to escape the bishops; they voice none of the necessary criticisms.

Endorsing "Economic Rights"

But the biggest bombshell in the bishops' letter has so far been overlooked. Several times the bishops call for new "economic rights" to go along with traditional U.S. political and civil rights. In stressing this point on television and in interviews, the bishops show that they are serious about this. At least one member of the bishops' writing staff has said they intend to inspire a "radical" restructuring of American society. The Jesuit who wrote the relevant sections, David Hollenbach, has even suggested: "The right to subsistence has never been a right protected by the Constitution, but the bishops are saying we need that basic right."

Such a move would surely alter the role of the state in the U.S. economy. For if the state is given the duty to supply every American with a job, income, and other benefits, the state will also gain immense new powers: to limit population, for example, and to send people where the jobs are (Siberia!). In many states today, economic rights do not supplement, in practice they replace, the rights of individuals. Conflicts of rights are inevitable. Granting the state such new responsibilities and powers is no light step.

"Economic democracy" and "economic rights" go far beyond the ideal of helping the poor. They offer a rival design for the U.S. political economy.

Indeed, many of us think, they are not compatible with it. One can, of course, speak of "the right to a job" merely in a declarative manner, not intending a fully formed constitutional right. In that case, the bishops do not really intend "radical restructuring."

Heavy debate is bound to continue during 1985. The bishops' second draft (due in May) and their third draft (due in November) are likely to be much improved.

Robert Royal, ed., *Challenge and Response: Critiques of the Catholic Bishops' Draft Letter on the U.S. Economy* (Washington, D.C.: Ethics and Public Policy Center, 1985), 30–32. Reprinted with permission of the author.

88. National Conference of Catholic Bishops, *A Pastoral Message: Economic Justice for All,* November 1986

...Chapter II, Section B, Part 2: Human Rights: The Minimum Conditions for Life in Community

79. Catholic social teaching spells out the basic demands of justice in greater detail in the human rights of every person. These fundamental rights are prerequisites for a dignified life in community. The Bible vigorously affirms the sacredness of every person as a creature formed in the image and likeness of God. The biblical emphasis on covenant and community also shows that human dignity can only be realized and protected in solidarity with others. In Catholic social thought, therefore, respect for human rights and a strong sense of both personal and community responsibility are linked, not opposed. Vatican II described the common good as "the sum of those conditions of social life which allow social groups and their individual members relatively thorough and ready access to their own fulfillment."[1] These conditions include the rights to fulfillment of material needs, a guarantee of fundamental freedoms, and the protection of relationships that are essential to participation in the life of society.[2] These rights are bestowed on human beings by God and grounded in the nature and dignity of human persons. They are not created by society. Indeed society has a duty to secure and protect them.[3]

80. The full range of human rights has been systematically outlined by John XXIII in his encyclical *Peace on Earth.* His discussion echoes the United Nations Universal Declaration of Human Rights and implies that internationally accepted human rights standards are strongly supported by Catholic teaching. These rights include the civil and political rights to freedom of speech, worship, and assembly. A number of human rights also concern human welfare and are of a specifically economic nature. First among these

1. Vatican Council II, *The Pastoral Constitution on the Church in the Modern World,* 26.
2. Pope John Paul II, Address at the General Assembly of the United Nations (2 October 1979), 13, 14.
3. See Pope Pius XII, 1941 Pentecost Address, in Vincent Yzermans, ed., *The Major Addresses of Pope Pius XII* (St. Paul: North Central, 1961), 1:32–33.

are the rights to life, food, clothing, shelter, rest, medical care, and basic education. These are indispensable to the protection of human dignity. In order to ensure these necessities, all persons have a right to earn a living, which for most people in our economy is through remunerative employment. All persons also have a right to security in the event of sickness, unemployment, and old age. Participation in the life of the community calls for the protection of this same right to employment, as well as the right to healthful working conditions, to wages, and other benefits sufficient to provide individuals and their families with a standard of living in keeping with human dignity, and to the possibility of property ownership.[4] These fundamental personal rights — civil and political as well as social and economic — state the minimum conditions for social institutions that respect human dignity, social solidarity, and justice. They are all essential to human dignity and to the integral development of both individuals and society, and are thus moral issues.[5] Any denial of these rights harms persons and wounds the human community. Their serious and sustained denial violates individuals and destroys solidarity among persons.

81. Social and economic rights call for a mode of implementation different from that required to secure civil and political rights. Freedom of worship and of speech imply immunity from interference on the part of both other persons and the government. The rights to education, employment, and social security, for example, are empowerments that call for positive action by individuals and society at large.

82. However, both kinds of rights call for positive action to create social and political institutions that enable all persons to become active members of society. Civil and political rights allow persons to participate freely in the public life of the community, for example, through free speech, assembly, and the vote. In democratic countries these rights have been secured through a long and vigorous history of creating the institutions of constitutional government. In seeking to secure the full range of social and economic rights today, a similar effort to shape new economic arrangements will be necessary.

83. The first step in such an effort is the development of a new cultural consensus that the basic economic conditions of human welfare are essential to human dignity and are due persons by right. Second, the securing of these rights will make demands on *all* members of society, on all private sector institutions, and on government. A concerted effort on all levels in our society

---

4. Pope John XXIII, *Peace on Earth* (1963), 8–27. See Pope John XXIII, *On Human Work* (1981), 18–19. *Peace on Earth* and other modern papal statements refer explicitly to the "right to work" as one of the fundamental economic rights. Because of the ambiguous meaning of the phrase in the United States, and also because the ordinary way people earn their living in our society is through paid employment, the NCCB [National Conference of Catholic Bishops] has affirmed previously that the protection of human dignity demands that the right to useful employment be secured for all who are able and willing to work. See NCCB, *The Economy: Human Dimensions* (20 November 1975), 5, in NCCB, *Justice in the Marketplace*, 470. See also Congregation for the Doctrine of the Faith, *Instruction on Christian Freedom and Liberation* [22 March 1986], 85.

5. Pope Paul VI, *On the Development of Peoples* (1967), 14.

is needed to meet these basic demands of justice and solidarity. Indeed political democracy and a commitment to secure economic rights are mutually reinforcing.

84. Securing economic rights for all will be an arduous task. There are a number of precedents in U.S. history, however, which show that the work has already begun.[6] The country needs a serious dialogue about the appropriate levels of private and public sector involvement that are needed to move forward. There is certainly room for diversity of opinion in the Church and in U.S. society on *how* to protect the human dignity and economic rights of all our brothers and sisters.[7] In our view, however, there can be no legitimate disagreement on the basic moral objectives.

Chapter II, Section B, Part 3: Moral Priorities for the Nation

85. *The common good demands justice for all, the protection of the human rights of all.*[8] Making cultural and economic institutions more supportive of the freedom, power, and security of individuals and families must be a central, long-range objective for the nation. Every person has a duty to contribute to building up the commonweal. All have a responsibility to develop their talents through education. Adults must contribute to society through their individual vocations and talents. Parents are called to guide their children to the maturity of Christian adulthood and responsible citizenship. Everyone has special duties toward the poor and the marginalized. Living up to these responsibilities, however, is often made difficult by the social and economic patterns of society. Schools and educational policies both public and private often serve the privileged exceedingly well, while the children of the poor are effectively abandoned as second-class citizens. Great stresses are created in family life by the way work is organized and scheduled, and by the social and cultural values communicated on TV. Many in the lower middle class are barely getting by and fear becoming victims of economic forces over which they have no control.

86. *The obligation to provide justice for all means that the poor have the single most urgent economic claim on the conscience of the nation.* Poverty can take many forms, spiritual as well as material. All people face struggles of the spirit as they ask deep questions about their purpose in life. Many have serious problems in marriage and family life at some time in their lives, and all of us face the certain reality of sickness and death. The Gospel of Christ proclaims that God's love is stronger than all these forms of diminishment. Material deprivation, however, seriously compounds such sufferings of the spirit and heart. To see a loved one sick is bad enough, but to have no possibility of obtaining health care is worse. To face family problems, such as the death of a spouse or a divorce, can be devastating, but to have these lead to the loss of one's home

---

6. Martha H. Good, "Freedom from Want: The Failure of United States Courts to Protect Subsistence Rights," *Human Rights Quarterly* 6 (1984): 335–63.

7. Vatican II, *Pastoral Constitution on the Church in the Modern World*, 43.

8. Pope John XXIII, *Mater et Magistra* (1961), 65.

and end with living on the streets is something no one should have to endure in a country as rich as ours. In developing countries these human problems are even more greatly intensified by extreme material deprivation. This form of human suffering can be reduced if our own country, so rich in resources, chooses to increase its assistance.

87. As individuals and as a nation, therefore, we are called to make a fundamental "option for the poor."[9] The obligation to evaluate social and economic activity from the viewpoint of the poor and the powerless arises from the radical command to love one's neighbor as one's self. Those who are marginalized and whose rights are denied have privileged claims if society is to provide justice for *all*. This obligation is deeply rooted in Christian belief. As Paul VI stated:

> In teaching us charity, the Gospel instructs us in the preferential respect due the poor and the special situation they have in society: the more fortunate should renounce some of their rights so as to place their goods more generously at the service of others.[10]

John Paul II has described this special obligation to the poor as "a call to have a special openness with the small and the weak, those that suffer and weep, those that are humiliated and left on the margin of society, so as to help them win their dignity as human persons and children of God."[11]

88. The prime purpose of this special commitment to the poor is to enable them to become active participants in the life of society. It is to enable *all* persons to share in and contribute to the common good.[12] The "option for the poor," therefore, is not an adversarial slogan that pits one group or class against another. Rather it states that the deprivation and powerlessness of the poor wounds the whole community. The extent of their suffering is a measure of how far we are from being a true community of persons. These wounds will be healed only by greater solidarity with the poor and among the poor themselves.

89. In summary, the norms of love, basic justice, and human rights imply that personal decisions, social policies, and economic institutions should be governed by several key priorities. These priorities do not specify everything

---

9. On the recent use of this term, see Congregation for the Doctrine of the Faith, *Instruction on Christian Freedom and Liberation,* 46–50, 66–68; *Evangelization in Latin America's Present and Future,* Final Document of the Third General Conference of the Latin American Episcopate (Puebla, Mexico, January 27–February 13, 1979), esp. pt. 6, chap. 1, "A Preferential Option for the Poor," in J. Eagleson and P. Scharper, eds., *Puebla and Beyond* (Maryknoll, N.Y.: Orbis Books, 1979), 264, 267; Donal Dorr, *Option for the Poor: A Hundred Years of Vatican Social Teaching* (Maryknoll, N.Y.: Orbis Books, 1983).

10. Pope Paul VI, *Octagesima Adveniens* (1971), 23.

11. Pope John Paul II, Address to the Bishops of Brazil, 6, 9, *Origins* 10, no. 9 (31 July 1980): 135.

12. Pope John Paul II, Address to Workers at São Paulo, 4, *Origins* 10, no. 9 (31 July 1980): 138; Congregation for the Doctrine of the Faith, *Instruction on Christian Freedom and Liberation,* 66–68.

that must be considered in economic decision making. They do indicate the most fundamental and urgent objectives.

90. a. *The fulfillment of the basic needs of the poor is of the highest priority.* Personal decisions, policies of private and public bodies, and power relationships must all be evaluated by their effects on those who lack the minimum necessities of nutrition, housing, education, and health care. In particular, this principle recognizes that meeting fundamental human needs must come before the fulfillment of desires for luxury consumer goods, for profits not conducive to the common good, and for unnecessary military hardware.

91. b. *Increasing active participation in economic life by those who are presently excluded or vulnerable is a high social priority.* The human dignity of all is realized when people gain the power to work together to improve their lives, strengthen their families, and contribute to society. Basic justice calls for more than providing help to the poor and other vulnerable members of society. It recognizes the priority of policies and programs that support family life and enhance economic participation through employment and widespread ownership of property. It challenges privileged economic power in favor of the well-being of all. It points to the need to improve the present situation of those unjustly discriminated against in the past. And it has very important implications for both the domestic and the international distribution of power.

92. c. *The investment of wealth, talent, and human energy should be specially directed to benefit those who are poor or economically insecure.* Achieving a more just economy in the United States and the world depends in part on increasing economic resources and productivity. In addition, the ways these resources are invested and managed must be scrutinized in light of their effects on nonmonetary values. Investment and management decisions have crucial moral dimensions: they create jobs or eliminate them; they can push vulnerable families over the edge into poverty or give them new hope for the future; they help or hinder the building of a more equitable society. Indeed they can have either positive or negative influence on the fairness of the global economy. Therefore, this priority presents a strong moral challenge to policies that put large amounts of talent and capital into the production of luxury consumer goods and military technology while failing to invest sufficiently in education, health, the basic infrastructure of our society, and economic sectors that produce urgently needed jobs, goods, and services.

93. d. *Economic and social policies as well as the organization of the work world should be continually evaluated in light of their impact on the strength and stability of family life.* The long-range future of this nation is intimately linked with the well-being of families, for the family is the most basic form of human community.[13] Efficiency and competition in the marketplace must be moderated by greater concern for the way work schedules and compen-

---

13. Vatican II, *Pastoral Constitution on the Church in the Modern World*, 47.

sation support or threaten the bonds between spouses and between parents and children. Health, education, and social service programs should be scrutinized in light of how well they ensure both individual dignity and family integrity.

94. These priorities are not policies. They are norms that should guide the economic choices of all and shape economic institutions. They can help the United States move forward to fulfill the duties of justice and protect economic rights. They were strongly affirmed as implications of Catholic social teaching by Pope John Paul II during his visit to Canada in 1984: "The needs of the poor take priority over the desires of the rich; the rights of workers over the maximization of profits; the preservation of the environment over uncontrolled industrial expansion; production to meet social needs over production for military purposes."[14] There will undoubtedly be disputes about the concrete applications of these priorities in our complex world. We do not seek to foreclose discussion about them. However, we believe that an effort to move in the direction they indicate is urgently needed.

95. The economic challenge of today has many parallels with the political challenge that confronted the founders of our nation. In order to create a new form of political democracy they were compelled to develop ways of thinking and political institutions that had never existed before. Their efforts were arduous and their goals imperfectly realized, but they launched an experiment in the protection of civil and political rights that has prospered through the efforts of those who came after them. *We believe the time has come for a similar experiment in securing economic rights: the creation of an order that guarantees the minimum conditions of human dignity in the economic sphere for every person.* By drawing on the resources of the Catholic moral-religious tradition, we hope to make a contribution through this letter to such a new "American Experiment": a new venture to secure economic justice for all. . . .

Published by United States Catholic Conference, Washington, D.C., November 1986. (Footnotes in original.) Printed with permission.

89. Rev. Edwin M. Conway, "The Forms of Homelessness: Testimony before a Subcommittee of the House Committee on Banking, Finance, and Urban Affairs," 4 February 1987

I am Father Edwin M. Conway, administrator of the Catholic Charities of the Archdiocese of Chicago and treasurer of Catholic Charities USA. We appreciate the invitation to testify today on a problem which imposes a heavy burden of suffering on many of our citizens: the problem of homelessness.

Catholic Charities of Chicago is a comprehensive human service agency serving Cook and Lake counties in Illinois. This year we will provide services

---

14. Pope John Paul II, *Address on Christian Unity in a Technological Age* (Toronto: 14 September 1984), *Origins* 14, no. 16 (4 October 1984): 248.

to approximately 570,000 individuals in all sorts of need. Catholic Charities of Chicago is the largest of the 600 human service agencies and 200 specialized institutions which are federated under the flag of Catholic Charities USA. Most of these institutions provide emergency assistance in the form of shelter, clothing and food, as well as advocacy and legal assistance to people in crisis....

Homelessness in Chicago is a serious and worsening problem, though its scope and magnitude are poorly understood. Estimates of the number of people who find themselves without housing at some time over the course of a year range from five [thousand] to 25,000.[1] Only one scientific study has been made, and this produced a low estimate: 4,000 to 6,000 homeless over the course of a year, 1,600 to 3,100 on any one night.[2] This study, however, employed an excessively restrictive definition of homelessness and a correspondingly narrow sampling methodology so that it measured only the number of people who spend the night either in shelters or in public places.

In truth, homeless people spend their nights in many other places. They spend them primarily in the homes of friends, relatives and acquaintances; in motels and flophouses; in church basements and spare rectory bedrooms; and in their cars. They also spend them hidden in culverts and under viaducts; in dangerous abandoned buildings and on rooftops; in railroad cars and truck trailers; and in a thousand other places where social scientists would not dare to visit but where homeless folk are desperate and ingenious enough to take refuge.

The extent of homelessness in Chicago, then, has not yet been credibly measured. But beyond a doubt, it is very much greater than 6,000 people over the course of a year, and in any case it vastly overwhelms existing efforts to address its underlying causes or even to shelter its victims. This is the experience of Catholic Charities and other Catholic service providers in Chicago.

Catholic Charities offers shelter to many different homeless populations, targeted by a variety of different types of shelters and residential programs.

First of all, we operate two emergency overnight shelters with a total capacity of 169 beds on the old Skid Row west of the Loop. These shelters are always full. Two other overnight shelters of 188 and 40 beds are maintained by Franciscan Fathers and Dominican Fathers in other depressed areas of the city. These shelters have slightly lower average occupancy rates, but on cold nights they are full and must turn away 10 to 590 applicants each. These turnaway counts are understated, however, because word spreads rapidly on the street that the shelters are full, and many who would avail themselves if there were room are discouraged before reaching the doors.

These shelters serve what I will call the hard-core homeless. Our social

---

1. U.S. Department of Housing and Human Development, Office of Policy Development and Research, "A Report to the Secretary on the Homeless and Emergency Shelters," May 1984, 11–14; and Peter H. Rossi et al., "The Conditions of the Homeless in Chicago," September 1986, 49.
2. Rossi et al., "Conditions," 44, 49.

workers estimate that 85 percent have been on the streets for a year or more, many have been homeless their entire adult lives or since they were deinstitutionalized years ago. More than half have disabling mental illness or are at least [so] highly eccentric as to make conventional conversation impossible. Ninety percent or more abuse alcohol. Clinical depression is the norm. Although all are eligible for the basic general assistance or welfare grant of $154 per month, only a small fraction receive it. None of the mentally disabled receive the more generous Supplemental Security Income to which they would be entitled if they had housing.

We have doubled overnight shelter beds in Chicago over the past four years and opened additional warming centers on very cold nights. Still, 26 people died of exposure this past winter. In a similar minimal sense, this population's need for food is met through the 75 soup kitchens and 500 food pantries that operate in metropolitan Chicago, of which Catholic Charities supports seven kitchens and 50 pantries out of its own funds supplemented by federal and other governmental monies. No one, however, would say that this population has nutritional needs adequately met.

These minimal solutions, however, are totally inadequate from the standpoint of basic human dignity. Intervention, sheltered housing and treatment are needed to attack the underlying causes of the desperate and demeaning condition.

Short-term psychiatric hospitalization or detoxification, to which most of this population are periodically subject, should be followed by placement in residential programs offering services such as supervision of compliance with medication regimes, Alcoholics Anonymous meetings, psychotherapy and employment counseling. Unfortunately, halfway houses for the mentally ill are badly oversubscribed in Chicago. One such Catholic-run residential program in Chicago's Pilsen area, which served 360 individuals in fiscal year 1986, turned away 720 referrals in the same period. Thus, homeless mental hospital patients are routinely discharged to overnight shelters and the streets. The prospects for newly detoxified homeless alcoholics are equally bad, since there are only two long-term residential treatment programs for them in the city. Catholic Charities operates one of these, accommodating some 70 clients, for which the waiting list is typically 35 names long and the delay before admission three months.

Additional "second stage" of long-term sheltered treatment programs are the key to making inroads into the entrenched homelessness of this population. Our 70 years' experience in the treatment of homeless alcoholics through such a program shows that modest success is possible. Likewise, those few community mental health centers that mount residential programs have succeeded in obtaining disability benefits or employment for mentally ill individuals and have established many in permanent living arrangements with ongoing outpatient support. But more of these programs are needed. In addition, very low-cost housing, such as was once supplied by the rapidly disappearing single room occupancy hotels, must be built to give permanent homes to rehabilitated hard-core homeless who are capable of only minimal employment or who must survive on disability benefits.

I strongly urge that generous provision be made in the legislation you are considering to fund residential treatment programs and very low-cost housing.

The hard-core homeless are not the only homeless. Catholic institutions in Chicago operate 11 transitional shelters serving, variously, homeless families and individuals, pregnant women and women with children, battered women and their children, and runaway youth who have been victims of sexual exploitation. Catholic Charities operates five of these, three of which are geared primarily to serving families and individuals experiencing temporary crises. In fiscal 1986, 376 individuals lived in these three shelters for an average stay of 45 days, and there were 98 families among this group. Last year, there were 1,603 requests for admission to these shelters, including 707 from families. Of these, we were able to accommodate only 170 or 10.6 percent of the total. The number of requests has grown at an average rate of 34 percent per year for the past seven years. This trend shows no sign of abating....

Origins 16, no. 37 (26 February 1987): 659–61. (Footnotes in original.)

Movies and Television

The emergence of film in the 1920s and the rise of television in the late 1940s and 1950s represent two of the most important benchmarks in American cultural history. Millions of Americans were attending the movies every week during the prosperous 1920s, and the numbers increased as the depression of the 1930s deepened. While Catholics joined the crowds at the theaters, many of their pastors worried about the impact of the new medium on manners and morals. Impatient with the results of industry self-regulation, Catholic leaders organized to combat the threat. By the mid-1930s, censorship, pledges, and threats of public boycott had become widely recognized signatures of Catholic influence in public life. The first document below takes readers back to Catholic efforts to influence movie industry self-regulation. The other two documents in this unit reflect early Catholic efforts to influence the use of television in American public life. By the early 1960s, 90 percent of all American homes had at least one television set. The rapid dissemination of television sets in American life and their use as home entertainment, baby-sitters, and companions for the lonely guaranteed that this medium would have a powerful impact on virtually every aspect of American life. Almost from the outset, there has been serious national debate on the impact of television on the values and morals of all Americans, especially young people. These documents reflect early Catholic comment on the issue.

90. Working Draft of the Daniel Lord–Martin Quigley [Moving Picture] Code Proposal, ca. November 1929

I. CRIMES AGAINST THE LAW

A/ The [cinematic] treatment of *crimes* must not:

1. Teach the *methods* of crime

2. *Inspire potential criminals* with a desire for imitation

3. *Make criminals seem heroic* and justified. *Revenge* in modern times shall not be justified. In lands and ages of less developed civilization and moral principles, revenge may sometimes be presented. This would be the case especially in places where no law exists to cover the crime because of which revenge is committed.

B/ Because of its evil consequences, the *drug traffic* should not be presented in any form. The existence of the trade should not be brought to the attention of audiences.

C/ The *use of liquor* should never be excessively presented even in picturing countries where its use is illegal. In scenes from American life, the necessities of plot and proper characterization alone justify its use. And in this case, it should be shown with moderation.

II. SEX

Out of regard for the sanctity of marriage and the home, the triangle, that is, love of a third party by one already married, needs careful handling. The treatment should not throw sympathy against marriage as an institution.

Scenes of passion must be treated with an honest acknowledgment of human nature and its normal reactions. Many scenes cannot be presented without arousing dangerous emotions on the part of the immature, the young, the criminal classes.

Even within the limits of *pure love,* certain facts have been universally regarded by lawmakers as outside the limits of safe presentation. In the case of *impure love,* the love which society has always regarded as wrong, and which has been banned by divine law, the following are important:

1. Impure love must *not* be presented as *attractive and beautiful.*

2. It must *not* be the subject of *comedy or farce,* or treated as material for laughter.

3. It must not be presented in such a way as to *arouse passion* or morbid curiosity on the part of the audience.

4. It must not be made to seem *right and permissible.*

5. In general, it must *not* be *detailed* in methods and manner. . . .

VI. COSTUME

General Principles:

1. The effect of nudity or semi-nudity upon the normal man or woman and much more upon the young and immature person, has been honestly recognized by all law makers and moralists.

2. Hence the fact that the nude or semi-nude body may be beautiful does not make its use in films moral. For, in addition to its beauty, the effect of the nude or semi-nude body on the normal individual must be taken into consideration.

3. Nudity or semi-nudity used simply to put a "punch" into a picture comes under the head of immoral actions. It is immoral in its effect on the average audience.

4. Nudity can never be permitted as being *necessary for the plot.* Semi-nudity must not result in undue or indecent exposures.

5. Transparent or translucent materials and silhouette are frequently more suggestive than actual exposure.

VII. DANCES

Dancing in general is recognized as an *Art* and as a *beautiful* form of expressing human emotions. But dances which suggest or represent sexual actions, whether performed solo or with two or more, dances intended to excite the emotional reaction of an audience, dances with the movement of the breasts, excessive body movements while the feet are stationary, violate decency and are wrong.

VIII. RELIGION

The reason why ministers of religion may not be comic characters or villains is simply because the attitude taken toward them may easily become the attitude taken toward religion in general. Religion is lowered in the minds of the audience because of the lowering of the audience's respect for a minister....

Gregory D. Black, *The Catholic Crusade against the Movies, 1940–1975*
(New York: Cambridge University Press, 1998), 249–51.

91. Administrative Board, National Catholic Welfare Conference, "Censorship," 17 November 1957

1. Censorship is today a provocative and sometimes misleading word. It generates controversy by provoking those who would deny in fact any restrictions, legal or moral, upon freedom of expression. It misleads, since few approach the problems of censorship without emotion.

2. Obviously the state does have some power of censorship. In times of war or great national danger, few will deny it a preventive power. In normal

circumstances, however, the state exercises only a punitive function, placing restraint on those who misuse liberty to deny equal or greater rights to others. The state's power of censorship is not unlimited.

Teacher of Morals

3. Morally, the Church can and does exercise what is called censorship. This right is hers from her office as teacher of morals and guardian of divine truth. Her decisions bind her people but her sanctions upon them are only spiritual and moral. She does, nevertheless, express her judgments to all men of good will, soliciting their reasoned understanding and their freely given acceptance and support.

4. Most commonly in civil affairs the particular freedom that is involved in discussions of the subject is freedom of the press, not only in newspapers and other publications, but also such dramatic expression as is represented in the theater, motion pictures, radio and television.

5. Because in modern times the press has been a major instrument in the development of knowledge and the chief means of its diffusion, freedom of the press is closely bound up with man's right to knowledge. Man's patient plodding ascent to the heights of truth evidences the spiritual powers given him by God and at the same time their wounding by sin. His search for truth is an enriching and ennobling experience, uniquely proper to man.

6. The right to know the truth is evidently broad and sweeping. Is the right to express this knowledge, whether through speech or press, equally broad? That man has a right to communicate his ideas through the spoken or written word is beyond challenge. And yet it can be recognized at the outset that expression adds a new element to knowledge. Directed as it is to others, it is an act that has social implications. Society itself must take cognizance of it. Although man must claim and hold to freedom of expression, he must also recognize his duty to exercise it with a sense of responsibility.

7. This is a freedom that is intimately bound up with other freedoms that man prizes. Freedom of the press is patently a key safeguard of civil liberty. Democracy does not exist without it. The day free expression of opinion is extinguished and all are constrained to fall into a single pattern of political thought and action, democracy has died.

8. As indispensable as is freedom of expression to us as citizens, it is no less indispensable to the Church in carrying out her mission to preach the Gospel. The content of man's knowledge of God derived through the use of his native powers has been immeasurably enriched and perfected and has been given certainty by the revelation made by God to man through Jesus Christ. This knowledge has been attained not through man's effort, but through the goodness and mercy of God. It is accepted by an act of faith made with the help of divine grace. Of this deposit of revealed truth the Church is the divinely appointed custodian.

9. Without an unfettered means of communication, the teaching office of

the Church is sorely hampered. She counts among her special blessings in our own country the important and fruitful Catholic press.

10. Because freedom of the press is a basic right to be respected and safeguarded, it must be understood and defended not as license, but as true rational freedom. The kind of uncritical claims for and defense of liberty which so often have been made in our day actually places that liberty in jeopardy. For this reason we feel that light must be thrown not only on its meaning but also on its limits.

Serve the Common Good

11. To speak of limits is to indicate that freedom of expression is not an absolute freedom. Not infrequently it is so presented. It is alleged that this freedom can suffer no curtailment or limitation without being destroyed. The traditional and sounder understanding of freedom, and specifically freedom of the press, is more temperate. It recognizes that liberty has a moral dimension. Man is true to himself as a free being when he acts in accord with the laws of right reason. As a member of society his liberty is exercised within bounds fixed by the multiple demands of social living. In the concrete this means that the common good is to be served. It will entail, among other things, a respect for the rights of others, a regard for public order, and a positive deference to those human, moral, and social values which are our common Christian heritage. It is within this context that freedom of expression is rightly understood.

12. This recognition of limitations has been given statement in recent decisions of the Supreme Court of the United States: "We hold that obscenity is not within the area of constitutionally protected free speech or press" (Roth v. United States, 77 S. Ct. 1304, Alberts v. California, 77 S. Ct. 1304–June 24, 1957). The decisions touching on this subject are encouraging to those who have been deeply concerned over trends that threatened to destroy the traditional authority exercised by the state over expressions and displays of obscenity.

Obscenity Demands Restraint

13. Contrary to this trend, the court has held that there is such a thing as obscenity susceptible of legal determination and demanding legal restraint; that laws forbidding the circulation of obscene literature are not as such in violation of the Constitution; that the federal government may ban such publications from the mail; that a state may act against obscene literature and punish those who sell or advertise it. The decisions reasserted the traditional conviction that freedom of expression is exercised within the defined limits of law. Obscenity cannot be permitted as a proper exercise of a basic human freedom. Civil enactments as well as the moral law both indicate that the exercise of this freedom cannot be unrestrained.

14. Ideally, we could wish that no man-made legal restraints were ever necessary. Thus, restraint on any human freedom would be imposed rather

by one's own reason than by external authority. In any case, restraint's best justification is that it is imposed for the sake of a greater freedom. Since, however, individuals do act in an irresponsible way and do threaten social and moral harm, society must face its responsibility and exercise its authority. The exigencies of social living demand it.

15. In his recent encyclical of September 8, 1957, Our Holy Father has spoken not only of the competence of public administrators, but also of their strict duty to exercise supervision over the more modern media of communication and entertainment — radio and television. He warns public officials that they must look on this matter not from a merely political standpoint — but also from that of public morals, the sure foundation of which rests on the natural law. What he has said applies with even greater force to the older media — the press and motion pictures — since they have been and continue to be subject to even greater abuse and supply so much of the material used in the programs presented through the more modern media. Pope Pius XII writes:

> Nor can it be asserted that this watchful care of the state's officials is an unfair limitation on the liberty of individual citizens, for it is concerned not with the private citizens as such but rather with the whole of human society with whom these arts are being shared.

16. Although civil authority has the right and duty to exercise such control over the various media of communications as is necessary to safeguard public morals, yet civil law, especially in those areas which are constitutionally protected, will define as narrowly as possible the limitations placed on freedom. The one purpose which will guide legislators in establishing necessary restraints to freedom is the securing of the general welfare through the prevention of grave and harmful abuse. Our juridical system has been dedicated from the beginning to the principle of minimal restraint. Those who may become impatient with the reluctance of the state through its laws to curb and curtail human freedom should bear in mind that this is a principle which serves to safeguard all our vital freedoms — to curb less rather than more; to hold for liberty rather than for restraint....

Hugh J. Nolan, ed., *Pastoral Letters of the United States Catholic Bishops* (Washington, D.C.: United States Catholic Conference, 1984), 2:192–98. Printed with permission.

92. "State of the Question: Catholic Code for Television Viewers," 2 August 1958

1. The Educators' Television Code is intended in the first place for parents who are anxious to know how to make the best use of their TV set with regard to their children. It is also meant to inform educators who, whether they be in boarding schools, classrooms or youth hostels, in hospitals or sanatoria, are wondering whether television should be regarded as a medium for

enlightenment and education, or at least as a means of entertainment for leisure hours.

2. Television has found its way into the lives of children: this is a fact nowadays. Consequently, educators must investigate the exact nature of the influence of television on children. They cannot be satisfied with merely expressing their wholehearted approval of it, and at the same time they would be unwise to be firmly set against it. They must avoid, on the one hand, the modern view of accepting it simply as a part and parcel of modern life and, on the other hand, the conservative attitude of contemplating it with instinctive distrust. It is their duty to assess the constructive elements in the change of milieu and of educational methods brought about by the impact of television, and to gauge the limitations and possible dangers of this medium.

3. It is obvious that, if our children become ever more frequent spectators of television, its effects upon them will be favorable or unfavorable according to whether the educators take the necessary precautions or not to ensure the reasonable use of this medium, by setting it in its proper place in the general pattern of modern educational methods.

But what is its proper place?

4. It has been said that television introduces the world into the home. Even if this is true to a very great and ever increasing extent, the fact remains that it is not the outside world, nature and mankind, that are to be seen on the TV screen, but merely pictorial images of them. These images are kaleidoscopic; they may be flattering or distressing, being magnified out of all proportion to anything our eyes can discern directly; and they reflect a breadth of vision far beyond our own natural perspective. Consequently, these visual, luminous, sound images can never be anything else than mere "signs" of mankind and of things. These must never be taken for reality; to do so would amount to a betrayal, since it is the duty of children and of men to face up to the realities of life and keep actively in touch with them. Therefore television must not serve as a substitute for the world, nor indeed can the TV world ever replace our tangible, visible world with all its human feelings and sufferings.

5. If television is not to dazzle us with the illusion of offering us a substitute for the real, living world, we must refuse to use it as if it could perform this conjuring trick, and we must not allow its fascinating properties to bewitch us. The TV screen will play its truly educational part on condition that *it does not become a screen between the child and the realities of this world and of human existence.* It will faithfully play its part as a "sign" if, through the high standard of its presentation of reality, it incites viewers to a deeper understanding of that reality, awakening and stimulating in them the urge to act as responsible beings in the world itself.

6. Television can discharge these functions in the fields of *information* and of *recreation*. It can give scientific information, as well as miscellaneous news in the form of current events from every part of the world and soon, perhaps, even from the intersidereal spaces. It can also provide recreation in the

widest sense of the word, from amusing games to cultural pastimes and artistic performances.

7. It is in this twofold manner that we should like to see television faithfully accomplishing its duty as a simple but ingenious and fascinating messenger of every possible kind of visible and audible reality. Its danger, of course, lies in its very fascination, since its brilliant costume of ambassador may well beguile adults and children into accepting it as the touchstone of reality. But this does not divest it of its wonderful possibility of irresistibly inviting us, without so much as leaving our homes, to acquire an enriching knowledge of life in its true perspective. Whether or not the danger is averted and this wonderful, enriching experience actually takes place, depends largely on educators. It is in the hope of assisting them in carrying out this task that we have written this code....

America 99 (2 August 1958): 472. Printed with permission.

Organized Labor

American Catholic support for organized labor burned bright during the heyday of CIO organizing in the 1930s. Wartime gains consolidated union power, and the strong support of the Democratic Party made it a considerable force in American society. Catholic leaders were present at the reunion of the AFL and the CIO. Support for unionism continued in the highly profiled efforts of Catholic labor leader Cesar Chavez to organize farmworkers and similar efforts by clothing workers to organize the textile industry.

Traditional Catholic support for the right of workers to organize and bargain collectively has been turned on the church itself as its own employment and wage practices have been held to the same standards expected of business and industry.

93. "AFL-CIO Is Born," 17 December 1955

Rumbling in the Wings

What history will one day record about the merger of the AFL and CIO is already partly known.

It will say that on December 5, 1955, in New York City, twenty years after John L. Lewis dramatized the rise of the CIO by punching "Big Bill" Hutcheson, president of the Carpenters, in the nose, the breach in the ranks of labor was closed.

It will record that nowhere, at no time, had the world seen such a large gathering of free trade unionists. The 1,450 delegates from 141 national and international unions who assembled in the huge Seventy-first Regiment Armory on lower Park Avenue represented somewhere between 15 and 16 million trade unionists. Only in Soviet Russia, where unions are servile arms of the state, are such numbers exceeded.

History will also note that the merger occurred with a surprising lack of fanfare and excitement. The separate conventions of the merging groups, which preceded by a few days their joint congress, were almost routine affairs. Only in the CIO gathering was there a brief flash of newsworthy drama when voluble Michael Quill, head of the small, 90,000-member Transport Workers Union, took the floor to oppose the merger. His perfervid charge that the new AFL-CIO constitution licensed raiding, racial discrimination and racketeering was heard in skeptical silence. Shortly thereafter the delegates voted 5,712,077 to 120,002 to dissolve the CIO and merge with the AFL. In the AFL meeting, the vote was unanimous.

Despite the smooth meshing of the AFL-CIO gears, the delegates nourished more doubts and apprehensions about the future than their public statements revealed. These, too, the historians will note. True, the delegates, in merging the AFL and CIO, were merely reaffirming the famous "Scranton Declaration" of 1901. They were once more recognizing, as 85-year-old John P. Frey, president emeritus of the AFL Metal Trades Department, explained to the press, that within the American labor movement there was room both for craft unions and industrial unions. Nevertheless, the craft unions could not forget overnight the whole divisive story of the past twenty years. Before the final act of AFL-CIO unity was achieved, they took certain precautions against any possible threat from their new brothers — the big CIO industrial unions.

Nor will the historians fail to observe that though Mr. Quill's oratory left his fellow CIO delegates unmoved, not a few of them also speculated that the idealism of their movement might suffer on coming into contact with the "realism" and "practicality" of certain old-line AFL affiliates. Would the fine words in the new AFL-CIO constitution about racial discrimination and racketeering remain only fine words?

In raising a question of this kind, we pass on to that part of the historical record which lies shrouded in the future. What verdict will historians, form the vantage-point of a half-century or more, eventually pass on the merger? Will they find that unifying the AFL and CIO was, indeed, a blessing for the workers? That it raised their living standards, enlarged their freedoms, enhanced their dignity as individuals? Will the historians judge that the merger benefited employers as well as workers, that it made for more responsible unionism, for a decline in jurisdictional strife, for better-informed, more creative collective bargaining? Or will the answer be negative?

And what about the impact of the merger on the country as a whole? Will history record that it contributed to building a better United States, to what the new AFL-CIO constitution describes as "the strengthening and extension of our way of life and the fundamental freedoms which are the basis of our democratic society"?

That last question seemed to weigh on the minds of both George Meany, first president of the AFL-CIO, and Walter Reuther, last head of the CIO, as they led their followers into a new and challenging future. In a pre-convention message to the AFL, Mr. Meany emphasized the contribution a united labor movement ought to bring not only to workers but to local communities and to the nation as a whole. The same thought was echoed in Mr. Reuther's presidential address to the CIO. Warned the CIO leader:

> If the new labor movement is just a big and more powerful pressure group, it will fail because the problems that need solution will not be solved by creating a more powerful competing pressure group in America.

To succeed, Mr. Reuther said, the AFL-CIO would have to cultivate "wisdom" and display "social and moral responsibility."

That these ideals will not be easily attained was emphasized, no doubt unconsciously, on the very eve of the merger. To the consternation of many delegates, the Teamsters, who only a few weeks ago concluded a mutual-assistance pact with the racket-infested International Longshoremen's Association, blandly announced on December 3 that they had signed a similar agreement with the Mine, Mill and Smelter Workers. Mine, Mill happens to be one of the unions which the CIO expelled five years ago as Communist-dominated.

An incident like this suggests that the real fight to build a unified, high-minded labor movement has only begun, though it was well begun. What New Yorkers saw last week was a honeymoon, signalizing the end of civil war in labor's ranks. But the infighting will go on. Two years hence, when the AFL-CIO again convenes, the future will be much clearer than it is today.

America 94 (17 December 1955): 325. Printed with permission.

94. Alice Ogle, "California Farm Labor," 19–26 December 1964[1]

California's major battle in the war on poverty is the farm-labor fight. The closer we get to December 31, 1964, expiration date of Public Law 78, which allows the importation of Mexican farm workers (braceros), the more furious it grows.

Anyone who thinks the issue is dead, that there can be no extension of the Mexican contract farm-labor program, doesn't know the power of "agribusiness." This label, supplied by the National Advisory Committee on Farm Labor, is one that it applies to the plantation-type farm to distinguish it from the family-type farm.

As the P.L. 78 deadline approaches, the possibility of some sort of extension looms constantly larger and more disturbing to everyone concerned. Max Awner, a California newsman and labor expert, writing in the August *Progressive*, said:

---

1. At the time this was written, Alice Ogle was a freelance writer living in San Francisco.

Like the ancient Pharaoh after he reluctantly allowed the Hebrew slaves to depart the land of Egypt, many growers are wondering whether they let a good thing slip out of their grasp too easily, and there is increasing evidence that they, too, are preparing an expedition to try to retrieve their lost treasure — or a suitable substitute.

One substitute under discussion is a stand-by section of the Immigration and Nationality Act, which could be used when P.L. 78 and the bracero treaty with Mexico ends.

Although its provisions differ in many ways from the bracero treaty, which brought 62,000 contract workers into California fields this year, the law can bring in temporary workers and send them back home again.

It brought in some 1,200 Japanese employed this year on California farm lands, hundreds of Filipinos and Basque sheepherders who were scattered about the whole West. These are the "H-2" laborers, so nicknamed from the section label in the 1952 Immigration Act that made their importation possible.

California's Alameda County is experimenting with another "substitute": welfare recipients are forced to do farm work or forfeit their aid payments. Some Californians were so shocked at the idea that they've been picketing county welfare offices regularly. Max Awner investigated this plan and reported: "The net earnings of some of these forced laborers were found to be less than their welfare payments would have been, while at the same time they were effectively prevented from seeking jobs more in line with their experience and capabilities."

The whole problem has become a football for politicians. One side quotes a University of Michigan report that it will require 25,000 domestic workers to do the work of 15,000 braceros, and wonders if "the so-called sociologists who have urged termination of the bracero program realize there are not sufficient domestic workers willing and able to do the tasks required in this type of agriculture." A famous politician, campaigning here in California, told his audience: "We are facing disaster because of government meddling in a farm-labor program that has worked well for years. We should return to the bracero program and the government should keep its hands off a relationship between employer and employee that has been successful so far."

He apparently forgot that the very foundation of the bracero program is government sponsorship, and the employer-employee relationship he talked about went out with the Mexican wetback.

In all this talk, no mention is made of the violent opposition of the farm lobby in Washington to legislative attempts at extending to the nation's domestic farm-workers social legislation — minimum wages, unemployment insurance, meaningful social security and the right to engage in free collective bargaining.

And the everlasting charge that Americans won't do "stoop" labor is nonsense. The hottest spot in California is the great Central Valley, where

American road crews tar and gravel highways for $2.25 an hour. Men will stand hip deep in slime repairing sewers for $2.75 an hour. The truth is that American workers have done and will go on doing hard, unpleasant work in any industry where they are able to earn a decent wage.

Public Law 78 makes possible an influx of foreign workers — and keeps wages down for domestic workers. But that isn't all it does.

No one is more aware of the evil of this law than bracero priests, who work across the United States whenever there is a concentration of Mexican braceros. A few years ago, while collecting material for an article on the problem, I visited Fr. Donald McDonald — who had devoted a dozen years to the bracero — in his cramped quarters of Our Lady of Guadalupe Mission in San Jose, California. He called the bracero program "a labor-camp system degrading the identity and life of a man."

He said it was nonsense that Americans won't do field work. "Give them decent wages and living conditions, and they'll be too numerous for work available." He added: "Surely Mrs. Jones can afford the few extra mills for her fruits and vegetables, the money needed to give domestic migrants a break."

When asked why the bracero comes to the United States, he replied:

The lure of the American buck. The real tragedy for him is that he's a good guy, usually, when he arrives here. But he and others like him, about 40 per cent, never return to their homes in Mexico after getting a taste of life here. This has caused a fearful number of broken homes in Mexico, something the Mexican bishops have long protested.

Then he quoted from Pope Leo XIII's *Rerum Novarum:* "Rich men and masters should remember this — that to exercise pressure, for the sake of gain, upon the indigent and the destitute, and to make one's profit out of the need of another, is condemned by all laws, human and divine." Looking down at his ranch boots, still covered with the dust of the previous night's Mass in the fields, he asked: "Could anything be clearer than that?"

He explained that migrants' efforts to organize themselves, to form a good union, can never come to anything so long as employers can say: "If you don't like the way we do things, we can always import workers." Even strikes have come to nothing, he said, "because braceros were brought in to help break them here in California — and men have been killed by deputy sheriffs in the process."

The wave of press releases by California growers' associations and their public-relations firms shows that the campaign for renewal of Public Law 78 is based on fear: fear that the crops will not be harvested, and fear that the cost of food will be increased.

You wonder, when you hear people out here express fear that they will have to pay a few cents more for a can of tomatoes or a sack of green beans, just what has happened to their instincts for justice and social compassion. When James P. Mitchell was U.S. Secretary of Labor, he said: "In this land, we do not choose to keep down our bills, including our food bills, at the cost of underpaying and overworking human beings."

As Fr. James L. Vizzard, S.J., says: "There can be neither moral nor economic justification for spending taxpayers' money for the antithesis of family farming, i.e., corporation or factory farming — one of the developments accelerated by the agricultural revolution."

America 111 (19–26 December 1964): 799, 802. Printed with permission.

95. Michael Novak, "Participatory Democracy at Work: The Grape Strike," 24 December 1965[1]

Some thirty years ago the vineyards and orchards of California were the setting of a moving novel by John Steinbeck, *The Grapes of Wrath*. In 1965, a new kind of story was being written in those hot, dusty valleys, but the story is not ended yet and the outcome is still in doubt.

The bare bones of the story are that the powerful financial and political interests whose strength rests upon the landowners and growers of California agriculture are being challenged for the first time by an indigenous, dignified, courageous group of domestic laborers. These local workers are staking their income and their lives on a strike they do not intend to end without success.

There have been many strikes in California since 1929. Almost all of them were very short, and none were effective. In agriculture, there are no factory gates to picket; there are hundreds of square miles of land (the present pickets must cover 400 square miles). Workers whose annual wage does not often reach $3000, and is usually less than $2000, in a state whose median income is $6,726, have slender resources. Great national unions which from time to time have sent in organizers and funds have always faced a double problem: (1) to call for a strike; and (2) to organize the scattered, poorly-educated, often skeptical and abject workers. For the first time, in 1965, there are in central California small but highly motivated cadres of local domestic laborers who have been organizing themselves for more than a year; who place their faith and their trust in one another and in the ultimate good sense of the growers; and who, when the moment came, had the discipline and the courage to sponsor a strike under their own auspices. Never has a strike lasted this long — at the present writing, nine weeks. Never has hope of success been so possible.

The dollar and cents issue of the strike, moreover, is far from being the fundamental issue. Wages for the workers vary from farm to farm, but before the strike they often did not reach $1.25 an hour, plus ten cents per basket (a fast worker might fill four baskets in an hour). Most workers have to have cars, and drive usually more than sixty miles round trip to the fields that are being worked on any given day. Only during harvest time are they paid at the

---

1. At the time of publication, Michael Novak was an assistant professor of religion at Stanford.

above rate; during the trimming season, the rate goes down; part of the year there is no work at all. The strikers are currently demanding $1.40 an hour and twenty-five cents per piece. Under the pressure of the strike, a few growers have taken steps toward meeting this demand. But the fundamental issue has not yet been met by even one single grower, not even by so much as a letter and a five-cent stamp.

That issue is the right of collective bargaining. Under the leadership of their soft-spoken, impressive and thoughtful spokesman, Cesar Chavez, the local laborers are asking for the dignity of being included in discussions concerning their own fate and that of the industry to which they are committed. They are even prepared to write a "no-strike clause" into their contracts, recognizing the perishability of the goods with which they deal. They are not prepared to allow the growers to go on paternalistically deciding what is good for the workers, or what the workers really want, or really need. They are asking to be treated as human beings — and to be granted at least the recognition that is granted to fertilizers, machinery and other factors in agribusiness. For the cost to the growers of all these items has risen in the last decade, but the cost of labor has remained almost stationary. The workers — and their traditional passivity and lack of organization — have been taken for granted.

Undoubtedly, the growers would like to continue running things the good old way — the way it was done, for many of them, in the old country of their fathers or grandfathers: Italy, Portugal, Yugoslavia, etc. The growers are willing to spend vast sums of money for political lobbying to keep things the good old way, and still further sums to bring in busloads of strikebreakers from as far away as Texas, and still further sums repacking fruit that the new, inexperienced workers mishandle. They have not yet come to the conclusion that a satisfied, skilled, local labor force is in the long run cheaper than their herculean efforts to avoid learning the lessons all other industries have learned. Every industry has special problems. Few industries have been blessed with strikers committed to nonviolence as the present strikers in the vineyards are. Few have been blessed with strikers who are unwilling to single out any one grower for their efforts, knowing that they could bring him to his knees. As Cesar Chavez has said: "It is a problem in which all the growers are involved, no single one; we do not wish to crucify one for the problem of all."

Chavez himself was born in Arizona, where his father worked a small farm. Like many other southwestern families, they lost their farm in the Depression and joined the caravans westward for work in California fields. Chavez spent his boyhood near Delano, and his wife's family is from Delano. It is largely because he is of the people there that, since his return in 1962 to begin his preparation for the present effort, they trust him implicitly as they would trust no outsider. He is a charismatic figure, who speaks quietly and warmly, simply and resolutely. Of medium stature, dressed in the heavy clothes of the worker, his shoes dusty, he stands calmly at a speaker's rostrum slowly choosing words of scrupulous honesty and sympathy.

Will the Churches Help?

Chavez worked for a time with Saul Alinsky. It is not surprising, then, that the churches of central California have from the beginning been invited to hear the cause of the workers. On a recent Sunday, Chavez spoke to six different gatherings, most of them church people. The reactions are mixed. Local ministers in the Delano area, in Kern county just south of San Francisco, have issued a statement attempting to dissociate themselves from the strike; they wish to separate such temporal matters from the purely spiritual concerns of their version of Christianity. Local political groups — city council, school board, and sheriff's office — have likewise tried to make the strike go away by denying that it exists, attributing it to outside agitation, or disclaiming its disturbances. A few growers are said to have reacted to sermons which seemed to support the strikers by stopping their financial contributions to the offending parishes; and some parishes rely heavily on the wealthy.

But throughout central California more and more congregations, or individual Christians, are sending food, clothing and money to the strikers and their families, who otherwise are totally without income. Some strikers have already lost their automobiles; others are beginning to forfeit their mortgages on their poor dwellings. The strike lives by charity. Without persevering gifts, it cannot succeed. If it is broken, a great hope will die.

Two main groups of workers are involved in the strike. One is a union of Filipino-Americans (affiliated with the AFL-CIO), the other a group of Mexican-Americans. It is the latter that is led by Chavez and attracts the most attention. In the very first days of the strike, Chavez contacted CORE and SNCC, asking them for trained leaders to come and instruct his men in the difficult art of nonviolence. The union members had for months been contributing dues of $3.50 a month to a fund which enabled Chavez to represent them. Before calling the strike — a decision made by a unanimous vote of the membership, together with the commitment of nonviolence — Chavez tried to contact each of the growers, personally, by registered letter, and by wire. Not a single one responded. The tactic of the growers is to avoid recognizing the workers. Neither the growers nor appointed representatives heed the invitations of Chavez, or of interested audiences, to debate the issues publicly. Chavez accepts all invitations, even from hostile audiences. From the other side, silence. And that is the fundamental issue.

Chavez says he cannot estimate the number of strikers, because the growers keep bringing in waves of strikebreakers. When the latter come to understand that there is a strike (in one case, a California priest with a flyer's license flew over the fields with a loudspeaker and helped to inform them), many of them leave the work. Many who do not stay to join the picketers move off to other areas of California for the sake of their family income. When some among these return to Delano after the harvest season, there may well be a crisis of food, clothing and income as the strike store dwindles.

The Newest Wine

Recently, the longshoremen in San Francisco refused to load a ship with grapes from a grower that the strikers were picketing. The growers have also taken to loading boxcars at night or in the wee hours of the morning, when the pickets are not yet in evidence. A new wave of pride seems to be reaching the workers in the valley, and *"Huelga"* (strike) and *"La Causa"* are words that are also beginning to stir the middle-class Spanish communities that have moved on to better things in the surrounding cities. At a recent meeting of an interfaith social justice forum in Palo Alto (which overflowed the school auditorium of St. Albert the Great parochial school), a member of the Redwood City Guadalupe Society who obviously had come for that purpose sprang to his feet during the question period and announced with choking voice the support and prayers of his society for the courage of Chavez and his men.

There is something new, then, in the central valleys this year. At the same meeting, a distinguished-looking lawyer rose to his full height at the rear of the hall and identified himself as a negotiator for management in labor disputes over the last thirty years. He said that the growers ought to learn from the mistakes of other industries. In the long run and even in the short run, it is cheaper and also better business to treat laborers as men, to give them security and take care of their medical insurance and the rest, than to try to pay for all the trouble one man like that — he nodded toward Chavez — could cause them. In the end, he said, they'll only have to pay both expenses anyway.

There also seems to be a general sentiment in the California air that the end of the *bracero* program, which the Labor Department enforced over heavy local opposition, has redounded, all fearful myths to the contrary, to the greater prosperity of California agriculture. Experienced workers do better work, and where the pay is decent, workers are even attracted from other jobs. Moreover, one local bureau (Salinas County) reports a drop in the number of families on welfare from 313 to 77, once domestic labor began to find steady work. Money earned by domestic laborers is spent in the locality. The growers do not have to pay to ship workers back and forth out of the country.

But perhaps this picture is too optimistic. Coverage by press and television is not extensive. The growers have not yet shown signs of grappling with reality, even though some moral prestige is shifting toward the strikers. They will meet the workers paternalistically, but not man-to-man. The strike is not seriously hurting the harvesting, though the work is not going smoothly. It is a bumper year for grapes. The growers are needled, the workers are hoping with a desperate but calm hope that the needle is sharp enough to puncture paternalism. And everything depends upon the charity of the larger Christian, Jewish and liberal community.

But what constitutes the newest wine in the central valley is not a longer strike than any before, but the new type of democracy which it represents. This is not the democracy of the 1930's, not the socialistic theory and the techniques of power and interest. Cesar Chavez was convinced that this movement had to come from the sentiments, intelligence and resolution of the community, without the benefit of national unions, their organizers and their funds. Moreover, each decision had to be participated in by the membership. The men have not committed themselves to a technique of power, for a clearly defined pragmatic goal. They have committed themselves to a way of life, to a sense of personal dignity, restraint and trust in one another and the organism of free societies. There is a humanism here which exceeds anything found in the literature of the 'thirties, a sense of community which is different from mere comradeship, a conviction that growers and workers alike are organically related and not merely separate centers of power to be brought into balance. If this is a liberalism, it is liberalism in a more human and more Christian dimension. If it is a democracy, it is more "participatory" than bureaucratic or structural.

There is, in short, a streak of what the British call "conservatism" in this new liberalism of the California fields. Its intellectual source is not the Enlightenment. Men are not atomic particles, but members of a community. There seem to be accents here of what the students across the bay at Berkeley are saying, in their own inimitable style: the birth of something new in American democracy, new wine about to rupture old skins.

Commonweal 83 (24 December 1965): 366–69. Printed with permission of the author.

96. "California Bishops Praise Farm Labor Law: Statement of the Catholic Bishops of California on Farm Labor Law," 5 June 1975

The California agricultural labor relations act is the first labor law in the nation to specifically provide for the collective bargaining rights of agricultural field workers. A compromise measure incorporating features advocated by each of the parties in the California farm labor dispute — the growers, the United Farm Workers of America, and the Teamsters union — the act defined the rights, powers and duties of the farm workers, their employers, and the unions which represent or seek to represent them. It permitted collective bargaining, strikes and secondary boycotts, but only after the union involved wins recognition as the workers' representative through secret ballot election. It also established an Agricultural Labor Relations Board to oversee elections and handle disputes.

We, the Catholic bishops of California, along with all men of goodwill, are appreciative of the signing into law of the Alatorre-Zenovich-Dunlap-Berman Agricultural Labor Relations Act of 1975.

The importance of this historic day lies not only with the enactment of legal provisions to afford agricultural labor peace in our state, but more especially, with the recognition and protection of the individual dignity and rights of the state's farm workers.

We salute the leadership and determination of our governor, Edmund G. Brown, Jr., for setting in motion the various elements to bring a legislative solution to this struggle in our fields. We are grateful to all who participated in working out this solution: the many and varied grower organizations, the United Farm Workers of America, AFL-CIO, the Western Conference of Teamsters, the authors of the bill in the Assembly and the Senate, the state legislators and the many advisors and staff who contributed to the finalization of the bill.

The mere signing of legislation does not guarantee an end to all the anguish and strife that has accompanied this dispute over the years. That can be accomplished only through a change of individual attitudes — a sincere change of heart, which will create the much needed atmosphere of trust.

Although the act does not become effective until late August, we believe the various parties can begin now to create a new era of mutual trust, which must be the first step toward peace in our fields. We see no justification for the parties to continue in last-minute hostility now that they are to be partners for peace and justice. We therefore call upon the parties to demonstrate their goodwill these three months in very concrete ways:

1. We urge the growers already with contracts to allow full access by the unions to the farm workers to acquaint them with the benefits of the union movement and participation in it.

2. We urge the growers and Teamsters to suspend at once all contract negotiations and contract signings until the act becomes effective and the workers have had the opportunity to express their wishes through secret ballot elections.

3. If the above can be implemented, we see no reason at all for economic and other pressures against growers and producers, and would, in good conscience, urge the UFWA and Teamsters to suspend at once, boycotts, strikes, slow-downs and other activities, until the terms of the new legislation become effective.

Only the parties to a dispute have the ability to demonstrate that the good faith which has brought them to this stage of agreement runs wide and deep in their attitudes, trust and determination to have peace now.

We ask God's special blessing upon the many people engaged in our state's agricultural industry, and ask him to sustain and strengthen that commitment to justice and peace in which we all share today.

Origins 5, no. 4 (19 June 1975): 49, 51. Printed with permission of the California Catholic Conference.

97. Msgr. George Higgins, Address to the National Catholic Educational Association on Unionism in Catholic Schools, 5 October 1976

Ever since lay teachers began to outnumber religious on Catholic school staffs, the trend toward the unionization of Catholic teachers has grown steadily. What has also grown steadily is a resistance to unionization by some school administra-

tors who see in the union movement the latest threat to the survival of Catholic schools.

. . . One of the great mistakes that was made by the American management in industry 40 years ago was that it completely underestimated the intelligence, the determination, the skill and the drive of the people it was dealing with. Forty years ago, management in the mass production industries thought that the workers' drive for unionization did not have to be taken seriously, but now I am sure they are happy, by and large, that it came to pass. The time has come, I think, for our Catholic institutions to do what everybody else in the United States had to do 40 years ago, and that is to begin to take seriously the right, or if you will, the obligation of people to organize into their own economic organizations — not to put our schools out of business but to enable them to carry on human relations in the economic field in the most sensible way that men have thus far been able to discover.

In a more perfect world, in a utopian world, there might be a better way to carry on human relations in the economic field than to do it through unions, but we do not live in that kind of world. And the notion that because we are connected in some way or another with Catholic institutions, or even worse, the notion that because we graduated from a Catholic nursing school and are now working in a non-Catholic hospital or health situation, and therefore should not get involved in this rather "dirty" business of trade unionism, is as dead as a dodo.

We live in a real world in which most people, in one form or another, are going to carry on an economic relationship through organization. To fight it under some confused understanding of the vow of poverty, or of the independence of church-related institutions, would be a serious mistake.

One very significant development in this area ought to teach us a lesson — namely, the rapid growth of teachers' unions and associations in the public school system and the increasing militancy of these organizations. Ten years ago, if any one had predicted this development, he would not have been taken seriously. Five years ago, nurses, teachers and people in similar professions simply had nothing to do with formal processes of labor-management relations. That couldn't go on forever. Industry is finding this out even in the case of highly skilled technicians and engineers. At long last — like teachers, nurses, and professionals — they are beginning to organize and to insist on their right to bargain collectively with their employers.

What I am suggesting is that rather than be the last, as we have so often been in the past, administrators of Catholic institutions should strike out on their own and, for once, take the lead in establishing progressive labor-management relations in their particular profession. There is no reason why they can't do it, and every reason why they should.

At the present time I think it would have to be said in all honesty that Catholic institutions, by and large, are not out in front in the field of labor-management relations in their particular profession. The time has come, then, to make up for lost time. The administrators of Catholic institutions can no longer ask for special treatment on the grounds that their institutions are serving society on a nonprofit basis and should therefore be exempt from the normal rules of labor-management relations.

If Catholic administrators want to be real professionals today, they must operate according to the highest standards of the communities in which their institutions exist. In the field of labor-management relations that means complete freedom for their professional and nonprofessional employees to exercise their right to organize and to carry on collective bargaining according to the procedures long since established, under the law of the land, in private industry....

Origins 6, no. 18 (21 October 1976): 277, 280–81. Printed with permission of Msgr. Higgins.

Human Sexuality:
Birth Control, Abortion, Homosexuality

In the postwar period, matters of human sexuality, previously often discussed in hushed tones and behind closed doors, burst into print and became a regular feature of American political, social, and cultural life. As the American Catholic community has become more thoroughly integrated into the mainstream of American public life, Catholic attitudes on matters of human sexuality have come to reflect the commonly held belief that such matters are essentially private and that the morality of sexual acts should be worked out by the individual conscience. It is difficult to pin down one, unified Catholic voice on these subjects.

Birth control is such a subject. Spurred by the Vatican, American church officials have not been shy in addressing the public aspects of this very private matter. Public voices on the birth control question often take up the issue of publicly funded population control programs, either at home or abroad. Official positions are consistently critical of such programs, yet even here, countervailing voices operating within the Catholic theological tradition have been heard.

A similar dynamic obtains in the matter of therapeutic abortion. The *Roe v. Wade* decision of 22 January 1971 struck down legislation forbidding elective abortion. Catholic opposition to this ruling and efforts to turn it back have become an important part of the political culture of the 1970s, 1980s, and 1990s. The response of Archbishop Rembert Weakland of Milwaukee to the women of his archdiocese offers a revealing view of Catholics struggling over this difficult subject.

Traditional strictures against homosexual acts have also come under serious discussion, especially with the onset of organized gay activism in the wake of the 1969 Stonewall Uprising in New York City. The public aspects of this debate revolve around issues of gay rights, discrimination directed against gay men and women, and the provision of spousal benefits for homosexual unions.

98. Administrative Board, National Catholic Welfare Conference, "Explosion or Backfire?" 19 November 1959

1. For the past several years a campaign of propaganda has been gaining momentum to influence international, national, and personal opinion in favor of birth prevention programs. The vehicle for this propaganda is the recently coined terror technique phrase, "population explosion." The phrase, indeed, alerts all to the attention that must be given to population pressures, but it also provides a smoke screen behind which a moral evil may be foisted on the public and for obscuring the many factors that must be considered in this vital question.

2. More alarming is the present attempt of some representatives of Christian bodies who endeavor to elaborate the plan into a theological doctrine which envisages artificial birth prevention within the married state as the "will of God." Strangely too, simply because of these efforts and with callous disregard of the thinking of hundreds of millions of Christians and others who reject the position, some international and national figures have made the statement that artificial birth prevention within the married state is gradually becoming acceptable even in the Catholic Church. This is simply not true.

3. The perennial teaching of the Catholic Church has distinguished artificial birth prevention, which is a frustration of the marital act, from other forms of control of birth which are morally permissible. Method alone, however, is not the only question involved. Equally important is the sincere and objective examination of the motives and intentions of the couples involved, in view of the nature of the marriage contract itself. As long as due recognition is not given to these fundamental questions, there can be no genuine understanding of the problem.

4. At the present time, too, there is abundant evidence of a systematic, concerted effort to convince United States public opinion, legislators, and policy makers that United States national agencies, as well as international bodies, should provide with public funds and support, assistance in promoting artificial birth prevention for economically under-developed countries. The alleged purpose, as already remarked, is to prevent a hypothetical "population explosion." Experts, however, have not yet reached agreement on the exact meaning of this phrase. It is still a hypothesis that must stand the test of science. Yet, pessimistic population predictors seizing on the popular acceptance of the phrase, take little account of economic, social, and cultural factors and changes. Moreover, it would seem that if the predictors of population explosion wish to avail themselves of the right to foretell *population increases*, they

must concede the right to predict *production increases* of food as well as of employment and educational opportunities.

5. The position of United States Catholics to the growing and needy population of the world is a realistic one which is grounded in the natural law (which, it should be made clear, is not the law of the jungle, as sometimes erroneously supposed) and in respect for the human person, his origin, freedom, responsibility, and destiny. They believe that the goods of the earth were created by God for the use of all men and that men should not be arbitrarily tailored to fit a niggling and static image of what they are entitled to, as conceived by those who are more fortunate, greedy, or lazy. The thus far hidden reservoirs of science and of the earth unquestionably will be uncovered in this era of marvels and offered to humanity by dedicated persons with faith in mankind, and not by those seeking short cuts to comfort at the expense of the heritage of their own or other peoples.

6. United States Catholics believe that the promotion of artificial birth prevention is a morally, humanly, psychologically and politically disastrous approach to the population problem. Not only is such an approach ineffective in its own aims, but it spurns the basis of the real solution, sustained effort in a sense of human solidarity. Catholics are prepared to dedicate themselves to this effort, already so promisingly initiated in national and international circles. They will not, however, support any public assistance, either at home or abroad, to promote artificial birth prevention, abortion or sterilization whether through direct aid or by means of international organizations.

7. The fundamental reason for this position is the well-considered objection to promoting a moral evil — an objection not founded solely on any typically or exclusively Catholic doctrine, but on the natural law and on basic ethical considerations. However, quite apart from the moral issue, there are other cogent reasons why Catholics would not wish to see any official support or even favor given such specious methods of "assistance."

Social Development

8. Man himself is the most valuable productive agent. Therefore, economic development and progress are best promoted by *creating conditions* favorable to his *highest development.* Such progress implies discipline, self-control, and the disposition to postpone present satisfactions for future gains. The widespread use of contraceptives would hinder rather than promote the acquisition of these qualities needed for the social and economic changes in underdeveloped countries.

Immigration

9. Immigration and emigration — even within the same country — have their role to play in solving the population problem. It has been said that migration to other countries is no ultimate solution because of difficulties of absorbing populations into other economies. But it is a matter of record that migration has helped as a solution. Sixty million people migrated successfully

from Europe to the Americas in the last one hundred fifty years. When the nomadic Indians roamed the uncultivated plains of North America before the coming of these immigrants, the entire country with its estimated Indian population of only 500,000 and its shortage of food, would have been regarded as "over-populated" according to the norms of the exponents of Planned Parenthood. Yet, the same plains today are being retired into a "land bank" because they are overproductive in a land of 175 millions. It is, therefore, apparent that to speak of a population explosion in the United States in these circumstances is the sheerest kind of nonsense.

Political and Psychological

10. The Soviets in their wooing of economically underdeveloped countries do not press artificial birth prevention propaganda on them as a remedy for their ills. Rather they allure them into the Communist orbit by offering education, loans, technical assistance, and trade, and they boast that their economic system is able to use human beings in constructive work and to meet all their needs. The Russian delegate to the relatively recent meeting of the United Nations Economic Commission on Asia and the Far East proclaimed, "The key to progress does not lie in a limitation of population through artificial reduction of the birthrate, but in the speedy defeat of the economic backwardness of these countries." The Communist record of contempt for the value of human life gives the lie to this hypocritical propaganda, but to peoples aspiring to economic development and political status, the deceit is not immediately evident. Confronted on the one hand by the prospect of achieving their goals without sacrificing natural fertility and on the other by the insistence that reducing natural fertility is essential to the achievement of such goals, how could these peoples be reasonably expected to reject Communism? Yet, the prophets of "population explosion" in alleging that contraception will thwart Communism naively emphasize its specious attractiveness in these areas.

Food and Agriculture

11. United States Catholics do not wish to ignore or minimize the problem of population pressure, but they do deplore the studious omission of adequate reference to the role of modern agriculture in food production. The "population explosion" alarmists do not place in proper focus the idea of increasing the acreage or acreage yield to meet the food demands of an increasing population. By hysterical terrorism and bland misrepresentation of data they dismiss these ideas as requiring too much time for the development of extensive education and new distribution methods and for the elimination of apathy, greed, and superstition. Such arguments merely beg the question, for the implementation of their own program demands the fulfillment of the same conditions. It seems never to dawn on them that in a chronic condition where we have more people than food, the logical answer would be, not to decrease the number of people but to increase the food supply which is almost unlimited in potential.

12. We make these observations to direct attention to the very real problem of population pressures. Such remarks are not intended to exhaust this complex subject, nor to discourage demographers, economists, agricultural experts, and political scientists in their endeavors to solve the problem. Rather, our intention is to reaffirm the position of the Catholic Church that the only true solutions are those that are morally acceptable under the natural law of God. Never should we allow the unilateral "guesstimates" of special pleaders to stampede or terrorize the United States into a national or international policy inimical to human dignity. For, the adoption of the morally objectionable means advocated to forestall the so-called "population explosion" may backfire on the human race.

> Hugh J. Nolan, ed., *Pastoral Letters of the United States Catholic Bishops* (Washington, D.C.: United States Catholic Conference, 1984), 2:221–25. Printed with permission.

99. Dexter L. Hanley, S.J., "The Catholic and Population Policy," 1966[1]

Tonight I wish to address myself to one major question: Can a Catholic support governmental family-planning programs without in some way compromising the power and right of the Church to teach men right from wrong? You, who are familiar with present-day debates and discussions of population and public policy, realize how explosive is the question, how delicate the nuances presented, how imperative the demand for a solution. It is then with some trepidation that I address myself to this topic.

Let me outline the premises upon which my discussion — indeed the problem itself — is based.

First, there is a concern of international and national dimensions arising out of the effort to match resources with manpower and to distribute the advantages of a temporal prosperity. Our information comes from demographic sources and points out a three-fold problem: the need of food, the lack of resources, the difficulty of distribution even in an affluent society. In the world today, there are vast areas of malnutrition and pockets of starvation. In many places with a fast-growing population, minimal or subminimal caloric intake is predicted for years to come. Most of the nations of the world and most of its people find that every effort to build a high standard of living is swallowed up in an increased population. Even the richest of countries finds that millions of its citizens are deprived of adequate education, opportunity, and a decent living — and the enormity and the complexity of the problems dwarf the attempts to improve the situation.

I shall not spell out the dire prophecies nor even quote from available statistics. This is the province of the sociologist and the demographer; their studies

---

1. This statement was delivered to the Catholic Roundtable, Washington, D.C., in April 1966. Father Hanley held an LL.B. from Georgetown University and was director of the Institute of Law, Human Rights and Social Values, Georgetown Law Center, Washington, D.C.

are available. Suffice it to say that the mass of independent information drives home both foreseeable limits upon resources and the challenge to the quality of daily living. There are threats of famine, of war, of declining standards, and of social disabilities brought about by a universally high birth rate....

It should be noted, however, that these studies do not tell us what to do about the problem. Nor are they anything more than projections based upon present birth rates. They point out the mathematical fact that if present birth rates continue, resources and living space will be depleted. Perhaps more importantly they point out that today's growth is one factor which has made it difficult, if not impossible, to achieve economic and social development in many areas of the world.

My second premise is a religious principle: according to the theological, moral, and authoritative pronouncements of the Catholic Church, the only morally acceptable form of voluntary family regulation is through continence, either total or periodic. Now I realize as well as you that a papal commission has been established to study Church doctrine in relation to birth control; I know that the Vatican Council, in speaking of the nobility of marriage and the family, has said that parents themselves must ultimately make a judgment in the sight of God as how best to fulfill their mission of transmitting human life and educating their children....

Yet, the clear statements of Pope Paul and the exquisite care with which the Council avoided decisions on fundamental questions and its insistence on objective standards make it clear that in matters of private morality the Church's position has not changed.

Perhaps it would interest you were I to enter into the speculations and debates on the question of private morality in the Church today: but I shall not. Indeed, if we are to study how to coordinate public policy and private morality, it is imperative that we assume that a conflict exists between the two. For, if the Catholic position at some later date were to be otherwise than I have outlined it, the problems of accommodating it to public policy would evanesce. Likewise, if there is no legitimate public concern over family regulation, then the government should stay out. The real challenge to democratic ideals is whether we can harmonize conflicting interests, not whether we can make all men agree. The basic issue then to which I am addressing myself is this: can a Catholic, believing that certain practices of birth regulation are immoral, still either permit or support governmental programs which are designed to meet the problems of population growth and which involve these forbidden practices? I believe the answer to this question is "yes." I also believe that the reasons for holding this position and the qualifications which are necessary are perhaps more important than the answer.

Let me then try this evening to show you why I maintain that an affirmative answer is consonant with the true notion of religious freedom, with the teachings of my Church, and with the principles of democratic government. This should be of equal interest to Catholic and non-Catholic alike, though for different reasons. For the Catholic it is a matter of his conscientious regard for his religious and civic obligations; for the non-Catholic it is the no less important question of assuring to his Catholic brethren full freedom of conscience.

The Catholic Church has made no definitive statements on matters of public policy in family planning. This is a matter for open public discussion. On June 23, 1964, Pope Paul VI reaffirmed the norms of private morality in saying: "No one should...for the time being take upon himself to pronounce himself in terms differing from the norm in force." His Holiness was not, however, addressing himself to political issues or to public morality. On his recent visit to the United Nations, the Pope indicated that man's concern should be for making the world's goods available to all men, rather than for limiting births. This expression of charity and of love is not determinative of the Catholic position on governmental family-planning programs. The Vatican Council has said: "Public authority should regard it as a sacred duty to recognize, protect and promote the authentic nature [of the family], to shield public morality, and to favor the prosperity of home life. The right of parents to beget and educate their children in the bosom of the family must be safeguarded." But, as we shall see, this must be read in the context of religious liberty and of an understanding of the function of government.

The place of government in family planning has been dealt with on three occasions by the hierarchy of the United States. In 1959, the Bishops stated their opposition to any proposal the aim of which, either at home or abroad, is to promote artificial birth prevention, abortion, or sterilization whether through direct aid or by means of international organizations. In August of 1965, the Pennsylvania bishops and the Administrative Board of the National Catholic Welfare Conference issued a statement which presented legal arguments against proposed government action in this area. And on August 29, 1965, the Archbishop of Washington expressed strong disagreement with the governmental programs on the basis of moral law and constitutional law. Although none of these statements is a definitive Church statement, they are all entitled to the highest respect and careful consideration by American Catholics especially where they bear on the moral law.

In these statements the authority of the moral law is invoked primarily on questions of private morality, in teaching and emphasizing the traditional forms of which I have spoken. Yet, if one disentangles the issue of public morality, it becomes clear that these statements either leave room for honest differences of opinion, or are based on private understandings of legal principles, or are directed to questions somewhat different from what I have proposed.

The most difficult statement to square with my position is the 1959 statement of the American hierarchy in opposition to any program to promote artificial birth prevention. I have always understood the words "to promote" as implying that the government itself supports artificial birth prevention as being moral, that is, as taking sides on a moral question. A brief reference to the history of the birth-control movement may make this clear. The early proponents of birth control were primarily engaged in selling a moral point of view. Of course, they were also engaged in an issue of civil rights inasmuch as they sought the overturn of those penal laws which forbade them to disseminate information. This latter battle finally culminated in the overthrow by the Supreme Court of the Connecticut Comstock Law. This decision has met with general acceptance and approval by Catholic commentators. But, if the government were now to step in and promote the moral philosophy of sexual freedom and of feminine emancipation from child bearing as originally conceived by the Birth Control League, it would, I suggest, clearly be taking sides in a religious and moral controversy. To this extent it would clearly be exceeding constitutional limits.

But I am suggesting that a meeting ground can be found wherein the government does no such thing. Rather than promote a moral position, the government can be concerned with a social problem; rather than take sides, it can remain neutral. It is our modern understanding of the population problem which makes this possible....

Reflection on a few more points may show how even the direct support of a government program can be harmonized with Catholic teaching. Perhaps most important is the growing understanding that the Catholic position on private morality and birth control is fundamentally a religious position. The existence of debates, the creation of the special commissions, the discussions of the Council, the papal declarations about the difficulty of arriving at definitive answers — all these indicate that any definitive teachings will be ultimately rooted in the infallible teaching authority of the Church. Reason alone has not proved a clear guide. Present discussion in the Church will be resolved finally in a clarification of past teachings, or in a statement founded on the power to teach, or in a declaration of discipline.

Out of all this, one thing is clear and pertinent to our discussion. Lacking or rejecting the guidance of the Catholic Church, men, even those of utmost good-will, can differ about these questions of private morality. Thus, the decisions reached by non-Catholics and by Catholics are religious decisions. Thus, as a matter of practical and political fact, neither position may be said to be right in the political order. And, just as we recognize religious freedom for theological convictions, we must grant civic freedom to moral convictions. Here, too, the common good is the regulating norm. This seems to be in accord with, though not required by, the Vatican Council's Declaration on Religious Freedom: "[N]o one is to be forced to act in a manner contrary to his own beliefs nor is anyone to be restrained from acting in accordance with his own beliefs, whether privately or publicly, whether alone or in association with others, within due limits...."

I suppose the Catholic's greatest difficulty in accepting the general proposition of this evening's discussion grows out of his understanding of his obligations toward his neighbor. One cannot give scandal, in the sense that he cannot offer another the occasion for sin. Nor may he cooperate, that is, concur in the evil intention of another nor, as a general rule, aid him in the commission of a sinful act. Now, to the Catholic, many of the procedures which the government will offer to the free choice of its citizens are sinful. How is he then to reconcile his own conscience, should he permit or support such programs?...

If one now assumes a purified and legitimate public purpose, the question of scandal and cooperation may be answered in the light of a statement already made: that decisions on private morality in the area of birth control are arrived at in good faith and are religious conclusions. When textbooks of Catholic moral theology speak of scandal and cooperation, they are generally concerned about formal sin on the part of one individual and about the direct act of another in private life. Very little guidance is found in the complex area of public responsibility and civic obligation and still less when one's support of a civic program does not involve formal sin, but only a violation of an objective order recognized by faith. Thus, the Catholic can support government programs because of their legitimate social aims and because of the civic value of religious freedom and choice. In doing so, he neither approves of what he thinks to be wrong nor does he support or in most instances give occasion to formal sin. In the language of the theologian, by his vote he gives remote cooperation to a program which itself is a material cooperation in private acts which for some will be objectively morally justified and for most others subjectively justified. That there may be some formal sin we may agree, but the Catholic's action, being remote and concerned with achieving legitimate social goals, does not offend against the love he must show his neighbor....

Originally published in *Catholic Lawyer* 12 (fall 1966): 330–36. Printed with permission.

100. National Conference of Catholic Bishops, "Statement on the Government and Birth Control," 14 November 1966

1. The good of the individual person and that of human society are intimately bound up with the stability of the family. Basic to the well-being of the family is freedom from external coercion in order that it may determine its own destiny.

2. This freedom involves inherent personal and family rights, including the freedom and responsibility of spouses to make conscientious decisions in terms of nuptial love, determination of family size, and the rearing of children. The Church and the State must play supportive roles, fostering conditions in modern society which will help the family achieve the fullness of its life and mission as the means ordained by God for bringing the person into being and maturity.

3. We address ourselves here to certain questions of concern to the family, with the special references to public policies related to social conditions and the problems of our times.

4. In so doing, we speak in the light of the *Pastoral Constitution on the Church in the Modern World* adopted by Vatican Council II. Faced with our

government's stepped-up intervention in family planning, including the subsidizing of contraceptive programs at home and abroad, we feel bound in conscience to recall particularly the solemn warning expressed in these words:

5. "...[There] are many today who maintain that the increase in world population, or at least the population increase in some countries, must be radically curbed by every means possible and by any kind of intervention on the part of public authority. In view of this contention, the Council urges everyone to guard against solutions, whether publicly or privately supported, or at times even imposed, which are contrary to the moral law. For in keeping with man's inalienable right to marry and generate children, the decision concerning the number of children they will have depends on the correct judgment of the parents and it can in no way be left to the judgment of public authority" (*Church in the Modern World*, Section 2, Number 87).

6. Therefore, a major pre-occupation in our present statement must be with the freedom of spouses to determine the size of their families. It is necessary to underscore this freedom because in some current efforts of government — federal and state — to reduce poverty, we see welfare programs increasingly proposed which include threats to the free choice of spouses. Just as freedom is undermined when poverty and disease are present, so too is freedom endangered when persons or agencies outside the family unit, particularly persons who control welfare benefits or represent public authority, presume to influence the decision as to the number of children or the frequency of births in a family.

7. Free decision is curtailed when spouses feel constrained to choose birth limitation because of poverty, inadequate and inhuman housing, or lack of proper medical services. Here we insist that it is the positive duty of government to help bring about those conditions of family freedom which will relieve spouses from such material and physical pressures to limit family size.

8. Government promotion of family planning programs as part of tax-supported relief projects may easily result in the temptation and finally the tragic decision to reduce efforts to foster the economic, social, and indeed moral reforms needed to build the free, enlightened society.

9. In connection with present and proposed governmental family limitation programs, there is frequently the implication that freedom is assured so long as spouses are left at liberty to choose among different methods of birth control. This we reject as a narrow concept of freedom. Birth control is not a universal obligation, as is often implied; moreover, true freedom of choice must provide even for those who wish to raise a larger family without being subject to criticism and without forfeiting for themselves the benefits or for their children the educational opportunities which have become part of the value system of a truly free society. We reject, most emphatically, the suggestion that any family should be adjudged too poor to have the children it conscientiously desires.

10. The freedom of the spouses to determine the size of their families must not be inhibited by any conditions upon which relief or welfare assistance

is provided. Health and welfare assistance should not be linked, even indirectly, to conformity with a public agency's views on family limitation or birth control; nor may the right to found a large family be brought properly into question because it contradicts current standards arbitrarily deduced from general population statistics. No government social worker or other representative of public power should in any way be permitted to impose his judgment, in a matter so close to personal values and to the very sources of life, upon the family seeking assistance; neither should he be permitted to initiate suggestions placing, even by implication, public authority behind the recommendation that new life in a family should be prevented.

11. For these reasons, we have consistently urged and we continue to urge, as a matter of sound public policy, a clear and unqualified separation of welfare assistance from birth control consideration — whatever the legality or morality of contraception in general or in specific forms — in order to safeguard the freedom of the person and the autonomy of the family.

12. On previous occasions we have warned of dangers to the right of privacy posed by governmental birth control programs; we have urged upon government a role of neutrality whereby it neither penalizes nor promotes birth control. Recent developments, however, show government rapidly abandoning any such role. Far from merely seeking to provide information in response to requests from the needy, government activities increasingly seek aggressively to persuade and even coerce the underprivileged to practice birth control. In this, government far exceeds its proper role. The citizen's right to decide without pressure is now threatened. Intimate details of personal, marital and family life are suddenly becoming the province of government officials in programs of assistance to the poor. We decry this overreaching by government and assert again the inviolability of the right of human privacy....

16. In the international field, as in the domestic field, financial assistance must not be linked to policies which pressure for birth limitation. We applaud food supply programs of foreign aid which condition our cooperation on evidence that the nations benefitted pledge themselves to develop their own resources; we deplore any linking of aid by food or money to conditions, overt or oblique, involving prevention of new life. Our country is not at liberty to impose its judgment upon another, either as to the growth of the latter or as to the size of its families....

18. Programs inhibiting new life, above all when linked to offers of desperately needed aid, are bound to create eventual resentment in any upon whom we even seem to impose them and will ultimately be gravely detrimental to the image, the moral prestige and the basic interests of the United States.

19. Obviously, therefore, international programs of aid should not be conditioned upon acceptance of birth control programs by beneficiary nations. Equally obvious, however, should be the fact that, in the practical administration of overseas assistance, neither direct nor indirect pressures should be exerted by our personnel to affect the choice of spouses as to the number of

children in their family. In the international field, as in the domestic field, both our government in its policy and our American representatives in their work, should strive above all to bring those economic and social advances which will make possible for spouses conscientious family planning without resort to contraceptive procedures fostered among them by controversial policies backed by American political power and financial aid.

20. Sobering lessons of history clearly teach that only those nations remain stable and vigorous whose citizens have and are encouraged to keep high regard for the sanctity and autonomy of family life among themselves and among the peoples who depend in any way upon them. Let our political leaders be on guard that the common good suffer no evil from public policies which tamper with the instincts of love and the sources of life.

Hugh J. Nolan, ed., *Pastoral Letters of the United States Catholic Bishops* (Washington, D.C.: United States Catholic Conference, 1984), 3:69–73. Printed with permission.

101. National Conference of Catholic Bishops, "Statement on Abortion," 22 April 1970

1. Last year, we stated our strong opposition to ongoing efforts to strike down laws prohibiting abortion. Our defense of human life is rooted in the Biblical prohibition, "Thou shalt not kill." Regrettably, there has been a radical turn of events during this past year, and a new effort has been directed to the total repeal of all such laws. At the same time, an effort has been mounted in the courts to have such laws declared unconstitutional.

2. Therefore we speak again on the important issue of public policy, addressing ourselves to the Catholic community and to all our fellow citizens. For the question of abortion is a moral problem transcending any particular sectarian approach. Our opposition to abortion derives from our conviction that whatever is opposed to life is a *violation* of man's inherent rights, a position that has a strong basis in the history of American law. The U.S. Bill of Rights guarantees the right to life to every American, and the U.N. Declaration on the Rights of the Child, which our nation endorses, affirms that the child, because of his dependent status, should be accorded a special protection under the law before as well as after birth (U.N. General Assembly, November 20, 1959).

3. In light of the attempts to remove all prohibition of abortion from our legal system, the life of the innocent unborn child is no longer given universal protection in the laws of our land. Moreover, the absence of all legal restraint promotes the acceptance of abortion as a convenient way for a woman to terminate the life of her child and the responsibilities that she has as its mother.

4. The implications of this proposed change in legal philosophy are enormous. Once we allow the taking of innocent human life in the earliest stages

of its development for the sake of convenience, how can we logically protect human life at any other point, once that life becomes a burden?

5. The assertion is made that a woman has a right not to be forced to bear a child against her will, but when a woman is already pregnant, this right must be considered in light of the child's right to life, the woman's responsibilities as its mother, and the rights and responsibilities of the child's father. The life of the unborn child is a human life. The destruction of any human life is not a private matter, but the concern of every responsible citizen.

6. We remain convinced that human life is a priceless gift, and our pastoral duty prompts us to reaffirm that "God, the Lord of life, has conferred on men the surpassing ministry of safeguarding life, a ministry which must be fulfilled in a manner which is worthy of man. Therefore from the moment of its conception life must be guarded with the greatest care, while abortion and infanticide are unspeakable crimes" (*Pastoral Constitution on the Church in the Modern World*, No. 51).

7. Once again, we declare our determination to seek solutions to the problems that lead some women to consider abortion. We pledge our efforts to do all that is possible to remove the social stigma that is visited on the woman who is pregnant out of wedlock, as well as on her child. We also pledge the facilities and the efforts of our Church agencies to provide counseling and understanding to the woman who faces a difficult pregnancy. At the same time, we are encouraged by the scientific advance of recent decades that has already provided us with ways to support and maintain the life and health of the mother and the development of the child in the womb.

8. Finally, we are aware that the value of human life is not exclusively a Catholic concern. Many Americans agonize over the loss of life involved in modern warfare, the serious ethical questions raised by recent scientific and surgical advances, the implications of pollution on our environment, and the long-range effects of drug use. But safeguarding the life of all men requires safeguarding the life of every individual, for our hold on life itself is only as strong as the weakest link in our system of law.

Hugh J. Nolan, ed., *Pastoral Letters of the United States Catholic Bishops* (Washington, D.C.: United States Catholic Conference, 1984), 3:254–55. Printed with permission.

102. Archbishop John Quinn, "A Pastoral Letter on Homosexuality," 5 May 1980

To the priests, deacons, religious and all the faithful of Christ in the Archdiocese of San Francisco: Grace and peace be yours from God our Father and from the Lord, Jesus Christ!

I. The Present-Day Situation

Vexing and serious questions arise with increasing frequency concerning the problem of homosexuality. While I cannot either treat or answer all possible questions on the subject, I feel it timely and important to offer some guidance and bring, I hope, some clarity to our understanding of the issue. It is with this purpose, then, that I write to you and commend to you the thoughts which follow in this pastoral letter.

A survey of the literature on the subject of homosexuality reveals that since 1974 especially there has been a growing public affirmation by individuals of their own homosexuality. At the same time pressures have been growing to remove prejudicial attitudes toward homosexual persons especially in regard to housing, hiring practices, teaching opportunities, etc. Still more there are growing pressures calling for recognition of the homosexual lifestyle as legitimate and worthy of societal, legal and ecclesiastical endorsement and approval.

In short, we are being besieged to move from a non-prejudicial attitude toward individuals to a point of view of total acceptance of homosexuality as a legitimate personal and public choice. Thus homosexuality is seen as a legitimate alternative to heterosexuality and the society is asked to support this position. Does this position warrant our agreement?

Several years ago, Jaroslav Pelikan attempted to crystallize the essence of the Catholic Church in the formula: identity plus universality. "By identity I mean that which distinguishes the church from the world — its message, its uniqueness, its particularity. By universality, on the other hand, I mean that which impels the church to embrace nothing less than all mankind in its vision and its appeal."

The general trend we are speaking of in regard to homosexuality reveals a determined bias toward the pole of universality, resulting in a distorted underemphasis on the pole of identity. Here it is well to recall Pope John Paul's reminder that the church must be a "sign of contradiction" to those elements of the world which threaten to distort, harm or destroy the authentic message of Christ.

And so as we move into the final decades marking 2,000 years since the birth of Christ, the church is keenly aware of a new and transforming consciousness of universality. But for the church this new consciousness stands within the perspective of a clear, certain and unambiguous Catholic identity which is embodied in the church's faith and witness to Jesus Christ.

An effort, then, to deal with the question of homosexuality must have clearly in mind both poles of universality and identity and must be built on the recognition that the Gospel is not a dichotomy between love and truth, for God, who is love, is also proclaimed by the scriptures as truth, and Jesus said of himself, "I am the truth."

1. Statement of the Question

There are several reasons why it is not easy to achieve a balanced and objective understanding of homosexuality. First of all, it is a highly charged emotional issue. Thus when certain mitigating factors at the subjective level are correctly pointed out, or when the human rights of homosexual individuals are defended, some wrongly conclude that this means an endorsement of homosexual activity.

In addition to the high emotions surrounding the issue, homosexuality in itself is enormously complex in its origins, its psychological vectors, medical ramifications, societal norms and in the application of valid moral principles to individual cases. Hence some of the aspects of the question do not admit of easy answers.

This does not at all say that the moral teaching of the church is unclear. It does say that it is necessary to recognize that we are dealing with an issue of considerable complexity in all dimensions.

Since not all persons who are homosexual engage in homosexual conduct, it is necessary at the outset to make the distinction between homosexual tendency and the acting out of homosexuality through specifically sexual encounters with persons of the same sex. It must also be pointed out that there is often a difference in understanding the language used in discussing homosexuality.

For instance, moral theologians tend to use the expression "homosexual orientation" to mean only the psychosexual attraction itself. On the other hand, legislative language often uses the expression "homosexual orientation" not merely for the psychosexual attraction, but also to include homosexual acts. For this reason the terminology used here is "homosexual attraction" or "tendency."

With this distinction in mind and respecting the contemporary data that in most cases the homosexual tendency has not been chosen, a working definition of homosexuality is a predominant, persistent and exclusive psychosexual attraction toward persons of the same sex; a homosexual person is one who feels sexual desire for and a sexual responsiveness to persons of the same sex, and who seeks or would like to seek actual sexual fulfillment of this desire by sexual acts with a person of the same sex. This definition rightly emphasizes the distinction between the homosexual condition, attraction or tendency, and homosexual acts.

2. Context for Our Response

The major theme of Pope John Paul's first encyclical *Redemptor Hominis*, is "again and always man" (n. 16). The whole encyclical is a powerful advocacy of respect and reverence for the dignity of the human person. Affirming that moral and spiritual progress is a necessity, the pope goes on to raise the question whether "man as man, is developing and progressing or is he regressing and being degraded in his humanity?" (n. 15)

The encyclical thus indicates an awareness of the tensions we have already mentioned between identity and universality. The Holy Father acknowledges the need to understand every person, every system, every legitimate right (universality). But he clearly notes that this does not mean "losing certitude about one's own faith or weakening the principles of morality" (n. 6).

This strong sense of certitude — identity — is seen in the encyclical always in the context of love, a love that is greater than sin and weakness, and the futility of creation. "It is stronger than death; it is a love always ready to raise up and forgive, always ready to go to meet the prodigal son, always looking for 'the revealing of the sons of God....' This revelation of love is also described as mercy; and in man's history this revelation of love and mercy has taken a form and a name: that of Jesus Christ" (n. 9).

The pope thus calls us to draw near to Christ — with all our unrest, uncertainties, weaknesses and sinfulness. We must learn to "appropriate and assimilate the whole of the reality of the incarnation and redemption" (n. 10) in order to find authentic meaning. Moral identity, in other words, must be rooted in the person of Jesus Christ, and it is to this end that the church must fully dedicate herself (n. 13).

And so the church must always safeguard and proclaim the true calling and the true dignity of humanity by holding in reverence the "transcendence of the human person" (n. 13) immeasurably enhanced by the incarnation, death and resurrection of the Son of God, who became like us in all things but sin so that we might become one with him.

In responding to any moral question, then, we must keep a correct perspective concerning human dignity and transcendence. Our perspective derives from the Gospel and not from any ideology. The teaching of the faith and the Lord's supreme commandment of love rooted in truth must always underlie our analysis of this and every other moral question.

Recent Catholic teaching on the subject of homosexuality has approached the subject from the point of charity and the inherent dignity of the human person. In 1974 the bishops of the United States issued a document titled *Principles to Guide Confessors in Questions of Homosexuality.* The document clearly reaffirms the objective gravity of homosexual acts.

At the same time it counsels sensitivity toward the individual homosexual person. The confessor, steering a course between harshness and permissiveness, should manifest great understanding, should give patient and loving encouragement to the individual in the often tedious and discouraging journey to grow in the image of Christ.

Similarly, in 1975 the Sacred Congregation for the Doctrine of the Faith issued a document titled *Declaration on Certain Questions Concerning Sexual Ethics.* This authentic document of the Holy See also reconfirms the objective wrongness of homosexual acts while drawing the important distinction between homosexual acts and a homosexual tendency or attraction.

Then in 1976 the American bishops wrote a lengthy pastoral letter touching on a variety of moral issues and bearing the title *To Live in Christ Jesus.* The teaching mentioned in the previous two documents is again stated.

In addition the pastoral letter adds the counsel that homosexual men and women should not suffer from prejudice on the basis of their sexual attraction. In fact, it states, the Christian community should provide a special degree of pastoral care and understanding for the problems of the homosexual person.

Most recently the pope himself spoke about homosexuality to the bishops of the United States in Chicago Oct. 4, 1979. He said "As men with the 'message of truth and the power of God' (2 Cor. 6:7), as authentic teachers of God's law and as compassionate pastors you also rightly stated 'Homosexual activity...as distinguished from homosexual orientation, is morally wrong.' In the clarity of this truth you exemplified the real charity of Christ; you did not betray those people who, because of homosexuality, are confronted with difficult moral problems, as would have happened if, in the name of understanding and compassion, or for any other reason, you had held out false hope to any brother or sister. Rather by your witness to the truth of humanity in God's plan, you effectively manifested fraternal love, upholding the true dignity, the true human dignity, of those who look to Christ's church for the guidance which comes from the light of God's word."

The recent teachings of the church therefore re-echo the clear teaching of the scriptures in declaring homosexual acts to be gravely evil and a disordered use of the sexual faculty. These same teachings also make clear the distinction between homosexual acts and homosexual orientation, and counsel sensitive and positive pastoral care in helping individual homosexual persons in their journey of discipleship.

The question then arises: What must be said to a subculture which advocates removing any distinction between homosexuality and heterosexuality? Given the fact that the authentic teaching of the church clearly affirms the objective gravity of homosexual acts, what must be said in light of the growing acceptance of homosexuality as a legitimate and alternative lifestyle?

3. The Real Problem

The term "homosexuality" is frequently used as if its meaning and connotations were self-evident. In fact, such is not the case. We have already noted how the term may apply either to a homosexual attraction or to homosexual conduct. In addition, we note that a fairly common view is that homosexuality represents an acquired condition that is both psychological and pathological. Yet many others do not accept homosexuality as pathological and view it as a variant form of sexual behavior. Some schools of thought hold that homosexuality is a purely physiological condition while others consider it only as a physiological pre-disposition.

These complexities in the data indicate the wide diversity of homosexual behaviors and only serve to increase the difficulty of arriving at a simple understanding of the problem. From a psychological point of view, homosexuality both in its origins and in its manifestations is a highly complex phenomenon and not always clearly understood even by experts.

Yet, it is because of developments in the fields of psychology and sociology that Catholic moral theology, guided by the distinction between sexual attraction and sexual behavior, is able to recognize more clearly factors which may in the case of individual conduct mitigate the gravity of such conduct on the subjective level.

But an additional problem arises for moral theology in a climate that increasingly encourages public revelation and proclamation of one's homosexual orientation. The emerging visibility of homosexuals and the militancy of the so-called "gay rights" movement only serve to heighten the problem. Still it is in light of this problem that the church must continue to uphold the human dignity and human rights of every person, including homosexual persons.

On the one hand, then, homosexuality cannot be treated simply as the manifestation of a consciously chosen depravity. Homosexual persons cannot, merely because they are homosexual, be visited with harassment and contempt. The lynch-gang approach cannot be justified.

At the same time, however, opposition to homosexuality as a form of conduct, opposition to homosexuality as an acceptable lifestyle by the church or by society cannot be regarded as a prejudice.

To agree that the persecution and harassment of homosexuals is incompatible with the Gospel is, therefore, not to say that the church and society should be neutral about homosexual activity. The church and society cannot and should not place the family which is and always will be the basic unit of society on a par with homosexual social units.

While we do not possess complete historical data on the subject, the fact is that in no culture has homosexuality been the dominant form of sexual expression and in Judaism and Christianity homosexual behavior has been clearly and consistently rejected as gravely contrary to the law of God....

III. Moral and Ethical Considerations

The moral teaching of the church on the scriptures themselves, and consistent in all periods of history, holds that homosexual behavior is objectively immoral, a human disvalue, disordered. The teaching of the church recognizes the fact that homosexuality has generally not been chosen by a person, but rather that most homosexual persons gradually come to the realization that they are homosexual.

Thus the church proposes various guidelines and pastoral approaches to assist and encourage the homosexual person's psychological and spiritual growth (cf. v.g. *Principles to Guide Confessors in Questions of Homosexuality*, 1974).

The church recognizes the complexity of the question as it exists in the life of an individual person as well as the complexity of the question in the fields of the behavioral sciences. There must be sensitivity in treating the question. Homosexual persons must be helped and encouraged to strive for wholeness and personal integrity as indeed all other persons must be encouraged, homosexual or heterosexual.

Sexual intercourse cannot be legitimated merely by individual preference or on the basis of sociological surveys or because of mutual consent between two parties. Sexual intercourse is legitimate and morally good only between husband and wife. Thus while it is claimed that homosexuality in a few instances is more or less fulfilling for a limited number of individuals, the homosexual condition and homosexual behavior cannot be morally normative.

The church always remains the church of the eucharist and of the sacrament of penance. Every member of the church should pray daily, and many times daily, the prayer the Lord has taught us: "Forgive us our trespasses as we forgive those who trespass against us." While the eucharist does manifest the community aspects of the church, "it cannot be treated merely as an 'occasion' for manifesting this brotherhood" (*Redemptor Hominis*, n. 20). More is required.

And so in this connection we must focus attention on the most recent letter of Pope John Paul II on the holy eucharist. He states: "We cannot allow the life of our communities to lose the good quality of sensitivity of conscience. A sensitive conscience is guided solely by respect for Christ who, when he is received in the eucharist, should find in the heart of each of us a worthy abode. This question is linked not only with the practice of the sacrament of penance but also with a correct sense of responsibility for the whole deposit of moral teaching and for the precise distinction between good and evil" (n. 11).

In order to receive the eucharist one must be in the state of grace, that is, in a living union with Christ characterized by the absence of grave sin. One must also be living in harmony with the moral and doctrinal teaching of the church.

Consequently, just as unmarried persons are not exempt from the moral teaching of the scriptures and of the church which has to do with sexual conduct, so homosexual persons are not exempt from this teaching either. Thus despite the difficulties, homosexual persons who wish to receive the eucharist must be honestly following the moral teaching of the church or at least sincerely striving to live up to that teaching.

This implies that like other Christians they must take advantage of the powerful graces that come from the reverent and frequent recourse to the sacrament of penance. In addition, of course, the natural aids they may need such as counseling, psychological help, etc., should and must be used where indicated and as needed.

In any case there is nothing to justify a departure from the church's normative pastoral and doctrinal teaching that one who has sinned gravely cannot approach the eucharist until he has been absolved from that sin in the sacrament of penance and this, of course, implies the firm amendment on the part of the penitent and his conscious intention to avoid that sin in the future.

Conclusion

Homosexual behavior cannot be viewed as an acceptable form of behavior morally or socially. At the same time persons who are homosexual must be treated with respect as human persons and they have a right to sound pastoral care.

It is the place of the church and her ministers to speak the whole moral teaching of the Gospel with clarity. The members of the church have the right to do this even when the moral teaching is difficult. But the ministers of the church must present that moral teaching in a way that also encourages homosexual men and women to begin or continue the journey toward the fulfillment of the law of Christ.

On the other hand, when homosexual men and women claim that their way of life is a morally healthy one, insist on their intention to affirm and promote it publicly and ask that it be in some way approved by the church, they are clearly in contempt of the Christian conscience and in conflict with the teaching of the scriptures.

Indeed the church holds that there is no place for discrimination and prejudice against a person because of sexual attraction. But this does not mean that there is nothing wrong with homosexual conduct.

While homosexuality may constitute a unique problem and challenge for the homosexual man and woman, it is a mistake to isolate the homosexual person from the general body of disciples. All believers in Christ young and old, men and women, experience the weight of sin in their lives. All must experience the struggle with evil.

All must hear the voice of Christ enjoining his followers to enter on "the narrow way that leads to life," or to "take up the cross each day and follow me." Christ chose the way of the cross. There is no other way for his followers. This is true of the homosexual as it is of all other Christians.

But in the eucharist and in the sacrament of penance supported by a life of daily prayer and growing faith, every believer finds that what is judged impossible by the world is indeed possible. For as Jesus said, "All things are possible to him who believes." Take to heart, then, the word of God which tells us:

> Get rid of all bitterness, all passion and anger, harsh words, slander and malice of every kind. In place of these, be kind to one another, compassionate and mutually forgiving just as God has forgiven you in Christ.... There was a time when you were in darkness, but now you are light in the Lord. Well, then, live as children of light. Light produces every kind of goodness and justice and truth (Eph. 4:31–5:9).

Origins 10, no. 7 (3 July 1980): 106–12. Printed with permission of Archbishop Quinn.

103. Archbishop Rembert Weakland, "Listening Sessions on Abortion: A Response," 20 May 1990

This response is written out of the context of having listened to women of the archdiocese at the six listening sessions, having studied the summary report of the sessions and having read the many letters sent to me since then. What a wealth of material!...

Why the Hearings

The abortion issue is one of the most divisive in our society and also in our church. It is an issue that touches our faith because it forces us to articulate how we view God's relationship to human life. It is, moreover, so sensitive that people are hesitant to speak frankly about how they feel on the issue, especially if they sense that the other person may not be on the same side of the argument. Rational discourse seems to have vanished in favor of slogans. It is not easy in the public forum to have a calm discussion about the moral principles involved.

The church's official position has been clear for decades now: Abortion is seen as the taking of human life and thus morally wrong. It could also be said that the church would like to see its moral position become the legal position in the nation as well. But listening is also an important part of any teaching process; the church's need to listen is no exception.

But this unequivocal position does not have the full support of many Catholics, especially of many women, because it seems to be too simplistic an answer to a complicated and emotional question and does not resolve all the concomitant problems surrounding the issue raised in a pluralistic society, especially where there is no political and societal consensus on the issue, either in its moral dimension or in its legal embodiment.

Moreover, this issue is often indicative of how women view their own identity and see their role in society, so that it has become the symbol for many other issues that touch feminism today.

For these reasons I felt that I had to do more listening to the voices of faithful women in the archdiocese. I have faith and trust in their wisdom and honesty. I knew I had much to learn from them that I had not heard yet. Listening seemed absolutely necessary to me. From the sessions I gained a clearer idea of why some women do not accept in its totality the church's official teaching. So many of these reservations can be found in the summary report....

What I Learned

No report could possibly respond to everything everyone said at all six sessions nor could it describe the different atmosphere each hearing displayed. The public ones differed from those by invitation only; among those by invitation there were remarkably different approaches and insights. I can only say what I learned and what I feel I would like to communicate to the people of the archdiocese at this moment as we continue to discuss the summary report.

1. I did not hear one Catholic woman defend abortion as a good in itself; they all considered it a tragedy in our society, a procedure that no one should have to resort to. Perhaps there were no representatives in favor of abortion on demand without grave cause present or perhaps they decided not to speak; but I feel my observation is correct when I say that there were so many women troubled by this issue and seeking some kind of shared common ground through a more profound and more sensitive dialogue than we have had up to now. Through such dialogue it was hoped that one could slowly begin to arrive at some here-and-now practical wisdom.

There is, thus, an urgent need for women to have more forums to keep up this dialogue. So many told me that they had never really talked about this vital issue in a reasonable way with other women, especially with those who had different experiences and different positions. Listening to others in a non-judgmental fashion on this issue was not easy for many, but so very necessary. Not only did I learn much, but most of the participants said they did.

Some felt that these sessions, because I listened to those who did not accept fully the church's official position, may have given the impression that the church was weak in its teaching. They expected me to take the opportunity of these listening sessions to come down hard and forcefully on those who disagree with the explicitness of the church's teaching on this issue. That would have negated the whole purpose of listening. I would have learned nothing. I always feel that those who are afraid to hear points of view that differ from their own are not really very secure in their positions.

2. One point was clear and emphasized by all: The church must maintain more consistency between its teaching and its actions. It must do more to help and encourage women facing most difficult life decisions, especially those carrying to term unplanned pregnancies.

It has to take seriously the consistent life ethic if it is to be credible in its teaching on abortion. I heard, as the summary report indicates, how many women applauded the U.S. bishops' emphasis on this consistent ethic of life as a means of showing that all life is sacred and that thus the taking of even one life is a serious moral decision, whether it be through abortion, war or capital punishment. They supported the teaching that each Christian has a responsibility, personally and socially, of protecting and preserving the sanctity of all life from womb to natural death and of fighting to eliminate in society all those structures and situations that deprive others of their rightful dignity and development.

At times I heard the pro-life movement criticized in this regard: It was felt that life was not consistently held in the same esteem after birth by some in that group. Others pointed out that the church excommunicates those involved in abortion but not in other kinds of attacks on human life. Women asked if the church was being consistent in admitting some circumstances that justify the taking of human life in other contexts (the just-war theory, unjust aggressors, etc.) but not in this instance. They called for further study of traditional teaching on such items as the principle of double effect and other moral teachings that could be helpful in forming the consciences of the faithful — without retreating from the position of respect for human life as such. If one were to characterize what I heard as the dominant position, it would be that which we usually title "respect for life."

In any case, this argument of consistency challenged me strongly and will be with me into the future.

3. Some members of the pro-life movement asked me why so many priests hesitate to preach publicly on the church's official teaching and do not support their political activity in favor of changing the present laws on abortion. It is true: I too know so many wonderful pastoral priests who do not want to be identified with the pro-life movement even though they are solidly against abortion on demand. I have talked many times to our priests in private about

this question. Although what I say may seem harsh, it is important that we all listen to such criticism. Many dislike the narrowness of so many in the pro-life movement, their tactics, their non-acceptance of the consistent life ethic approach, their lack of compassion, their alliances with groups that often are very anti-Catholic in other areas, their lack of civility and so on. In other words, such a perception of the pro-life movement does not lend itself to attracting not just priests but so many others who are searching for what is best for our society. Many priests, moreover, feel uncomfortable with some of the political and other aggressive activities of the pro-life movement. Some of the rhetoric and literature seems ugly and demeaning. Further discussion on these observations is truly needed so the root reasons for lack of support can be verified.

4. My ears are still ringing after hearing so many women say bluntly that they are angry about the church's stance on birth control. The listening sessions were not about that question, but it kept coming up over and over again. I did not sense that there was much support even among those who were strong in their opposition to abortion for the church's position about contraception. Even those advocating natural family planning as a solution seemed at times to approach the question with a contraceptive mentality, with little discussion of motives and intentions.

The phrase one woman used to express her non-acceptance of the church's teaching in this regard still lingers in my ears: "We want to be pro-choice before conception." I noticed how far the gap is between the official teaching in this area and its non-receptivity by some very conscientious women.

5. I could not help but notice some strong cultural differences that seemed to accompany the positions taken on abortion. Women who saw their identity as women in childbearing, in raising a family, in being a homemaker tended to be stronger in their convictions and stances on the pro-life spectrum. Those who saw childbearing as important, but only one aspect of their full identity as women and who were concerned about developing other aspects of their gifts through involvement in world and society tended to be more open on the issue. I could not help but reflect on the fact that this latter group seemed to dominate on our college faculties and could represent the thinking of many of the younger women they come into contact with daily.

6. Likewise, I noticed cultural influences I had not thought about previously on the part of those who were more favorably disposed to a more open stance on the issue of abortion. From the literature, but less so among the participants at the listening sessions, I noticed that some seemed to fall into the Cartesian dualism between body and soul that looks upon the body as a machine or instrument to be controlled as one wills. The church has never accepted this point of view, namely, that one has control over one's body to do with it what one wants. The body is not a mannequin or a machine. Cutting off any part of the body just to show that one has control over this "machine" is contrary to the whole approach our faith takes to the body as integral to the identity of the whole person. Control over the forces that affect one's life made more sense to me.

One heard also an occasional reference to "rights" over one's body or "rights to an abortion." We all use expressions such as this. It is true that in common speech we have come to use that word *rights* for almost anything we wish, so that it has begun to lose its full meaning. In a discussion as serious as this one about abortion, I see the need for us Catholics to be very precise in its use. I was never quite sure how the term was being used.

Because of my involvement in the economic pastoral letter of the U.S. bishops, in which economic rights are crucial to the central argument of the letter, I have become more sensitive to the need to clarify exactly what is meant when the word *rights* is used, what corresponding responsibilities result and on whose shoulders they fall. If we could only agree on what personal rights our society guarantees us and how they are to be fulfilled and what happens when there is a conflict in rights — but this is a discourse that goes beyond the scope of this response.

7. I came away from the listening sessions making a few resolutions. I would never be so glib in talking about the "moment of conception," since from a medical point of view that is far from accurate: Conception is a long process, not a moment. I have learned much from letters and from the discussion among the health care women that the first days and weeks of the growth of a fetus are, from a medical point of view, anything but simple. I know I must be more precise and correct in talking about those stages of development.

I also learned from listening to women to be more careful about the need to treat in a pastoral fashion infertility and miscarriages. Especially in the latter case, I sense that for many women much grieving is needed, and a sense of loss can be very real. Nor will I talk so glibly about bringing the baby to term and then "just give it up for adoption," since I learned that there can be so much grieving here too and a deep sense of loss that often needs to be faced. I have to do more listening to women about those questions and the pastoral cares involved.

8. From the discussion I became aware of the implications of the terms *pro-choice* and *pro-life*. A good overview is given in the summary report. So much emotion is hidden in the terms one uses!

Some said they felt many in the pro-life movement were really just anti-abortion because of their lack of support for a total range of life issues. In each case this would have to be verified.

The term *pro-choice* was much more ambiguous and the term itself did not seem to cover the range of differences. Abortion on demand was one extreme. Some used it in a legal way implying the right to the process of choice, even though they did not feel that they personally could have an abortion; the choice, however, would be theirs and not the government's. Others limited the choice to certain circumstances — rape, incest, the life of the mother. In any case, I will continue to use the term *pro-life* for the church's position and try to distinguish the ranges of meaning within the pro-choice groups to do justice to the variety of points of view found there.

9. I was disappointed that the pro-life women who were politically in-

volved in trying to reverse present laws and legally to eliminate all abortions in the land were not more articulate for me about what the consequences of such a total prohibition would be in our society. Would the wealthy, because they could afford to do so, then go to other countries where abortions would be permitted? Would there be again the back-alley, illegal practitioners? These are urgent questions, especially if there is no clear consensus of the population on this issue.

10. I was surprised and disturbed by the strong influence of fundamentalist positions on some of the pro-life women who have been politically involved in this issue. I say disturbed, because they did not seem to know the Catholic approach to Scripture and fell into proof-texting in ways that are not our tradition. I will have to talk much with the priests and other pastoral ministers in the diocese about this unwholesome influence and what it means. It might also account for some of the narrowness of vision on the part of some of the pro-life people one meets.

11. Finally, I was much impressed with the caring and compassionate qualities of the women who attended the hearings and were trying to see other points of view.

I came away from the listening sessions in great admiration for so many Catholic women who very quietly and without fanfare are involved in crisis-pregnancy counseling, for example, those involved in Birthright. Many showed those caring and compassionate qualities that come from a deep respect for the dignity of each person and that seek to integrate faith and life options.

I applauded those involved in care at all stages of life and thus who have contributed much time and means to helping others, especially younger women faced with bringing a pregnancy to term under difficult economic and psychological situations. Institutional support for such women and men must not only continue, but become better known and increased....

Origins 20, no. 3 (31 May 1990): 33, 35–38. Printed with permission of Archbishop Rembert Weakland.

104. National Conference of Catholic Bishops Committee, "Always Our Children," Pastoral Message to Parents of Homosexual Children and Suggestions for Pastoral Ministers, 27 November 1997

The purpose of this pastoral message is to reach out to parents who are trying to cope with the discovery of homosexuality in a child who is an adolescent or an adult. It urges families to draw upon the reservoirs of faith, hope and love as they face uncharted futures. It asks them to recognize that the church offers enormous spiritual resources to strengthen and support them at this moment in their family's life and in the days to come....

The meaning and implications of the term *homosexual orientation* are not universally agreed upon. Church teaching acknowledges a distinction between a homosexual "tendency" which proves to be "transitory" and "homosexuals who are definitively such because of some kind of innate instinct" (Congregation for the Doctrine of the Faith, Declaration on Certain Questions Concerning Sexual Ethics, 8).

In light of the possibility, therefore, it seems appropriate to understand sexual orientation (heterosexual or homosexual) as a fundamental dimension of one's personality and to recognize its relative stability in a person. A homosexual orientation produces a stronger emotional and sexual attraction toward individuals of the same sex. It does not totally rule out interest in, care for and attraction toward members of the opposite sex. Having a homosexual orientation does not necessarily mean a person will engage in homosexual activity.

There seems to be no single cause of a homosexual orientation. A common opinion of experts is that there are multiple factors — genetic, hormonal, psychological — that may give rise to it. Generally, homosexual orientation is experienced as a given, not as something freely chosen. By itself, therefore, a homosexual orientation cannot be considered sinful, for morality presumes the freedom to choose.

Some homosexual persons want to be known publicly as *gay* or *lesbian*. These terms often express a person's level of self-awareness and self-acceptance within society. Though you might find the terms offensive because of political or social connotations, it is necessary to be sensitive to how your son or daughter is using them. Language should not be a barrier to building trust and honest communication.

You can help a homosexual person in two general ways. First, encourage him or her to cooperate with God's grace in order to live a chaste life. Second, concentrate on the person, not on the homosexual orientation itself. This implies respecting a person's freedom to choose or refuse therapy directed toward changing a homosexual orientation. Given the present state of medical and psychological knowledge, there is no guarantee that such therapy will succeed. Thus, there may be no obligation to undertake it, though some may find it helpful.

All in all, it is essential to recall one basic truth. God loves every person as a unique individual. Sexual identity helps to define the unique persons we are. One component of our sexual identity is sexual orientation. Thus, our total personhood is more encompassing than sexual orientation. Human beings see the appearance, but the Lord looks into the heart (cf. 1 Sm. 16:7).

God does not love someone any less simply because he or she is homosexual. God's love is always and everywhere offered to those who are open to receiving it. St. Paul's words offer great hope:

"For I am convinced that neither death nor life, nor angels, nor principalities, nor present things, nor future things, nor powers, nor height, nor depth, nor any other creature will be able to separate us from the love of God in Christ Jesus our Lord" (Rom. 8:38–39).

Accepting God's Plan and the Church's Ministry

For the Christian believer, an acceptance of self and of one's homosexual child must take place within the larger context of accepting divinely revealed truth about the dignity and destiny of human persons. It is the church's responsibility to believe and teach this truth, presenting it as a comprehensive moral vision and applying this vision in particular situations through its pastoral ministries. We present the main points of that moral teaching here.

Every person has an inherent dignity because he or she is created in God's image. A deep respect for the total person leads the church to hold and teach that sexuality is a gift of God. Being created a male or a female person is an essential part of the divine plan, for it is their sexuality — a mysterious blend of spirit and body — that allows human beings to share in God's own creative love and life. "Everyone... should acknowledge and accept his sexual identity" (Catechism of the Catholic Church, 2333).

Like all gifts from God, the power and freedom of sexuality can be channeled toward good or evil. Everyone — the homosexual and the heterosexual person — is called to personal maturity and responsibility. With the help of God's grace, everyone is called to practice the virtue of chastity in relationships. Chastity means integrating one's thoughts, feelings and actions in the area of human sexuality in a way that values and respects one's own dignity and that of others. It is "the spiritual power which frees love from selfishness and aggression" (Pontifical Council for the Family, "The Truth and Meaning of Human Sexuality," 16).

Christ summons all his followers — whether they are married or living a single celibate life — to a higher standard of loving. This includes not only fidelity, forgiveness, hope, perseverance and sacrifice, but also chastity, which is expressed in modesty and self-control. The chaste life is possible though not always easy, for it involves a continual effort to turn toward God and away from sin, especially with the strength of the sacraments of penance and Eucharist. Indeed God expects everyone to strive for the perfection of love, but to achieve it gradually through stages of moral growth (cf. John Paul II, "On the Family," 34). To keep our feet on the path of conversion, God's grace is available to and sufficient for everyone open to receiving it.

To live and love chastely is to understand that "only within marriage does sexual intercourse fully symbolize the Creator's dual design as an act of covenant love with the potential of co-creating new human life" (U.S. Catholic Conference, *Human Sexuality: A Catholic Perspective for Education and Lifelong Learning*, p. 55). This is a fundamental teaching of our church about sexuality, rooted in the biblical account of man and woman created in the image of God and made for union with one another (Gn. 2–3).

Two conclusions follow. First, it is God's plan that sexual intercourse occur only within marriage between a man and a woman. Second, every act of intercourse must be open to the possible creation of new human life. Homosexual intercourse cannot fulfill these two conditions. Therefore, the church teaches that homogenital behavior is objectively immoral, while making the important distinction between this behavior and a homosexual orientation, which is not immoral in itself.

It is also important to recognize that neither a homosexual orientation nor a heterosexual one leads inevitably to sexual activity. One's total personhood is not reducible to sexual orientation or behavior.

Respect for the God-given dignity of all persons means the recognition of human rights and responsibilities. The teaching of the church makes it clear that the fundamental human rights of homosexual persons must be defended and that all of us must strive to eliminate any form of injustice, oppression or violence against them (cf. Congregation of the Doctrine of the Faith, "The Pastoral Care of Homosexual Persons," 10).

It is not sufficient only to avoid unjust discrimination. Homosexual persons "must be accepted with respect, compassion and sensitivity" (Catechism of the Catholic Church, 2358). They, as is true of every human being, need to be nourished at many different levels simultaneously.

This includes friendship, which is a way of loving and is essential to healthy human development as well as one of the richest possible human experiences. Friendship can and does thrive outside of genital sexual involvement.

The Christian community should offer its homosexual sisters and brothers understanding and pastoral care. More than 20 years ago we bishops stated that "homosexuals...should have an active role in the Christian community" (National Conference of Catholic Bishops, "To Live in Christ Jesus: A Pastoral Reflection on the Moral Life," p. 19). What does this mean in practice? It means that all homosexual persons have a right to be welcomed into the community, to hear the word of God and to receive pastoral care. Homosexual persons who are living chaste lives should have opportunities to lead and serve the community. However, the church has the right to deny public roles of service and leadership to persons, whether homosexual or heterosexual, whose public behavior openly violates its teachings.

The church recognizes the importance and urgency of ministering to persons with HIV/AIDS. Though HIV/AIDS is an epidemic affecting the whole human race, not just homosexual persons, it has had a devastating effect upon them and has brought great sorrow to many parents, families and friends.

Without condoning self-destructive behavior or denying personal responsibility, we reject the idea that HIV/AIDS is a direct punishment from God. Furthermore:

"Persons with AIDS are not distant, unfamiliar people, the objects of our mingled pity and aversion. We must keep them present to our consciousness as individuals and community, and embrace them with unconditional love.... Compassion — love — toward persons infected with HIV is the only authentic Gospel response" (NCCB, "Called to Compassion and Responsibility: A Response to the HIV/AIDS Crisis").

Nothing in the Bible or in Catholic teaching can be used to justify prejudicial or discriminatory attitudes and behaviors. We reiterate here what we said in an earlier statement:

"We call on all Christians and citizens of good will to confront their own fears about homosexuality and to curb the humor and discrimination that offend homosexual persons. We understand that having a homosexual orientation brings with it enough anxiety, pain and issues related to self-acceptance without society bringing additional prejudicial treatment" (*Human Sexuality: A Catholic Perspective for Education and Lifelong Learning*, p. 55)....

Patrick W. Carey, ed., *Pastoral Letters of the United States Catholic Bishops* (Washington, D.C.: United States Catholic Conference, 1998), 6:840–50. Printed with permission.

Catholics and Electoral Politics

The candidacy of the Roman Catholic John F. Kennedy opened once again the question of whether Catholics were fit to hold high office. Kennedy's definition of the relationship between his private faith and his public life, though criticized by some as too secularist, set the parameters of Catholic interaction with the politics of the next generation.

The ever-changing political landscape of America reflected at first Kennedy's smooth secularism, but after the trauma of Vietnam, the assassinations of popular leaders, and the Watergate scandal, American voters were far more receptive to the expression of religious beliefs and sensibilities within the political sphere. Evangelical Protestants led the way, helping to elect Georgia governor Jimmy Carter in 1976. But the real beneficiaries of a renewed emphasis on religion in politics were the Republicans under Ronald Reagan who won the presidency in 1980. Catholic office-holders, especially those in the Democratic Party, found themselves seriously challenged over the party's official endorsement of a woman's right to an abortion. Since this position involved indirect participation in the destruction of innocent human life, Catholic legislators had to find a way to maintain their own loyalty to the church of their baptism while at the same time dealing with the realities of popular support for abortion. Similar challenges, although not of equal intensity, have been made around the issues of support for capital punishment, assistance to totalitarian regimes, and welfare reform.

105. John F. Kennedy, Address to the Houston Ministerial Association, September 1960

...I believe in an America where the separation of church and state is absolute — where no Catholic prelate would tell the president (should he be Catholic) how to act, and no Protestant minister would tell his parishioners for whom to vote — where no church or church school is granted any public funds or political preference — and where no man is denied public office merely because his religion differs from the president who might appoint him or the people who might elect him.

I believe in an America that is officially neither Catholic, Protestant nor Jewish — where no public official either requests or accepts instructions on public policy from the pope, the National Council of Churches or any other ecclesiastical source — where no religious body seeks to impose its will directly or indirectly upon the general populace or the public acts of its officials — and where religious liberty is so indivisible that an act against one church is treated as an act against all.

For, while this year it may be a Catholic against whom the finger of suspicion is pointed, in other years it has been, and may someday be again, a Jew — or a Quaker — or a Unitarian — or a Baptist. It was Virginia's harassment of Baptist preachers, for example, that helped lead to Jefferson's Statute of Religious Freedom. Today I may be the victim — but tomorrow it may be you — until the whole fabric of our harmonious society is ripped at a time of great national peril.

Finally, I believe in an America where religious intolerance will someday end — where all men and all churches are treated as equals — where every man has the same right to attend or not attend the church of his choice — where there is no Catholic vote, no anti-Catholic vote, no bloc vote of any kind — and where Catholics, Protestants and Jews, at both the lay and pastoral level, will refrain from those attitudes of disdain and division which have so often marred their works in the past, and promote instead the American ideal of brotherhood.

That is the kind of America in which I believe, and it represents the kind of presidency in which I believe — a great office that must neither be humbled by making it the instrument of any one religious group, nor tarnished by arbitrarily withholding its occupancy from the members of any one religious group. I believe in a president whose religious views are his own private affair, neither imposed by him upon the nation nor imposed by the nation upon him as a condition to holding that office.

I would not look with favor upon a president working to subvert the First Amendment's guarantees of religious liberty. Nor would our system of checks and balances permit him to do so — and neither do I look with favor upon those who would work to subvert Article VI of the Constitution by requiring a religious test — even by indirection — for it. If they disagree with that safeguard, they should be out openly working to repeal it.

I want a chief executive whose public acts are responsible to all groups and obligated to none — who can attend any ceremony, service or dinner his office may appropriately require of him — and whose fulfillment of his presidential oath is not limited or conditioned by any religious oath, ritual or obligation.

This is the kind of America I believe in — and this is the kind I fought for in the South Pacific and the kind my brother died for in Europe. No one suggested then that we might have a "divided loyalty," that we did "not believe in liberty" or that we belonged to a disloyal group that threatened the "freedoms for which our forefathers died."

And in fact this is the kind of America for which our forefathers died — when they fled here to escape religious test oaths that denied office to members of less favored churches — when they fought for the Constitution, the Bill of Rights, and the Virginia Statute of Religious Freedom — and when they fought at the shrine I visited today, the Alamo. For side by side with Bowie and Crockett died McCafferty and Bailey and Carey — but no one knows whether they were Catholics or not. For there was no religious test at the Alamo.

I ask you tonight to follow in that tradition — to judge me on the basis of my record of fourteen years in Congress — on my declared stands against an ambassador to the Vatican, against unconstitutional aid to parochial schools, and against any boycott of the public schools (which I have attended myself) — instead of judging me on the basis of these pamphlets and publications we all have seen that carefully select quotations out of context from the statements of Catholic church leaders, usually in other countries, frequently in other centuries and rarely relevant to any situation here — and always omitting, of course, the statement of the American Bishops of 1948 which strongly endorsed church-state separation and which more nearly reflects the views of almost every American Catholic.

I do not consider these other quotations binding upon my public acts — why should you? But let me say with respect to other countries, that I am wholly opposed to the state being used by any religious group, Catholic or Protestant, to compel, prohibit or persecute the free exercise of an other religion. And I hope that you and I condemn with equal fervor those nations which deny their presidency to Protestants and those which deny it to Catholics. And rather than cite the misdeeds of those who differ, I would cite the record of the Catholic Church in such nations as Ireland and France — and the independence of such statesmen as Adenauer and De Gaulle.

But let me stress again that these are my views — for, contrary to common newspaper usage, I am not the Catholic candidate for president. I am the Democratic party's candidate for president, who happens also to be a Catholic. I do not speak for my church on public matters — and the church does not speak for me.

Whatever issue may come before me as president — on birth control, divorce, censorship, gambling, or any other subject — I will make my decision in accordance with these views, in accordance with what my conscience tells me to be the national interest, and without regard to outside religious pressures or dictates. And no power or threat of punishment could cause me to decide otherwise.

But if the time should ever come — and I do not concede any conflict to be even remotely possible — when my office would require me to either violate my conscience or violate the national interest, then I would resign the office; and I hope any conscientious public servant would do the same.

But I do not intend to apologize for these views to my critics of either Catholic or Protestant faith — nor do I intend to disavow either my views or my church in order to win this election. If I should lose on the real issues, I shall return to my seat in the Senate, satisfied that I had tried my best and was fairly judged. But if this election is decided on the basis that forty million Americans lost their chance of being president on the day they were baptized, then it is the whole nation that will be the loser, in the eyes of Catholics and non-Catholics around the world, in the eyes of history, and in the eyes of our own people.

But if, on the other hand, I should win the election, then I shall devote every effort of mind and spirit to fulfilling the oath of the presidency — practically identical, I might add, to the oath I have taken for fourteen years in the Congress. For, without reservation, I can "solemnly swear that I will faithfully execute the office of president of the United States, and will to the best of my ability preserve, protect and defend the Constitution . . . so help me God."

Taken from John F. Kennedy Library website (http://www.cs.umb.edu/jfklib/).

106. Statement of 166 Catholic Laymen on Religious Freedom in a Presidential Campaign, 5 October 1960

The present controversy about the Catholic Church and the Presidency proves once again that large numbers of our fellow-citizens seriously doubt the commitment of Catholics to the principles of a free society. This fact creates problems which extend far beyond this year's elections and threaten to make permanent, bitter divisions in our national life. Such a result would obviously be tragic from the standpoints both of religious tolerance and of civic peace.

In order to avert this, we ask all Americans to examine (more carefully, perhaps, than they have in the past) the relationship between religious conscience and civil society. We think that, in the present situation, Catholics especially are obliged to make their position clear.

There is much bigotry abroad in the land, some of it masquerading under the name of "freedom." There is also genuine concern. To the extent that many Catholics have failed to make known their devotion to religious liberty for all, to the extent that they at times have appeared to seek sectarian advantage, we must admit that we have contributed to doubts about our intentions. It is our hope that this statement may help to dispel such doubts.

To this end we make the following declarations of our convictions about religion and the free society. We do this with an uncompromised and uncompromising loyalty both to the Catholic Church and to the American Republic.

1. We believe in the freedom of the religious conscience and in the Catholic's obligation to guarantee full freedom of belief and worship as a civil right.

This obligation follows from basic Christian convictions about the dignity of the human person and the inviolability of the individual conscience. And we believe that Catholics have a special duty to work for the realization of the principle of freedom of religion in every nation whether they are a minority or a majority of the citizens.

2. We deplore the denial of religious freedom in any land. We especially deplore this denial in countries where Catholics constitute a majority — even an overwhelming majority. In the words of Giacomo Cardinal Lercaro, the present Archbishop of Bologna: "Christian teaching concerning the presence of God in the human soul and belief in the transcendent value in history of the human person lays the foundation for the use of persuasive methods in matters of religious faith and forbids coercion and violence." The Catholic's commitment to religious liberty, therefore, he says, "is not a concession suggested by prudence and grudgingly made to the spirit of the times." Rather, it is rooted "in the permanent principles of Catholicism."

3. We believe constitutional separation of Church and State offers the best guarantee both of religious freedom and of civic peace. The principle of separation is part of our American heritage, and as citizens who are Catholics we value it as an integral part of our national life. Efforts which tend to undermine the principle of separation, whether they come from Catholics, Protestants or Jews, believers or unbelievers, should be resisted no matter how well-intentioned such efforts might be.

4. We believe that among the fundamentals of religious liberty are the freedom of a church to teach its members and the freedom of its members to accept the teachings of their church. These freedoms should be invulnerable to the pressures of conformity. For civil society to dictate how a citizen forms his conscience would be a gross violation of freedom. Civil society's legitimate interest is limited to the public acts of the believer as they affect the whole community.

5. In his public acts as they affect the whole community the Catholic is bound in conscience to promote the common good and to avoid any seeking of a merely sectarian advantage. He is bound also to recognize the proper scope or independence of the political order. As Jacques Maritain has pointed out, the Church provides Catholics with certain general principles to guide us in our life as citizens. It directs us to the pursuit of justice and the promotion of the common good in our attitudes toward both domestic and international problems. But it is as individual citizens and office holders, not as a religious bloc, that we make the specific application of these principles in political life. Here we function not as "Catholic citizens," but as citizens who are Catholics. It is in this spirit that we submit this statement to our fellow Americans.

Catholic Mind 59 (March–April 1961): 179–80; also in John Tracy Ellis, ed., *Documents of American Catholic History* (Wilmington, Del.: Michael Glazier, 1987), 2:652–54. Printed with permission of the estate of John Tracy Ellis.

107. Administrative Board of the U.S. Catholic Conference, "Political Responsibility: Reflections on an Election Year," 12 February 1976

This year marks the 200th anniversary of the founding of our republic with its remarkable system of representative democracy. It is also a year that will test the workings of this democracy. A national election is time for decisions regarding the future of our nation and the selection of our representatives and political leaders. As pastors and teachers, we address this statement of political responsibility to all Americans in hopes that the upcoming elections will provide an opportunity for thoughtful and lively debate on the issues and challenges that face our country as well as decisions on the candidates who seek to lead us....

II. The Church and the Political Order

It is appropriate in this context to offer our own reflections on the role of the church in the political order. Christians believe that Jesus' commandment to love one's neighbor should extend beyond individual relationships to infuse and transform all human relations from the family to the entire human community.

Jesus came to "bring good news to the poor, to proclaim liberty to captives, new sight to the blind and to set the downtrodden free" (Luke 4:18). He called us to feed the hungry, clothe the naked, care for the sick and afflicted and to comfort the victims of injustice (Matt. 25).

His example and words require individual acts of charity and concern from each of us. Yet they also require understanding and action upon the broader dimensions of poverty, hunger and injustice which necessarily involve the institutions and structures of economy, society and politics.

The church, the people of God, is itself an expression of this love, and is required by the gospel and its long tradition to promote and defend human rights and human dignity.[1] The 1971 Synod of Bishops declared that action on behalf of justice is a "constitutive dimension" of the church's ministry and that, "the church has the right indeed the duty, to proclaim justice on the social, national and international level, and to denounce instances of injustice, when the fundamental rights of man and his salvation demand it."[2]

This view of the church's ministry and mission requires it to relate positively to the political order, since social injustice and the denial of human rights can often be remedied only through governmental action. In today's world concern for social justice and human development necessarily require persons and organizations to participate in the political process in accordance with their own responsibilities and roles.

The church's responsibility in the area of human rights includes two complementary pastoral actions: the affirmation and promotion of human rights

---

1. Synod of Bishops, *Human Rights and Reconciliation* (1974).
2. Synod of Bishops, *Justice in the World* (1971).

and the denunciation and condemnation of violations of these rights. In addition, it is the church's role to call attention to the moral and religious dimensions of secular issues, to keep alive the values of the gospel as a norm for social and political life, and to point out the demands of the Christian faith for a just transformation of society.[3] Such a ministry on the part of every Christian and the church inevitably involves political consequences and touches upon public affairs.

Christian social teaching demands that citizens and public officials alike give serious consideration in all matters to the common good, to the welfare of society as a whole, which must be protected and promoted if individual rights are to be encouraged and upheld.

In order to be credible and faithful to the gospel and to our tradition, the church's concern for human rights and social justice should be comprehensive and consistent. It must be formulated with competence and an awareness of the complexity of issues. It should also be developed in dialogue with other concerned persons and respectful of the rights of all.[4]

The church's role in the political order includes the following:

- Education regarding the teachings of the church and the responsibilities of the faithful;

- Analysis of issues for their social and moral dimensions;

- Measuring public policy against gospel values;

- Participating with other concerned parties in debate over public policy;

- Speaking out with courage, skill and concern on public issues involving human rights, social justice and the life of the church in society.

Unfortunately, our efforts in this area are sometimes misunderstood. The church's participation in public affairs is not a threat to the political process or to genuine pluralism, but an affirmation of their importance. The church recognizes the legitimate autonomy of government and the right of all, including the church itself, to be heard in the formulation of public policy....

A proper understanding of the role of the church will not confuse its mission with that of government, but rather see its ministry as advocating the critical values of human rights and social justice.

It is the role of Christian communities to analyze the situation in their own country, to reflect upon the meaning of the gospel, and to draw norms of judgment and plans of action from the teaching of the church and their own experience.[5] In carrying out this pastoral activity in the social arena we are confronted with complexity. As the 1971 Synod of Bishops pointed out: "It does not belong to the church, *insofar as she is a religious and hierarchical*

---

3. Ibid.
4. Pope Paul VI, *A Call to Action* (1971), 4, 50; Vatican II, *The Church in the Modern World* (1965), 43.
5. Vatican II, *Church in the Modern World*, 76.

community, to offer concrete solutions in the social, economic and political spheres for justice in the world."[6] (Emphasis added.)

At the same time, it is essential to recall the words of Pope John XXIII:

> ...it must not be forgotten that the church has the right and duty not only to safeguard the principles of ethics and religion, but also to intervene authoritatively with her children in the temporal sphere when there is a question of judging the application of these principles to concrete cases.[7]

The application of gospel values to real situations is an essential work of the Christian community. Christians believe the gospel is the measure of human realities. However, specific political proposals do not in themselves constitute the gospel. Christians and Christian organizations must certainly participate in public debate over alternative policies and legislative proposals, yet it is critical that the nature of their participation not be misunderstood.

We specifically do not seek the formation of a religious voting bloc; nor do we wish to instruct persons on how they should vote by endorsing candidates. We urge citizens to avoid choosing candidates simple on the personal basis of self-interest. Rather, we hope that voters will examine the positions of candidates on the full range of issues as well as the person's integrity, philosophy and performance....

> Hugh J. Nolan, ed., *Pastoral Letters of the United States Catholic Bishops* (Washington, D.C.: United States Catholic Conference, 1984), 4:129-37. Printed with permission.

108. Archbishop John Roach, "The Need for Public Dialogue on Religion and Politics: Address to the National Conference of Catholic Bishops," 17 November 1981

...As a rule of thumb for keeping friends, "Never discuss religion or politics" has a long history in our culture. It has received the status of a secular commandment. At times it is even taken as a corollary of the constitutional principle of separation of church and state.

I agree fully with the principle of separation of church and state. I do not agree that absence of dialogue about and between religion and politics serves either the church or the state. Three complementary considerations support the proposition that we should reverse cultural custom and initiate an explicit, public, systematic dialogue about the relationship of religious communities and the political process in the United States.

The first case can be drawn from the content of existing public policy discussion in the land. Whether we like it or not, a whole range of policy choices are permeated by moral and religious themes today: From the debate

---

6. Synod of Bishops, *Justice in the World*, 1971.
7. John XXIII, *Pacem in Terris* (1963), 160.

on abortion to decision making about Poland, from care for the terminally ill to the fairness of budget cuts, the direction our society takes must include an assessment of how moral and religious convictions relate to the technical dimensions of policy.

The second case is based on the content of the religious traditions as they are understood and expressed today. Our own faith community is an example, but not an isolated instance, of how the social vision of faith increasingly calls the church to a public theology and public witness on political questions.

The third case is drawn from existing attitudes in our country. Recently the Connecticut Mutual Life Company sponsored a survey on "American Values in the 1980s." The report concludes: "Our findings suggest that the increasing impact of religion on our social and political institutions may be only the beginning of a trend that could change the face of America."

This conclusion is based on data showing that people with strong religious convictions influence the political process out of proportion to their numerical strength. This fact can be evaluated in different ways. History teaches vividly that the expression of religious conviction through the political process is not necessarily a blessing to a society. The key question is how religious belief is related to political practice. This is the question which requires that a systematic discussion of religion and politics take place within our religious organizations and in the public arena, where people of all faiths and no religious faith are called as citizens to set the direction of society....

A focal point in the debate about religion and politics has been the role played by the Moral Majority. In my judgment two points should be made.

First, some have argued that the Moral Majority's role is an example of why religion and politics should be kept absolutely separate, and religious organizations should be silent on political questions. I reject this contention while defending the right, in the terms defined above, of the Moral Majority or any religious organization to address the public issues of the day.

The right of religious organizations of varying views to speak must be defended by all who understand the meaning of religious liberty and the social role of religion. But religious organizations should be subjected to the same standards of rational, rigorous presentation of their views as any other participant in the public debate. Moreover, religious organizations which address the moral dimensions of public issues are to be judged by the standards of competent moral analysis. Particularly relevant are the issues of how one defines a moral issue and the consistency with which moral principles are defended across a range of moral issues.

These same standards of discourse are the ones by which our position should be tested. Neither the rigor of reasonable argument nor the controversy which surrounds the role of religion and politics should make us timid about stating and defending public positions and key issues. Allow me to indicate the direction of a consistent moral vision rooted in Catholic social thought.

On a global scale, the most dangerous moral issue in the public order today is the nuclear arms race. The church in the United States has a special responsibility to address this question, a responsibility underscored by Pope John Paul in his remarks at the White House in 1979. The U.S. Catholic Conference has addressed the issue often, most notably in Cardinal Krol's testimony in the SALT II agreements.

It is an unhappy fact that strategic arms control discussions are presently stalemated, even as the technological and strategic dynamics of the arms race proceed. It is perhaps the convergence of these two themes which has moved a number of American bishops to address the arms race recently in terms that are both prophetic and profoundly important.

Certainly the sense of moral urgency about the arms race is what stands behind the establishment of our committee on war and peace about which Archbishop Bernardin, its chairman, will speak at this meeting. Without prejudging the complex work of the committee as it sets our future direction on the arms race, it is useful to say clearly what we already know from Catholic teaching. The church needs to say "no" clearly and decisively to the use of nuclear weapons. This is surely the direction of Vatican II teachings on the arms race and its condemnation of attacks on civilian centers. The "no" we utter should shape our policy advice and our pastoral guidance of Catholics.

It is not useful to blur the line of moral argument about the use of nuclear weapons at a time when the secular debate is openly discussing the use of limited nuclear weapons and winnable nuclear wars.

Second, the abortion issue: The horrors of nuclear war, though hardly fantasies, are possibilities at present. But the horror of legalized, permissive abortion is tragically real. The destruction of unborn life now occurs in the nation at the staggering rate of 1.5 million abortions annually.

Nearly nine years after the Supreme Court decision of 1973 initiated this carnage, who can doubt that it is time to say, "Enough!" Human dignity and human rights are mocked by this scandal. The concept of just law is mocked by the evasions used to create and continue it.

There is, thank God, some reason for encouragement at present. Our elected representatives increasingly recognize the need to correct the situation. As you know, Senate hearings are now taking place on proposals for this purpose. Our conference has recently given its support to one of these, a realistic constitutional remedy which holds out hope for undoing the damage done by the abortion decision. I call upon all pro-life people to unite at this crucial moment....

Third, the poor among us. Papal statements on the arms race have consistently condemned it because of the misallocation of scarce resources it entails. These statements have typically referred to the global level of the issue, but at a time of scarce resources here they take on meaning in a domestic debate on social policy. The proposed expenditure of $1.5 trillion for defense during the next five years stands in stark contrast to budget cuts which threaten the food, the health care and the education of the poor. In the past it was presumed in the United States that we could spend whatever we decided for defense and still be a compassionate society. That assumption is today denied in fact; what is spent for guns directly reduces what is available for the quality of care and life for the least among us.

In the past few years we have often heard from the church in Latin America the pastoral principle of "the option for the poor." Implementing that principle in our more complex economy faces different challenges. But the principle also has meaning for us. It means that while we are concerned about the larger "macro" questions of the economy, we will give specific weight to how any overall solution touches the poor.

We are called to this role of advocacy for the poor not only by our social teachings but also by our experience in the Campaign for Human Development and Catholic Charities across the country. This ministry with and for the poor confirms the moral vision of our teaching. The Old Testament prophets were right: The quality of our faith is tested by the character of justice among us.

We know from experience the impossible choices the poor face in our society: not between guns and butter, but between bread and rent, between money for heating oil and the need to pay for health care for children. We know also that private agencies of the nation cannot fill the gap created by recent cuts. We have neither the resources nor, I suppose, even the mandate to do this. We will do our part, but our own social teaching calls upon the state to do its part.

Religion and politics always come back to the person, to the way society respects or fails to respect a person. The church must raise its voice clearly about justice, because choices now before us as a nation can erode the conditions which support human dignity.

Today those of us who visibly represent a religious vision must be clear about our task. We must carry forward the debate about religion and politics, because both have a central contribution to make to preserving all that is valuable in the life of each person and the lives of all the people who constitute this society. To serve the person is to honor the Creator. We are called to reverence both in our ministry.

Origins 11, no. 25 (3 December 1981): 389, 391–93. Printed with permission of Archbishop Roach.

109. Mario Cuomo, "Religious Belief and Public Morality: A Catholic Governor's Perspective," University of Notre Dame, 13 September 1984

I would like to begin by drawing your attention to the title of this lecture: "Religious Belief and Public Morality: A Catholic Governor's Perspective." I was not invited to speak on church and state generally. Certainly not Mondale vs. Reagan. The subject assigned is difficult enough. I will not try to do more than I've been asked. . . .

In addition to all the weaknesses, dilemmas and temptations that impede every pilgrim's progress, the Catholic who holds political office in a pluralistic democracy — who is elected to serve Jews and Moslems, atheists and Protestants, as well as Catholics — bears special responsibility. He or she undertakes to help create conditions under which all can live with a maximum of dignity and with a reasonable degree of freedom; where everyone who chooses may hold beliefs different from specifically Catholic ones — sometimes contradictory to them; where the laws protect people's rights to divorce, to use birth control and even to choose abortion.

In fact, Catholic public officials take an oath to preserve the Constitution that guarantees this freedom. And they do so gladly. Not because they love what others do with their freedom, but because they realize that in guaranteeing freedom for all, they guarantee our right to be Catholics: our right to pray, to use the sacraments, to refuse birth control devices, to reject abortion, not to divorce and remarry if we believe it to be wrong....

Almost all Americans accept some religious values as a part of our public life. We are a religious people, many of us descended from ancestors who came here expressly to live their religious faith free from coercion or repression. But we are also a people of many religions, with no established church, who hold different beliefs on many matters.

Our public morality, then — moral standards we maintain for everyone, not just the ones we insist on in our private lives — depends on a consensus view of right and wrong. The values derived from religious belief will not — and should not — be accepted as part of the public morality unless they are shared by the pluralistic community at large, by consensus. That values happen to be religious values does not deny them acceptability as a part of this consensus. But it does not require their acceptability, either....

Ultimately, therefore, the question whether or not we admit religious values into our public affairs is too broad to yield a single answer. Yes, we create our public morality through consensus, and in this country that consensus reflects to some extent religious values of a great majority of Americans. But no, all religiously based values don't have an *a priori* place in our public morality. The community must decide if what is being proposed would be better left to private discretion than public policy; whether it restricts freedoms and if so to what end, to whose benefit; whether it will produce a good or bad result; whether overall it will help the community or merely divide it....

Today there are a number of issues involving life and death that raise questions of public morality. They are also questions of concern to most religions. Pick up a newspaper and you are almost certain to find a bitter controversy over any one of them: Baby Jane Doe, the right to die, artificial insemination, embryos *in vitro*, abortion, birth control — not to mention nuclear war and the shadow it throws across all existence. Some of these issues touch the most intimate recesses of our lives, our roles as someone's mother or child or husband; some affect women in a unique way. But they are also public questions, for all of us....

As a Catholic I have accepted certain answers as the right ones for myself and my family and because I have, they have influenced me in special ways, as Matilda's husband, as a father of five children, as a son who stood next to his own father's deathbed trying to decide if the tubes and needles no longer served a purpose.

As a governor, however, I am involved in defining policies that determine other people's rights in these same areas of life and death. Abortion is one of these issues, and while it is one issue among many, it is one of the most controversial and affects me in a special way as a Catholic public official.

So let me spend some time considering it.

I should start, I believe, by noting that the Catholic Church's actions with respect to the interplay of religious values and public policy make clear that there is no inflexible moral principle which determines what our political conduct should be. For example, on divorce and birth control, without changing its moral teaching the church abides the civil law as it now stands, thereby accepting — without making much of a point of it — that in our pluralistic society we are not required to insist that all our religious values be the law of the land.

Abortion is treated differently.

Of course there are differences both in degree and quality between abortion and some of the other religious positions the church takes: Abortion is a "matter of life and death," and degree counts. But the differences in approach reveal a truth, I think, that is not well enough perceived by Catholics and therefore still further complicates the process for us. That is, while we always owe our bishops' words respectful attention and careful consideration, the question whether to engage the political system in a struggle to have it adopt certain articles of our belief as part of public morality is not a matter of doctrine: It is a matter of prudential political judgment. Recently, Michael Novak put it succinctly: "Religious judgment and political judgment are both needed," he wrote. "But they are not identical."

My church and my conscience require me to believe certain things about divorce, birth control and abortion. My church does not order me — under pain of sin or expulsion — to pursue my salvific mission according to a precisely defined political plan. As a Catholic I accept the church's teaching authority. While in the past some Catholic theologians may appear to have disagreed on the morality of some abortions (it wasn't, I think, until 1869 that excommunication was attached to all abortions without distinction), and while some theologians still do, I accept the bishops' position that abortion is to be avoided.

As Catholics, my wife and I were enjoined never to use abortion to destroy the life we created, and we never have. We thought church doctrine was clear on this, and — more than that — both of us felt it in full agreement with what our hearts and our consciences told us. For me, life or fetal life in the womb should be protected, even if five of nine justices of the Supreme Court and my neighbor may disagree with me. A fetus is different from an appendix or a set of tonsils. At the very least, even if the argument is made by some scientists or some theologians that in the early stages of fetal development we can't discern human life, the full potential of human life is indisputably there. That — to my less subtle mind — by itself should demand respect, caution, indeed — reverence.

But not everyone in our society agrees with me and Matilda.

And those who don't — those who endorse legalized abortions — aren't a ruthless, callous alliance of anti-Christians determined to overthrow our moral standards. In many cases the proponents of legal abortion are the very people who have worked with Catholics to realize the goals of social justice set out in papal encyclicals: the American Lutheran Church, the Central Conference of American Rabbis, the Presbyterian Church in the United States, B'nai B'rith Women, the Women of the Episcopal Church. These are just a few of the religious organizations that don't share the church's position on abortion.

Certainly we should not be forced to mold Catholic morality to conform to disagreement by non-Catholics however sincere or severe their disagreement. Our bishops should be teachers, not pollsters. They should not change what we Catholics believe in order to ease our consciences or please our friends or protect the church from criticism. But if the breadth, intensity and sincerity of opposition to church teaching shouldn't be allowed to shape our Catholic morality, it can't help but determine our ability — our realistic, political ability — to translate our Catholic morality into civil law, a law not for believers who don't need it but for disbelievers who reject it.

And it is here, in our attempt to find a political answer to abortion — an answer beyond our private observance of Catholic morality — that we encounter controversy within and without the church over how and in what degree to press the case that our morality should be everybody else's, and to what effect.

I repeat, there is no church teaching that mandates the best political course for making our belief everyone's rule, for spreading this part of our Catholicism. There is neither an encyclical nor a catechism that spells out a political strategy for achieving legislative goals. And so the Catholic trying to make moral and prudent judgments in the political realm must discern which, if any, of the actions one could take would be best....

Respectfully and after careful consideration of the position and arguments of the bishops, I have concluded that the approach of a constitutional amendment is not the best way for us to seek to deal with abortion. I believe that the legal interdicting of abortion by either the federal government or the individual states is not a plausible possibility and even if it could be obtained, it wouldn't work. Given present attitudes, it would be Prohibition revisited, legislating what couldn't be enforced and in the process creating a disrespect for law in general. And as much as I admire the bishops' hope that a constitutional amendment against abortion would be the basis for a full new bill of rights for mothers and children, I disagree that this would be the result....

Apart from the question of the efficacy of using legal weapons to make people stop having abortions, we know our Christian responsibility doesn't end with any one law or amendment. That it doesn't end with abortion. Because it involves life and death, abortion will always be a central concern of Catholics. But so will nuclear weapons. And hunger and homelessness and joblessness, all the forces diminishing human life and threatening to destroy it. The "seamless garment" that Cardinal Bernardin has spoken of is a challenge to all Catholics in public office, conservatives as well as liberals. We cannot justify our aspiration to goodness simply on the basis of the vigor of our demand for an elusive and questionable civil law declaring what we already know, that abortion is wrong.

Approval or rejection of legal restrictions on abortion should not be the exclusive litmus test of Catholic loyalty. We should understand that whether abortion is outlawed or not, our work has barely begun: the work of creating a society where the right to life doesn't end at the moment of birth; where an infant isn't helped into a world that doesn't care if it's fed properly, housed decently, educated adequately; where the blind or retarded child isn't condemned to exist rather than empowered to live....

The Catholic Church has come of age in America. The ghetto walls are gone, our religion no longer a badge of irredeemable foreignness. This newfound status is both an opportunity and a temptation. If we choose, we can give in to the temptation to become more and more assimilated into a larger, blander culture, abandoning the practice of the specific values that made us different, worshiping whatever goods the marketplace has to sell while we seek to rationalize our own laxity by urging the political system to legislate on others a morality we no longer practice.

Or we can remember where we come from, the journey of two millennia, clinging to our personal faith, to its insistence on constancy and service and on hope. We can live and practice the morality Christ gave us, maintaining his truth in this world, struggling to embody his love, practicing it especially where that love is most needed, among the poor and the weak and the dispossessed. Not just by trying to make laws for others to live by, but by living the laws already written for us by God, in our hearts and minds.

We can be fully Catholic: proudly, totally at ease with ourselves, a people in the world, transforming it, a light to this nation. Appealing to the best in our people, not the worst. Persuading not coercing. Leading people to truth by love. And still, all the while, respecting and enjoying our unique pluralistic democracy. And we can do it even as politicians.

Origins 14, no. 15 (27 September 1984): 234–40. Printed with permission of Mario Cuomo.